This book may be ⟨⟩ P9-BVM-927
FOURTEEN DAYS
A fine will be charged for each

RELEASED

BUSINESS AND POLITICS
UNDER JAMES I

Lionel Cranfield, Earl of Middlesex, Lord High Treasurer of England
1575–1645

BUSINESS AND POLITICS UNDER JAMES I

LIONEL CRANFIELD AS MERCHANT
AND MINISTER

BY

R. H. TAWNEY, F.B.A.

*Professor Emeritus of Economic History in the
University of London*

32697

ST. JOSEPH'S UNIVERSITY   STX
HF 3505.4 .T23b
Business and politics under James I;

3 9353 00089 3386

CAMBRIDGE
AT THE UNIVERSITY PRESS
1958

PUBLISHED BY
THE SYNDICS OF THE CAMBRIDGE UNIVERSITY PRESS

Bentley House, 200 Euston Road, London, N.W.1
American Branch: 32 East 57th Street, New York 22, N.Y.

©

CAMBRIDGE UNIVERSITY PRESS
1958

H F 3505.4
T 23 b

Printed in Great Britain at the University Press, Cambridge
(Brooke Crutchley, University Printer)

To

T. S. ASHTON, F.B.A.

WITH GRATITUDE AND
AFFECTION

PREFACE

This book had its origin in a study begun in the early 1930's of certain aspects of English economic life, in particular foreign trade and financial policy, in the critical half-century preceding the Civil War. The papers of Lionel Cranfield, Earl of Middlesex, were an obvious source to which to turn. The late Professor A. P. Newton, who was then engaged in editing for the Historical Manuscripts Commission the volume published by it in 1940 under the title *Cranfield Papers, 1551–1612* (*MSS. of Lord Sackville*, vol. I), was most generous in allowing me to consult his transcripts and in helping me with advice. Circumstances subsequently compelled me to turn to other tasks, and it was not till some years after the close of the war that work on the subject could be resumed. Its fruits were originally intended to appear as a supplement to *The Economic History Review*, but ended by outgrowing the limits of a brochure. The following pages are the result. Omitting, as they do, the long concluding chapter of Cranfield's career which followed his political eclipse, and touching both on the European background of English enterprise and on the peculiarities of the English financial system at greater length than would be appropriate in a *Life*, they have no pretension to provide the full-length biography which the labours and achievements of their central figure, for all the spots on him, deserve. Such contribution as the volume offers is of a more pedestrian, but not, it is hoped, a superfluous or unrewarding, kind. Merchants and finance ministers function within a framework of international connections, domestic institutions and conditions, and —not least important—political assumptions, aspirations and beliefs, without a grasp of which their activities and vicissitudes are hardly to be understood. To throw some light, with the aid of evidence supplied by one eminent in both capacities, not only on his own successes and defeats, but on the characteristic features of the two contrasted, though interacting, spheres in which, in an age of approaching revolution, his lot was cast, is the object of the present work.

It remains for me to express my gratitude to those whose assistance has made this book somewhat less imperfect than it would otherwise have been. My thanks are due to Major-General Lord Sackville, K.B.E., C.B., C.M.G., for permission to examine and transcribe the Cranfield Papers deposited in the Public Record Office and to reproduce the portrait of Cranfield; to Mr S. C. Ratcliff and Mr R. L. Atkinson, secretaries successively of the Historical Manuscripts Commission, for facilitating my work on them; to Mr Raymond Smith, formerly Librarian and Curator of the Guildhall Library of the Corporation of London, for clues to Cranfield's part, apparently a minor one, in London civic life; and to Professor A. P. Newton for his encouragement and counsel. I am indebted to Mr V. H. Treadwell for information concerning Cranfield's interest in the reform of the government of Ireland, and to Mr Robert C. Johnson, of the University of Minnesota, for generously allowing me to see his transcripts of two unprinted diaries of the Parliament of 1624, as well as of letters from Cranfield to Buckingham and others in the Harleian and Egerton MSS. Among the colleagues and friends who have aided me with advice and information, I must thank, in particular, Professor F. J. Fisher, from whose knowledge of the period I have profited greatly and whose forthcoming edition for the Historical Manuscripts Commission of the second volume of the *Cranfield Papers* will, doubtless, suggest additions to the account here given of Cranfield's foreign trade and other business activities; Professor T. S. Ashton who, in matters of economic theory, has done his best to keep my feet on the strait and narrow path; Professor T. F. T. Plucknett, who introduced me to discussions of the conduct of Middlesex's impeachment by legal authorities of the seventeenth and eighteenth centuries; Dr J. Hurstfield, who suggested amendments in my treatment of the Court of Wards; Mrs A. M. Millard, who kindly allowed me to draw on her knowledge of the import trade of London under the early Stuarts, and Mr Robert Ashton who, on problems of customs-farming procedure, has done the same. I am deeply grateful to an old friend and fellow-worker, the late Miss Mildred E. Bulkley, who was good enough to read the whole of the following pages and to suggest numerous improvements; to Mrs G. Cornwell, by whom the laborious task of typing the book has been performed, to Miss O. P. Coleman, who has compiled the bibliography and helped me to correct the proofs, and to the author of the index, Mrs F. J. Fisher. My debt to my wife is beyond acknowledgement.

R. H. T.

LONDON
June 1958

NOTE ON REFERENCES TO
CRANFIELD MSS.

The *Cranfield MSS*. used in the present work are principally those in the Public Record Office. They fall into two main divisions, consisting of (1) the business papers of Lionel Cranfield and to a small extent of his father (Thomas Cranfield), his uncle (William Cranfield), and his father-in-law (Richard Sheppard); (2) the papers of Lionel Cranfield relating to his work as an official and minister of the Crown. These two categories of papers are separately numbered.

1. *Business Papers*. These include (*a*) letters from the clothiers from whom Cranfield purchased cloth for export or who made it to his order; (*b*) letters from and to his factors in his principal continental markets and other agents employed by him from time to time abroad; (*c*) business accounts. According to the classification adopted by Professor Newton, the first of these series is marked 'X', the second 'S', and the third 'T', the letter in each case being followed by a number. It should be noted, however, that Cranfield's ledger is numbered separately, without a preceding letter, 354. These papers were re-numbered by Professor Newton shortly before his death. The numbers referring to them cited here are the latest given by him.

2. *Official Papers*. These also, when the present writer began to work on them, had been numbered throughout by Professor Newton. He appears to have begun re-numbering them as well, but did not live to complete the task. The result is that a considerable proportion of them are now marked by two numbers, the later numbers being distinguished from the earlier by the fact that they are preceded by the letter 'M'. In the references to these papers given in the following pages, the old numbers have, except in one or two cases, been used throughout.

CONTENTS

Part I

CRANFIELD AS MERCHANT

Part II

CRANFIELD AS MINISTER

CONTENTS

PART III

THE FALL OF MIDDLESEX

The frontispiece, a portrait of Lionel Cranfield, Earl of Middlesex, Lord High Treasurer of England, 29 Sept. 1621—25 April 1624, attributed to Daniel Mytens, hangs in the Leicester Gallery at Knole and is reproduced by kind permission of Major-General Lord Sackville, K.B.E., C.B., C.M.G.

PART I

CRANFIELD AS MERCHANT

CHAPTER I

INTRODUCTION

'Whosoever commands the sea', wrote Raleigh in a famous passage, 'commands the trade; whosoever commands the trade of the world commands the riches of the world, and consequently the world itself.'[1] Confirmed, as it was thought, by all recent history—by the partial eclipse of Venice, the sensational start into a brief opulence of Portugal and Spain, the miracle of the pyramid balanced on its point by the ingenious Hollanders—the conviction that commerce, shipping and manufactures were the El Dorado of the future had become by the beginning of the seventeenth century a dogma overriding political and confessional frontiers. All States, by different methods, rang discordant changes on it. It emerged strengthened from convulsions which shook more venerable creeds. Its hold was tighter, and its empire wider, in 1650 than in 1600, and in 1700 than in 1650.

As an essay in theory or an exercise in statesmanship, the commercial politics prompted by these assumptions hardly merit, perhaps, the attention sometimes given them. They were not infrequently an effort to secure, at great expense, exclusive access to the point where the rainbow ends, and perpetuated poverty in pursuing wealth. But, in spite of its extravagances, the doctrine inspiring them touched at moments solid earth. The expansion of economic enterprise in range, volume and variety was a fact not to be denied. The new resources released by it, if misused, were incontestable. The reaction of both on the societies in the van of the commercial movement, if less immediately obvious, could not remain unobserved. Hence, when glittering fallacies have been exposed, and grandiose pretensions deflated, two prosaic realities remain which seemed significant to contemporaries, and which deserve consideration.

The first is an enlargement of the scope of the activities composing, in the language of the day, 'the circle of commerce', and a corresponding increase in the number and intricacy of the political tasks

[1] W. Raleigh, 'A Discourse of the Invention of Ships', from *The Works of Sir Walter Raleigh* (1829), vol. VIII, p. 325.

undertaken by rulers disposed to regard the expanding ambitions of international business as impinging on spheres too important and too profitable to be resigned to the untutored self-interest of acquisitive business men. The second result, if slower to become apparent, was productive of consequences more enduring and profound. It consisted in the erosion of traditional social systems by the pressure of new interests; in the struggle of those interests to survive and grow in States eager to exploit, but not organised to accommodate, them; in the novel conceptions of economic and political expediency with which, as their self-confidence increases, they arm themselves for their campaign; in the attempts of authority to harness them to its own ends, the unanticipated consequences both of its failures and its successes, and the emergence, when the environment is propitious, of political systems which find in the forces which menaced the stability of their predecessors a buttress of their own. All Governments are agog to capture the new dynamic for their service. All discover that its operation is not certain, but conditional on its treatment, and that the servant, to be commanded, must at times be obeyed. The world of business enterprise develops, as it grows, a formidable complexity. How manipulate it without courting the consent and invoking the advice of the classes who daily handle the capricious springs of the machine? Those classes are themselves a power not to be despised, and, though far from homogeneous, can act on occasion as a State within the State. Can the blessings of Judah and Issachar, in spite of Bacon's aphorism, be made to meet? Is it possible to ensure that the adolescent Leviathan is sufficiently sturdy to aid Governments by its vigour, and sufficiently docile not to embarrass them by its strength?

Questions of this order, couched in varying terms in different regions, if not among the most conspicuous issues of the day, were on any but the shortest view not the least important. 'It is not our conquests, but our commerce,' the Long Parliament was reminded in 1641, 'not our swords, but our sails, that...eternise the English honour and name.'[1] Attempting, half a century later, when the era of revolution had run its course, to sift the wheat from the chaff, a subtler and more sophisticated pen enunciated two morals, both of which cut deep. 'We are to consider', wrote Halifax, 'that we are a very little spot in the map of the world, and make a great

[1] Lewis Roberts, *The Treasure of Trafficke or a Discourse of Foraine Trade...* *dedicated to the High Court of Parliament now assembled* (1641).

figure only by trade, which is the creature of liberty; the one destroyed, the other falleth to the ground.'[1] The writer's exaltation of the unspectacular prose of commercial progress above the sublime, but perilous, ardours of the stormy past reflected not only his own utilitarian temper, but an unquiet generation's sigh of relief that the ghost of an unforgotten anarchy had at last been laid; nor can his unilinear pedigree of freedom be accepted without a closer scrutiny than the Trimmer undertook. But, while his interpretation of the epic age of English history has no claim to finality, it none the less opens vistas which deserve to be explored. The following pages attempt to examine, at a point higher up the stream, some features of the economic rivers on whose majestic lower reaches the national fortunes seemed to him to float. Their subject is commerce, finance, and policies concerned with both, as seen under James I by one who, as merchant, official and minister, possessed a knowledge of the interactions of these dynamic, but unruly, forces more intimate than most of his contemporaries could boast.

Lionel Cranfield, later Earl of Middlesex, belonged by birth to the age of the great Elizabethans. The second half of the succeeding reign saw his fortunes at their height; and he survived to hear, in his seventieth year,[2] the news of Naseby. His varying roles in the strenuous quarter of a century preceding his political eclipse, with which alone the present study is concerned, are recounted below; but the reader may be aided to find his way through the windings of a not too easily epitomised career by a brief preliminary reminder of its successive phases. The foundation of it all was, of course, Cranfield's opening two decades in the City, which not only provide the stepping stones for his ascent, but impress on the style and procedure of his subsequent official labours a distinctive and, to some of his aristocratic colleagues, an unpleasing stamp. English commerce was, however, too heterogeneous for the conventional rubric 'merchant' to supply an adequate clue to the specific interests of the different groups of practitioners so described. As an introduction to the first, commercial, chapter of the future Treasurer's life, a reminder of the limitations, as well as of the range, of the experience offered by it is, perhaps, to the point.

[1] 'A Rough Draft of a New Model at Sea (1694)', in *The Works of George Savile, the Marquis of Halifax*, ed. by Sir Walter Raleigh (Oxford, 1912).

[2] The date of his burial is given by Professor A. P. Newton, on the authority of the Westminster Abbey Register, as 13 August 1645.

Chronology, in the first place, determined that certain major spheres of enterprise should lie outside his scope. Born in 1575, Cranfield started trade on his own account in 1597; wound up his export business in 1613; and, after eleven years in the service of the Crown, was driven from public life in 1624. It is not surprising, therefore, that he played a leading part neither in his country's belated, though decisive, entry on the quest for the riches of the golden East nor in the subsequent partial diversion of English enterprise in Europe from its traditional northern targets to a more intensive exploitation of business possibilities in Spain, Italy and the Levant. It is true that, like other merchants of repute, he makes his bow to fashion by acquiring shares in the East India, Virginia and Somers Island Companies; but his papers reflect neither the vision of an English economic empire to East and West, which inspired Hakluyt's epic, nor the laborious commercial staff-work by which a Sir Thomas Smythe toiled to give the iridescent dream effect. The gravity, again, of the blow later dealt by the Thirty Years War to the long-established Anglo–German system of connections did not escape his eyes; but the commercial change of front accelerated by it was a development whose full significance there was little in his experience to aid him to foresee. Apart from an occasional consignment of guns to the Mediterranean, and of textile wares to Venice, trade with southern Europe, as he told a business correspondent, was off his beat;[1] while it was not till the middle 1620's, when he was temporarily in the depths, that the counterstroke by which English enterprise, with Leghorn as its base, sought in the Levant a compensation for markets lost in Germany, began to yield its fruit. To one, in short, brought up in Cranfield's school the North Sea and the Baltic were better than all the waters of the South. It is a question whether, even had he still retained in the early years of Charles the adventurous audacity of his eager, though discreet and calculating youth, the opportunities opening in the latter would have allured him.

Judged by his commercial interests, therefore, Cranfield is a man of the old world rather than the new. He belongs, as a merchant, to the age, not of the East India Company, of fantastic margins on re-exported spices and of the precocious multilateralism of Mun, but of the Merchant Adventurers, of strictly regulated sales and of the defence of that cautious restrictionism by their secretary,

[1] See below, p. 64, n. 6.

John Wheeler, whose ingenuous panegyric[1] on the Company employing him was published in the year when Cranfield makes his first, and not it seems too creditable,[2] appearance as a member of the ring. It is on this conservative core of long-established, prosperous and exclusive enterprise, the source of more than half the exports shipped from London,[3] not on the glittering fringe of experimental new departures, that his business correspondence, memoranda, and, when power comes his way, the policies sponsored by him, throw their light. The striking feature here—a feature more significant than the inevitable limitations of his geographical horizons—is the brilliance of his success in his own chosen field. His quickly won position among the leading figures of a celebrated trade marked him out as a force of whom discerning eyes must take account.

Of the nature and dimensions of his export business more is said below. Here it is sufficient to note its effect in preparing the way for a further stage in his ascent. Employing the profits yielded by it for financial operations on the London market, partly by way of speculations in private deals and Government concessions, partly to expand his money-lending activities, he at once adds to his pecuniary resources and—not less important—establishes personal relations with influential dignitaries, whose support may in future stand him in good stead. Before, in short, the age of thirty-five, he not only is a power in the City, but is known outside it both as a discreet and obliging banker, and as a sagacious man of affairs, whose judgment on matters beyond his counting-house is not to be despised. Gardiner[4] does his customary justice to Cranfield's official competence and zeal; but had the latter been in fact no more than the 'City tradesman' to whose 'true spirit of a London shopkeeper' the author refers at times in somewhat slighting terms, it is improbable that opportunities to exhibit his admired administrative genius would have come the humble huckster's way. In reality, Cranfield was a shopkeeper only in the same sublimated sense as a catalogue of later political notabilities too familiar to recite. Animadversions on his economic status, if such are in order, would be nearer the mark in reproaching him, not as a typical specimen of the *petite*

[1] John Wheeler, *A Treatise of Commerce* (1601).
[2] See below, p. 12.
[3] Astrid Friis, *Alderman Cockayne's Project and the Cloth Trade* (1927), p. 70.
[4] S. R. Gardiner, *History of England, 1603-1642*, vol. III, p. 200, and vol. IV, pp. 46, 57.

bourgeoisie, but as too faithful an embodiment of the outlook of the capitalist plutocracy alleged by unfriendly critics to exploit it.

No logical frontier divides Cranfield's business activities from his subsequent labours in the service of the State. Like a modern economic magnate appointed in an emergency to advise a Government Department or preside over a Control Board, he owes his public position to a reputation won on the stricken fields of private trade. It is as a potential source of cash and counsel that he secures the *entrée* to ministers in need of one or both; as spokesman for his Company that, by his lucid and trenchant exposition of its grievances, he makes on the Council the impression of a coming man; as an exporter familiar with a market abruptly closed by its intransigent ruler to English textiles that he is summoned by the Lord Privy Seal, with the approval of the King, to prescribe the measures required to bring the vexatious prohibitionist to heel; as a speculator, with the tricks of the trade at his fingers' ends, that he calls the customs-farmers' bluff, and extorts from the reluctant concessionaires terms beyond his royal client's hopes.[1] Judged by the subjects with which he deals and the power wielded by him, a change in his position hardly less important, though more difficult to date, than his initial appointment in 1613 to an official post is the transition which occurs when he already has some years of public life behind him. It consists in the conversion of the economic expert, charged with the duty of advising the Government on commercial technicalities, into the embryo statesman influencing decisions on large issues of policy and ultimately making them himself. It is not possible to specify with precision the moment when that watershed is crossed. Cranfield's projected reconstruction of the tariff in 1615-16 shows the upward movement under way. By the time when, in January 1619, as Master of the Court of Wards and Liveries, he becomes head of one of the most important revenue departments of the State, the transformation is complete. Its sequel is the mounting load of financial responsibilities, and of exasperation caused by his efforts to discharge them, which, combined with hostility in high places, five years later brings him down.

If such are the outlines of Cranfield's career, what of its ante-

---

[1] See below, pp. 123-4, and G. Goodman, *The Court of King James I*, ed. J. S. Brewer (1839), vol. I, pp. 302-3. The Company referred to here is the Mercers' Company.

cedents? In a study restricted to the business and official chapters
of his life, a summary treatment of his early years may, perhaps,
be excused. The contempt later voiced by D'Ewes[1] for a *parvenu*
'started up suddenly to such great wealth and honour from a base
and mean original' was not surprising in one whose learning, unfortunately, was not equally matched by sense; but, in Cranfield's case,
the oft-repeated sneer missed the mark. By birth the supposedly
offensive upstart represented the common alliance of land and trade.
His maternal grandmother, Elizabeth Dennis, belonged to a respected,
though apparently not too affluent, Gloucestershire family, which
owned, in addition to a manor in Kent, a small estate at Aust on the
Severn, where the ferry, then part of its property, crosses the river
to Beachley at the confluence of the Severn and the Wye. It had
given at different dates half-a-dozen sheriffs to the county, including
two during the two preceding reigns; and, in the early years of the
great Queen, Sir Maurice Dennis stood well enough at Court to be
appointed Treasurer to the heroic, but ill-fated, expeditionary force—
'as noble a garrison as ever served a prince'—left by the Government in the winter of 1562 to starve and freeze at Le Havre.
Elizabeth, his only daughter, married Vincent Randall, a London
mercer[2] with an export business to Antwerp, then on its last
legs as the principal continental market for English textiles; and
her daughter, in her turn, became the wife of one of Randall's
employees, Thomas Cranfield, like him a mercer, and also, it
appears, an original member of the recently established Baltic
Company. Of Randall Cranfield, the eldest of their four children,
little is heard till he is jobbed long after by his brother, when a
power, into the Mastership of the Mint, from which he was quickly

---

[1] *The Autobiography and Correspondence of Sir Simonds D'Ewes, Bart*, ed. by James
Orchard Halliwell (1845), vol. I, pp. 245-6.

[2] A point which arises frequently below had better here be stated once for all. By the
rule known as 'the custom of London' a member of any one of the twelve principal
Companies was entitled, as a freeman of the City, to engage not only in the craft by
which he was described, but in whatever other he might please. Hence the designation
'mercer', 'draper', 'fishmonger', etc. after a name indicates merely the Company to
which the individual in question belonged, not the trade which he pursued. At any rate
by the early seventeenth century a single Company might include among its members
practitioners of a dozen or more different trades. For some striking examples see
A. H. Johnson, *History of the Worshipful Company of Drapers of London* (1914-22),
vol. I, p. 73, and vol. III, pp. 93-4, where it is stated that, in 1641, out of 538 freemen
paying quarterage only twenty-five were drapers or woollen drapers, and that the great
majority had no connection with the craft.

ejected on the Treasurer's fall.[1] Lionel was the younger son. It may be remarked in passing that, as a result of the marriage of one of his sisters to a rising Exchequer official, then secretary to Lord Treasurer Dorset and later Comptroller of the Household, he became in due course uncle to the hard-drinking courtier, soldier and agreeable minor poet, the younger Sir John Suckling.[2]

In their attitude to education, to judge by their liberality in endowing it, the English commercial classes of the century between the Reformation and the Civil War were on the side of light. London, in particular, 'the third University of England',[3] was well supplied with schools. Lionel's family connection with the Mercers made it natural that he should attend St Paul's, the government of which Colet, a believer in the lay control of education, had vested in their Company. Of his school-days we know little more than that long after, when a financier of some note, he thought kindly enough of his former High Master to assist him with a loan;[4] that, whether because of his education or in spite of it, he acquired a command of vigorous and hard-hitting prose; and that enough of his classical studies remained with him in middle age to enable him to burst, at moments of emotion, into agreeably vituperative Latin, rebuking public lethargy and sloth, and, more surprisingly, denouncing with citations from St Bernard the nauseating greed of the parasitic courtiers who preyed upon the King.[5] His task, on leaving school, was that of all aspiring youth. The Cranfields, though reasonably well-to-do, had no large margin for manœuvre. The estate of £1700 odd, together with a house in the City, some scraps of other property in London and Hertfordshire, and the Greyhound Inn at

[1] Knighted July 1623; dismissed from Mastership July 1624 (Chamberlain, *Letters*, ed. McClure, vol. II, pp. 511, 569).

[2] The few particulars of Cranfield's family connections here given are taken principally from Hist. MSS. Comm., *Cranfield Papers, 1551–1612* (*MSS. of Lord Sackville*, vol. I), ed. A. P. Newton. For the statement as to the Dennises made Sheriffs see Th. Fuller, *The Worthies of England* (1840 ed.), vol. I, pp. 573–85, and for the Le Havre episode, J. B. Black, *The Reign of Elizabeth, 1558–1603* (1936), pp. 54–61. The Dennis manors were Hamon Hey in Gloucestershire and Sutton-at-Hone in Kent (Hist. MSS. Comm., *op. cit.* p. 24).

[3] The title of a book on the educational resources of London by Sir George Buck (1615). For business benefactors of education see J. Stow, *Survey of London* (1633 ed.), and N. Carlisle, *Endowed Grammar Schools in England and Wales* (1818). A convenient list of such schools, 1600–60, with dates of foundation, is given by W. A. L. Vincent, *The State and School Education* (1950), pp. 120–35.

[4] Hist. MSS. Comm., *op. cit.* p. 212. John Harrison, to whom the loan is made, was High Master of St Paul's School from 1581 to 1596.

[5] *Cranfield MSS.* no. 2330 (1616). See below, pp. 149–50.

Ware, left by Thomas Cranfield at his death in 1595, suggests that, in his later years, his export business may not have fared too well; while the income received by his widow from her share in the former Dennis manors was a bagatelle.[1] In such circumstances, Lionel's future would depend upon himself. Nor, with his strong practical bent, and a home where piece-goods, price-lists and continental markets were the air that he breathed, can he have remained long in doubt what line to pursue. His problem, it may be suspected, was not whether textiles should be his walk in life, but, given that objective, what approach to it to choose.

Opportunity came in the not too convincing guise of a business acquaintance of his father and uncle. Richard Sheppard, a member of the Grocers' Company, ran a general export and import business, which, while handling spices and some other articles appropriate to the name by which he was described, included the sale of woollen textiles in the Netherlands and north Germany, against Italian velvets, silks and satins, Dutch linens, the German specialities known as Osnaburgs and Munsters, and grain from the great cereal entrepôt of Amsterdam.[2] Apprenticed to him in 1590, at the age of fifteen, Lionel accompanied his employer on visits to the fairs at Bristol, Beverley, Stamford and elsewhere at which clothiers exhibited their wares; acted as a buyer for the firm, as well as for his uncle, William Cranfield, at home and abroad; learned the continental end of the trade by spells of residence at Stade and Middelburg, and dealt, while still serving his indentures, in occasional parcels on his own account.

Thanks partly to such ventures, partly to a small legacy left him by his father, but most of all, it may be suspected, to his own brains and drive, he was in a position, when, in 1597, at the end of his seven years' apprenticeship, he was formally admitted to the freedom of the Mercers' Company and set up in business for himself, to make a flying start. Two years later he married his master's daughter, Elizabeth Sheppard, in the approved manner of the books, though not, since later he had to keep his father-in-law, with the orthodox results.[3] Sharing with his mother, as home, office, and warehouse

<hr>

[1] Hist. MSS. Comm., *op. cit.* pp. 17, 24–5.
[2] *Ibid.* pp. 1, 9, 10, 13, 19, 23–4.
[3] *Ibid.* p. 23 (admission to Mercers' Company) and pp. 52–3, 55, 62–3 (financial embarrassments of Sheppard). Later, after his purchase in 1610 of the manor of Pishobury (Herts), Cranfield kept his father-in-law afloat by employing him, till the latter's death in 1621, to manage the estate.

in one, the family mansion in the parish of St Michael Bassishaw, he is of sufficient local standing to act in the last year of the old century as one of the collectors of the subsidy in his ward. In the second year of the new, when he gives the net value of his assets as £6000 to £7000, he is, as a cloth exporter, firmly on his feet, and can afford two years later, in 1603, to put in hand the building of the new house in Wood Street which was long to remain his home. It is characteristic, perhaps, of his not too docile disposition that our first conclusive evidence of his membership of the vigilant organisation to which, as a Merchant Adventurer, he owed allegiance, should be the imposition on him of a fine for disobedience to its rules.[1]

---

[1] Hist. MSS. Comm., *op. cit.* p. 28 (household arrangements and collectorship of subsidy); p. 43 (draft will of July, 1601); pp. 55, 59–61, 74–5, 102 (new house in Wood Street); p. 49 (receipt dated April 1602, by the Treasurer of the Merchant Adventurers' Company of a fine of £57 imposed on Lionel Cranfield by the Governor of the Company on 22 Nov. 1601).

CHAPTER II

THE EUROPEAN BACKGROUND

I. THE INTERLUDE OF PEACE

Nature, in endowing Europe with a long and deeply indented coast-line and two inland seas to north and south, has made commerce accessible to most of her regions and indispensable to some; but it is a commonplace that geography and state-craft have found it difficult to live at peace. It was Cranfield's fortune to launch his bark at a moment when political storms, though not yet allayed, showed signs of dying down, and an interlude of peaceful intercourse seemed for the moment to be more than on the way. At the turn of the century the ruin of the former economic power-house of the Continent lay twenty years in the past. The ruin of central Europe in a more appalling catastrophe lay twenty years in the future. In the first part of the generation and a half between the destruction of Antwerp and the Thirty Years War old fires still blazed. In the second, though not extinguished, they burned low. Gardiner has remarked that the pacific predilections of James were not merely a personal idiosyncrasy, but an attitude dictated by the facts of a situation in which it appeared for a time not impossible that the Iron Age was over, and that wars of religion might at last have spent their force.[1] A contemporary historian of the reign hinted the same verdict. 'The truth is that the Christian world was weary of these wars, for merchants will be merchants, and will always contrive that, if any goods are taken, they shall always belong to such as are in league with us. Towards the end of Queen Elizabeth's reign, all Christian kings...were resolved to have a peace.'[2]

It may be doubted whether, save in the form of exhausted treasuries, the economic considerations stressed by Goodman were a decisive factor in the change of front; but fiscal paralysis was a nightmare which few belligerents, save the United Netherlands, saw their way to dispel. Spain, in the later 1590's, was just over her third repudiation and not far from her fourth. The French finances, when in the

---

[1] Gardiner, *Cambridge Modern History*, vol. III, p. 558.
[2] Goodman, *op. cit.* vol. I, pp. 58–9.

same decade Sully took them in hand, were in ruins. England had fared better, but the debt left by Elizabeth at the end of her reign was, on paper, not far short of twice that inherited by her at its beginning.[1] In these countries, therefore, the financial incentive to a *détente* was strong. It caused moderation, a policy of mutual concessions, a suspicion that business might be as profitable as embargoes and trade as privateering, to make converts in unexpected places. 'The halcyon days' of which an observer brought up in them wrote long after that, not only in England, but in France, Spain and Germany, 'the habiliments of war grew rusty',[2] were not the oasis of tranquillity on which, in a harsher age, his memory dwelt; but, compared with past and future, they were, at least, a haven between storms. Whatever the motives and intentions of her rulers, Europe, though not free from wars and rumours of wars, slid half-unconsciously into one of her brief lucid intervals, and the political environment, long unfriendly to enterprise, became for a period propitious to it.

The treaty of 1598 between France and Spain, which reopened to each country its most important foreign market; the Anglo–Spanish treaty of 1604, applauded in the City, though unpopular outside it; the treaty of the same year, which meant much to southern trade, between France and the Porte; and, two years later, the belated common sense of the treaty of commerce between England and France, may reasonably be seen, against that background, not as isolated episodes, but as milestones on one road. The exchange of Ambassadors between England and Venice, which gave Wotton his chance, had, at least for James, larger ends in view, but was partly designed to cope with the scandal of English privateering in the Mediterranean and to dissuade rival monopolists from cutting

---

[1] On the successive bankruptcies of the Spanish Government in 1557, 1575, 1596 and 1607 (the last a moratorium) see R. Ehrenberg, *Das Zeitalter der Fugger*, vol. II, pp. 153–7, 205–10, 259–61; for the financial situation of France, *ibid.* vol. II, pp. 263 *seq.*, and Sully, *Economies Royales* (the latter a doubtfully reliable source); and on the debts at the beginning and end of Elizabeth's reign, F. C. Dietz, *English Public Finance, 1558–1641*, pp. 7–8, 113, and W. R. Scott, *The Constitution and Finance of English, Scottish and Irish Joint-Stock Companies to 1720* (1912), vol. III, pp. 494 and 509. Scott points out that at her death three of the four subsidies voted in 1601, i.e. above £300,000, still remained to come in and suggests that the debt of £400,000, mentioned in 1606 by Lord Treasurer Dorset (Gardiner, *Parliamentary Debates in 1610*, p. 5 n.), should be reduced by that amount. On the other hand, part at least of the military expenditure to meet which the subsidies had been granted continued under her successor.

[2] Arthur Wilson, 'The Life and Reign of King James I', in *A Complete History of England* (1719), vol. II, p. 703.

throats for currants.[1] The half-hearted enforcement and early with-drawal of the imperial embargo—'a ban, rather ridiculous than formidable'[2]—excluding from German markets the wares of the greatest of English export rings was a minor item on the same side of the account. The high landmark of the twelve years' truce of 1609 between Spain and the United Netherlands overshadowed them all. The instability of the equilibrium depicted in that year by an English notability[3] on tour abroad was only too obvious; but the 'balance'—to use the term then in fashion—survived, if precariously, the shocks of the best part of another decade. In the event, it fell a victim less to its own inherent unrealities than to an explosion, half nationalist, half religious, in eastern Europe.

Charmed by that milder climate, the reader is tempted to recall the famous lines saluting the advent of an era in which

> Incertitudes now crown themselves secure,
> And Peace proclaims olives of endless age.[4]

Our data are too scanty to permit a detailed demonstration of the scale on which political pacification bore its usual economic fruits. Such fragmentary evidence, however, as we possess suggests that the English recovery from the post-Armada depression ascribed by Professor Scott[5] to the early years of James is best regarded, not as an insular vagary, but as part of a more general movement in which several regions shared. The increase after 1606 in the export from Danzig, the granary of Europe, of the international staple in widest demand; the simultaneous rise in the receipts from the lastage dues levied on vessels traversing the great northern artery of the Sound and the upward movement in several of the most important wares, including the two key commodities of salt and of timber in the form

[1] *Cal. S. P. Ven. 1603–7*, Introd. p. xlvii; Logan Pearsall Smith, *The Life and Letters of Sir Henry Wotton* (1907), vol. II, chs. IV and V.

[2] J. Howell, *Familiar Letters*, sect. VI, letter no. iii; R. Ehrenberg, *Hamburg und England im Zeitalter der Königin Elizabeth* (1896), pp. 195 *seq.* (order of 1 Aug. 1957, for-bidding trade between subjects of the Empire and Merchant Adventurers), pp. 200 *seq.* (inefficient enforcement of the order) and p. 220 (permission of 29 September 1607, to English merchants to reside, trade and make rules for the conduct of the trade at Stade).

[3] *The Observations of Sir Thomas Overbury in his Travels*, in *Harl. Misc.* vol. III, pp. 97–109.

[4] The date generally favoured for these lines appears to be one between 1600 and 1609, with a preference for 1602 or 1603, and the allusion is thought to be to the peaceful accession of James (Shakespeare, *Sonnets*, ed. H. E. Rollins, in *The New Variorum* edition).

[5] W. R. Scott, *op. cit.* vol. I, pp. 129–30.

of planks, shipped east and west; the striking advance, in an age when the manufacture of greatest international significance was woollen textiles, in the value and volume of cloth exports from London, as well as in the output of the factories of the famous textile town of Leyden—such are a handful of examples in point.[1] Similar information on the trade of southern Europe is still, it seems, to seek; but a memorandum produced in 1610 by one Richard Gore, later the Merchant Adventurers' deputy at Hamburg, gives us a glimpse of the developments which his ever-tearful company believed to have occurred.[2] The article which occupied somewhat the same place among raw materials as cereals among foodstuffs was wool. Spain, the Australia of the day, had seized, it was alleged, the opportunity given by the Peace of 1604 to flood the

[1] The sources of the statements made above are as follows:

(a) Grain shipments from Danzig. The most recent work on the subject is that of D. Krannhals, *Danzig und der Weichselhandel in seine Blütezeit vom 16 zum 17 Jahrhundert* (1942). His figures indicate that, after allowance has been made for the export of grain to other ports on the Baltic, the total exports in the five-yearly periods, 1601–5, 1606–10, 1611–15 and 1616–20, were respectively 8% below, 16% above, slightly 2% below, and 22% above, the average of 1591–1600. Aksel E. Christensen's *Dutch Trade to the Baltic about 1600* (1941) contains much valuable information on the same subject.

(b) Trade through the Sound. The principal source of information is *Tabelle over Skibsfart og Varetransport gennem Øresund, 1497–1660 (Tables de la Navigation et du Transport des Marchandises passant par le Sund, 1497–1660)*, ed. Nina Ellinger Bang. Especially before 1618, when the methods of collection were improved, the figures are apparently open to criticisms which the present writer is incompetent to discuss. Useful assistance in interpreting them is offered by Christensen, *op. cit.*; see in particular pp. 444–5 (figures of lastage, 1574–1639), and his account of the system in ch. VI. In addition to the wares mentioned several others showed a rise, e.g. herrings, wines and woollen stuffs (west to east), and cereals, flax, hemp, ashes, pitch, hides and skins (east to west).

(c) Textile exports from London. The figures of the yield of the Petty Customs (6/8d per cloth exported by English and 13/4d per cloth exported by other merchants), which I owe to the kindness of Professor F. J. Fisher, are taken for 1598–1604 from the *Enrolled Accounts* for 1606–9 from *Lans. MSS.* 152, ff. 175–9, and for 1613 and 1614 from those of Cranfield and Wolstenholme in *Cranfield MSS.* (see e.g. nos. 4540, 4541, 4534, 4388, all 1615). They indicate an increase in cloth exports from London which raised them on the average of the four years 1606–9 to 28%, and on that of 1613 and 1614, the last two years of the boom, to 32% above the level of 1598–1601. See also Professor Fisher's table of 'short cloths' exported from London in 'London's Export Trade in the Early Seventeenth Century', in *Econ. Hist. Rev.* vol. III (1950), no. 2.

(d) Textile production at Leyden. N. W. Posthumus, *De Geschiedenis van de Leidsche Lakenindustrie* (1908–1939), vol. II, p. 129, gives a table showing the production of says, fustians and bays over a term of years. Their average aggregate output appears to have been in 1605–9 28%, and in 1610–14 45% above that of the last five years of the preceding century.

[2] *Lans. MSS.* 152, no. 45, ff. 232–3: 'The Reasons of the Decay of Clothes and Clothiers in England', by Mr Richard Gore, 20 September 1610.

international market with her long pent-up supplies. During a
generation of disorder—civil war in France, civil war in Germany,
war and revolution in the Low Countries, banditry on land and
piracy at sea—continental textile industries had fallen on evil days,
and, as later during the Napoleonic Wars, the English lead had
lengthened. Now, the indignant Adventurers complain, the tide has
turned against them. Aided by cheap and high-grade raw materials
from Spain, their competitors are in a position, not merely to recover
old markets, but to capture new, in half-a-dozen countries, from
Portugal to Turkey, where formerly the English article was wont
to reign alone. Such laments from such a source are commonly to
be taken with a grain of salt. In this case, however, less dubious
evidence lends some colour to them. The reliance of the Leyden
textile industry on bulk supplies of Spanish wool begins, it seems,
about the middle of the second decade of the century. The dependence of Italian textiles on raw materials from the same quarter is
both then and later a recurrent theme of the Venetian Embassy in
London.[1]

Such sporadic symptoms of a revival, swelling here and there, as
in England, into a more than ordinarily active trade, do not, it may
readily be admitted, take us far. It may be noted, however, that they
receive a measure of confirmation from indications of a less specific
kind. Professor Scott's evidence that companies were doing well;
the ease with which capital for new ventures appears to have been
raised in Amsterdam and London; the doubling of the former's
customs revenue in just over twenty years, and the speculative fever
accompanying in the latter the intermittent boom of James' opening
decade are cases in point.[2] To place a too implicit reliance on contemporary expressions of opinion would be naïve. But economic
meteorologists in London were more prone to ban than to bless, and
the unanimity with which, once the Spanish war was over, they proclaimed all set fair cannot simply be dismissed. It is illustrated from
one angle by the enthusiasm which hailed the recently granted contract
for the farm of the Great Customs, as a presage of 'open traffic with

---

[1] Posthumus, *op. cit.* vol. III, pp. 755–6, and *Cal. S.P. Ven. 1619–21*, no. 608 (on the
importance of imported wool to the United Provinces). For the dependence on it of
Italian textile industries, see *ibid. 1613–15*, no. 66; *1623–25*, no. 8; *1625–26*, nos. 744,
745.

[2] W. R. Scott, *op. cit.* vol. I, pp. 130–1; Violet Barbour, *Capitalism in Amsterdam
in the Seventeenth Century* (1950), p. 17 and *passim*; Ben Jonson's plays, especially *The
Alchemist* (1610) and *The Devil is an Ass* (1616).

the universe';[1] from another by the characteristically sardonic comment of the Venetian Embassy that there was now no arguing with the City, which, exulting in the prospect of long-closed markets once more at its feet, clamoured for concessions to trade where and how it pleased, while persistently refusing to grant a *quid pro quo* itself;[2] from a third by the transition from the sanguine self-congratulation which saluted in the House of Commons James' golden dawn to the embittered disillusionment that scowled on his reign's unhappy close. The complacent exhilaration, voiced in the Parliament of 1605 by a Jacobean Mr Podsnap—'of a weak, feeble and breathless estate [England] is become the most mighty, rich and opulent empire of Christendom'—showed optimism on the way to carry all before it; the storm of economic lamentation from every quarter of the House which met in January 1621—'All the grievances of the kingdom a trifle in comparison of the decay of trade'—gave expression to the mood of its melancholy successor.[3] The spokesmen of the Government, while labouring to set the contrast in a less repulsive light, were driven, in spite of themselves, to pay tribute to its truth. 'The staple commodities of the kingdom, viz., wool, corn, yea and even land itself,' wrote Cranfield in some notes for a speech to be delivered in the autumn of 1621, 'hath been improved one third part at the least since his Majesty's reign, and hath so continued all his Highness's reign until this last two years.... The general cry is the poverty of the people. If eighteen years with a flourishing trade, and one third part improvement of all the staple commodities of the kingdom, will not make the people rich, they have strangely abused God's blessing under his Majesty's government.'[4]

2. THE PATTERN OF EUROPEAN TRADE

The career of successful enterprise which gave the speaker's words their weight is recounted below. Detached, however, from its context, the trade, not only of an individual, but of a single country,

---

[1] Hist. MSS. Comm., *MSS. of the Earl Cowper*, vol. I, p. 58 (S. Naunton, M.P. for Helston, to John Coke, 29 October 1605).

[2] E.g. *Cal. S.P. Ven. 1603–7*, no. 278 (6 October 1604).

[3] *Commons' Journals*, 10 February 1605 (speech of Mr Bond); *Proceedings and Debates of the House of Commons in 1621* (Oxford, 1766), 29 May 1621 (speech of Sir Edwyn Sandys).

[4] *Cranfield MSS.* no. 7495, printed in Notestein, Relf and Simpson, *Commons' Debates, 1621* (1935), vol. VII, pp. 617–19.

is a rope thrown into the void. The map is more important than the pieces composing it; and, though studies of the commerce of particular nations have their use, the localised activities depicted in them gain in significance and point, if seen on occasion in the setting of the larger pattern which together they produce. During his early years in the City, Cranfield's eyes were fixed on foreign markets, and later, when officially confronted by the task of grappling with domestic distress, he was quick to discern among its causes the political breakdown abroad, whose disastrous repercussions only peace could arrest. As an introduction, therefore, to his export business, a glance at some features of the international economy determining the character and scope of the trade by which he rose, is not a mere digression. It is, on the contrary, a concession to realism which, both as merchant and minister, he himself would have approved.

One corner of the scene need not detain us for long. It was to be remarked by a contemporary with a flair for economic synthesis, whose name more than once occurs in Cranfield's ledger, that, reduced to essentials, the world commerce of his day consisted in the exchange of the mineral wealth of the new Indies in the west for the luxuries and refinements of the old Indies in the east.[1] Mun's picture of a vast and slender arch spanning oceans and continents, an arch with one pier firmly planted in Peru, Mexico and Bolivia and the other in the Spice Islands, over-simplified the reality; but, in his emphasis on the role of the mistress of South America as, in Bacon's phrase, 'the money-breeder of Europe',[2] he spoke as history now speaks. No statesman, and no merchant with extensive foreign connections, could be incurious as to the migrations of the treasure which streamed, 'like rain pouring off a roof',[3] through the fingers of the least commercial-minded of peoples to Genoese bankers, Spanish officials, secret service agents and soldiers, and finally—since, given a deficiency of alternative means of payment, the first link in the mercantilist argument was not a fallacy but a platitude—to the countries with a credit balance on their merchandise account. Cranfield's papers show him in both capacities alive to their significance.

[1] T. Mun, *England's Treasure by Forraign Trade* (1664), ch. VI. (The date at which the work was written is uncertain; that suggested by McCulloch is 1635 or 1640.)

[2] F. Bacon, *Considerations touching a War with Spain.*

[3] Quoted by M. Ansiaux, 'Histoire économique d'Espagne au XVIe et au XVIIe siècles', in *Revue d'Economie Politique* (1893), vol. VII, p. 1031.

The two other branches of extra-European trade hardly came within his purview. One, with an El Dorado as its goal, was to make, when luck favoured, the fortunes of investors in Amsterdam and London, but remained, during the greater part of Cranfield's apprenticeship, the as yet unrealised aspiration of sanguine Dutch prospectors and disillusioned English Turkey merchants. The other wooed a Thule for fish, later brightened by tobacco. For both—the Eastern and the North American—fate reserved a brilliant future, and during its first two decades the former, at least, did well; but, in spite of contemporary paeans on it as a pearl beyond price, it is a question whether the much advertised enterprise did not, at this stage of its history, do more for the imagination of England than for its stomach or its industries. While, in short, a single East Indiaman might return with a king's ransom of exotic treasures in its hold, the student of the English company's achievements during the years when Cranfield was engaged in foreign trade may, perhaps, be pardoned if his exhilaration is tempered by reflections of the kind which prompted Gibbon's dry grimace—'splendid and trifling'—at the oriental traffic of Rome.[1] The latter, the American, was of moment to the re-export business of Plymouth and other south-western ports, and, subsequently, as Virginia developed her single-crop economy, to the English Exchequer; but the contribution to the European market made by a scattered handful of under-manned and under-capitalised settlements in North America remained for long on too modest a scale to count for much. It was not till Cranfield was about to abandon commerce for public life that he showed an interest in either. If then he invested in the Virginia and East India Companies, it is possible that his motive was less profit than prestige.[2]

The traffic of Europe with other continents remained, therefore, during Cranfield's career as an exporter, not a closely woven fabric, but a skein composed of few and slender, if often brilliant, threads. The traffic of Europe with itself, an affair, not of annual or biennial expeditions to distant Golcondas, but of intercourse between

[1] Gibbon, *The History of the Decline and Fall of the Roman Empire*, ed. J. B. Bury (1897), vol. I, p. 54.

[2] Cranfield invested £12. 10s. in 1611 'for my adventure in the voyage to Virginia'; £25 in 1613; and two further sums of £25 each in 1617 for his first year's adventure in the second joint-stock. He bought in 1617 Sir Edward Villier's £1000 venture in the East India Company, and may have made another investment in it. In 1614 he lent £10 to Sir Thomas Smythe on two shares in the Somers Island Company, but the shares were presumably merely the security for the loan (Hist. MSS. Comm., *Cranfield Papers, 1551–1612*, p. 236; *Cranfield MSS*. nos. 6149, 4792–3, 4930, 4931, 4935).

neighbours long specialised to different roles, was less spectacular, but more important. Its note in an age supposedly the heir of a commercial revolution was less change of direction than growth in scale. Except—an important qualification—that some routes which had debouched on the Levant now ended on the Atlantic, the strategy of European trade had been little altered by the Discoveries, which had added a circumference of new connections, but which had not yet, save at a few critical points, superseded the old. The high degree of integration, which was its most significant characteristic, was not novel, but of long standing. It existed because, given the facts of geography, it could not but exist.

The fundamental feature of the economy of Europe can be simply stated. It was a contrast of climate, of natural resources, and probably of population, between north and south, resembling in miniature that later to become important between Europe as a whole and the extra-European world. The former contained within itself its own small equivalent of North America, and, if not its own tropics, its partial substitute for them. At one end, the regions adjacent to the Baltic remained semi-colonial. Thinly settled, heavily wooded, with the trapper giving way to the lumberman, and lumbering to agriculture as the timber-line retreated and the cereal frontier advanced, they were a still unexhausted reservoir of raw materials and foodstuffs. At the other, Spain and Portugal, with a surplus of textile fibres, vegetable oils, dye-stuffs, iron ore and southern fruits, reinforced by colonial wares, supplied primary products complementary to those of the north. Commanding the resources of a more genial environment, a denser population and a more sophisticated civilisation than the first, and less disposed than the second to 'employ themselves in arms, not in manufactures',[1] the chief industrial areas of Europe lay between these two extremes. To such a statement there are, of course, numerous exceptions; but the larger currents of trade had their source in the regional differentiation which such contrasts caused. As in the Middle Ages, and indeed, well into the last century, they flowed south and north, from forest, corn land, territories rich in copper, lead or iron, and seas in fish, to vineyard, olive grove, sheep pasture, salt lagoon, textile workshop, smithy and shipyard, meeting, crossing and re-starting in the great junction of the Netherlands, and, at different

---

[1] *S.P.D. Chas. I*, XVIII, no. 21 (18 January 1626). The document contains the views of the City on the economic effects of war with Spain.

points, feeding or fed by subsidiary streams. Of these tributaries, some were themselves no trifling rivers; but the circulation along the minor veins depended on the pulse of the great north to south artery. If that were blocked or cut, the whole organism languished. The knot-points were Amsterdam and London; Danzig and Hamburg: Frankfurt-am-Main, Leipzig and Nürnberg: Rouen, Bordeaux and Marseilles: Venice and Leghorn. The international exchange, to which most staples found their way, was Amsterdam. The financial experts were Italians, in particular the Genoese, the south Germans and the Dutch, with the last rapidly gaining on the two first. The bullion on which their operations were based came, largely via Barcelona and Genoa, from Spain. The ligament which held the whole structure together was the shipping of the Dutch.

The key positions were obvious. International politics and naval strategy repeatedly underlined them. The trade which passed between them, to modern eyes a trickle, was a system, not a chaos. The wares moving east and west through the Sound offer one glimpse of the interlocking wheels at work; the business done by one of the great entrepôts, which handled the imports and exports, not of a single country, but of a large part of Europe, another and more instructive one.[1] On the question of values little useful can be said. It is a truism that a country's commerce is merely one aspect of its total economy, and that no conclusions as to wealth or poverty, prosperity or its absence, can be deduced from it alone. Figures of foreign trade are for that reason uninstructive in the absence of the means to relate them to other aspects of its economic life. Accompanied, as, for example, later in Petty's hypothetical correlations, by estimates of population and of income,[2] they may contribute to

[1] For trade through the Sound, see above, pp. 15 and 16, n. 1. A good example of regional differentiation, though one subsequent to Cranfield's retirement from public life, is supplied by the re-export trade done by Dover, which, partly as a result of the economic agreement accompanying the Cottington Treaty of 1630, had become by the thirties the greatest of English entrepôts. Among the re-exports, other than silver, from Dover to Hamburg, the Spanish Netherlands and the United Provinces, rather more than 40% consisted of southern raw materials for the textile industries, in particular silk and wool, together with subsidiaries such as dye-stuffs, potash and Spanish oil. Food, drink and tobacco came to just over a quarter, with sugar and molasses and wines at the head of the list. Manufactures, chiefly textiles, amounted to slightly over a tenth. In the re-exports from Dover to Spain, Italy and the Straits the picture is reversed. Virtually the whole of them consisted of manufactures, and above nine-tenths of them of textiles (*Exchequer King's Remembrancer Port Books*, 659/12/1638).

[2] For Petty's views on population see *Verbum Sapienti*, probably written 1665 (C. H. Hull, *The Economic Writings of Sir William Petty*, vol. 1, p. 105), *Political*

light; unaided by those auxiliaries, they leave the inquirer little wiser than before. Contemporary calculations of English commodity imports and exports, which yield an average of just over £4,000,000, or, at a guess, in the region of 23s. per head, for three years under James,[1] may in future, if complementary data come to hand, be of service; but the only conclusion that can at present be drawn from them is disappointingly banal. It is that the results of these few rudimentary attempts at trade returns are, at least, not inconsistent with the marked degree of integration between different economies which the more convincing non-statistical evidence shows to have been a fact.

As a clue to the nexus between nations, the character of the wares exchanged is in Cranfield's day both less uncertain and more illuminating than official valuations put on them at ports. The venerable legend of medieval commerce as an affair of high values in small bulk has recently sustained at the hands of Professors Postan and Lopez some corrective shocks.[2] The infectious glamour of Milton's 'barbaric pearls and gold', which clings to the first predatory phase of European expansion, requires, if to a somewhat less degree, the same deflating touch. The part played by costly superfluities in the trade of Cranfield's generation was, doubtless, more conspicuous than later it became, and his own import business appears to have done well on them; but, apart from the East Indian and South American fleets, bulk consignments were predominantly of a different stamp. Except for the virtual absence of crude minerals, and the paucity of capital goods other than timber, ships

Arithmetic, begun, according to the editor, in 1671, and completed not earlier than 1676 (*ibid*. vol. II, p. 310), and *Observations on England* (*The Petty Papers*, ed. the Marquis of Lansdowne, vol. I, p. 206); for the national income or output, *Verbum Sapienti* (Hull, *op. cit.* vol. I, pp. 105, 108, 110); and for foreign trade, *Political Arithmetic* (*ibid*. vol. I, pp. 295-7). To describe Petty's estimates as hypothetical is an understatement.

[1] The years in question are 1612-13, 1613-14, and 1621-2 (*Lans. MSS.* 152, ff. 175 *seq*., and E. Misselden, *The Circle of Commerce* (1623), p. 127). See also G. N. Clark, *Guide to English Commercial Statistics, 1698-1792*, pp. xi-xii. In the first of these years trade was good, in the second exceptionally good, in the third exceptionally bad. N. S. B. Gras, *The Evolution of the English Corn Market* (1915) gives 4,000,000 and 4,500,000 as approximate estimates of the population of England in 1605 and 1634; a later work by G. Davies, *The Early Stuarts* (1937), p. 259, suggests 'between 4,000,000 and 4,500,000 inhabitants for the reign of James I. The figure of 23s. odd assumes a population in the region of 4,200,000.

[2] M. Postan and E. E. Rich, *The Cambridge Economic History of Europe* (1952), vol. II, ch. IV (by M. Postan) and ch. V (by R. S. Lopez) on the trade of medieval Europe, north and south.

and guns, the international staples which kept tonnage moving were at once insignificant in number compared with those of today, and in kind not less prosaic. Handling, as it did, three essential foodstuffs, the raw materials of a dozen or so industries, and one large group of manufactures flanked by several minor ones, international commerce had as its backbone, not the luxuries of a romantic legend, but commodities catering, if not for a mass demand, which, outside a few great cities, hardly yet existed, for the elementary needs of a large consuming public.

In an economy destitute of the auxiliaries and substitutes supplied by science, and in which production depends less on a generalised technology than on traditional crafts, goods must be sought where nature supplies them. Hence the primary products of differently endowed regions occupied, it is probable, a larger space in freights than in the Europe of today. A catalogue would be tedious, and a handful of specimens must suffice. Corn is one example. The world's chief cereal-importing countries tend in our own age to be those whose high population density and low acreage per head causes land to be dear; the chief cereal exporters those where the opposite conditions make it cheap. Except that rye, not wheat, was the principal export crop, a similar situation obtained in the past. Four permanent deficiency areas, the Netherlands, northern Italy, Spain and Portugal, and parts of Scandinavia, the two first the most densely populated countries in Europe, the two last with natural disadvantages which made cereal-farming a gamble, depended regularly on imported grain, as at moments of emergency did several more. Poland with Prussia—which a climate and soil suitable for rye, if not for wheat, excellent river communications between the interior and the sea, and a population per square mile a third or less that of the Netherlands, prepared for the role of a European Middle West—was the principal source of the surplus which supplied them.[1] Minor contributions came from Esthonia; from Russia, described, when trade with it had been developed by Dutch capital,

---

[1] Krannhals, *op. cit.* gives the average annual export of grain, mostly rye, from Danzig as, in 1601–5, 45,779 last; in 1606–10, 58,095 last; in 1611–15, 48,659 last; and in 1616–20, 61,347 last. According to G. Malynes (*Consuetudo vel Lex Mercatoria* (1656 ed.), p. 30) the English equivalent of the last of rye, which was slightly smaller than that of wheat, was approximately 1 ton, 17 cwt. For the important grain trade of southern Europe at a slightly earlier date, see Fernand Braudel, *La Méditerranée et le Monde méditerranéen à l'Époque de Philippe II* (1949), especially pp. 268–92 and 421–503.

as 'the Sicily of Holland'; and in southern Europe from Sicily itself, Sardinia and France. The export specialty of the last, wheat, not rye, went to Spain, the Netherlands, and, when the English harvest failed, across the Channel.

Fish—at a period whose agricultural technique made fresh meat almost the seasonal delicacy that game is now, not a supplement to flesh food, but a substitute for it—was another article in the same category. Cheap, easily packed, and standing transport well, it travelled from the 'golden mines' of the North Sea as far as Venice in one direction, and Archangel in the other; entered eastern Germany by the Sound, and western by the Rhine; set nations by the ears; reconciled Protestant sailors to Popish fasts; and produced for the edification of posterity a library of pamphlets unique even in economic literature for their singular blend of credulity and dullness. The reader, exasperated by the intolerable tedium of odes to the herring, must solace his sufferings with the princely aphorism that the humble kipper was the pebble in the sling with which the Dutch David laid at last the Spanish Goliath low.[1]

Salt, Bacon's 'most excellent of minerals', served an even wider market. Not only a universal condiment, but indispensable for curing fish, meat and leather, it played in the infancy of chemical science a role later to be divided between a score of different preservatives and antiseptics. The principal bulk demand came partly from the pastoral peoples, to whom salt was essential for their cattle and the industries based upon them; partly, and more important, from the maritime nations of the North-West, who plied their craft in waters rich in fish, but too cold to provide the means to make it an article of commerce. The ideal return-cargo for northern vessels trading south, bay-salt recovered by evaporation—Bodin's 'manna bestowed by Heaven on France'—journeyed, mostly in Dutch vessels, to all parts of northern Europe not served by the rock-salt—itself a much-travelled article—of Germany and Franche-Comté. The Netherlands import was on a scale to enable them, after meeting the requirements of their vital fish-curing industry and supplying the regions served by the Rhine, to re-export through the Sound something over 90,000 tons a year. On the proposal under Charles to prohibit, in the interests of a monopolistic ring, salt imports into England, the usually docile officials of Trinity House

---

[1] The remark is ascribed to Prince Maurice (H. G. R. Reade, *Sidelights on the Thirty Years' War* (1924), vol. I, p. 29).

for once took the bit between their teeth. By forcing English merchantmen trading to the Mediterranean to come home in ballast, the embargo, they warned the Government, would cause a third or more of the country's shipping to be laid up.[1]

Salt was more important as a raw material than as a foodstuff; and when, in 1641, Sir Thomas Roe told the House of Commons that 'the northern trades...are the root of all others',[2] it was to another, and hardly less essential, raw material that he referred. With the increase in mercantile marines, the expansion of fuel-consuming industries, and the advance of agricultural frontiers, Venice, Spain, France and England—the last rich in woodlands, but reckless in plundering an asset which Pepys, jealous for his beloved Navy, defines in one of his few savage passages as 'an excrescence of the earth created by God for the payment of debts'— if they did not actually experience a timber famine, lived in constant fear that one was looming up.[3] In such conditions, 'the Indies of the materials of shipping'—the one great area combining virgin forests with easy river-transport to the sea—had an importance all its own. Baltic timber not only gave the Dutch the largest mercantile marine in the world, but provided them with re-exports in the shape of ships to a substantial part of the rest of commercial Europe. To Governments with naval ambitions the importance of the region supplying it had at times some resemblance to that which oil-fields were later to acquire. It is hardly an exaggeration to say that from Philip II to Cromwell, and from Cromwell to Napoleon's continental system, the Baltic question was largely a timber question.

All countries manufacturing textiles produced some of the raw materials required, but none produced all. Spanish silk was important to the French silk industry and essential to the Dutch. France and Holland relied mainly on home-grown flax, but also imported it. The exotic connections of the cotton industry are an old story. A trickle of wool found its way into trade from a dozen countries from Poland to Greece, but supplies from the one great specialist, Spain, were essential to the textile industries of not less

---

[1] *Cal. S.P.D. Chas. I, 1635–36*, CCVIII, no. 11, 1635(?): 'The greatest part of these [i.e. English] ships have their employment to the Straits, most of them being freighted only outwards. For freight home they expose themselves to chance, being encouraged by the certain lading of salt, when all better employment fails. If the importation of salt fails, a third part of the merchant ships in this land will want employment'.

[2] 'Sir Thomas Roe's Speech in Parliament', in *Harl. Misc.* vol. IV, pp. 456–62.

[3] Pepys, *Diary*, 5 May 1667. See R. G. Albion, *Forests and Sea Power* (1926), p. 146.

than four. England, while buying abroad such indispensable subsidiaries as oils, alum, potash and dyestuffs, and producing minor
specialties from Spanish wool, was the least dependent on foreign
fibres. It may be noted, however, that, within less than a decade of
Cranfield's death, a level-headed business man was urging that the
English Government, by way of bringing continental competitors
to heel, should negotiate with Spain for the bulk purchase of her
annual clip.[1]

In most of these cases diversities of climate and resources called
the tune; but such physical factors, if relatively more decisive than
today, did not act alone. Their effect was heightened or counteracted
by differences of energy, initiative and taste of the kind which
prompted Mun's encomium on the resourcefulness that enabled
the sagacious Genoese, when 'forced to leave their trades which
they cannot keep from other nations, who have better means...to
perform those affairs with more advantage',[2] to achieve, nevertheless,
a high level of prosperity by the intensive cultivation of those which
they retained. The regional differentiation characteristic of the
greatest manufacture of the day was the product of both influences
combined. The student of mercantilist literature may be pardoned
for some perplexity at the limelight lavished on it, as though the
grand end of economic statesmanship were to deluge with an ever-
mounting flood of fabrics a world already wallowing in superfluous
piece-goods. In reality, the industries concerned were not one, but
five, and, if their sub-divisions be included, not five, but legion.
Italian looms supplied the larger part of the small demand for silks,
satins and velvets. France rivalled Italy in the luxury trade, but her
longest suit was based on flax, which then met the needs later
served by cotton. Producing everything, from coarse canvas and
trade goods for South America to linens, damasks and cambrics,
Picardy, Normandy, and Brittany, if not yet the Lancashire of the
day, were on the way to become it. The specialty of south Germany
was fustians; that of the Spanish Netherlands tapestries and carpets.
The United Provinces shipped to London half-a-million yards of
linens of their own production, together with three-quarters of
a million yards of linen re-exports,[3] at a time when they were

---

[1] Henry Robinson, *Certain Proposals in order to the Peoples' Freedom and Accommodation in some particulars* (1652).
[2] T. Mun, *England's Treasure by Forraign Trade*, ch. XIV.
[3] *Cranfield MSS.* no. 6796. The date is Christmas 1619 to Christmas 1620.

themselves the second largest market for English woollens. England, while importing linen warps from the Netherlands and cotton yarns from Turkey, supplied the former with the grey cloths which were the raw material of its finishing industry, and sent kerseys to be dressed and dyed at Bremen and Nürnberg. Nor do these familiar examples stand alone. Venetian glass; French *bimbeloterie*; the products of Nürnberg's mechanical ingenuity, which were to be found, according to a younger contemporary of Cranfield,[1] in every corner of Europe; above all, in spite of every disadvantage, the miraculous pre-eminence in shipbuilding of the Dutch, are further instances of a specialisation which owed less to nature than to art.

An expanding commerce required a financial backing as elastic as itself. The last and not least important of the articles passing in international trade supplied the dynamic which kept the remainder on the move. 'These kingdoms', wrote an Italian observer of Spain and Portugal in the 1620's, in words which would have been equally valid half-a-century before, 'cannot exist unless relieved by others, nor can the rest of the world exist without the money of Spain.'[2] The conditions which caused the treasure of the Indies to fly from the embraces of its helpless host as quickly as it reached him hardly need to be explained. Like an heir endowed by the accident of an eccentric will with an estate which he is too poor to maintain, and too proud to resign, the Spain of Philip III, a super-national system rather than a nation, bore a crushing load of political and military liabilities abroad. Agriculturally and industrially retarded, she not only relied, like some of her more prosperous neighbours, on imported foodstuffs and manufactures to meet essential needs at home, but, in spite of valuable raw materials, exported her native products on too small a scale to pay the bill. In such circumstances it is not surprising that American silver should have been used to bridge the gap.

An attempt to trace the movements of the re-exported bullion would take us too far afield. Part of it went to France, on which Spain depended for wheat, linens, paper, minor manufactures, and trade goods for her colonies; part to England for woollen textiles, fish, grain, tin, lead and hardware to the tune, it was reported in

---

[1] Lewis Roberts, *The Merchant's Map of Commerce* (1638), ch. cxc. The first draft of the book was written some ten years earlier.

[2] Reade, *op. cit.* vol. II, pp. 332–3, quoting from a letter of Tarantaise, 22 January 1626.

1626, when the approach of war caused the English Government to call for figures, of half the value of English imports from Spain.[1] More, it is probable, was shipped to Genoa, which, from the fall of Antwerp in the 1570's till the ruin of the south German banking houses and their Italian consorts by the southward march in the 1630's of the Swedes, was the financial mainstay of the Spanish empire. Most of it, whatever its first destination, drifted north, raising prices on the way by irregular jerks, to arrive in the end at Amsterdam. An unrivalled foreign trade, a warehousing, agency and factoring business done on commission for foreign firms, and an international shipping service which made the United Provinces the universal carriers, drew remittances in. Dutch enterprise in lending to foreign customers and in opening under-developed regions in Europe, from Sweden and Russia to the Levant, as well as in Asia and America, carried part of them out in a stream so continuous that a Dutch historian can write that his country's single largest export was specie. Once founded in 1609, the Bank of Amsterdam became the pulse of the machine. The quadrupling of its deposits in its first fifteen years is a comment, not only on its own success, but on the dimensions of the market which it served.[2]

3. THE GROWTH OF ECONOMIC UNITY

Together with shipping—largely, in spite of navigation policies, an international business—and a thin, but growing, trickle of foreign investment, the movements of these staples gave the economic life of Europe a measure of unity and cohesion which it would be absurd to exaggerate, but which made commerce a link not to be snapped without formidable reactions. In his great *Study of History*, Dr Toynbee has used words implying that, before the age of coal and iron, foreign trade, except for a handful of 'lucrative super-fluities', was of minor significance, and to the mass of mankind, who could not afford such luxuries, of next to none.[3] Such was not the world as seen by Cranfield and his contemporaries. Their calculations were based on the assumption that, as far as certain major products were concerned, the coastal regions of Europe, and large parts of its

---

[1] *S.P.D. Chas. I*, xviii, nos. 20, 21 (18 January 1626).

[2] J. G. van Dillen, 'Amsterdam als Wereldmarkt der edele Metalen in de 17de en 18de Eeuw', in *De Economist* (1923). The brief allusions to Amsterdam made above are principally based partly on Dr van Dillen's article, partly on Violet Barbour, *op. cit.*

[3] Arnold J. Toynbee, *A Study of History*, vol. IV, p. 7.

interior, formed a single market. Two generations were to elapse before a merchant, who was also an economic thinker, could enunciate the axiom that 'the whole world as to trade is but as one nation or people';[1] but, in the interlude of comparative tranquillity preceding the plunge into general war, conditions of a kind to lend some colour to that view were slowly gathering way.

Examples offered by the trade of Cranfield himself will be found below; nor would it be difficult to add to them further illustrations both from the correspondence of his factors and from sources of a slightly later date. News received via the Netherlands of a wet August in England send September corn prices sky-high at Danzig. A good harvest in Spain means a slump in English textile exports to Hamburg, since, selling less grain in southern markets, the German agriculturist contracts his purchases of English cloth. Heavily hit by the failure of a leading Dutch grain importer, 'that devil, Krill', his English creditors take payment of a bad debt in saltpetre, and watch anxiously the Amsterdam and London markets before deciding where to send it. Polish leadmines increase their output, and Welsh lead becomes a drug. German tin and lead producers, and Dutch coal-owners, are on the alert to capture the French market the moment that political friction between England and France checks supplies from the former. French exporters of hardware and toys to Spain find their prices cut by cheap stuff from Nürnberg. At one end of Europe, Venice is both elated at the prospect of new markets opened to her textiles by the imperial embargo on the English article, and, a few years later, dismayed by the heightened severity of English and Dutch competition in the Mediterranean as a result of the Treaty of 1604 and the Truce of 1609. At the other, the English Eastland Company cries and cuts itself with knives at the thought of the injury inflicted on its trade by the sinister arts of the French, who buy up English rabbit-skins to make hats for the Italian market.[2]

This fabric of commercial intercourse was repeatedly torn by embargoes and blockades. Then, as always, progress in the arts of peace added weapons to the arsenal to be employed in war. When,

---

[1] *Discourse upon Trade*, preface, in J. R. McCulloch, *Early English Tracts upon Commerce*. The tract is anonymous but is probably by Dudley North.

[2] For the above examples see letters from factors to Cranfield, *Cranfield MSS.*, Ser. S., nos. S.660, S.635, S.644, S.652, S.653; *Wynn Papers* (Nat. Library of Wales), nos. 1031, 1154; A. Girard, *Le Commerce français à Séville et Cadix au temps des Habsbourgs*, p. 370 (*temp*. Hen. IV); *S.P.D. Jas. I*, XLV, no. 90; *Cal. S.P. Ven. 1592–1603*, no. 611; *ibid. 1610–13*, no. 383; *S.P.D. Chas. I*, CCCXLI, no. 383.

after more than a decade of expanding trade, half-a-dozen conflicts exploded in a general conflagration, both the importance and the vulnerability of the international economic nexus was emphasised by plans and, less often, by operations which included commercial key-points among their principal targets of attack. The strategy, for example, of the Dutch was to preserve at all costs their northern connections, in confidence that, if that link, on which their economy depended, continued to hold, they would in the end wear the ancient enemy down. The strategy of Spain was that to be expected of a military power engaged in 'a duel with fishes and water'. It was to throttle from a base on the North Sea or Baltic the Netherlands' vital trade in northern corn and timber. A further, and not more realistic, ingredient was added to that design by the Imperial project of reversing the trend of a century and restoring Venice to her position as an entrepôt through which an economically revivified Mittel-Europa was to be supplied with southern wares, in particular the products of Italian, instead of English, looms.[1] Of the English counter-strokes that most often canvassed was the seizure *en route* of the south-bound shipping of Hamburg, Lübeck and other Hanse towns, without whose cargoes of masts, pitch and tar, cordage and other shipping requisites neither the Spanish naval forces nor the all-important West Indian treasure-ships could put to sea. Applied both in the opening and the closing years of James, and expounded by Cranfield in one of the last State-papers produced by him before his fall, the policy was less nebulous than some of those favoured by continental powers, but was open to the objection of provoking retaliation in important markets for English cloth.[2] The last consideration, however, lost part of its weight through the inevitable repercussions of international conflicts on neutrals, however pacific, depicted by one who himself experienced the partial paralysis produced. 'Since coming to these parts', wrote in June 1622, from Hamburg a youthful Merchant Adventurer to his father in Wales, our trade 'has one half part decayed, and that is [*sc.* in] four years. Usually heretofore we used to have 15, 16 or 18 ships a year laden with cloth, and now it is come but to 6 for this place; and these few will not sell what with dearness and want of vent in regard of wars

[1] E.g. H. G. R. Reade, *Sidelights on the Thirty Years' War* (1924), vols. II, pp. 574-5, 580-1, and III, pp. 86-7, 230-8, 383-9; *Cal. S.P. Ven. 1628-9*, no. 28 (15 March 1628).

[2] *Cal. S.P. Ven. 1592-1603*, no. 1160 (20 March 1603), *1623-5*, no. 790 (10 February 1625), *1625-6*, nos. 645 (10 July 1626), 710 (4 September 1626), 727 (11 September 1626); *Cranfield MSS.* no. 8436 (1624?).

and base money, and also the store of Dutch [*sc*. German] woollen cloth made in these parts.'[1] Nor, in considering the political risks which commerce had to run, must it be forgotten that, if total war was not the fashion of the age, no more was total peace, and that, in the absence of hostilities between States, piracy was an ever-open wound.

The fact remains, nevertheless, that the threads of commercial intercourse were closer, and its texture more resilient, than at first sight might appear. Opinion, as usual, lagged in the rear of realities, and the doctrinal economic militancy, which laboured rivalries, not mutual benefits, was partly, as often since, a cry of alarm at the impact on nervous interests of the reduction of protective barriers by the practical logic of commercial facts. Economic interdependence, as the authors of the *Cambridge Economic History of Europe* have recently reminded us,[2] is not a phenomenon of recent growth; and in Cranfield's day, though embracing a wider area than in the centuries depicted by them, it remained rudimentary. The important fact was its existence. When, as on an unhappy occasion in the England of James I, statesmen treat the system as a machine to be speeded up, arrested or reconstructed at will, it proves convincingly that it is an organism by the convulsions into which it falls.

---

[1] *Wynn Papers*, Nat. Library of Wales, Aberystwyth, no. 1023 (letter of June 3, 1622, from Maurice Wynn at Hamburg to his father, Sir John Wynn).

[2] Postan and Rich, *op. cit.* vol. II, pp. 119–33, 284–354, 372–428.

CHAPTER III

CRANFIELD'S EXPORT BUSINESS

1. THE CHARACTER OF ENGLISH COMMERCE

During Cranfield's two decades in the City, the economic bonds between England and her continental neighbours grew in strength, but the principal links composing them underwent little change. The salient features of her commerce can be simply stated. Its older bases in northern markets more than held their own;[1] while, apart from eastern and a trickle of American imports and re-exports, English foreign enterprise was as conservative in the wares which it handled as in the directions which it took. Writing in the 1620's, an English author described as an advantage superior even to his country's geographical position 'the richness and quantity of our native commodities to make trade withal, which far exceeds any one kingdom in Christendom or in the known world'.[2] Foreign

---

[1] For the markets to which London exports went, see F. J. Fisher, 'London's Export Trade in the Early Seventeenth Century,' *Econ. Hist. Rev.*, 2nd series, vol. III, no. 2, 1950. He shows a slight decline between 1614, the Merchant Adventurers' peak year, and 1640 in the percentage of short cloths exported by English merchants from London to Russian, Baltic and North Sea ports, and a somewhat larger increase in that of short cloths exported to Spanish, African and Mediterranean ports. In the case of commodities other than short cloths a similar movement is more marked. For information on London imports, as evidenced by the Port Books in two of the few years of the early seventeenth century for which data are available, I am indebted to Mrs Millard, who allows me to quote her conclusions as to their regions of origin and the principal commodities composing them (see below, pp. 34–5). She estimates that in the nine months September 1601–July 1602, roughly two-thirds in tonnage of London imports by English and alien merchants came from France, the Low Countries and Germany; just over one-seventh from the Baltic, Norway and Russia; one-tenth from Spain, Portugal and the Islands; rather more than one-twelfth from the Levant, Italy and Barbary, less than 1% from the West Indies and *nil* from the East; and that, as a result of the relative increase of southern and extra-European trade, the corresponding percentages in the twelve months Christmas 1620–Christmas 1621, were in terms of values 56, 6, 18, 12, 1 and 5. Such figures are, of course, at best a rough approximation, and can be used to illustrate only the most general features of the pattern of trade. For a critical discussion of the uses and defects of the Port Books as a source of historical information, see G. N. Clark, *op. cit.* pp. 52–6; for an account of them in the reign of James I, Friis, *Alderman Cockayne's Project and the Cloth Trade*, App. B; and for some further observations applying specially to provincial Port Books, J. H. Andrews, 'Two Problems in the Interpretation of the Port Books', in *Econ. Hist. Rev.*, 2nd ser., vol. IX, no. 1 (August 1956), and R. H. W. Hinton, 'Dutch Entrepôt Trade at Boston, Lincs.', *ibid.* vol. IX, no. 3 (April 1957).

[2] Sir John Watts, *A Discourse upon Trade* (1625?), quoted Hist. MSS. Comm., *Third Report*, App. p. 66.

observers of English economic enterprise, if in other respects more critical, were equally impressed by the ample reserves of pastoral and mineral wealth at its command.

It was from the first of these assets, aided, as Professor Carus-Wilson has shown, by precocity in the industrial use of water-power,[1] that, down to the age of coal and iron, English commerce took its stamp. Three-quarters to nine-tenths in value of London exports were estimated under James to consist of woollen textiles, and there are indications that the preponderance of textiles among the exports of provincial England was not much less marked.[2] Thus, if the differences, some of them important, between varying types of fabric be for the moment ignored, English shipments abroad were predominantly a one-commodity affair. It was not, in short, by the range of the wares offered by her, but by her concentration on a few long lines, that the hold of England on foreign markets was, in Cranfield's day, maintained. The characteristic feature of her exports, compared with the miscellaneous cargoes of more versatile rivals, was another aspect of that fact. It was the preponderance among them, not merely of manufactures, but of manufactures, in the words of a Jacobean business man, of 'great bulk and massie'.[3]

Imports into England were, by contrast, a heterogeneous host; but here, too, a rudimentary pattern can be discerned. Later, when preparing, as part of his official duties, a statement on the balance of trade, Cranfield classified imports under the three main heads of manufactures competing with native products; raw materials and semi-manufactured goods; and articles 'for the food and sustenance of the nation', with which, when it becomes important, tobacco may, perhaps, be grouped. A consecutive series of figures is, as usual, lacking, but for three dates, 1560–1, 1621–2 and 1633–4, the principal items in the import trade of London are approxi-

---

[1] *Cambridge Economic History of Europe*, vol. II, pp. 409–14.

[2] Friis, *op. cit.* pp. 70, 246. The figure nine-tenths is Sir Edward Coke's estimate of the proportion of cloth exports to English exports as a whole. The Port Books for a small number of years between 1600 and 1620 of ten provincial ports, including those of Hull and Newcastle, cited by Miss B. Hall, *The Trade of Newcastle-on-Tyne and the North-East Coast, 1600–1640* (Ph.D. Thesis, University of London, 1933), show that in the case of three (Bristol, Plymouth and Yarmouth) textiles accounted for the value of under half the exports, and in the case of seven (Exeter, Dartmouth, Lyme Regis, Southampton, Dover, Hull and Newcastle) for that of over three-quarters. The years represented, however, are too few to permit a confident generalisation.

[3] *The Circle of Commerce or the Balance of Trade*, by E[dward] M[isselden], Merchant (1623).

mately known.[1] Data so widely spaced do not permit any but general and tentative deductions; but two conclusions suggested by them are, perhaps, both valid and to the point. The first is the stability of the chief components of the three categories specified by Cranfield, linens, mixed fabrics and silkstuffs heading at each date the list of manufactured imports, and textile fibres, dyestuffs and other subsidiaries, together with yarns and threads, that of raw materials and semi-manufactured articles. Imports under the last of his three rubrics point to a slight extension in the range of consuming habits. Wines retain throughout an easy lead; but in the 1620's, as also in the 1630's, sugar, tobacco, currants and pepper are much in demand. In other respects the changes worth noting in the kind, as distinct from the value, of imports are few. A second, and more significant, development is the alteration in the relative importance of the different groups themselves. Manufactures, which accounted in 1561-2 for over two-fifths of London imports in value have declined to one-third of them in 1621-2 and to a quarter in 1633-4. Raw materials, semi-manufactured goods and foodstuffs have increased correspondingly from under three-fifths at the first date to two-thirds at the second, and three-quarters at the third.

The foreign trade of Cranfield's London had as its backbone, therefore, the sale of woollen textiles, partly, though in a diminishing proportion, against other textile fabrics, in particular linens and silks, partly, and to an increasing extent, against raw materials and foods. Woollen textiles, a comprehensive category, became, as specialties multiplied, an increasingly ambiguous one; but, in the early years of the century, one species of the genus, cloth in the custom-house sense of the term,[2] stood in importance, and still more in reputation, in a class by itself. The commerce concerned with it had, as events were to show, its Achilles' heel, in the shape of an excessive dependence on the Central European market; but, exporting in good years 120,000 to 130,000 pieces[3] to the value of

---

[1] The statements here made as to the character of London imports at different dates are based on figures kindly shown me by Mrs Millard.

[2] For the length, width and weight of cloths, as prescribed by the Acts of 1552 and 1607, and for the duty charged, see Friis, *op. cit.* pp. 47–50. A more detailed contemporary statement of the dimensions of different kinds of cloths is printed in *Camden Miscellany*, vol. xv, pp. 25–7.

[3] Friis, *op. cit.* p. 61, where the exports of cloths from London by English merchants are given as in 1606 about 125,000, of which over three-fourths went to markets in Germany and the Netherlands in which the Merchant Adventurers were privileged. Cranfield in 1615 put the average value of a cloth at £7, other Customs officials at £8 (*ibid.* p. 70).

£800,000 to £1,000,000, politically influential, controlled for the most part by an organisation led at times by men of some note, which aimed at securing favourable terms in foreign markets by restricting sales, and which, though unpopular in the provinces, knew to a nicety, in dealing with Governments, when to bluff and when to whine, this famous trade—'the gold of our Ophir, the milk and honey of our Canaan, the Indies of our England'[1]—was a power in the City, and was invested with something of the dignity of a national enterprise. It was natural that an ambitious young man should be attracted by it. Cloth was far from reigning alone; and, even before its later resounding crisis, the lighter fabrics known by the unhelpful name of the New Draperies[2] were gaining on it. Cranfield did not meddle with the latter, but he was not the man to keep all his eggs in one basket, and he dealt in both the more expensive and the cheaper kinds of cloth. The former he exported chiefly to the Netherlands, the latter to Germany.

2. CLOTHIERS, FACTORS AND MARKETS

Cranfield's career as an exporter opened in the later years of a depression which did not completely pass till 1604, and ended at a moment when an even graver crisis in the cloth trade was about to begin. During most of the intervening period, for reasons recounted above, he had the wind behind him.[3] The business of a cloth merchant included the purchase of piece-goods from manufacturers, their sale in continental markets, and the provision of returns in the

---

[1] *Free Trade or the Means to make Trade flourish*, by E[dward] M[isselden] (1622), p. 40.

[2] For an account of the growth of the New Draperies in the eastern counties, see J. E. Pilgrim, *The Cloth Industry in Suffolk and Essex, 1558–1640* (M.A. Thesis, University of London, 1939).

[3] For the duration of the depression, see W. R. Scott, *op. cit.* vol. I, pp. 100-2, 129-30, and F. J. Fisher, 'Commercial Trends and Policy in sixteenth-century England', in *Econ. Hist. Rev.* vol. X, no. 2 (1940). It would have been desirable, had our data permitted, to illustrate the effect on Cranfield's exports of the boom. It happens, however, that a journal kept by one of his factors, Richard Rawstorm (*Cranfield MSS.* no. S.2743: 'A journel for the accounts of Mr Lyonell Cranfield of London, mercer'), containing exact particulars of his sales in Germany and of the returns shipped by him, is available only for the period January 1601 to May 1603. It has seemed best, therefore, to make use of it, and to leave the reader to remind himself, with the aid of such occasional figures as are to hand, that, from at least 1604 onwards, conditions favoured an expansion of Cranfield's trade. It may be added that the journal is kept in Hamburg money (25s. Hamburg = 20s. sterling), and is followed by a balance sheet dated 21 May 1603 (*ibid.* no. S.2744).

shape of foreign wares to be disposed of in London, to which must be added, in Cranfield's case, more speculative transactions facilitated by contacts established through his textile interests, but not directly connected with them. His papers throw some light on all.

The first of these operations cannot here be treated at length, but the student of the woollen industry will find some features of Cranfield's dealings with clothiers of interest to him.[1] He will note, in the first place, that, while five or more different counties supplied the merchant with his wares, forty-six of the seventy-nine firms with whom between 1603 and the end of 1608 he dealt belonged to Wiltshire, Gloucestershire and Somerset, and twenty-eight to Yorkshire, and that the famous textile region of East Anglia was represented by only one. He will contrast, in the second place, the fastidious discrimination shown in the purchase of the expensive and highly individualised cloths, costing anything from £7 to £15 a piece, produced by West Country specialists with a reputation for excellence in particular lines, and commonly ordered in small quantities of ten, five, three, or even less, with the bulk purchase methods applied to the cheaper brands of northern kerseys—the dhooties of the woollen trade—which were destined for consumers too poor to afford a better article, and were bought in lots of 150 to 1250 at a time. He will be struck by the varying methods of payment employed before the general use of inland bills—cash remittances by carriers, settlements at the next fair, the discharge by the buyer of the seller's debts to London creditors, and, in the case of large orders, payment in instalments spread over many months. He will note that credit may run either way, but that, since many of the clothiers are men in a small way of business, who work from hand to mouth, Cranfield increasingly finds it expedient to finance them, and that from 1605, when his purchase of the Receivership of Crown Revenues in Somerset and Dorset enlarges his command of ready money, his advances to them mount, Bath, where the Receiver had an office, becoming a centre to which

---

[1] The chief sources of information on this aspect of Cranfield's business are (1) *Cranfield MSS*. Series X, containing letters from clothiers, 1600–8; (2) *ibid*. no. 354 (Cranfield's ledger), which contains individual accounts relating to the clothiers and other persons connected with the cloth trade with whom he dealt. It should be noted that Cranfield bought and shipped much cloth in addition to that manufactured to his order. He is also stated to have dealt in cloth on commission (Hist. MSS. Comm., *Cranfield Papers, 1551–1612*, p. xx). Hence the payments for cloths and kerseys made by him to clothiers are not a reliable index of the scale of his business.

borrowers have recourse.[1] He will remark, finally, that, while Cranfield's relations with the firms working for him appear on the whole —to judge by their letters—to have been reasonably human, occasions are not absent when tempers get out of hand. Recurrent complaints of his critical eye for quality, of his failure to pay to date, of his propensity to cut prices and reluctance to follow the market when it rises—of, in short, a 'hardness' which leaves one correspondent threatening to take his wares 'to the Halls, to yield what they list', and another concluding reproachfully, 'I leave you to the Lord, whom I beseech to send his blessings on your body and grace on your soul to the increase of your faith'—convey hints of the exasperation which caused disputes between provincial manufacturer and metropolitan merchant occasionally to flare up into an issue of which both Council and Parliament had to take account. These aspects of Cranfield's affairs belong, however, to the industrial history of textiles, and need not now detain us. He is primarily, at this stage of his career, a commercial entrepreneur, whose fortunes depend on his continental sales. It is that side of his activities which best repays attention.

A group to whose significance justice has hardly yet been done consists of the foreign representatives of English commercial houses. Stationed in the strategic centres of commerce; buying and selling; lending, borrowing, and dealing on the local bourse; from time to time making tours in their adopted countries in search of a specialty or to get in debts, these agents, factors and servants knew the life of the communities in which they resided with an intimacy that makes the narratives of travellers, such as Moryson and Howell, read like tourists' gossip. Many of their letters to their principals are dull business documents, but, even so, there are few without flashes of light on features of economic life which commonly escape our view. It is not easy to follow the movements of exports once their country of origin has been left behind them, and our knowledge of international trade too often ends at the point where its most instructive chapter is about to begin. The correspondence of factors partially fills the gap. It reveals the destinations to which, once they have surmounted the customs barriers of the importing country,

---

[1] Hist. MSS. Comm., *Cranfield Papers*, pp. 107, shows moneys paid to Cranfield as Receiver at Bath, Yeovil and Shaftesbury. His ledger contains from 1605–8 a good many advances to clothiers, an ordinary entry being: 'A.B. of Wilts. Paid him at Bath to be repaid in London £100.'

wares slowly trickle through; the impediments and risks which beset them on their way; the ever-changing conditions which raise and lower the demand; the competition encountered from native and imported products. Nor is the discourse of factors exclusively of trade. The poverty or wealth of the population amid whom their lot is cast; the relations of rulers and subjects and on occasion of landlords and tenants; the prospect of disturbances provoked by religious animosities—such topics, as well as the effects of tariff policies, unstable currencies and depreciation, are grist to their mills. There are, in short, aspects of public affairs which leave few traces on State papers, but which the historian cannot afford to neglect. On such matters there are grains of information to be gained and stray hints to be pondered in the unpretentious notes of these realistic observers.

Some seven individuals appear to have served Cranfield in different continental centres, and four or five to have been at times employed by him at once. The letters which have interested the present writer most have been those of Richard Rawstorm, Cranfield's factor in Germany; Daniel Cooper, who acted for him at Middelburg; Samuel Passfield, employed off and on at Amsterdam; and Richard Perrott, who, in addition to visits to Stade, Middelburg and Flushing, worked for him for an uncertain period in 1608–9 at Danzig.[1] The pages which follow owe something to all of them, but most to the two first. Rawstorm and Cooper served Cranfield in his two most important markets, but they ran oddly in harness. The former is too intelligent not to have an eye beyond his books; but he is a master of his business, and his heart is in it. Industrious, conscientious, precise in his statements and punctilious in his accounting, a man of system and method, he is the professional factor at his best. Cooper, a friend of Cranfield as well as an employee, and the cousin of the John Cooper of the Fishmongers' Company who was Cranfield's partner in not a few of his London *coups*, is at the opposite extreme. He is the inspired, not always the too happily inspired, amateur. He had broken with his former employer in London in circumstances which

---

[1] The letters which I have studied in detail belong principally to the years 1600–6, but they include some between the latter year and December 1610. Vol. II of the *Cranfield Papers*, edited by Professor F. J. Fisher for the Historical Manuscripts Commission, will doubtless contain much of interest that I have missed. In addition to those mentioned above, other persons intermittently employed abroad by Cranfield included Thomas Wright, 'my man'; Thomas Wootton, the servant of Cranfield's father-in-law, Richard Sheppard; and one Francis Otley.

left the latter with some claims upon him; and his earlier letters ring with denunciations of 'my tyrant', whom he characteristically endeavours to intimidate into leaving him in peace by the ingenious device of threatening that, if he returns to London, he will be obliged to marry—'a great hindrance unto me and to him, which bone...I give him to gnaw upon'. Sanguine and credulous; full of wise saws—'the world is naught, and faithful friends are few'; expecting impossible profits from deals which reduce his employer to despair, and sometimes, contrary to all reason, appearing to make them; persuaded—'ask William Quarles, brother [to] the Counsellor'—that the death of Elizabeth will be the signal for a revolution, he is a figure who, if works on the romance of trade had been the fashion under James that later they became, might appropriately have been chosen as the hero of one of them.[1] Cranfield, who is all for trade but has doubts about romance, regards him with a mixture of affection and dismay.

At the time when Rawstorm was writing his first letters to Cranfield, the cloth markets of northern Europe were in a state of some confusion.[2] The Merchant Adventurers' traditional policy of concentrating their commerce at certain staple towns—in effect treaty ports—was not without its advantages; but harmonious relations between the interests concerned—the 'good order and amity' praised by its admirers—were not always among them. The successive migrations of the Adventurers from the 1560's to the 1580's had left a legacy of friction, which the policies of States locked in struggle had aggravated and exploited. For nearly two decades from the later 1580's the trade was bedevilled by a six-cornered conflict. Officially the Company regarded Middelburg, to which it had moved its continental headquarters in 1586, as its sole foreign staple. It endeavoured to insist that German, as well as Dutch, merchants should buy their textiles there, and pilloried as interlopers English cloth-exporters trading without its permission elsewhere. Not a few of its members, reluctant to break established connections, persisted, in defiance of its orders, in shipping to Emden, or more generally,

---

[1] *Cranfield MSS.* nos. S.172, S.67, S.247.

[2] The most useful accounts of the mart towns of the Merchant Adventurers and the disputes mentioned below are given by R. Ehrenberg, *Hamburg und England* (1896), of which chs. IV and V deal with Stade and the imperial embargo; C. Te Lintum, *De Merchant Adventurers in de Nederlanden* (1905); Friis, *op. cit.* chs. I and II; E. Lipson, *The Economic History of England* (1931), vol. II, ch. II, especially pp. 199–214; see also Hist. MSS. Comm., *Cranfield Papers*, pp. 31–4.

from 1587 onwards, to Stade. Stade, on its side, was naturally all agog to seize the prize dropped nine years before by Hamburg. Hamburg, together with the majority of the Hanse towns, while continuing to import the English textiles required for her dyeing industry, denounced the erring sister as a traitor to the League, which finally expelled it. Pressed by the League, the imperial authorities imposed in 1597 the celebrated embargo, which, though ineffective from the start,[1] was not formally rescinded till 1607. Spain, which had strong economic reasons for supporting the Hanse towns, and strong political reasons for crippling English trade, backed the policy of the Empire. The realities behind this imposing façade of intrigue and diplomacy were much what might have been expected. The trade of the Company with the United Netherlands was centralised at Middelburg. The trade with Germany went to Emden or Stade, but, especially after 1600, preponderantly to the latter.[2] Cranfield exported to all three. Rawstorm, his representative in Germany, was stationed, when we first encounter him, in December 1600, at Emden. From April to August, 1601, when he was winding up his affairs at Emden, he was on the move between that town and Stade, where he settled for good in August. His subsequent letters, with hardly an exception, are written from Stade.[3]

3. CRANFIELD'S GERMAN TRADE

Rawstorm's duties as a factor need no lengthy explanation. Stated summarily, they were to receive, warehouse and sell piece-goods consigned to him by Cranfield; to buy and ship returns; to transact the financial business which both proceedings involved; and, not least important, to ensure that his principal, whose policy depended on advices from Germany, was kept fully informed as to the state of markets, the demand for different brands of textiles, the prices

[1] From the beginning the embargo was riddled by imperial licences to import the prohibited textiles (Ehrenberg, *Hamburg und England*, p. 205, and the letter of November, 1598, from the Lübeck Council there quoted).

[2] Ehrenberg, *op. cit.* pp. 207–8, for the number of English residents in Emden in August 1600, and the decline of the trade with Emden from the spring of 1601; Hist. MSS. Comm., *Cranfield Papers*, p. 34, for eighteen English ships, with 2000 pieces per ship, trading to Stade between June 1598 and June 1599; Friis, *op. cit.* p. 77, for figures of London merchants trading with Stade, Middelburg and other ports in 1606. It would appear that, by that year, the trade in textiles from London to Emden had ceased.

[3] The journal kept by Rawstorm mentioned above (see p. 36, n. 3) was begun at Emden and continued at Stade.

being charged for wares likely to sell well in England, and generally as to all conditions affecting trade, from ice in the Elbe or pirates just outside it to the temporary closing of the Sound and rumours of war in Poland or the Balkans. Communications by sea, if less difficult than by land, left a good deal to be desired. The initial operation, therefore, of assembling supplies was not always so simple as it sounds. It is evident that a good many tramps wandered in and out of Stade; but Rawstorm, except in the last resort, has little truck with them. Sharing the organised trader's conviction of the virtues of orderly marketing, he has no love for shipping which 'comes in so disorderly, one in the neck of another' and which 'makes our [sc. German] merchants refrain, expecting better penny-worths to come'.[1] In general, he relies on the vessels chartered by the Company. It is by these—'the fleet', 'our ships', 'the appointed ships'—that the bulk of his cargoes reach him and that he normally despatches his returns.

That procedure, however, whether adopted in compliance with the Company's regulations or for business reasons, produced problems of its own. It meant that the factor's sales and purchases at Stade must be timed to keep in step with the official sailings. If Rawstorm makes 'a clear packhouse' too soon, then a delay in the arrival of the fleet causes him to be caught short of wares, to miss profitable deals, to be compelled to appease his employer as best he may, with the excuse that 'had the ships come, as they might if it had pleased God, since Christmas, I might have performed the bargain'.[2] If, to avoid that reef, he keeps large stocks on hand, he risks running on a worse one. Stray interlopers cut in—'small reason to come hither...in regard they have good sales...at Danzig'[3] —to poach in markets not their own; local buyers hold back, anticipating, if they wait—since 'according to the quantity the markets will be ruled'—better prices later. The uncertainties of maritime time-tables, largely inevitable, but not always, to judge by his complaints, the act of God, aggravate his difficulties.

It was all very well for the Company to eulogise the benefits secured by 'our regularity in shipping'[4]; but, if one thing is clearer than another from Rawstorm's letters, it is that the arrival of the fleet is not only the most important date in his business calendar, but a highly unpredictable one. In theory there were, at least, two

---

[1] *Cranfield MSS.* no. S.474.   [2] *Ibid.* no. S.119.
[3] *Ibid.* no. S.112.   [4] E. Lipson, *op. cit.* p. 238.

sailings a year, one in spring, and one in autumn. The first was that which most mattered to him: two-thirds of his sales at Emden, and nine-tenths of those at Stade, took place in the six months between March and August. The names of the seasons, however, are not terms of precision, and, from shortly after Christmas, Cranfield's factor is on tenterhooks. He snatches at scraps of local gossip, pesters for news correspondents at Middelburg and Amsterdam, and scans the skies in a fever of anxiety—will the ice hold or will it break? will a west wind bring the laggards in or an east wind keep them out?—only to find, after all, that the vessels for which his watch had begun in January fail to discharge, in one year, till late in March and, in another, till the end of May. And, if delays in the delivery of his consignments from London are a recurrent exasperation, the difficulty of despatching his returns is hardly less acute. The orthodox course, and that which he favours, is to seize the opportunities offered by the return voyage of the Company's ships; but, here again, timing is not too easy. His employer is fastidious. Not all that he demands is to be had in Stade. If, however, Rawstorm waits to make up his cargoes till the great fairs of the interior —above all, that of Frankfurt—have done their business, and the high-quality silks of Venice, Florence and Lucca have been moved to the port, will the regular fleet still be in harbour to lade them?[1] Such dilemmas are tormenting; there are occasions when they are too much for him. Harassed beyond endurance, he at times falls back, in spite of himself, on the unprofessional expedient of preferring the convenient by-way of individual enterprise to the strait and narrow path of collective control. Cranfield, he urges, instead of missing the market by waiting for official ships which show no sign of sailing, would do better to employ an interloper, or to ship by a vessel bound for Hamburg, or to despatch his wares to Middelburg or Emden for forwarding to Stade.[2] At a pinch, he himself, though not without qualms as to the reactions of his fellow-factors, lades his linens on a Hamburg fly-boat.[3]

Rawstorm's trade consisted in the sale of English cloths and kerseys against Italian silks, satins, velvet, cloths of gold and silver, and other luxury wares, together with 'Augsburgs' from southern Germany and an occasional parcel of German linens. Germany was much frequented by foreigners; and, as recurrent references in his

---

[1] *Cranfield MSS.* no. S. 348.   [2] *Ibid.* nos. S. 399, or S. 483, S. 352.
[3] *Ibid.* nos. S. 349, S. 352.

letters to 'the strangers' show, the German depot of the Merchant Adventurers, though not a cosmopolitan city like Frankfurt or Cologne, attracted traders of several nationalities, interested in English textiles or with wares to catch the taste of the London market. Though he relied on Italy for the greater part of his returns, and watched anxiously changes in that country likely to affect their price, he does not appear to buy direct from Italian merchants, and his journal makes it evident that he did not sell to them. His wares went off in a variety of different ways. A handful was bought by other English firms in Stade, presumably at a loss to complete an order, and occasionally he dealt with local shopkeepers, or a householder on the look out to pick up a bargain.[1] The great bulk of his sales were made, however, to wholesale merchants, who either resided in the mart town or, more often, resorted to it when the ships were expected, spent some weeks or months in doing their business there, and then returned home to distribute their purchases throughout regions as distant from it and from each other as Poland, Saxony, Bavaria, Austria and Alsace. Of the ninety to a hundred separate individuals with whom we find him dealing between January 1601, and May 1603, nine-tenths at least must be placed in that category. They include some Dutchmen, who, on occasion, buy heavily for Amsterdam; but the majority—though certainty is impossible—appear to be Germans. Such wares as remain unsold when the busy season at Stade is over are packed and despatched, sometimes to Hamburg, but more often farther afield, to Frankfurt, Nürnberg, or some other market in the interior of the country. Occasionally instructions are received from London to move them as soon as unloaded, without waiting for the exhaustion of appetites at Stade.

Rawstorm's business differed markedly from that of his colleague at Middelburg. The latter resided among a population distinguished, in the eyes of observers, by its social equality, and reputed to enjoy the highest standard of life of any in Europe.[2] Rawstorm's lines were cast in less pleasant places. Some twenty years later a member of his Company stationed at Hamburg, to which the Adventurers had returned in 1611, accompanied his applause of German mechani-

---

[1] The occasional allusions in Rawstorm's letters to 'townsmen' may relate to such persons. It is possible, on the other hand, that they merely refer to wholesalers residing in Stade. The names of persons buying from him are stated in his journal. They are usually also mentioned in his letters to Cranfield.

[2] *The Observations of Sir Thomas Overbury in his Travels*, in *Harl. Misc.* vol. VIII, p. 363 and James Howell, *Familiar Letters*, vol. I, ch. XIV.

cal *expertise* with supercilious comments on the backwardness of north German agriculture, and dwelt with indignation on the exploitation of the peasant, low-rented, indeed, by comparison with his English fellows, but 'tied to great slavery, to bring in his landlord's corn, and, in fine, to do him all the servile work that is to be done, and [his landlord] hath so much power over him as to take away all his estate, and his life'.[1] While we know that Cranfield's textiles travelled far afield, we have no direct clue to the classes which bought them. It was necessary for the exporter, however, to play to the score, and it is evident that it was expedient for him, in choosing the line to push in Germany, to have an eye to the peculiarities of a market whose purchasing-power was lower than that of the Netherlands. Rawstorm's specialty, therefore, was not cloths, but kerseys. His receipts from each were in 1601 approximately equal, but the kerseys sold outnumbered the cloths by not far short of five to one. His journal makes it clear that the marketing of the two proceeded on different lines. The expensive cloths went off in ones and twos, rarely more than ten at a time, and only once over sixty. The kerseys were sold, as they had been bought, in bulk, most of them being despatched in lots of one hundred to a thousand or more. The merchant who takes the first is catering, in the main, for the individual tastes of well-to-do consumers. The purchaser of the second is concerned to meet a mass demand. The buyer who lays out as much as £600 on a single purchase of seventy pack-cloths at once is a rare exception. Of Rawstorm's two chief stand-bys for kerseys, one takes 628 at £1360 in a single deal, and the other 1259 at £3339. Kerseys, therefore, since they involve relatively few large transactions, were less troublesome to sell than cloths, and cost less in overheads. Cranfield, though he decides that they are not suitable for the Netherlands, continues to deluge the German market with them. It is noticeable that his large syndicated sales, undertaken in conjunction with groups of partners, were all deals in kerseys.[2]

Cranfield was an importer, as well as an exporter. He did a considerable home trade in continental wares, and he looked to the proceeds of his sales in Germany to enable him to expand it. Rawstorm's activities, therefore, as a purchaser of supplies for the London market occupied as much of his time as the task of selling

[1] *Wynn Papers*, no. 1154 (letter of 18 October 1623, from Maurice Wynn at Hamburg to his father, Sir John Wynn).
[2] See, for example, below, p. 59.

textiles, and—to judge by his correspondence—made heavier demands on his knowledge and discrimination. The consignments which he shipped were bought partly on specific instructions from his employer, partly—since Cranfield appears to have felt more confidence in his judgment than in that of the temperamental Cooper—at his own discretion on the basis of advices from London. His choice of wares to make up his cargoes may, at first sight, cause surprise. Germany was a magazine of raw materials. She also, though not an industrial specialist of the standing of France in linens, Italy in silks, England in woollens, or the Netherlands in shipbuilding, had won a reputation in mining, metallurgy and some branches of textiles, as well as by the mechanical ingenuity of her 'subtle inventions in manual works and cunning arts'[1]. If these sides of her economy have left little trace on Rawstorm's letters, the reason is to be sought, not in ignorance, but in the character of his employer's business. The domestic market for which Cranfield catered is suggested by the long list of sixty to seventy mercers, drapers, haberdashers, cloth-workers and tailors, who figure in his books.[2] It was the fashionable world of London. One need not take the moralists *au pied de la lettre*, but it is probably true that, till Puritanism made sobriety of dress a form of distinction, competitive extravagance in apparel—'velvets, satins, cloth of gold, pearls, yea, pearl-lace, which scarce Caligula wore on his birthday'[3]—became for a time almost a point of honour. Sumptuousness in domestic furniture—'cloth of gold, arras, tapestry and such other rich ornaments, pendices and hangings'[4]—ran riot hardly less. For Rawstorm, concerned as he is to meet the appetite for ostentation of the tiny class to whom money is no object, Germany, except as a market, hardly exists as an economic entity with distinctive characteristics and a life of its own. She is primarily an emporium of southern wares, with a shop-window on the North Sea.

Italian luxury fabrics were much in demand—'good vent for them in Poland, France and the Low Countries'[5]—to which may be added, as Rawstorm's letters show, Spain and Portugal, England

---

[1] Lewis Roberts, *The Merchant's Map of Commerce*, ch. CXC.
[2] I take the list from that compiled by the late Professor Newton from Cranfield's ledger.
[3] Robert Greene, *A Quip for an upstart Courtier* (1592), in *Harl. Misc.* vol. II, pp. 215-49.
[4] Philip Stubbes, *Anatomy of Abuses in England* (c. 1583), ch. II.
[5] *Cranfield MSS.* no. S. 346.

and Germany herself. They reached Stade, partly, it seems, by sea, possibly via Amsterdam, but also from Frankfurt, to which they were sent by the historic routes across the Alps. Rawstorm purchased them, not from traders of their country of origin, but from German or Dutch merchants, often, it would seem, the same individuals as those to whom he sold his cloths and kerseys. Two of his invoices for this period have survived. They show that Italian textiles formed over nine-tenths of both the cargoes concerned, the small balance being made up in one case by Augsburg fustians and Spanish and Portuguese silk, in the other by German linens. The documents in question cover less than half of his total purchases from January 1601 to May 1603. It cannot be assumed, therefore, that all his homeward freights were similarly composed; and we find him later, at a time when, as he explains to Cranfield, the prices of high-class goods have reached prohibitive levels, lading a couple of vessels with cheap local stuff.[1] It is evident, however, both from his recurrent solicitude concerning developments in Italy and from his replies to Cranfield, with their constant references to sipers, white and coloured taffeties, jeans and satins, luccas and coloured luccas, where his and his employer's preferences lay. The conclusion suggested by his letters is that he fell back on commodities of German origin to complete a cargo or when more attractive wares were too expensive, but that he devoted his main energies as a buyer to combing Germany for the products of Italian looms.

Cranfield's trade with Germany was done on credit.[2] Stade—the same was true of Emden—was not among the capitals of international trade whose moods were watched with anxiety by all commercial Europe. Compared with Hamburg, the range of its connections was narrow and its resources slender. The rates at which currencies were quoted on its bourse were governed by those of its wealthier neighbour[3], and contemporary English lists[4] of the leading exchanges, from Elizabeth to Charles I, rarely troubled to include it. But its money-market, if inferior even to some of the second rank, such as

[1] *Ibid.* no. S.404.

[2] The separate transactions by way of sales in the period covered by Rawstorm's journal appear under number 115. Of these three were for ready money, and the rest on credit, three for over eight months, twenty-two for eight months, thirty-two for seven months, thirty-five for six months, and the remainder (which include eight sales for wares and two for wares and money) for an uncertain period.

[3] *Cranfield MSS.*, no. S.112: 'The exchange here is fallen 4*d.* per pound, which cometh in regard it is fallen there' [*sc.* Hamburg].

[4] E.g. *S.P.D. Eliz.* CVI, no. 6, and Lewis Roberts, *op. cit.* ch. CCLXXIV.

Rouen, Strasbourg and Seville, had a specialised importance of its own. Situated at one of the key-points of trade between England and the Continent, it served the considerable body of traders, of several different nationalities, interested, as buyers or sellers, in English textiles and the wares exchanged for them. When the local bourse could not meet their needs, they had recourse to Hamburg. In their daily operations they made use of the facilities provided by Stade. The sterling exchange both on Emden and on Stade was quoted in Hamburg shillings, and is noted by Rawstorm at the end of every letter. Its movements are the subject of explanatory comment, pessimistic or cheerful, for the benefit of his employer.

'The merchant', it had been remarked by one of them, in the days when Antwerp ruled the roost, 'can no more be without exchange than a ship can be without water.'[1] Stade, however, was not Antwerp, and, as a method of obtaining payments for his exports, a bill drawn by Cranfield on their foreign buyer or his London agent played in his German trade a minor part. The reason was, presumably, the deficiencies of the credit mechanism. The commerce of the day retained some traits reminiscent of the pedlar. German merchants were often peripatetic, and few of them were of a standing to maintain representatives in London, while the hour of specialist accepting houses had not yet, as far as England was concerned, arrived. Since, in such conditions, accepters were to seek, bills of exchange, at least in this branch of Cranfield's commerce, were not the international currency which later they became. Other expedients required to be employed.

The alternatives on which Rawstorm relies are simple. Occasionally, when all else fails, he exchanges English for foreign goods; but these barter transactions are the exception, and are in the main, it seems, confined to inferior stuff. The ordinary form in which he receives payment for his wares is a promissory note—or, to use his own term, a 'bill'—commonly at six to eight months, which he can either employ to discharge his liabilities to the foreign vendor of his returns, or discount on the local bourse, or hold till, on its maturity, he collects the sum due. Commercial paper is normally abundant. It is transferred regularly by endorsement from hand to hand, and when good names are on it, will 'sell', he writes, 'at

---

[1] Richard Gresham to Thomas Cromwell, 1536, in Schanz, *Englische Handelspolitik gegen die Ende des Mittelalters* (1881), vol. II, pp. 632–3. I owe the following account of Rawstorm's financial transactions mainly to Professor F. J. Fisher.

9 or 10 per cent'. Debts owing by him for his imports sometimes, it is true—since he works on small margins—involve him in borrowing, which he hates; but normally he contrives to make his sales and purchases keep in step. His remittances to London are made in three ways. The most obvious and regular consists in the despatch of cargoes for his employer to sell. There are moments, however, especially, for example, the seasons at which stocks for export require to be renewed, when Cranfield is too hard pressed for cash to wait till the marketing of his imports relieves the strain. The usual procedure on such occasions is for him to bring money home by drawing a bill on his factor which the latter accepts, and which, since he is known to be Cranfield's agent, his principal can sell in London, Rawstorm paying it at Stade to its buyer's foreign representative out of the proceeds of sales of cloth, or by borrowing the funds to meet it, or by himself drawing a bill on Cranfield and selling it on the local bourse. The last procedure—'charging and recharging'[1] as it is called—is a convenience, since money may be easy or tight at the continental end of the trade when in London it is the opposite, and Cranfield and his factor may not be equally in funds at once. Not unnaturally, it is accompanied by gusts of mild bickering. Cranfield, who has no hesitation in drawing on Rawstorm, is apt to be indignant when Rawstorm draws on him, and issues an occasional veto which leaves the latter lamenting that, having strained his credit and wearied his friends, he is driven to raise money locally at exorbitant interest.[2] But the constant recurrence of similar transactions suggests that the prohibition was not intended to be of general application.

A third expedient, remittances *in specie*, revives the memory of controversies more resounding than Rawstorm's prosaic references

---

[1] Three examples out of many may be cited in illustration. 'Your bill of exchange payable to Richard Bladwell....I have accepted and will see orderly discharged without recharging anything upon you, because, as I perceive by your writing, money is marvellous scant there [*sc.* in London], but here, God be thanked, very plentiful' (*Cranfield MSS.* no. S.110): 'The exchange here is fallen 4*d.* per pound...so that I wish I had charged you when it was so large, but am loth (in regard it is not your desire) so long as I can find other means' (*ibid.* no. S.112): 'Finding the exchange favourable, have taken up of Thomas Balie £100 sterling at 24/4 payable there [*sc.* in London] to Mr John and William Goode the 28th of March, which I pray you to make payment of at the day, being also minded to charge you with some more if the exchange continue at this rate, for I have both taken up money at interest and used my friends for discharging of your debts, hoping either of the ships coming or some better means of provision, which I now see no likelihood of' (*ibid.* no. S.117).

[2] *Ibid.* nos. S.117, S.369, S.483.

to it would suggest. The theory of the matter, expounded by Gresham, and later, in laborious detail, in memoranda compiled for Burleigh,[1] had long been a commonplace. The proceedings described in Cranfield's correspondence are merely another illustration of it. The mint-par of exchange between Stade and London was 25 Hamburg shillings to the pound. The market, though over short periods fairly stable, sometimes fluctuated sharply, on one occasion as much as 92% in a week. These oscillations, as Rawstorm more than once remarked, set on foot corresponding movements of bullion. Given —a condition not always realised—a sufficiency of shipping, high rates for sterling have as their results 'good means to send home money in specie to a better reckoning'; and such remittances to London might be, and were, made. If the converse situation arises —if sterling 'is like to come under 25s.'—then 'no man sends any ready money in specie', and cheaper alternatives are preferred.[2] We have no direct evidence as to the scale on which these movements took place. The impression made by Rawstorm's references is that they were the exception.

So much for the dusty routine of a factor's affairs. The details of Rawstorm's operations are, however, less instructive than the glimpses which he offers of the business life of central Europe in the days when foreign enterprise, if from time to time it met rough weather, was not yet paralysed by war. The problems depicted in his correspondence sprang partly from the character of the commerce in which he was engaged, partly from the environment in which it was carried on. His trade, it is evident, was a highly competitive one. Particular firms, including his own, agree on occasion to act temporarily together; but, if his Company discouraged—a charge which it denied—under-cutting between its members, that mollifying influence has left few traces on his letters. He sells against his fellow-factors, north-country and Dutch exporters, and Germans trafficking in the cheap native article. The silks and satins which he buys are in keen demand with three of these four, who regularly bid against him, as well as in Poland, France and Spain;[3] while the Italians supplying them, who 'stand much on their reputations',[4] may decide, if offers in Germany are disappointing, to close down

[1] Burgon, *The Life and Times of Sir Thomas Gresham*, vol. I, pp. 483–6; *S.P.D. Eliz.* LXXV, no. 54; Tawney and Power, *Tudor Economic Documents*, vols. I, pp. 146–9, and III, pp. 346–59.

[2] *Cranfield MSS.* nos. S.434, S.927.

[3] *Ibid.* nos. S.346, S.127.   [4] *Ibid.* no. S.383.

in Stade and take their wares direct to London. Prices, both for exports and returns, fluctuate sharply. The arrival of an unexpected cargo, internal changes in the producing country, exceptional foreign demands, a political crisis, administer a jolt. Kerseys rise 3s. to 4s. in a month, or fall twice as much; coloured jeans stand at 12s. in the first week of March, and are 13% up by the end of the second.[1] Cranfield's factor must advise his employer both as to prices to be charged for exports and as to wares worth buying. If unwary, he may find himself caught between the blades of the scissors.

Naturally, such movements, the causes producing them and their probable consequences are the constant preoccupation. His obsession with quality is, perhaps, less expected, but is equally, or more, insistent. The doctrine that reliable standards of workmanship were the first condition of success in foreign trade was, of course, common form. It had been the premise of the long series of English Cloth Acts,[2] themselves a mere shadow of the more elaborate continental codes; was expounded at length by authors with some claim to write as experts;[3] and had been underlined by formal remonstrances from the Dutch ambassador at the sorry stuff, all holes and under-sizes, alleged to be inflicted on his countrymen.[4] The views of Rawstorm on the subject contain, therefore, nothing novel. What gives them their significance is that they are expressed, not by a doctrinaire, but by a practical business man wrestling daily with buyers, and only too conscious that not infrequently he is condemned to sell the unsaleable. In the worst cases, the offending article, if despatched at all, is taken by the purchaser before the magistrates, and a certificate issued in his favour, with the result that Cranfield has a bill for tares. More often the effect is either that the wares cannot be marketed, or, if they are, unpleasant remarks at a later stage, and —since textiles are largely sold on the maker's name—the discredit of the latter's future products. 'Marvellous narrow; one stop-list sold Adrian van Porten was narrow throughout'; 'they are weary of coarse rags, and desire no more at any price'; 'northern kersies now

[1] *Ibid.* nos. S.399, S.480 (kerseys); S.126, S.127 (jeans).
[2] The most recent Act was that of 1597 (39 Eliz. c. 20). It dealt solely with cloths produced north of the Trent, including the northern kerseys with which Rawstorm was specially concerned.
[3] E.g. Leake's *Treatise on the Cloth Industry* (1577), in Tawney and Power, *Tudor Economic Documents*, vol. III, pp. 210–25; and J. May, *The True Estate of Clothing in the Realm* (1613), quoted H. Heaton, *The Yorkshire Woollen and Worsted Industries* (1920), p. 144.
[4] E.g. Heaton, *op. cit.* pp. 138–9.

unvendable and wholly unrequested in regard of the great quantity of coarse rags formerly vented'; 'Cullimore has sold 200 pieces of northern kerseys at 52s.... in regard you are quit of all this tag and rag, I thought it a good match'; 'such as have any experience of the Bath cloths will not buy any more, for they say they fall out very badly in dyeing and dressing'; 'have been fain to allow Cornelius Jansen £16 Hamburg money for tare on the twenty cloths of Tylers, he having provided a certificate from the lords of Stade, with John Heming his oath, for verifying the shortness and narrowness in the said twenty cloths'; 'I doubt not to find sales for your King's, but I fear I shall not bring them above £12, except he have mended his hand since his last shipping, for all complain of them and divers certificates are brought for narrowness in them; so you must put him in mind to keep his former hand, else his cloth will be discredited; Hendrick Berentts, that hath often had them, hath now order not to buy a piece more of them'[1]—such are a handful from a mountain of complaints. The difficulty of supervising domestic workers, carelessness in checking cheap fabrics before export, and the fact that, in the pre-mechanical era, the readiest way of reducing costs in bad times was to economise on materials and labour,[2] are the obvious explanations. Whatever the reason, Rawstorm's letters leave little doubt that, among the trials of his trade, the problem of inferior quality was not the least vexatious.

The mart town of the Merchant Adventurers, for all its importance, did not form a closed world. Sales, supplies of wares available for returns, and the prices of both, were determined by conditions beyond the control of the traders who gathered there. Except for periodical journeys to Hamburg and occasional visits to his colleague at Middelburg, Rawstorm is too busy to have time for travel; but he scans from his counting-house horizons beyond it. Selling textiles not for local consumption, but to wholesalers with interests in every corner of the country, and buying wares most of which have been imported, he cannot afford to be indifferent to the shifting economic currents, both in Germany and outside it, which affect the demand for and supply of both. Nor is that the whole story. A German historian has lamented the lethargy which caused, as he thinks, cities once famous among commercial capitals, instead of re-

[1] *Cranfield MSS.* nos. S. 119, S. 127, S. 349, S. 374, S. 386, S. 399, and Rawstorm's letters *passim*.
[2] I owe this suggestion to Professor F. J. Fisher.

doubling their efforts to wrestle with the foreigner on the international battle-field of the Netherlands, to relapse into helpless passivity before the onslaught of the audacious English trader, who seizes the initiative, penetrates the interior from north to south and west to east, and markets his wares at the very doors of firms whose exports, in the past, he had been happy to buy.[1]

The reversal of fortune may well be over-dramatised; but the accounts of English business methods given by Cranfield's correspondents lend some colour to it. While most of the trade of the English community at the port is done with German merchants who resort there, it is far from being confined to them. Stade is a point of departure, as well as a terminus. Not only do English textiles go far afield, but English factors on occasion accompany them on their travels. Among the multitudinous laws, customs and ordinances of the Merchant Adventurers' Company compiled in 1600 by the industrious Wheeler, none was rehearsed by it with greater unction than that which sought to preserve a united front by prohibiting, with one exception,[2] all sales outside the mart town. Whatever the exact interpretation to be placed on this ban upon a 'straggling trade', there is no doubt that, in the case of kerseys sold in Germany, nothing of the kind was operative in practice. The representatives of English firms at Stade had well-established connections with half-a-dozen or more leading German cities. It was inevitable that they should move their wares from one to another in accordance with suggestions conveyed in letters from acquaintances, the rumours of the market-place, and even—a lapse which might have shocked their decorous secretary—instructions received from their principals in London. The picture which emerges from Rawstorm's correspondence is different, therefore, from that sometimes painted from a study of the official pronouncements of the famous Company. It is not of a well-ordered trade restricted to a treaty port, where sellers wait sedately till customers approach them, for fear that, if they take the initiative, their 'pedlar-like dealing'[3] will spoil the market. It is, on the contrary, of enterprise starting from its coastal base to conquer an extensive hinterland, in which information is disseminated with surprising rapidity, different markets

---

[1] R. Ehrenberg, *Hamburg und England*, especially pp. 39–41 and 118–22.

[2] The exception was Frankfurt (see Lipson, *op. cit.* vol. II, p. 222).

[3] John Wheeler, *Treatise of Commerce*, in Tawney and Power, *Tudor Economic Documents*, vol. III, p. 293.

react quickly on each other, and a movement of prices in any one of them sends traders scurrying to catch a rising tide or fly a falling one.

In such circumstances, an eye for the economic weather blowing up from different quarters was as indispensable a part of a factor's qualifications as the horse-trader's capacity for driving a hard bargain; and Rawstorm is not less alert to divine premonitory symptoms of activity or stagnation in regions remote from his own than to make the most of transactions within it. A postal service[1] seems to have functioned with fair regularity between Stade and London, Middelburg, Amsterdam, Frankfurt and Nürnberg. It is of some importance to him, since advices from home may fix a minimum price for the sale of kerseys, and delay in the arrival of his letters may cause the articles demanded by his employer 'not only [to be] enhanced in price but also engrossed and bespoken'. Most of his evidence, however, he must gather for himself. As a seller, he is all ears for reports of changes influencing the demand for woollen textiles in the different quarters of a diocese stretching from Bremen to the Russian frontiers and from the Rhineland to the Balkans; as a buyer, for news that Augsburg fustians are in short supply, costs of production in Italian silk factories rising, heavy purchases by the Netherlands and Spain driving the prices of jeans and satins up, and the plague in England pulling them down. He is not without a slightly supercilious interest in the singular country in which his lot is cast; but, if he packs into a single letter[2] references to Poland, Sweden, Nürnberg, Hungary, the Empire, the rebellious 'Sebenburger', and the encroaching Turk, the reason is neither scientific curiosity nor the mere loquacity of the traveller. It is the conscientious vigilance of a hard-headed Yorkshireman determined to omit no scrap of information which may assist his employer and himself to make 'good pennyworths' out of cloth.

The market which interested Rawstorm least was that which, next to the mart town, lay nearest to him. He reports occasional sales to representatives of Hamburg firms who visit Stade; from time to time goes to Hamburg himself to dispose of remainders—'odd rests'—not sold elsewhere; despatches to it the few consignments

---

[1] For references to posts, see *Cranfield MSS.* nos. S.119, S.348, S.352, S.378, S.379, S.436, S.472, S.479, S.481. Some letters for Stade came via Middelburg and Amsterdam. For inconveniences caused by delays see nos. S.348 and S.352.

[2] *Ibid.* no. S.127.

sent him of specialties outside his ordinary trade, such as guns and pepper, which are less likely to find a market in Stade than in the most cosmopolitan of German ports; and, when money is tight in the former, has recourse to Hamburg bankers.[1] But, though Hamburg, with its important dyeing and finishing industry, was importing from Stade, on the average of 1601–3, over 19,000 pieces a year, including 3800 odd kerseys,[2] Cranfield's textiles contributed little to the total. Rawstorm's Eastland connections—a far more substantial affair—were also a more vexatious one. The long northern winter; the maddening habits of traders from Hull—'no truth in Hull men'[3]—who turn up when least expected, unload on Stade wares which by rights should have gone on to Melvin,[4] and, having knocked to pieces English business at the former, deluge Danzig with kerseys to the point that transactions in them have temporarily been suspended; political disorders in Poland resulting in a fall of 8s. or more in the price of piece-goods; the attitude of the principal Danzig buyer—'hard in his dealings' and 'so near in beating prices now that he hath the market in his hands, as there will be no good done by him'—all these misfortunes combine to exasperate the unhappy seller.[5]

The Eastland trade, nevertheless, had its compensations, as well as its drawbacks. Poland and Prussia were an important outlet for the northern kerseys which were Cranfield's largest export to Germany. They took, if no better was forthcoming, inferior stuff, so that, when wares prove unsaleable in more fastidious markets, the first suggestion to be made is, 'send them to Danzig'; took it, not in driblets, but by thousands at a time; and took it on a scale which caused it subsequently to be stated in the House of Commons— an argument famous two centuries later—that the northern textile industry would be ruined if, as a concession to the cereal-farmers' clamour, the imports of Polish rye, which paid for its products, were prohibited in England.[6] A market with such merits was not

---

[1] *Ibid.* nos S.386 (odd rests); S.475, S.482, S.483 (guns); S.410, S.411 (pepper); S.476, S.477 (Hamburg bankers).   [2] Ehrenberg, *Hamburg und England*, p. 332.

[3] *Cranfield MSS.* no. S.335. The words are those of another of Cranfield's employees, Richard Perrott, writing of the arrival of a Hull ship at Stade in November 1601. The sentiments of Rawstorm were, however, the same.

[4] Probably a variant for Elbing. See *Hanserecesse*, vol. II (1431–76), ed. G. von der Ropp (Verein für Hansische Geschichte, Leipzig, 1878), p. 407. I am indebted for this reference to Professor E. Carus-Wilson.

[5] *Ibid.* nos. S.386, S.480, and (on Hans Cornelius of Danzig) S.110, S.119.

[6] Notestein, Relf and Simpson, *Commons' Debates,1621*,vol. II, p. 178; vol. IV, p. 358.

one which a faithful factor could afford to neglect, nor did its embarrassments last for ever. The ice at last breaks. Civil strife in Poland is temporarily appeased. Even the obnoxious buyer, if his commercial morality is that of a shark, has also its voracity, and is good, it is thought—a hope not fulfilled—for 3000 kerseys. So Rawstorm sells, groans, and sells again. It is with a crow of triumph that he reports to his employer that he has succeeded in inducing Hans Cornelius—'the bargain we stood upon four or five days'[1]— not only to take 1200 odd pieces, but to agree to buy all future consignments of kerseys that Cranfield may send.

Of the textiles not disposed of at the mart town, some went that way; but the bulk of them, to judge by Rawstorm's correspondence, reached other destinations. We hear of two well-known Dutch capitalists buying up 'blues' wholesale, including some of Cranfield's, for the Amsterdam market; of the movement of coloured cloths from Stade to Leipzig; of the despatch of kerseys to Bremen to be dyed and dressed, amid ritual curses at 'rotten rags'; of gaudy fabrics for Alsace known as 'Strassburgs', as well as of 'Königs-bergs', called after the capital of the cheerless region for which they were designed.[2] German economic civilisation, however, had reached its zenith in the cities of the south, which had felt at first-hand the magic touch of Italy. It was to such cities that the English factor who moved his kerseys from the coast looked for his best sales.

If the wars of the Reformation had any beneficiaries, Frankfurt had some claim to be included among them. Not only a *commune emporium inter inferiores et superiores Teutones*,[3] but an entrepôt serving Italy, Switzerland, the Low Countries and France, it had offered an industrious haven of commercial peace to refugees and their businesses up-rooted from surrounding regions, including, from the sixties of the previous century onwards, English traders no longer at home in an Antwerp in convulsions. Its reputation as an international textile exchange stood high; and, when complaints of the sinister arts of the English cloth-exporting company shocked imperial ears, it was to the expert buyers of Frankfurt that perplexed officials first turned for advice.[4] To the foreign colony at Stade its importance was that of at once a market, a source of supply and, not

---

[1] *Cranfield MSS.* no. S.383.

[2] *Ibid.* nos. S.133, S.470, S.359.

[3] The words are those of Piccolomini (quoted by J. Kulischer, *Allgemeine Wirtschaftsgeschichte des Mittelalters und der Neuzeit* (1929), vol. II, p. 253).

[4] Ehrenberg, *Hamburg und England*, p. 161.

least, a centre of commercial information. Liveliness at Frankfurt is news for London; a bankruptcy worth reporting. Particular qualities of cloth—'Frankfurt sorts'—are specially ordered for it. 'Packing for Frankfurt' is a regular routine at the beginning of every August. The prices paid for textiles at its celebrated fair—a European institution—are accepted as an index of their movements elsewhere, so that Cranfield must wait for firm quotations till 'the Frankfurt merchants are returned'. Northern sellers seek at Frankfurt southern wares in exchange for their own; 'no more [sc. coloured luccas] to be had till the Frankfurt goods come' is the factor's excuse for delay in buying returns. So keen is the scramble among English traders for its 'coloured taffetas, velvets and Venice [cloth of] gold and silver', that an enterprising individualist, who steals a march on his competitors by starting for Frankfurt a week in advance of them, can send them empty-handed home.[1]

If Frankfurt was one barometer of the state of trade, a second, and for Rawstorm, it would seem, an even more important one, was provided by another southern city. 'Dead doings at Nürnberg' breaks the news of a depression. 'Good hope we shall find good markets...at Nürnberg' announces a revival.[2] The rubbish which exporters expect their unhappy factors to sell at Nürnberg, of all places, is a perpetual irritation to him. The news that the Netherlands traders, after helping to spoil the Nürnberg market, have moved their wares to Italy, only to burn their fingers there as well, brings a ray of consolation.[3] It is evident, in short, that Nürnberg stood high among the markets for Dutch and English textiles, and no locality recurs more constantly in Rawstorm's letters. When Cranfield forms a consortium with two other London firms for the joint selling of kerseys, though Frankfurt and Danzig figure in the partners' programme, it is mainly on Nürnberg that the changes are rung.[4]

The role of the city as a centre of the European trade in textiles was partly due, no doubt, to its finishing and dyeing industry, partly to the demand of a populous region, with towns such as Regensburg, Ulm and, above all, Augsburg, whose fustians Rawstorm patronised, and to which the English trade was vital,[5] at no

---

[1] *Cranfield MSS.* nos. S.110, S.119, S.348, S.364, S.387, S.471, S. 477, and *passim* in Rawstorm's letters.
[2] *Ibid.* nos. S.112, S.387.   [3] *Ibid.* no. S.386.
[4] *Ibid.* nos. S.376, S.369, S.378, S.379, S.387, S.399, S.469, S.471, S.475, S.480.
[5] On Augsburg see Ehrenberg, *Hamburg und England*, pp. 203–4, and the report there printed of December 1598, in which the Augsburg merchants state (i) that English

great distance; but it was primarily the result of its geographical position. The remoter connections which that position gave it were of not less importance, and are of greater interest to the historian, than the business done within walls. Down to the Thirty Years War, Nürnberg was the distributing centre from which western textiles reached south-eastern Europe. Yorkshire kerseys, dyed and finished there, went to Austria, the Bürgerland and Transylvania. They travelled, indeed, still farther afield. The reader who meets the assertion that the greatest of European kersey markets is Hungary is inclined, at first, to rub his eyes; but the statement is not an unconsidered lapse, for its author elaborates it. No one, writes Rawstorm to his employer, with things as they are in Hungary, 'where kerseys are most vented', will venture to trade there. 'Cannot encourage you', he repeats some years later, 'to buy any more till we see further how matters will go in Hungary and some vent at Nürnberg.' The thought that the hapless Hungarians are cheated with 'rotten rags, whereof, now they are dyed and dressed and come to be worn, they find the discommodity', moves him to indignation. The news that, owing to irrelevant international complications, 'there is yet no encouragement out of Hungarie' plunges him in gloom.[1]

Rawstorm's correspondence is that of a business man immersed in an exacting trade; but he was too intelligent not to have an eye for affairs beyond prices and packing. His views on commercial politics were those to be expected. At Stade 'our company', in the sense of the ninety to a hundred odd merchants, factors and clerks engaged in selling textiles, is a reality to him. He quotes its opinions to reinforce his own, and refuses, though hard-pressed, to take the unorthodox course of shipping by a Hamburg vessel till satisfied that his colleagues are prepared to do the same. Except, however, for recurrent groans—late again—at the unpunctuality of the cloth fleet, there is little evidence that the higher direction of 'the most famous company of merchants in Christendom', which made so much noise in London and was a power in Middelburg, meant anything to him; nor were all his practices such as it would have approved.

textiles are indispensable, and that their exclusion involves the doubling in price of German woollen fabrics; (ii) that Augsburg fustians are exported to England to the value of 400,000 fl. yearly, and that the interruption of the trade with England must cause the ruin of the industry.

[1] *Cranfield MSS.* nos. S.127, S.374, S.434, S.471, S.473, S.474, S.475.

He shares, but not without reservations, the official objection to a 'straggling' trade; regards interlopers as often a nuisance, but sometimes a blessing; and regrets unashamedly that Cranfield does not see fit to make a larger use of them.[1] For the rest, he is all in the orthodox tradition, denouncing with vehemence the unforgivable sin of 'overcloying' the market, turning a suspicious eye on foreigners, and delighted to learn that 'the strangers, [who] thought to make a prey of us, and hung their dear ware upon us', are now all scowls at having over-reached themselves.[2] His favourite remedy for undercutting is the ever-green specific of collective selling. So he first urges his employer to join an export cartel—'seven or eight thousand will make no glut, and if you could agree with Mr Venn and the rest to buy and sell here together, it should be the more profitable for you all'[3]—and then, when the ring looks like breaking down, adjures him to cut his losses by persuading a well-known figure in the world of international finance to take over his quota. Such things were easier said than done; but Cranfield, an adept in keeping several balls together in the air, characteristically contrived to follow both counsels at once. While not doing too badly out of his temporary association with the firms of Samuel Hare and Richard Venn—both old cronies in the City—he appears to have managed in addition to dispose of just under 1400 kerseys to the slippery Burlamachi.[4]

The author of a useful little manual on *The Office of a Counsellor* had recommended that a Secretary of State, when concerned with German affairs, should consult 'some discreet person of...those which trade into those parts to advertise you...what they understand at Stade or Elvinge'.[5] Herbert might have done worse than turn for light to Cranfield's factor. Rawstorm's small drama of business stratagems, triumphs and defeats is played on a stage that itself is felt to rock. There are moments when the shadow of more awful issues falls across his sober pages. He does not seek to probe its message, but neither can he repress a shudder at the chill which the intruder spreads. In the jungle of factious principalities

---

[1] *Ibid.* nos. S. 352, S. 399.   [2] *Ibid.* no. S. 378.

[3] *Ibid.* no. S. 399. A similar view is expressed in a letter from Rawstorm to his fellow-employee, Richard Perrott: 'and I hope our masters will join together again, and get most part into their own hands' (no. S. 387). Other references to the consortium are nos. S. 369, S. 378, S. 379, S. 469, S. 471, S. 475, S. 480.

[4] For Burlamachi see *ibid.* nos. S. 469-471, S. 478.

[5] Robert Beale, *A Treatise of the Office of a Counsellor* (1592), in W. H. Dunham and S. Pargellis, *Complaint and Reform in England, 1436–1714* (1938), p. 396.

and implacable creeds composing the Germany—though he does not think of it as one entity—of his commercial pilgrimage, much gunpowder is lying about, and more than a whiff of it creeps into his letters. The feature which impresses their reader is less the recurrent explosions than the poisoned atmosphere, the hints of worse catastrophes to come, the background of strained apprehension, as of men waiting for a dam to burst. The writer's discourse is of textiles; but profitable trade is impossible without a stable peace. Where look for stability? The temporary closing of the Sound, though it means congested markets and low prices at Stade, is lightly dismissed as a passing evil; nor is Rawstorm much perturbed, 'now that we have got so mighty and gracious a Prince to defend us', by the pressure of the Hanse towns on the Empire to caulk the leaks in the embargo.[1] But worse storms are blowing up. Hostilities threatening between Poles and Swedes; civil war in Poland between the nobles and the King; war between the Duke and the city of Brunswick; a state of all but war—'greater than ever was'—for half a year on end between the Empire and Russia; war in Hungary, with 'the Pope and the Jesuits' as the villains of the piece; revolts in Transylvania, where 'the Emperor would bring in papistry' and the counter-Reformation is more hated than the Turk; the Hamburg money-market drained to finance archducal wars; merchants repudiating contracts as the hope of peace recedes; from Danzig to Nürnberg and Nürnberg to Vienna 'no encouragement for kerseys'—such, at different moments during an anxious six years, are the spectres which haunt him.[2] Among his letters to Cranfield in the summer of 1606 there are few which omit to refer to the vicissitudes of the negotiations between the Emperor and the Great Turk. It is curious that his one ray of light in the darkness of those months should be a report that the prospective belligerents have at last been induced to patch up their quarrels by the news that the Persians are within three days' march of Constantinople. Business for a moment looks up. 'You may be the bolder to venture upon kerseys or cloths.'[3]

[1] *Cranfield MSS.* nos. S.346, S.348.
[2] *Ibid.* nos. S.127, S.434, S.469, S.473–9, S.482, S.483.
[3] *Ibid.* no. S.479. See also no. S.478, 'Pack-cloth at Nürnberg is since the news of peace somewhat amended in price, and we hope there will be some store vented that way if the peace continues, which we doubt not. You cannot do amiss in buying, now cloth is at a reasonable rate there.' Later letters show that Rawstorm's optimism was premature: 'The peace between the Emperor and Russky holds not; so there is no encouragement for kerseys, except good and very cheap' (no. S.483).

4. CRANFIELD'S TRADE WITH THE
UNITED NETHERLANDS

The activities of Daniel Cooper, Cranfield's representative at Middelburg, did not differ in principle from those of Rawstorm. On his daily labours and their problems—the routine tasks and trials of a factor's existence—it is needless to elaborate a tale already told. Cooper's sphere of operations, however, was the second[1] most important port of a nation whose unchallenged pre-eminence in commerce and shipping was already proverbial. Both his activities and his correspondence took their stamp from that environment. The textiles, in the first place, which formed his staple ware were a different article from the greater part of those shipped to Stade. The northern kerseys, which provided Rawstorm with more than half his receipts, were not a commodity to appeal to the opulent and fastidious Dutch; and Cranfield wrote to Cooper in the autumn of 1600 announcing his decision, as far as Middelburg was concerned, to abandon or drastically reduce that part of his trade.[2] Nearly nine-tenths in value, therefore, of Cooper's sales consisted in the following year of cloths, fetching on the average £17 to £18 per piece; while such few kerseys as he dealt in were principally not the cheap Yorkshire, but the superior Devonshire, variety.

The relatively homogeneous market, in the second place, for which he catered was at the opposite pole from the central European jungle. Rawstorm must follow the politics of some half-dozen or more rulers, and plan his sales with his eyes on markets several hundred miles apart. Cooper also is not concerned solely with conditions in the mart town. He watches comparative prices in London, Emden and Stade; resorts to Amsterdam to inquire for supplies of Seville oil and to purchase a specialty—borrall cloth—demanded by his employer; disposes of remainders by sending them to the same voracious market; suggests that kerseys unsaleable in Middelburg shall be despatched via Amsterdam to Hamburg; and periodically makes a tour of Holland, his largest customer, to get in over-due debts. Even in wartime, however, the order, tranquillity and, in spite of provincial rivalries, superior unity of a people 'wholly

---

[1] C. Te Lintum, *op. cit.* pp. 63-4.

[2] *Cranfield MSS.* no. S.96: 'I note your resolution to cease your great dealing in northern kerseys, and to convert your trade into cloth whereby you write you shall be the more trouble to me.'

given over to their greed of gain by trade',[1] preserve him from the unpredictable complications, economic and political, which make Rawstorm's life a burden.

That part of Cooper's business, therefore, which consisted in selling cloths was, to judge by his letters, on the whole plain sailing. The arrival of the cloth fleet is followed by the organisation of a show-day by the English merchants at Middelburg, and by an influx of Dutch buyers.[2] Then unless, as in 1600, trade is abnormally bad, cloth goes off quickly, half Cooper's sales in 1601 being crowded into a feverish three weeks in December, and more than another third taking place in June, so that only between one-sixth and one-seventh of his textiles require to be despatched in the remaining ten months. Merchants from some seventeen towns were represented among his customers; but the majority of localities required only small consignments of from two to twenty-eight pieces. What mattered was the mass demand of a few large centres. Haarlem, and Middelburg itself, each took about one-tenth. Buyers from Amsterdam, who dominated the market, bought not far short of half. Cooper's dealings in returns were a more exacting business, which seem to have caused him, and still more his employer, not a few sleepless nights. The correspondence between the realistic Cranfield and his enterprising agent—the former all for speculations provided that they are certainties, the latter indignant at 'your tieing me express to meddle with no unvendable wares'; consoling his principal for a consignment of black velvets which no one will look at with the tranquil assurance that, having bought his experience, he has now put 'that crotchet out of my head'; and retorting, when upbraided for sending shoddy grograms and linens, that they are perfection compared with Cranfield's kerseys bartered for them[3]— is not without its comic side. Here again, however, the most striking feature of Cooper's trade is the comparative facility with which it is conducted. His problem was not the deficiency of wares which the universal emporium of the Netherlands provided for export. It was the difficulty of selection from an *embarras de richesse*.

If the economic pre-eminence of a country organised, as an observer remarked, like a business undertaking makes Cooper's letters barren of the hazards and vicissitudes which give colour to

---

[1] H. G. R. Reade, *Sidelights on the Thirty Years' War* (1924), vol. III, p. 12, quoting Scaglia (May 1627).

[2] *Cranfield MSS.* no. S.247. [3] *Ibid.* nos. S.173, S.225.

those of Rawstorm, it also confers on them a sober interest of their own. He writes with the cosmopolitan outlook of a citizen of the world. He is interested, of course, in conditions both in central Europe, particularly Frankfurt, whose prices for textiles react on his own, and also in Italy, which provides him with most of his consignments for England; but, residing within easy reach of the greatest of commercial capitals, he has glimpses of more distant horizons than were visible from Stade. He barters Dutch textiles in Bayonne—'where there is good profit to be done if a man had an honest factor, which is hard to be found there'[1]—for pearls to be sold through his employer in London. It seems natural to him to suggest that linens, which fail to find a market in England, can easily be re-exported as trade goods to North Africa or the West Indies.[2] The excitement with which the East India fleet is awaited; its competition with the Portuguese, who, if they can elude the English men-of-war, may beat it by a short head; the fever of speculation which follows its arrival; and the stratagems of importers bent on rigging the spice market, are recurrent sensations enlivening his letters.[3] The prospects of his own investments in the trade— '£300 flemish ventured for the East Indies in ships of Middelburg and Amsterdam, which if I would sell presently, I could have £110 profit, and they to step into my shoes'—are reported to Cranfield in an outburst of exhilaration, qualified, by way of touching wood, with the pious ejaculation, 'but God bless them all'.[4]

Compared with these glittering prizes, the English cloth trade was a humdrum affair; but the importance of the Netherlands market to the organised exporters caused them to guard their monopoly of it with jealous care. To judge by Cooper's sales—virtually all at the staple port—the success of the Company in suppressing its bugbear of 'straggling' was greater in the Netherlands than it could be in Germany, and the necessity of deferring to its formidable authority lay heavier on him than it did on Rawstorm. The circle in which he moved was not above reproach. Richard Sheppard, whose daughter Cranfield had married, had a bad reputation. 'Men's judgments are very hard on your father-in-law's courses.... I perceive by some friends that came from Amsterdam that John Wootton

---

[1] *Ibid.* no. S.250.   [2] *Ibid.* nos. S.210, S.225, S.120.
[3] See especially *ibid.* nos. S.71, S.72, S.77, S.78, S.80, S.165, S.207, S.210, S.225, S.247, S.251, S.264.
[4] *Ibid.* no. S.264.

[Sheppard's servant] is noted there for a great interloper'.[1] Cranfield himself, for all the later respectability of his middle age, was in his youth something less than a model Adventurer, and snatched more than once at the forbidden fruit of surreptitious sales outside the mart town. His factor, torn between loyalty to an employer and alarm at his imprudence, alternately warns him not to play with fire, and advises him how best, if the temptation is too much for him, to avoid being burned.

In few words, touching your trade with Amsterdam, it is noted, and the Company will stomach you for it....If you do interlope that way with some Devonshire and northern kerseys....Thomas Armitage would be a fitter man than Wootton....If I were you, I would chide you for venturing so much in a small Dutch bottom. God send him in safety. Doubt you nothing of my care to take them up forth of the Company's danger and to despatch them to profit with as much speed as I can.[2]

The struggle between the metropolitan export-cartels and the provincial ports led by Devonshire and Yorkshire, always simmering below the surface, was shortly to produce one of its recurrent explosions.[3] Cooper reads with a sigh of relief a letter from Cranfield renouncing for the future the perilous profits of the blackleg;[4] but his personal sentiments on the issues at stake are expressed with the reservations of a discreet Laodicean. 'I think that there will be all good means used that may be to make the Company all good brethren. If not, a man finding profit hath no reason but to take advantage of every way as well as others.'[5] So tepid an enthusiasm for the sacred principle of a well-ordered trade would hardly have satisfied a Wheeler or a Misselden; but it may well have represented the prevalent attitude of all those on active service abroad.

Germany and the United Netherlands were not the only markets for Cranfield's textiles;[6] but they were much the most important

---

[1] *Cranfield MSS.* no. S. 165.   [2] *Ibid.* nos. S. 183, S. 165, S. 255.

[3] See e.g. *Commons' Journals*, vol. 1, p. 218 ('Instructions touching the Bill for Free Trade', 1604).   [4] *Cranfield MSS.* no. S. 190.   [5] *Ibid.* no. S. 183.

[6] For cloth sent to Antwerp in 1604, see below, p. 66 and the references there given. Cranfield had already, in 1601, received an order from a foreign correspondent at Stade to ship on his account to Venice 300 to 600 kerseys—'no rags among them; they serve not in any wise for that place' (*ibid.* S. 233). In another letter referring to tincal sent to Venice in 1605, he asks for a return 'in currants or other commodities at your discretion, for I am but a stranger in the course of trade in those parts' (*ibid.* no. S. 379). Tincal, a crude borax found in late deposits in Persia and some other Asiatic countries, was presumably a re-export.

ones. Is it possible to offer an estimate of the quantity and value of the piece-goods sold in both of them together? Any answer must be tentative, but an approximate figure is not beyond our reach. Rawstorm's journal shows that, for the period of just under two years and five months covered by it, his sales per twelve months averaged 444 cloths, 2070 northern kerseys, and 16 Devonshire kerseys, and his receipts, when converted from Hamburg money into sterling, £3278, £3281, and £37, a total of £6596 sterling.[1] No similar account has been left by Cooper; but such of his letters as survive—some, no doubt, are missing—make it possible to arrive at a minimum figure of his sales and receipts in 1601. It was not less, at any rate, than 488 cloths, realising £8653 sterling, and 405 kerseys at £1382, so that his total receipts were £10,035. It will be seen that his cloths sold at over twice per piece those of Rawstorm (£17. 14s. against £7. 7s.), while his kerseys, a much less important item to him than to Rawstorm, also fetched, being predominantly Devonshires, a higher price than the latter's northerns. If Rawstorm's average[2] sales per twelve months are combined with Cooper's for 1601, it would appear that, in his German and Netherlands markets together, Cranfield was selling something in the region of 930 cloths and 2500 kerseys a year, yielding together some £16,630. The returns bought were on a somewhat smaller scale. Rawstorm's average outlay on them per twelve months was £6604 sterling. Cooper's was in 1601 not less than £6650, and was probably over £7750.

These figures are offered with diffidence; but they are near enough to the mark to convey an impression of the business done in the opening years of the century by a reasonably prosperous textile merchant. The later chapters of Cranfield's career in the field of foreign trade still remain to be thoroughly explored; but some fragmentary data, though too meagre to permit of a confident statement, suggest that, though increasingly occupied with other interests, as a textile exporter he more than held his own. There is the despatch of some 2700 kerseys to Stade alone in 1603,[3] which puts a different

---

[1] *Ibid.* no. T. 53.

[2] The average figure is used, instead of that for 1601, because Rawstorm's sales of cloth in 1601 appear to have been abnormally high (795 cloths for £4872 sterling). If Rawstorm's figure for 1601 be taken, then the cloths sold by Rawstorm and Cooper together in 1601 were 1283 for £13,525, and the value of their sales of cloths and kerseys together £18,189, instead of £16,630. The minimum figure of Cooper's sales is probably an under-statement.

[3] *Cranfield MSS* no. T. 194.

complexion on Rawstorm's meagre figure for the early months of that year. There is the striking episode—a consequence, it seems, of the peace with Spain—of Cranfield's incursion into the long-closed market of the Spanish Netherlands. To an inquiry of April 1604, from a correspondent at Antwerp whether he could undertake to deliver 6500 pieces, mostly coloured cloths but including some whites and kerseys, he replied that, while he himself would 'manage the business...a matter of great moment...and well worth the entertaining', it would be necessary for him to secure partners, and, subject to agreement on patterns and prices, accepted the order. He took into partnership James Cullimore, Samuel Hare and Richard Venn, for the purchase of coloured broad cloths up to £2800. The wares were duly shipped; but the deal, the largest which had as yet come Cranfield's way, did not turn out too well. It passes from sight in a storm of plaintive letters from the exasperated agent who managed the business at Calais and Gravelines, exclaiming at the outrageous customs and port-dues at the latter, upbraiding his principal for having tendered at an impossibly low figure, and reporting unhopeful conversations with the consignee on the subject of an advance in prices.[1] There is the fact, in the third place, that, on the evidence of the Port Books, Cranfield was the second largest exporter of kerseys from London in 1606, when he was entered for 2685,[2] and that, in 1607, his Stade consignment in May alone was 1362, sold for £2790 sterling, which was followed in July by another considerable shipment of 570 kerseys and 100 cloths at £1768 sterling, on account of Philip Burlamachi.[3] Evidence, finally, of a different kind that his trade was on the ascent is provided by the record of his purchases of cloth. In 1606, his payments to clothiers for textiles supplied by them were 42%, and in 1607, the last full year for which data exist, 31%, above the average of the three preceding years, 1603-5.

Obviously, such scraps of information do not by themselves amount to proof. All that can be said is that, so far as they go, they point in one direction. The important point, however, for an understanding of Cranfield's career is, perhaps, less the absolute dimensions of his

---

[1] *Cranfield MSS.* nos. S. 407, S. 408 (Jehan van den Varent's inquiry and Cranfield's reply). Cranfield cancelled the contracts for the reason, or on the pretext, of 'the danger I stood in by the law of our land'; but proposed a new one, which was accepted (no. S. 349). For the partnership with Cullimore, etc., see no. T. 245. For shipping of the cloths and Cooper's difficulties, see nos. S. 442, S. 443, S. 447.

[2] Friis, *op. cit.* p. 130.   [3] *Cranfield MSS.* no. T. 308 and ledger.

trade, which, in the absence of comparable figures, do not tell us much, than his relative position *vis-à-vis* competitors engaged in the same line of business. On that question, thanks to the book of Professor Friis, we are not wholly without light. She has shown that, out of 219 firms shipping cloth from London in 1606, 142 exported up to 400 pieces, fifty-one from 401 to 1000, and only twenty-six above 1000.[1] If, therefore, Cranfield's exports of cloths alone to Stade and Middelburg be considered, he was well up in the second flight. If his kerseys be included, at Rawstorm's rate of between four to five northern kerseys to one cloth, he was easily in the first.

5. MISCELLANEOUS SPECULATIONS

'I will not by any means', a friend once wrote to him, 'encourage you to have too many irons in the fire.'[2] The hint was not superfluous. The taste for backing his fancy grew on Cranfield with success. While his domestic interests, being largely concerned with Government contracts, followed a well-defined pattern, his foreign speculations were highly heterogeneous. They took the form of raids on a variety of different markets, and must be touched on lightly. Not unnaturally, in view of his Netherlands connections, pepper was among his early loves. Cooper, whom he pesters with instructions to buy it, has burned his own fingers, and preaches caution—'it is more uncertain venturing therein than in any commodities whatsoever'—with the enthusiasm of a convert. The unexpected arrival of a single East Indiaman may knock the market to pieces. Portuguese supplies—'for store of Lisbon, with these westerly winds, will be dispersed into all kingdoms of Christendom' —defeat calculations based on Dutch shipments alone; 'no wisdom to adventure upon any quantity, considering it comes flying from all places'. One group of importers are bears, who spread rumours to depress the price and buy cheap; another are bulls and combine to sell dear, with Amsterdam and Middelburg agreeing to fix a minimum. Both have to reckon with the hazards of war. 'You expect that pepper will keep about 3s. 4d. or 3s. 6d. middle sort, but you are deceived... If the Queen's ships meet with a carrack, as I hope they will, then under 3s. it will come.... All that at Amsterdam is sold to the corn coopers and the cheese coopers at 70d., but they had better have remained at their selling of corn and cheese, for they

---

[1] Friis, *op. cit.* p. 78. [2] *Cranfield MSS.* no. S. 165.

sink with their pepper already, and would gladly sell at 60*d*.' Even when the East India fleet arrives in strength, it may bring so little as to upset all plans, and even that little—'this sudden engrossing of spices is strange'—may be cornered by a ring. Pepper, in short, is 'a vile commodity...as dangerous for loss...as hazardous of gain....For the love of God, do not be too hasty upon that biting weed.'[1]

Whether Cranfield was bitten or not, we do not know; but, in spite of Cooper's nerves, he took the risk. He was buying pepper in 1601, and again in 1604, in each case partly for export, and receiving, in the latter year, unhopeful reports from his representatives abroad as to the prospects of selling it. A second tropical product, with which he conducted a prolonged flirtation, consisted of dyewood. The small quantities which reached Europe, and particularly England; the fact that it was a 'prohibited' commodity, the export of which required a licence, to be obtained by influence or intrigue; and, according to Professor Newton, a recent invention which greatly increased its value, enhanced its charms for the speculator. Cranfield's attempt, with a group of partners, not only to monopolise the London market, but to corner the continental supplies, the bulk of which naturally came to the Netherlands, began in 1607. It met at first with some success. He could write in May of the following year a letter addressed jointly to two of his factors, Perrott and Rawstorm, in which he stated that he had heard from the latter that 50,000 lb. had been bought by him, and expressed approval of his action in going to Hamburg to arrange for the purchase of 25,000 lb. more. Large amounts, he remarked, were already in the syndicate's hands at Middelburg and Amsterdam, where prices had risen to 50*s*., at which he hoped to sell. 'Let me hear how they rule there [*sc.* at Stade and Hamburg] for that commodity. It is worth here £20 per ton ready money, and, did not the great quantity with you fear us, we would have made it here within this month or six weeks £40 per ton; but, by reason of that, we do not proceed as we intended.' The profits realised by the partners by September 1609 were £8044, or something under £900 per head; and in 1610 Cranfield was still pressing Passfield, his Amsterdam agent, to go forward with fresh purchases. By that time, however, the scene

[1] For these and other references to pepper see *Cranfield MSS.* nos. S. 71, S. 72, S. 77, S. 78, S. 80, S. 82, S. 96, S. 195, S. 207, S. 210, S. 215, S. 225, S. 241, S. 247, S. 251, S. 295. For cloves see nos. S. 165, S. 207, and for nutmegs, no. S. 250.

had changed. Passfield could only reply that the bottom had dropped out of the market; that logwood bought by him at 35*s.* per lb. was now selling at 17*s.* or 18*s.*; and that, having paid for it out of his own pocket, he did not know where to turn to meet his debts. Apart from the winding up of the account, which dragged on for another three years, the last that we hear of the transaction is that the stocks unsaleable at Amsterdam have been shipped home to London.[1]

Two other commodities which attracted Cranfield's attention were less exotic. His textile interests in Poland gave him a footing in what was then the European granary; and his deals in grain of 1608 and 1609—the former a year of famine prices in England— may be cited as an illustration of his occasional skirmishes on the corn-market. In May 1608 he gave instructions to his Danzig agent, Perrott, that the whole proceeds of his kersey sales at Danzig were to be returned to him in rye and wheat. Perrott, as ordered, shipped in August just over 3000 qrs, at a cost of £2129 paid to the sellers and £118 in customs duties, a transaction which was followed early next year by further consignments of 1600 qrs of wheat and 9600 qrs of rye, while negotiations undertaken by Cranfield himself with Burlamachi, who was also buying in Danzig, resulted in his acquisition of another 1500 qrs. Apart from sales to the Bakers' Company totalling down to the end of March 1610 some £1870, and private sales in 1608 for another £1300 odd, we do not know how Cranfield disposed of his purchases, or what, if any, profits he made; but Perrott was not optimistic. Prices at Danzig, which ruled those elsewhere, fluctuated sharply—there 'is no meddling with it at present until the price be settled'. In January 1609 they declined, and the fall continued in April. 'I hope'—a vain hope—'you have not gone through with Burlamachi for the wheat. If you have, I could wish you to clear your hands of it again as soon as possible.'[2]

Among commodities passing in international trade munitions of war held a place of some importance. Cranfield's contact with one of them—saltpetre—was a matter less of choice than of necessity;[3]

---

[1] Hist. MSS. Comm., *Cranfield Papers, 1551–1612*, pp. 146–50, which gives particulars of the partners' purchases in London, but not, unfortunately, of their total outlay, which was, of course, much larger (*Cranfield MSS.* nos. S. 557, S. 643, S. 651, S. 669, S. 674, S. 675).

[2] *Cranfield MSS.* nos. S. 557, S. 579, S. 642, S. 634, S. 637, S. 653, S. 659, and ledger, ff. 202, 228.

[3] Cranfield's factor at Danzig was obliged to accept saltpetre in payment for a bad debt due from a Dutch firm of corn-importers, which had failed in 1609. For the attempts

his interest in another, and more important one, was for several years recurrent. Till later knocked out by Swedish competition, England was among the leading gun-founders of Europe, to whom not only Governments, but companies and individual traders, looked for part of the indispensable armaments. Cranfield's ventures in the export of ordnance were neither large nor continuous, and he handled a tonnage derisory to modern eyes; but they went on inter-mittently from 1604 to about 1610, and the markets with which they dealt ranged from the North Sea to the Mediterranean. The two men, Arthur Ingram and William Massam, associated with him in the business were both among his intimates. The latter, Passfield's brother-in-law, was a partner in not a few of Cranfield's enterprises. The former, an influential Customs official of whom more is said below, was in this matter, as in several others, in a position to pull strings. He dealt in the forbidden ware himself, and it was through him that Cranfield more than once secured his supplies.

The principal markets concerned were Amsterdam and Hamburg, both not only the possessors of mercantile marines which required equipment, but great distributing centres. Into the details of particular transactions it is needless to enter. It is sufficient to say by way of illustration, that in 1604 Cranfield sent guns to Amsterdam to be sold by Passfield, and to Hamburg, where they were handled by Rawstorm, while smaller consignments went to an English agent in Spain, for the benefit, it is thought, of English privateers in the Mediterranean; that in 1606 and 1607 he repeated his shipments to Amsterdam and Hamburg; that he also, in the former year, sent a small cargo to Leghorn, as well as a larger one to La Rochelle; and that his interest in the business continued for another five years. The trade, in addition to its other difficulties, was one which was peculiarly at the mercy of international politics; and Cranfield, it seems, risked holding on to it longer than was good for him. In 1609, of all years, he is pressing his unhappy agent at Amsterdam, who has 200 tons

to dispose of it, see *Cranfield MSS.* nos. S. 637, S. 644, S. 653, S. 659, S. 668–78. Perrott, the individual in question, who took the view that the truce between the Netherlands and Spain had killed the Dutch market, suggested unloading the stuff on Burlamachi—an unhopeful victim—and then sent it home. In answer to Cranfield's inquiries, Passfield, his agent at Amsterdam, reported that rumours of war there caused gunpowder to be in demand. He insisted, however, that since saltpetre varied in quality and the Dutch were not the people to buy a pig in a poke, nothing could be done unless Cranfield sent him samples.

on his hands, to make a quick despatch of them. Not unnaturally, Passfield's first reaction is a cry of dismay. Peace has broken out. Disarmament is in the air. The East Indiamen carry fewer guns than they did. 'The Admiralty of this town is selling much of their ordnance.' Six months later Passfield's drooping spirits show signs of reviving. He has persuaded one buyer to take thirty to forty pieces, and another to take twenty. He even suggests that, if Cranfield cares to transfer to Amsterdam the guns shipped to La Rochelle, a market may be found for them among the Dutch.[1]

Compared with Cranfield's textile business, these intermittent raids on regions off his beat were too trivial to count. Such interest as belongs to the former attaches less to the detailed operations involved than to the glimpses offered by it of a few important strands in the economic network linking the different provinces of the Europe of his day. The golden age of the Merchant Adventurers, against which this chapter of his career must be seen, was not destined long to last. Royal state-craft and the Great Depression of the early 1620's combined to bring them low; while later the dislocation, if not the actual ruin, of considerable tracts of German economic life accelerated a change already under way both in the principal markets for English textile products and in the nature of the fabrics shipped. The first two catastrophes were surmounted. The effect of the last was that long-term economic currents, which formerly had favoured the Adventurers, ceased to set their way. In Cranfield's day, however, that shift of commercial interests south, the opening segment of the majestic curve which, combined with other influences, was to make England a Mediterranean power, had hardly yet begun. During the last two-thirds of his period as an exporter, the northern trade in heavy woollens, which was his own and his Company's specialty, not only enjoyed a unique prosperity, but seemed assured of equally illustrious days to come. Its pre-eminence as the leading branch of English continental enterprise lends something of a representative quality to his commerce and connections.

It was not till 1613 that Cranfield's interests at Stade and Danzig were finally wound up, but some years before that date his

---

[1] Hist. MSS. Comm., *Cranfield Papers*, pp. 64–6, 122–3, 135, 170, 258, 310, 348; *Cranfield MSS.* nos. S. 474, S. 475, S. 482, S. 483 (letters from Rawstorm), S. 636, S. 651, S. 656, S. 661, S. 666, S. 667–70, S. 674 (letters from Passfield), T. 202 (bond by Ingram assigning ordnance to Cranfield and Massam), and ledger, ff. 100, 182).

withdrawal from active commerce had, it seems, begun.[1] The significance for his future eminence of his fifteen years of foreign trade is
not easily appraised. For all his initiative and drive as an exporter, he
was not of the merchants the bulk of whose fortunes came from
enterprise overseas. His largest gains were to be made when his
textile interests were behind him; and, if he was later conspicuous,
not merely as a public figure, but as a master of great possessions,
it was less his early business triumphs than his career in the service
of the Crown which was to supply the most imposing, as well as
the most quickly acquired, additions to his wealth.[2] To the annual
profits of his export and import business no clue, it appears, exists.
His periodical statements of his financial position—net assets
£2500 odd in August 1598; £12,800 at the end of December 1606;
£20,000 in July 1611; £24,200 in January 1613[3]—suggest an unspectacular, but continuous and respectable, ascent. The margins
revealed by his expenditure point in the same direction. He does
not as yet attempt, like his crony, Ingram, to cut a dash in London
society; but his erection, six years after he set up in business, of a
new London house; his purchase in 1605 of the Receivership of
Somerset and Dorset; the facility with which he finds money for
speculative ventures abroad and at home; and his considerable
investments in real property, are not the traits of one cramped by
lack of means. Since from 1604 onwards he had other strings to his
bow, the progress of his fortunes cannot be ascribed to the success
of his export business alone; but the pedestrian routine of a cloth-
merchant's counting-house had given him his start. Of the methods
by which he turned to account that initial success something is said
below.

[1] Cranfield's statement of his assets in January 1613 (*MSS.* no. 4096) includes small
debts due to him, presumably on account of textiles sold, at Stade and Danzig. According
to Professor Newton (Hist. MSS. Comm., *Cranfield Papers*, p. xxiii) 'he was dropping
mercantile business' (in or before 1612), 'and the letters from his correspondents on the
Continent ceased before 1612'. The last of such letters which I have myself read
(*Cranfield MSS.* no. S. 677) is from Samuel Passfield, 19 February 1611, who was
selling ordnance for him at Amsterdam.

[2] See below, pp. 194-5, n. 1 and 2.

[3] Hist. MSS. Comm., *Cranfield Papers*, pp. 26, 131, 346-51 (for 1598, 1606, 1611);
Cranfield MSS. no. 4096.

CHAPTER IV

CRANFIELD IN THE CITY

1. THE METROPOLITAN BACKGROUND

Cranfield's second chapter opens in the later months of 1604, towards the end of his first seven years of independent business. It does not supersede his activities as an exporter, nor does it last for ever; but for almost a decade the transactions characteristic of it are increasingly prominent in his papers. His aim, to judge by the turn taken by his interests, was not merely a fortune, but a fortune quickly made; and he was not one to permit conventional obligations or sentimental claims to impede its pursuit.

> Nature sent man into the world alone,
> Without all company, but to care for one,
> And that I'll do.[1]

Cranfield, with his political ambitions and genial facility in making useful friends, was far from a Bartervile. It must be confessed, however, that the comment of the attendant demon on that unsocial gospel—'true City doctrine, sir'—contained a warning not irrelevant to this phase of his career.

Local politics—the civic *cursus honorum* which might carry the industrious apprentice to the office of Alderman, Sheriff and Lord Mayor—are not, indeed, ignored by him, but are treated with an indifference which caused malicious tongues to wag.[2] Custom

---

[1] T. Dekker, *If it be not good, the Devil's in it* (1612) (*Dramatic Works* (1873 ed.), vol. IV, p. 312). I owe this quotation to Professor L. C. Knights, *Drama and Society in the Age of Jonson*, p. 243.

[2] Cranfield was nominated an alderman for the ward of Farringdon Without in October 1613, and for Bridge Ward in July 1615, but was not elected on either occasion (A. Beaven, *Aldermen of the City of London* (1908), vol. II, p. xliv). He was chosen Sheriff 11 July 1614, but refused to serve, and, on again being chosen on 24 June 1615, was discharged without a fine on 28 August (Cockayne, *Some Account of the Lord Mayors and Sheriffs of London, 1601–25* (1897), p. 68). A letter of 7 August 1615, from Sir Ralph Winwood, then Secretary of State, to the Lord Mayor (*Cranfield MSS*. no. 4432) repeats an order already given that Cranfield should be discharged of the shrievalty in order that his more important duties might not be neglected. A letter of 12 August from Cranfield to the Lord Mayor (*ibid*. no. 1518) gives his answer to attacks by his critics for his failure to attend the Common Council. He complains that 'we have some devils abroad in the shape of men who, by raising slanderous speeches, seek to make a

encouraged the successful merchant to make his bow to the proprieties by serving as a committee-man or governor of one or other of the famous Companies. Cranfield, a mercer of standing, evades office in his own till offered it as an honorific tribute to an eminence already won. Shortly after his appointment as Lord Treasurer he receives the cordial commendations of its court for the 'special affection' which he has shown it, and which—more important—he is confidently expected to continue to display. So far as is known, however, beyond paying his dues, he reveals on only one occasion, when his championship of his Company before the Council made some stir, a realistic and effective interest in its affairs.[1] Not only these ritual obligations, but, apart from the transactions with clothworkers, drapers and haberdashers necessitated by his trade, the whole world of London industry, vivid with the mingled gaiety and squalor of a street in Pekin, in which organised craftsmen fight their long, losing battle against the conscienceless individualism of encroaching capitalists, and the pioneers of new arts seek in the unchartered freedom of the suburbs a sanctuary for enterprise immune to both, rarely comes within his purview. The light cast by his papers falls, not on these familiar themes, but on regions whose importance has rather deepened than diminished the obscurity surrounding them. The London which supplies his stage is neither the historic corporation whose decorous magnificence dazzled foreign observers, nor the hive of industrial energy whose congestion east of Temple Bar, and ceaseless expansion west of it, were the perplexity of Governments. It is principally composed of the minority of commercial and financial magnates—successful traders, bankers,

difference between the City and me'; repudiates the charge that his bad attendance has been due to 'pride and contempt'; protests that he will make it apparent 'how much I honour and desire the prosperity of our City', and begs the Lord Mayor to call a meeting, 'where I shall attend, if I know the time'.

[1] G. Goodman, *The Court of King James I*, vol. 1, p. 398, states that he became Master during his tenure of the Lord High Treasurership, i.e. between October 1621, and May 1624. The topic on which he addressed the Council on behalf of his Company was the allocation between the different City Companies of the contribution to be made by them to the cost of a plantation in Ireland, an occasion on which he appears to have convinced it that the burden imposed on his Company was excessive. His speech brought him some *réclame* in high places: 'this was the first notice that was taken of Mr. Cranfield at Court' (*ibid.* pp. 202–3). On 14 November 1621, the Court of the Mercers' Company, in granting a request from Cranfield for a lease of a property owned by it, referred appreciatively to 'what place his Lordship had heretofore borne in this Company' and also to 'that [*sc.* place] his Lordship now is in, wherein he may show the effects of the same his honourable affection' (*Cranfield MSS.* no. 7135).

tax-farmers, middlemen and brokers, with, not least important, a sprinkling of influential officials—which forms the apex of the economic pyramid. In the language of today, which, though not yet quite a cliché, was on the way to become one, it is the City.[1]

This business aristocracy had a distinguished history behind it and a dazzling future still to come. The opening year of James washed wealth to its shores. Peace, the revival of trade, both in England and abroad, probably an industrial expansion which gathered impetus from both, enlarged its resources. An inflated and impecunious Court; the growth of the professions, in particular law and medicine; the change in social habits described by Professor Fisher[2] which was turning town houses for the wealthier gentry from a rare extravagance into a conventional necessity and was soon to launch a London season; a nobility prone to the 'magnificence in expense' deplored by Bacon[3] and crumbling Crown finances, combined to swell the clientele which looked for enrichment or relief to the potentates courted and denounced as the 'usurers of the City'. The dominant position of the capital in English economic life—a dominance unpopular in the provinces and by some of them, at moments of crisis, angrily attacked, but as yet unshaken—was never more pronounced. Three-quarters of the country's foreign trade paid toll in its custom-house. The tonnage in the service of London shipowners may well have been not far short of half that of all other ports together.[4] In industries dependent on raw materials moved by water, as well as in most of the older crafts, its preeminence was unquestioned. Nor was its radius of influence

[1] The transition from 'this city', or 'the city of London', to 'the City' *tout court*, in the sense of London business, can be observed in the debates of the Parliament of 1621. See, e.g. Notestein, Relf and Simpson, *Commons' Debates, 1621*, vols. II, pp. 446–7, and VI, p. 321.

[2] F. J. Fisher, 'The Development of London as a Centre of conspicuous consumption in the Sixteenth and Seventeenth Centuries', in *Trans. R.H.S.* 4th series, vol. XXX (1948), pp. 37–50.

[3] Bacon, *Of the True Greatness of Kingdoms and Estates.*

[4] On the average of the seven years 1605–11 the customs receipts from London were just over 74% of those from all ports together (Hist. MSS. Comm., *Cranfield Papers, 1551–1612*, p. 289). No satisfactory figures of shipping are available. For such information as exists, see Lawrence A. Harper, *The English Navigation Laws* (1939), who states that 'by Charles I's reign London possessed one-third of the country's shipping' (p. 282 and n.); G. G. Marston, 'English Ships in the reign of James I', in *Trans. R.H.S.* new series, vol. XIX (1905), pp. 309–42; and a return (possibly incomplete) of February 1629 of ships of 100 tons and upwards belonging to several ports, in *S.P.D. Chas. I*, LXXXII, 135. London shipping was, on the whole, of larger burden than provincial.

restricted to the metropolis. As the greatest of consuming centres, London affected cereal prices and farming methods as far as Berkshire in one direction and Norfolk in another; dairy produce came to it, not only from Essex, but from Yorkshire and Wiltshire; Northamptonshire and Wiltshire wools were handled by its distributors; while cattle from North Wales and Scotland, some of them finished on Romney Marsh, and sheep from the western Cotswolds, found a market in Smithfield. London merchants were concerned in the export from other ports, both in England and abroad, of wares bought and sold through agents to an extent which makes their shipments from the Thames an inadequate index of the scale of their activities. Provincial industries—Cornish tin, Welsh and Derbyshire lead, Yorkshire alum, Durham and Northumberland coal, the iron of Sussex and the Forest of Dean, Cumberland copper, Midlands hardware and brass, textiles in half-a-dozen counties—were partly financed, directly or indirectly, with money raised in London. As the chief market for the larger transactions by mortgage and sale in real estate, London had its thumb on a considerable section of the landed gentry. The whole increasing mass of Government financial business, with its formidable reactions on public revenues and private fortunes, was virtually its monopoly.

The foundations of it all were, of course, of great complexity. Of the different elements composing them that which, in view of Cranfield's interests, most concerns us here is the position of London in the world of international commerce. Neither in the dimensions of its trade, nor in financial resources, nor in business *expertise*, could the English capital, if contemporary opinion may be trusted, rival Amsterdam, but the currents by which both were floated forward, if different in volume and speed, were similar in kind. In the early seventeenth century the natural resources of Europe were still but little depleted, while new worlds outside it had been made accessible by an advance in geographical knowledge and the science of navigation, unaccompanied by a corresponding progress in the productive arts. The result was a combination of business precocity with technical conservatism which gave the economies of the day a distinctive stamp, and which, until failing resources and rising costs compelled attention to the search for improved techniques, made the triumphs of enterprise less intensive than extensive. It was more profitable and less precarious to exploit expanding markets

76

and sources of supply by way of trade than to tread, with alchemist and projector, the perilous paths of technological innovation.

In such circumstances, the social pattern of the past, though enlarged and elaborated, was not remade. It continued, as in previous centuries, to be predominantly commerce, not manufactures or mining, which, if territorial wealth be excepted, yielded the great fortunes; commercial, not industrial, profits which contributed the lion's share of the small surplus for investment; trading, not producing, interests which steered to its victorious conclusion the conquest, long before begun, of the historic crafts, and which launched new forms of industrial enterprise organised from the start on a capitalist basis; commercial magnates, not industrialists, who pulled the strings of City politics, mixed on equal terms with the landed aristocracy, and on occasion ended, far from the dust and roar of Cheapside and Lombard Street, as themselves the lords of great estates. Dekker's genial craftsman, made Lord Mayor for honest worth, may delight the groundlings; but, in the prose of daily life, the spokesman who, whether as civic functionary, governor of a great company, or mere successful capitalist, voices the demands or discontents of London business, is a suppler and more sophisticated figure, of the type commemorated in the same versatile dramatist's Mayoralty Pageant of 1612,[1] who needs no lessons in the refinements of the diplomatic art from the harassed Ministers with whom he deals. He may, and often does, have rural roots,[2] which, when he comes to make his will, he occasionally recalls, and enjoy the practical advantages and honorific distinction of membership in one or other of the twelve historic companies; but, whether described as a grocer, merchant tailor, goldsmith, ironmonger or mercer, it is normally commerce and finance that have made him. He is pre-eminently 'the master of the mysteries of trade, the steward of the kingdom's stock, the perfect merchant'.[3]

The triumph of this commercial capitalism—to use the conventional, if ambiguous, term—produced two consequences, both of

---

[1] The pageant in honour of Sir John Swinnerton, who was Lord Mayor in 1612, was the work of Thomas Dekker, the author of *The Shoemaker's Holiday*.

[2] The list of Lord Mayors, with particulars of their parentage, given by Stow (*Survey of London*, ed. J. Strype (1720), vol. II, pp. 37 *seq.*) shows that, of 53 Lord Mayors from 1591 to 1640, only eleven were natives of London, Westminster and Middlesex, and thirteen of the home counties (Essex, Kent, Surrey, Herts, Berks), while more than half came from more distant regions.

[3] Thomas Mun, *England's Treasure by Forraign Trade*, p. 1.

which cut deep. It maintained or heightened the barriers separating classes. It lowered or suppressed the divisions between different occupational groups within them. Owing to the overhead costs of warehouses, factories and agents, foreign commerce tended, even in the provinces, to be predominantly in the hands of a minority of substantial firms.[1] In London, with its greater volume of transactions and powerful monopolistic corporations, the concentration of control is seen at its height. The proportion of its total exports handled by the Merchant Adventurers is thought to have exceeded one-half;[2] and Professor Friis, while citing the astute Wheeler's commendation of the protection to the smaller fry offered by the Company, has shown that, in reality, in the opening years of the century, more than half its members shipped less than one-tenth of its exports, while just over one-tenth accounted for almost half of them.[3] The criticism passed, some sixteen years later, in 1622, by the Standing Committee on Trade which emerged from the depression, on arrangements that permitted 'two third parts of all the commodities of the kingdom [to be] borne and managed by fifty hands only',[4] has a slightly rhetorical ring; but the sponsors of the Report were sobriety itself, and, if they exaggerated, they did not invent. In such circumstances, the sides of the pyramid were obviously steep. The objective sought by corporate restrictions, which excluded 'retailers, shopkeepers, handicraftsmen' and other inferior persons from engaging in wholesale trade to the prejudice of 'the mere merchants', was attained, in effect, by the logic of economic facts. Nor, of course, was that happy condition confined to foreign commerce. As disputes, petitions and legislation show, rigid apprenticeship rules, high fees for admission to the grade of master, growing costs of setting up in business, and the increase in the number of journeymen per firm, had combined to entrench a similar oligarchy in control of not a few of the London crafts. In both cases, whatever

---

[1] Some provincial Port Books, 1600–40, e.g. those of Bristol, Exeter, Dartmouth, Plymouth, Southampton and Yarmouth, offer cases in point.

[2] Friis, *Alderman Cockayne's Project and the Cloth Trade* (1927), p. 70. The period to which her statement refers is the first decade of the seventeenth century.

[3] *Ibid.* pp. 77–80. The Eastland Company, which did not love the Merchant Adventurers, was equally emphatic both on the large proportion of the total cloth export shipped by the Adventurers and on the concentration of the trade in the hands of a small minority of members: 'the greatest part of their trade, being above the three-fourth parts of all broad cloth transported, is driven by less than forty persons' (Hist. MSS. Comm., *Cranfield Papers, 1551–1612*, p. 36, *c.* 1600).

[4] *S.P.D. Jas. I*, CXXXIII, no. 35.

the constitutional forms of company organisation, a dominant minority is, in fact, in command.

This feature was accompanied by another. 'The only glory' of merchants, it was remarked half-a-century later by Hobbes, who did not love them, is 'to grow excessively rich by the wisdom of buying and selling'; while their alleged services to the State he dismissed as nothing more recondite than the art of 'making poor people sell their labour to them at their own price'.[1] The primary interest of the commercial entrepreneur was, not production, but markets. His disposition to merge his employees, whether nominally independent small masters or hired wage-earners, in an undifferentiated mass of hands, irrespective of diversities of professional status, rule and custom, had long been an old story. A movement which, for our purpose, is more significant is a second aspect of the same propensity. It is the partial obliteration of traditional distinctions within the higher ranges of the economic hierarchy, and the emergence, side by side with separate bodies of practitioners, each with its own sphere of interests, of more heterogeneous and more mobile groups. Commercial capital was easily diverted from one venture to another. Means, tastes and connections confined the majority of traders to their distinct and varying grooves; but not a few of the leading figures in the London of James I, like the corresponding class today, owed their importance less to their eminence in this line or that, than to their versatility as economic pluralists. The activities of these precocious individualists cut across conventional divisions. Their attachment is less to the particular trade by which they are described than to the elusive goddess profit, wherever she may lead.

Professor Thrupp, in her study[2] of the business world of medieval London, has written of the fifteenth-century merchant as essentially 'a man of mixed enterprise', who combined 'a preferential interest either in the special branch of trade with which his company was connected or in some one of the great staple commodities' with a readiness 'to deal in any other merchandise that came his way'. A century and a half later the economic virtuosity described by her appears on a more imposing scale. The variety of different irons kept in the fire by some of Cranfield's associates, who, without abandoning

---

[1] *Behemoth*, in F. Maseres, *Select Tracts relating to the Civil Wars in the reign of Charles I* (1815), vol. II, p. 576.

[2] Sylvia Thrupp, *The Merchant Class of Medieval London* (University of Chicago Press, 1948).

the trade which is their speciality, move in a continuous whirl of temporary and shifting partnerships to exploit a commercial *coup* or a grant by the Crown, is a case in point. To such men, however, their speculative plunges seem rarely to be more than an exhilarating adjunct to the main body of their affairs; nor is it commonly they by whom the most rewarding ventures are initiated and controlled. The personalities best qualified to discover or invent opportunities for profitable deals and to set the machinery to exploit them at work move, as a rule, on a more exalted plane. They are less often traders harnessed to the tactical routine than business notabilities who have already arrived, and whose standing in the City, combined, as on occasion it is, with the asset of a post in the customs or a pull at Court, ensures that, when windfalls are the order of the day, they will hear of them in advance and be in at the start. With a footing in more than one world and fingers, if they please, in every pie, from silk, starch or dye-woods,[1] as the market turns, to deals in Crown lands and the Great Farm itself; so closely interlocked that the ledger of one important figure can contain a substantial assortment of them; propitiating, when expedient, ministers and courtiers with tips as to possibilities in the wind, and sometimes, if rumour told the truth, with more material rewards, this open oligarchy of successful merchants and financiers provides the leaders of the class known in France—though in England, with its fusion of land and commerce, the phrase is infelicitous—as *la haute bourgeoisie*. Its members wield, whatever their nominal professions, a reality of influence extending far beyond them.

The monarchy, on its side, finds their existence a convenience, and, sometimes of set purpose, sometimes inadvertently, plays into their hands. James was not of the princes to whom it came easy to be hand in glove with business men. Merchants, he complained,[2] regard the commonwealth as existing to serve their turn, and do not scruple to feather their nests to the public loss. But, if the King in his personal capacity has little love for traders, he is conscious as a ruler that without them he cannot keep afloat. The Crown has necessities to meet and favours to bestow. It requires an increased revenue and loans to meet emergencies, as well as expert advice on difficult questions—tariffs, currency and credit, the state of trade,

---

[1] See below, pp. 100–5, and *Cal. S.P. Ven. 1621–23*, no. 16, 26 April 1621 and no. 603, 21 September 1622, for alleged bribes to ministers.

[2] *Basilikon Doron*, Bk. II, in *Opera Regia* (1619), pp. 150–1.

commercial diplomacy, the prospects of the textile industries, the merits of free trade and company control—which, in a country so dependent on foreign commerce as England, are matters vitally affecting both the Treasury and public order. Its patronage is extensive. In addition to grants of real property—most of which, though not all, go to courtiers—import and export licences, customs-farms, patents and monopolies, a host of profitable offices, are in its gift. The practitioners best qualified to supply its needs and exploit its concessions are the capitalists at home in the intricacies of the ambiguous *demi-monde* between politics and business. It is they who lease the customs; make or arrange for advances to the Government; mobilise the funds to handle Crown lands in bulk; offer—in spite of Bacon's sneer at traders who 'look ever to their present gain'— indispensable counsel on those technical aspects of public policy where aristocratic statesmen are liable to be at sea; and earn, on occasion, the gratitude of an impecunious minister by hints how to cause his private accounts to show a less cheerless face. An over-dramatised portrait of the influence of a group so formless and heterogeneous would be a caricature. The fact remains that, in so far as the Government is in contact with business, it is these discreet tycoons who stand closest to it.

2. CRANFIELD'S BUSINESS ASSOCIATES

The relations between political authority and the classes whose *métier* was commerce and finance, if a minor aspect of the age, were not an unimportant one. The dealings of Governments with the City, and of the City with Governments, were a particular case of that general problem. It is a question whether the picture of the City Corporation as the centre of a growing opposition to royal policies has not been overdrawn. The composition of its governing organ was not such as to make it a sounding-board of popular discontents. Financial distrust did not necessarily imply political hostility, and the seven years' cessation after 1617 of municipal loans needs no explanation more recondite than the caution natural in a creditor whose previous advances had not been repaid. In reality, during the early years of James, issues of that order hardly yet arise. The opening decade of the reign, when the economic climate smiles, is the period of an informal *entente* between London business and the Crown, an *entente* which is disturbed by recurrent friction such as that occasioned in 1608 by Salisbury's additions to the tariff, and which later, from 1615 onwards, dissolves under the impact of unanticipated shocks, but which, while it lasts, is profitable to one party and a necessity to the other. Cranfield's career as a speculator must be seen against that sanguine background.

A principal part of the equipment for fishing in these sometimes turbid waters consisted, apart from personality, in capital and connections. The profits of his export and import business supplied the former; the latter he acquired partly from the same source, partly by a judicious cultivation of useful acquaintances. It was an age, in which success, like death, came young. Cranfield was thirty-eight when, in 1613, he entered the public service. For most of the ten years or so before that date, to judge by the names appearing in his papers, his standing in the City was not to be despised. A galaxy of past and present Lord Mayors—Sir Thomas Bennett; Sir Thomas Campbell; Sir William Ryder; Sir John Swinnerton, the 'worthy gentleman' of Dekker's ode; Sir William Craven, who was said to have died worth half-a-million, and whose son, an ardent royalist, became in 1643 Baron Craven—did business with him. Sir Thomas Smythe, governor of three companies, treasurer of another two, and member of two more, at whose house are reported to have met, as at an unofficial headquarters, the courts of half those organisations in London; Sir Nicholas Salter, one of the heads of the syndicate which took in 1604 the first farm of the Great Customs, and who later acquired extensive other interests of a similar kind; Sir John Ferne, who was to help to finance the last fatal voyage that brought Raleigh to the scaffold; Baptist Hicks, later Lord Campden, brother to Michael Hicks, the secretary of Robert Cecil; the two Baynings, Paul and Andrew, of whom Paul became, like Hicks, a peer; Duncombe and Viner, names destined to fame or notoriety among those of the Restoration bankers who squeezed Charles II; the ubiquitous cosmopolitans, at home wherever they caught the smell of money, Van Lore and Burlamachi; and, of all the distinguished phantoms alone remembered now, Thomas Mun, economist and East India merchant —such is a small selection from the gallery in his books.[1]

In adding to his previous interests the series of new ventures which began in 1604, Cranfield did not cease to make the cloth trade the backbone of his affairs. It was natural, however, that an aspiring

---

[1] The majority of the names here mentioned occur in *Cranfield MSS.* no. 354 (Cranfield's Ledger), which covers the years 1603-11.

young man should be intrigued by the possibilities of the seductive border region where politics grease the wheels of business and polite society smiles hopefully on both. Apart from the Receivership of Somerset and Dorset, which he bought in April 1605, it was not till August 1612, that his first official work for the Government was done;[1] but his business transactions had brought him before that date into contact with ministers, and he had long had connections in quarters which counted. One of his brothers-in-law, John Suckling, the father of the poet, had been, since 1602, secretary to Dorset, the Lord Treasurer; another, Henry Osborne, and two of Cranfield's friends,[2] were officials in the Exchequer. He employs them, as required, to open awkward doors, and drops, in return, succulent morsels in their way. To one on the watch for profitable *coups*, a key position was the Customs. Sir Henry Billingsley, a former Lord Mayor and Customer of London, who, after sowing his cheerless wild oats by producing the first English translation of Euclid, had played a part in the reorganisation of the Elizabethan customs, was on friendly terms with Cranfield; while three acquaintances, later both allies and opponents, Wolstenholme, Garway—'old Garway the chief of the Customers'—and one Richard Wright, a universal factotum, who, whenever a job under a syndicate is vacant, slips into it like an eel, held posts in the same strategic service. A fourth, who, not merely as a partner in his deals, but as his most intimate friend, left the deepest mark on this phase of his career, was a more spacious, and by common repute a more sinister, figure.

'A scandalous fellow' was the verdict quoted by a genteel correspondent on Arthur—recently made Sir Arthur—Ingram.[3] The gossip of Chamberlain, a garrulous snob, ought, perhaps, to be taken with a grain of salt; but less fastidious gorges rose at Ingram. The testimonial[4] to his virtues, signed by well-known names and posted in

---

[1] Hist. MSS. Comm., *Cranfield Papers*, p. 275, and below pp. 123-4. For his earlier business associations with ministers see *ibid.* pp. 68-9, 86-92, 154-6. In May 1612, as one of a group of contractors for Crown lands, Cranfield assisted Northampton to obtain a piece of land required by the latter for his hospital at Greenwich (*ibid.* pp. 265-6). It was probably this service which caused Northampton to write of him on 12 August 1612 as 'a special friend of mine own' (*ibid.* p. 274).

[2] John West, Secondary of the King's Remembrancer of the Exchequer, and William Pitt of the Exchequer, Surveyor of the Crown's property in Dorset, with whom Cranfield transacted business relating to his Receivership.

[3] N. B. McClure (ed.), *The Letters of John Chamberlain*, vol. i, p. 585 (2 March 1615). Ingram had been knighted 9 July 1613.

[4] *Ibid.* p. 319 (27 November 1611), and Hist. MSS. Comm., *Cranfield Papers*, p. 252. Its signatories, who included 'three or four principal counsellors', asserted that 'they

the Exchange at one of his crises, was a two-edged gift—for why, if he was all that it said, should the tribute be required?—and, some years later, on the news that he had purchased the post of Cofferer of the Household,[1] the whole considerable department, from grave dignitaries to scullions, was alleged to be up in arms, partly at the infringement of the principle of promotion by seniority, but partly at the insult of so disreputable a chief. The truth is that 'Ingram, the undertaker', was not merely, in addition to his official avocation, a company-promoter who knew every trick of his trade and meant to make the most of it; he was also one of the unforgivable characters who infuriate their critics by a shameless exhibition of appetites which the latter are anxious both to gratify and to conceal. As Controller of the Port of London, he had his hand on not a few commercial ropes; was first on the scent of a patent to grab or a concession to exploit; knew the way to aristocratic hearts—within six months of celebrating the wedding of the murderous Frances Howard to James' favourite inanity by the present of a kitchen suite in silver, he had captured two peers and a peeress as godparents to his son[2] —and added, as a consequence, to his experience of the City useful contacts in Whitehall. His affection for 'friend Lionel'—rare gushes of authentic feeling in the financial desert of his letters—gives him at times an almost human air; but, that redeeming spark apart, the impression left by the London chapter of his exploits remains, it must be confessed, that of the gross, predatory animal which unfriendly contemporaries thought him. The final phase of his career was not the least odd. He had bought in 1612, though he did not apparently take up, the secretaryship for life of the Council of the North. Retreating to his native Yorkshire, he acquires a substantial estate; loses heavily, amid malicious cackles from Chamberlain, in that grave of reputations and fortunes, the alum business; founds Bootham Hospital at York; basks, during the second Bishops' War, in the lustre of the purveyor of the best billets in that city—'the inventory of his dishes as long as these country miles'—and, two years later, when a sterner struggle is about to open, entertains the King.[3]

held him for an understanding officer, a good citizen and an honest man'. The occasion of the testimonial was presumably a rumour that Ingram 'is broken for great sums' (McClure, *op. cit.* vol. I, p. 316, 20 November 1611).

[1] *Ibid.* pp. 584–5 (2 March 1615).
[2] *Ibid.* pp. 498 (5 January 1614) and 545 (30 June 1614).
[3] For the secretaryship see *Cal. S.P.D. 1611–18*, p. 125, 16 March 1612; *ibid. 1623–5*, CL, no. 28, 5 August 1623 (suggestion by Middlesex (i.e. Cranfield) to Sec.

'To join together faithfully to raise our fortunes by such casualties as this stirring age shall afford'[1] is the programme with which, in their unregenerate youth, the future Lord Treasurer woos the genial pirate's heart. In company with a group of kindred spirits, they proceed to act upon it.

The part played by the State in the economy of the day is a much-bedevilled topic. Its significance can be exaggerated; but one aspect of the problem deserves, perhaps, more attention than it has commonly received. It was the opportunities for speculation offered by the co-existence of an embarrassed Exchequer with a mass of valuable rights of which Governments could dispose, and an ambitious structure of economic regulation which they lacked the means to enforce. It is that unstable compound which provides the material for most of Cranfield's deals. The formal procedure of the business possessed no novelty. The grant by the Crown of a profitable privilege; its sale or lease whenever, as commonly, the first concessionaire is too exalted to do more than take his rake-off, to a syndicate of business men organised in the mobile and individualistic form of a partnership; its division into shares; brisk dealing in them, and fractions of them, by the small groups in the know; the admission, when all goes well, of additional partners; sometimes a proliferation of secondary enterprises—such, with the omission of the preliminary squaring of influential personages and the incidental intrigues, shifts, and sleights of hand, though not the unvarying, is the standard, pattern. The Crown gets a rent or other payment, though not, unless it deals with the business world direct—and not always then—a competitive one. The parasitic intermediary, when such exists, who secures the grant and sells or sublets it, is a minister, favourite or courtier, whom the Crown thus rewards from pockets

---

Conway that the deputy-secretary, Sir Arthur's brother, having died, the post should be filled by the latter, 'a man very useful to the King and paying £9000 a year in alum rents); and *ibid. 1625-6*, IV, no. 93, 20 July 1625 (complaint by Ingram to Conway that, though he is secretary, his name has, contrary to precedent, been omitted from the Commission of the North). For the alum business, see Hist. MSS. Comm., *Var. Coll.*, vol. VIII *passim*, and numerous entries in *Cal. S.P.D.*, especially for 1623-5. For Ingram's open house in 1639 and later hospitality to the King, see *S.P.D. Chas. I*, CCCCXVII, no. 107, 16 April 1639, and CCCCLXXXII, no. 11, 3 July 1641. Ingram's old age—'a generous, free and grave old knight'—is depicted in *A Relation of a Short Survey of 26 Counties observed in a seven weeks Journey 1634*, ed. L. G. Wickham Legg (1904), p. 20. The travellers were three military men, a Captain, a Lieutenant, who did the writing, and an Ancient.

[1] Hist. MSS. Comm., *Cranfield Papers, 1551-1612*, p. 138 (18 August 1607)

other than its own. The operative organ, which puts up the capital, bears the cost of promotion—including, on occasion, *douceurs* to these potentates and their hangers-on—manages the business, and takes the profits, is the syndicate.

Our information on several of Cranfield's incursions into this fertile field is not too abundant; but they seem to have numbered, in the ten years from 1604 to 1613, approximately a score, exclusive of a crop of subsidiaries, and they may well have considerably exceeded that figure. Yielding, perhaps, to the excitement of a novel game, he appears to have plunged at the outset more heavily than later. In 1604, when he starts it, five deals follow each other in quick succession, and during the four years 1605 to 1608 his speculative irons simultaneously in the fire, exclusive of the great deals in Crown property, which begin in 1607 and reach their height in 1609–10, average approximately eight a year. Naturally, he did not operate alone, but relied, when he could, on a clique of familiars, with the result that the different individuals associated with him as partners are less numerous than, in view of the range of his transactions, might have been expected. Apart from the inevitable handful of gilded supernumeraries,[1] those whose names are recorded number forty to fifty,[2] of whom a third participated only in a single venture. Of the pack of half a dozen or so with whom for choice he hunted, two, Arthur Ingram and Richard Wright, were customs officials, and two, Samuel Hare and Richard Venn, Merchant Adventurers, as was also George Lowe, a less regular partner. William Massam, a member of the Armourers' Company and at this time, next to Ingram, Cranfield's closest crony, may have done a little business as a Merchant Adventurer; but, if he had any regular occupation other than that of a sanguine, pertinacious and

---

[1] E.g. Suffolk (duties on currants); Salisbury (duties and 'improved rates' on silks); Nottingham and Lord Howard of Effingham (patent to license retailers of wines); Northampton (duties on starch).

[2] The actual number was, no doubt, considerably larger, as commonly only the names of the patentees, i.e. the leading partners, to whom the Letters Patent were granted and who were legally liable for the rent due to the Crown, can be traced. When, in 1614, Cranfield made an unsuccessful bid for the Great Farm of the customs, he was one of a group of twenty-four (*Cranfield MSS.* no. 4351). Dietz, *English Public Finance, 1558–1641* (1932), p. 332, states that the syndicate holding it from 1604 to 1621 comprised 'about thirty merchants'. The evidence given by the farmers at Middlesex's trial before the Lords shows that the partnership which took form in 1621 consisted of four patentees and twenty-eight other members (*L.J.* vol. III, p. 351 and *passim*, 7 and 18 May 1624).

unlucky bargain-hunter, it is not apparent that he followed it. His bankruptcy, followed by his despatch by friends fatigued by his laments to make a fresh start, out of reach of his creditors, in the cheerless asylum of the Irish Customs—the then equivalent of the Victorian berth in the colonies—is not, perhaps, surprising.

The most notable figure in the outer ring of Cranfield's business acquaintances and occasional associates was John Wolstenholme, a Merchant Adventurer with interests in the East India, Virginia and Somers Island Companies, a leading figure in the customs service on whose advice the Government relied, and, together with the head of a dynasty of Levant merchants, Sir William Garway, a prince of farming magnates. The smaller fry included William Angell, a fishmonger who, unlike some of his Company, dealt in fish, and who served the Royal Household; William Duncombe, a speculative haberdasher, of whom little is known; and Thomas Dalby, secretary for a time to the Mercers' Company and a Merchant Adventurer—though an interloping one—later seduced by the plausible Cockayne; Richard Croshaw, a goldsmith and money-lender; and Richard Martin, a member of James' first Parliament, later Recorder of London, and legal adviser to several of Cranfield's syndicates. Some of the group were to have, like Venn and Francis Jones, distinguished careers in municipal politics. Others, such as Nicholas Salter, Wolstenholme and Garway, were, to all concerned with the customs, household words. Others again, without climbing high, belonged, like Hare and Dalby, to the category of substantial and experienced merchants whose opinion the Crown, in considering a revision of the tariff, thought it worth while to seek. Of the thirty or so as to whose activities we possess information, five-sixths were business men, or in a few cases, such as Ingram, Wolstenholme, Salter and Wright, customs officials so closely connected with business as to be indistinguishable from them. The great majority either were or had been engaged in foreign trade. We cannot say whether, in their zest for hazards and rewards off the beaten track, they were exceptional or typical of an attitude widely shared. That uncertainty apart, they offer, it is probable, a not unrepresentative sample of the middle and upper layers of City life.

3. MINOR VENTURES

Cranfield's speculations, since he was at pains to spread his risks, were a mixed bag. They ranged from grandiose operations, which touched interests in every corner of the country, and in which considerable sums were at stake, like the Wine Commission and the contracts for the purchase of Crown property, to the casual freaks of a light-hearted gambler with cash to back his fancy. Some were mere raids made with an eye to capital appreciation and quickly wound up; others, sober investments which he continued to hold for a decade or more. On occasion he himself prepares the ground, plans the *coup*, and sees it through; sometimes he comes in later, through the purchase of a share in a concern already launched. In other cases, again, his interest in the initial enterprise is small, and he devotes himself mainly to transactions consequential on it. Classification is arbitrary; but for convenience his ventures may provisionally be divided into two main types. A feature common to both was their origin in a situation created by some departure, whether legislative enactment or executive order, in the sphere of public policy. They differed in the character of the particular objects to which the deals related and in the methods employed to put the latter through. The first and least significant group consisted of random shots at what-ever game chance, aided on occasion by judicious beating, might bring the sportsman's way. The second and more important had as its target the financial prizes offered by contracts to farm some branch of the Crown revenues, in particular, though not exclusively, those derived from duties collected at the ports.

To illustrate the former a few examples must suffice. A Portuguese prize-ship, freighted with spices, expensive fabrics and other oriental wares, is docked in London. A Commission, including, in addition to the invaluable Ingram, Wolstenholme and Wright, the last as registrar, is appointed to auction the cargo. Presents in the right quarter give Cranfield and Massam a finger in the pie to the tune of several thousands. The subsequent sales are spread over two years or more, and an estimate of the former's profits would be a guess; but that he did not do too badly on his share of the calicoes disposed of by him, partly to the well-known firm of cloth exporters mentioned above, Samuel Hare and Co., partly to the King's grocer, Simon Harvey, is suggested by the pious ejaculation, 'Almighty God be praised', which enlivens his ledger. The contents of the *St*

Valentine are hardly off the partners' hands when a second similar windfall drops into their lap. With the aid of 'gratifications' to the Lord High Admiral's two secretaries, they secure a selection of the plums in the hold of a pirate brought to berth at Portsmouth, with results, when the indigo and cochineal are marketed, equally or more rewarding.[1]

Export prohibitions and controls—to turn to a different topic— might reasonably be regarded by some of the parties handling them as twice-blessed. The Crown could make a modest profit by selling licences of exemption; while the privileged licensee had the choice between disposing of his wares in a protected market or—since Government paper floated readily from hand to hand—of reselling the licence to a purchaser willing to pay more than its face value for the right to do the same. Early in 1604 two courtly notabilities, Sir Philip Herbert, better known as Earl of Montgomery and fourth Earl of Pembroke, and a gentleman of the Bedchamber, Sir James Hay, later Viscount Doncaster and Earl of Carlisle, secure an authorisation to export 17,500 cloths, undressed and undyed, in derogation of the Merchant Adventurers' charter and of a similar grant already held by the Earl of Cumberland. They promptly cash their concession by selling it to a certain John Harris, apparently a professional go-between, acting on behalf of a syndicate formed in May 1604, and composed, in addition to himself, of five partners, including Ingram, Wolstenholme and Wright, who between them put ·up the £3000 required. Cranfield does not appear among the original shareholders; but he finances to the extent of one-half Ingram's purchase of a share; buys the remaining half six months later; and, after subsequently selling half to Samuel Hare and Richard Venn, makes, according to Professor Newton, a profit of $28\frac{1}{2}\%$ per annum on the fraction retained. One Julius Hues acquires another licence to ship abroad wares whose export was forbidden. Ingram buys it from him; sends, on the strength of it, ordnance to Amsterdam; and sells a quarter of it to Cranfield. Cranfield despatches another consignment of guns to the same voracious market; sells what remains of the hard-worked paper to an ironmonger, John Bull, who uses it to export hides; and clears,

---

[1] For the Portuguese carrack see Hist. MSS. Comm., *Cranfield Papers, 1551–1612*, pp. 49–62, and Cranfield's ledger (*Cranfield MSS.* no. 354), pp. 70 and 81, and for the pirate cargo, Hist. MSS. Comm., *Cranfield Papers*, pp. 137–9, 158–60, and ledger, 208.

with his customary acknowledgements to Heaven, a profit not to be despised.[1]

Side by side with this minute transaction may be set another not more imposing, but redeemed from insignificance by the comedy of its occasion. 'Fabian Scarecrow', laments Mistress Tenterhook in *Westward Ho!* 'used to frequent me and my husband..."Master Tenterhook", says he, "I must trouble you to lend me 200 pound about a commodity which I am to deal in", and what was that commodity but his knighthood?' Two years after the first performance of Dekker's play, the enterprising Ingram goes one better. Six knighthoods are in the market. The right to confer them is an article of commerce. Ingram buys it at a price which, as such things go, appears not immoderate, and then floats a partnership to take both that venture and another off his hands, with the usual group, Cranfield, Massam and Duncombe subscribing each one-sixth, and Hare and Co. plunging for three-sixths. The accounts of that and the preceding deal are too inextricably entangled in Cranfield's books for the profits of converting grubs into butterflies to be stated with precision. They appear, not surprisingly, to have been unimpressive.[2]

4. THE CUSTOMS-FARMING SYSTEM

Diversions of this type—the exhibition by a playful elephant of his trunk's virtuosity in manipulating pins—are, of course, the exception. The majority of Cranfield's speculations were all seriousness and calculation. On two of them, which were in the nature of special cases—the deals in Crown lands and the farm of the patent to license retailers of wine—something is said below. The remainder, over half the total, were species of one genus. They found their oppor-

---

[1] For the above transactions see Hist. MSS. Comm., *Cranfield Papers*, pp. 116–21, 323 (licence to export cloths); *ibid.* p. 66, and Cranfield's ledger, f. 193 (licence to export prohibited wares).

[2] Hist. MSS. Comm., *Cranfield Papers*, pp. 122–4. The transaction was not so eccentric as might be thought. In unfolding at Cranfield's impeachment the fourth charge against him, the Attorney-General referred to an undertaking alleged to have been given by him to one Sir Thos. Mounson, whose lands he was in treaty to buy, to the effect that, as part of the payment for them, he should procure Mounson the right to make six baronets. The scandal in that case appears to have consisted, not in the bargain made, but in the alleged failure to implement it. The King having already disposed of the baronetcies, Mounson petitioned in lieu of them for the right to enfranchise copyholders on the Crown manor of Wakefield (*L.J.* vol. III, p. 370, 10 May 1624).

tunity in doors opened by the Exchequer in the year which saw the start of Cranfield's operations on the London market. The experiment in the direct administration of the customs had reached its climax in Burghley's closing decade as Treasurer. Its abandonment was an act of policy, not the result of negligence or chance. Long canvassed in official circles, it was one of a series of measures[1] by which, during the first half of the reign, it was sought to give the new regime a hopeful start. Certain duties, such as those on French and Rhenish wines and silks had already, at the turn of the century,[2] been leased; but it was not till early in the second year of James, when further minor grants had seen the light, that the issue of principle was faced. A general reversion to farming, it was urged, was at once a fiscal necessity and the appropriate response to the economic circumstances of the moment. By substituting a certain for a fluctuating revenue, it would enable 'the King to know how much he has'[3] and the Government to plan its course. It would arrest the loss of income 'occasioned by the corruption and negligence of the officers in the latter end of Queen Elizabeth and the practice of sundry merchants with them combining'.[4] With the expansion of trade to be expected as a result of 'this happy and blessed peace', the customs, competently managed, would rank as a gilt-edged investment. What firmer security could be offered for economy and efficiency than the appetite for profits of 'particular persons having ...some particular interest therein, [who] did on their own use and benefit...upon a reasonable...yearly rent thereupon reserved, undertake and attend the whole care and charge thereof by way of farm'.[5] Later, when the contract was through, optimism was increased by the favourable terms on which it had been placed, and which 'the world', as a member of Parliament wrote to Coke, Charles' future Secretary of State, 'takes for an argument that we shall have open traffic with the universe'.[6] Acceptable on public

---

[1] E.g. the increased tariff of 1604; the impositions of 1608; the surveys of Crown estates, with a view to raising rents, set on foot by Salisbury; the abortive Great Contract.

[2] 1599 (wines) and 1601 (silks).

[3] *Cal. S.P. Ven. 1603–7*, no. 295 (17 November 1604).

[4] *Stowe MSS.* 326, f. 89, quoted by W. P. Harper, *Public Borrowing, 1640–1660* (thesis for University of London, May 1927).

[5] *S.P.D. Jas. I*, VIII, no. 134, quoted as view of Buckhurst by Dietz, *op. cit.* pp. 328–9. A. P. Newton, 'The Establishment of the Great Farm of the English Customs' in *Trans. R.H.S.*, 4th series, vol. 1 (1918), remains the best account of the genesis and organisation of the Farm.

[6] Hist. MSS. Comm., *MSS of the Earl Cowper*, vol. I, p. 58 (R. Naunton, M.P. for Helston, to John Coke, 29 October 1606).

grounds to the Government, and on private to London business, the lease, in December 1604, of the Great Farm of the Customs, as well as the crop of minor farms which preceded and followed it, seems at the outset to have been accorded a measure of approval which few of the monarchy's subsequent essays in financial reform were destined to enjoy.

'Thus', wrote a contemporary, 'did Henry VIII with his customs, and since his time the late Queen, and now our Sovereign Master; and it was so then in use in the best governed state, Rome, which let out portions and *decims* to publicans.'[1] Experience caused the expedient which appealed to the pious antiquarianism of Cotton to be viewed with less unqualified favour by vulgar eyes. The reputation of the farmers, if less odious than that of *cette vermine de gens* in France,[2] did not smell too sweet. Plain men were nauseated by the spectacle of an upstart plutocracy—'poor men...by deceipt and fraud become rich',[3] too dishonest to trust and too powerful to punish. Sharp practice in the custom-house—'such deceipt in the farmers that, if you saw it, you would say publicans and sinners'[4] —was a recurrent theme in Parliament. That 'we shall be able to dissolve the patent of the wines, which according to that of the Proverbs hath made the heart of the merchants merry'[5] was the prayer wrung from a ministerial cynic by the alleged enormities of the capitalists concerned. From the denunciation of abuses to the suggestion of remedies was not a long step. 'If those farmers get many thousands a year, as the world knows they do', why, inquired Raleigh, should they not be compelled to declare their gains on oath and become collectors for the State?[6] Expert opinion walked with a sedater mien in the direction suggested by him. In a paper which reached Cranfield in his salad days as an official, Ingram, not a financial purist, but with the technical equipment of gamekeeper

---

[1] 'The manner and means how the Kings of England have from time to time supported and repaired their Estates', in *Cottoni Postuma* (1661), p. 191.

[2] Germain Martin, *L'Histoire du Crédit en France sous le Règne de Louis XIV* (1913), pp. 127–33, gives many examples.

[3] Hist. MSS. Comm., *Buccleugh MSS.*, vol. v, p. 173 (1615). The examples mentioned by the writer include Garway, Salter, Hyde, Wolstenholme, Ingram and others.

[4] Notestein, Relf and Simpson, *Commons' Debates, 1621*, vol. III, pp. 393–6. The speaker was Coke, who also remarked, 'Zacchaeus was a customer, but he was converted ...and he held himself to be a thief'. See also vols. II, p. 287, and IV, p. 228.

[5] Hist. MSS. Comm., *Cranfield Papers, 1551–1612*, p. 299 (8 October 1612). The writer was Northampton.

[6] Oldys and Birch, *The Works of Sir Walter Raleigh*, vol. VIII, pp. 200–1.

and poacher in one, voiced a warning that the only sound policy was to substitute for the farming of the customs direct administration by the Crown.[1] Sir John Harrison, an experienced and apparently an honest man, who, after entering the service as a protégé of Wolstenholme, rose to be one of the famous six dismissed and fined by the Long Parliament, and who lived to be saluted by Pepys, when the deluge had receded, as a 'very fine grave gentleman', more than once, in his long career as a farmer, pressed on the Government the superior advantages of management by a Commission.[2] Whether, as his friend Bishop Goodman asserts, Cranfield himself had earlier reached the same conclusion, we do not know. His memoranda[3] are, however, evidence that, for all his determination to make hay while the sun shone, he retained few illusions as to the merits of the arrangements which provided the crop.

If, in spite of popular growls and official doubts, the policy revived and systematised in 1604, though modified in detail, in essentials stood, one reason at least is not far to seek. In a period of rising costs and sticky or depreciating receipts, it was inevitable that the strains of mounting expenditure, except in so far as met by parting with capital, should increasingly be thrown on the greatest elastic source of income. In England, for example, the revenue derived by the Crown from rents of land fell, on Cranfield's estimate, between the last year of the Queen and 1620-1 by approximately one-quarter, while that from duties collected at the ports appears in the course of the same period to have more than doubled.[4] In such

---

[1] *Cranfield MSS.* no. 4462 (18 November, 1615). Ingram's counsel was 'to resume the King's customs and imposts into his own hands when they fall, and never to grant things of that nature above four or five years at once'. The paper appears to have been prepared, not for Cranfield, but for the guidance of the then Lord Treasurer, Suffolk. It was natural, however, that its author should send his friend a copy.

[2] *Stowe MSS.* 326, ff. 89-89 b, quoted by W. P. Harper, *Public Borrowing, 1640-1660* ch. v, and Robert Ashton, *Government Borrowing under the first two Stuarts* (thesis for University of London, 1953), ch. v.

[3] E.g. Hist. MSS. Comm., *Cranfield Papers*, pp. 293-4 (October 1612): 'If they [the farmers of the Great Customs] had been as careful of his Majesty's profit as of their own, they might have brought into his Majesty's coffers many thousand pounds per annum which they have gained to themselves.' A suspicion of the farmers, and a determination to be stiff with them, as for example in 1621, is one of Cranfield's permanent traits.

[4] *Cranfield MSS.* no. 7887 (1621, see below, App. 3) gives the 'certain rents of the lands of the Crown' (i.e. Receivers General, Duchy of Lancaster and Duchy of Cornwall) as in the last year of Elizabeth £128,257, and in 1621 as £95,403. *Cotton MSS.* Titus B IV, ff. 285 b-293 b (Scott, *op. cit.* vol. III, p. 517) gives the annual average of the customs and impositions 1598-1603 as £127,080, and *Cranfield MSS.* no. 6894 (October 1621) puts the revenue from customs and impositions in 1620-21 at £285,000. At the

circumstances, it is intelligible that not the least urgent of the problems confronting an impecunious ruler should have been to harness the resources accruing from expanding trade to the service of the State. The establishment of a *modus vivendi* with the masters of commercial wealth was one of the conditions of solving it. An arrangement under which governments, in return for capital payments and fixed annual rents, entrusted the collection of substantial blocks of revenue to the self-interest of syndicates of business men cemented the not too easy alliance by a series of partnerships profitable to both. Tax-farming had already a long history behind it, and was destined to remain to the end a characteristic feature of most continental old regimes. It is neither surprising not discreditable to James' advisers that, scanning rocks ahead, they should have determined to have recourse to an improved, but still modest, version of so venerable and ubiquitous a device.[1]

That initial achievement was accompanied by a second. Once firmly on its feet, the organisation fathered by them, in addition to the other virtues claimed for it, revealed an adaptability not at first foreseen. Mr Ashton, in his valuable study of Government indebtedness under James and Charles,[2] has shown that the principal source of short-term loans to which the Crown could turn consisted of the patentees of the Great Farm, without whose advance payments of rent, together with the overdrafts accorded by them, a prodigal regime could hardly have kept afloat. It was, he suggests, these indispensable by-products of farming, rather than the more widely publicised conveniences of a predictable revenue and reduced administrative charges, which made it inevitable that James and his successor should turn a deaf ear to suggested improvements on it. Not only, indeed, the King, but influential elements among his subjects, from the groups in the City immediately concerned to the noble grantees of farms no sooner bestowed than sublet, found in the system attractions which they were reluctant to forego. It is possible

first date the land revenue and the customs and impositions each supplied approximately 42% of the gross ordinary revenue. At the second the former provided about 23%, and the latter slightly more than 60%.

[1] With the exception of the fees collected from licensed retailers of wines (see below, pp. 118–19) the only really important taxes farmed under James appear to have been the import and export duties collected at the ports. Further, it should be noted that the additional duties imposed in 1608 under the name of impositions were not farmed, but collected by Crown officials.

[2] R. Ashton, *op. cit.* chs. v and vi, and 'Revenue Farming under the Early Stuarts' in *Econ. Hist. Rev.*, 2nd series, vol. VIII, no. 3 (April 1956).

that the foreign observer who, in commenting on the exasperation aroused in high places by rumours of Parliamentary interference with the fountain whence these blessings flowed, remarked that 'the great Lords of the Council...have a deep interest in the customs',[1] hit the nail on the head. An institution appealing to interests so diverse and powerful was armed to survive both the strictures of its enemies and the malpractices of its friends. Superseded in the upheaval of the 1640's by a series of Commissions and Committees, it was reintroduced in 1657 by Cromwell's last Parliament, after a debate in which a member for the City commended farming as both acceptable to Big Business and advantageous to the State.[2] It was not till the appearance in 1671 of the new Board of Customs that the creation of Dorset and Cecil was finally wound up.

5. CRANFIELD'S FARMING SPECULATIONS

The process of partial unification which produced in 1604 the establishment of the Great Farm did not end with it. It advanced intermittently throughout the reign through the piecemeal absorption of minor concessions by the Great Farm's patentees, with the result that consolidation, though not formally systematised till 1632, was by the later 1620's virtually complete. An observer of the tendencies at work in James' early years might have expected the currents to run the other way. A characteristic feature of the new regime's sanguine youth was a proliferation of grants, and among them of favours which took the form of remunerative opportunities on the farming front. The reactions evoked by the latter in the business quarters to which such prizes appealed somewhat resembled those to be observed at times today in communities which lease their public utilities, instead of operating them. A series of concessions, some large, some small, but which, if secured on favourable terms, might be highly profitable, and in obtaining which a pull in the right quarter could tilt the scales, was dangled before the public eyes. In the early years of James, a wave of economic optimism born of the peace, reopened markets, a consequent export boom,

---

[1] *Cal. S.P. Ven.*, *1603–7*, no. 435 (20 October 1605).

[2] M. P. Ashley, *Financial and Commercial Policy under the Cromwellian Protectorate* (1934), ch. VI. The author points out that, though an Act was passed in June 1657, appointing a Parliamentary Committee to farm the customs, the farmers drew back from the contract, with the result that the customs 'remained in the hands of the Commissioners till the Restoration'. See also Harper, *Public Borrowing*, especially ch. V.

and a continued, but not abrupt or alarming, rise in prices, was beginning to run high. The spectacle of the Crown offering bargains to investors accelerated its advance.

The procedure employed in marketing and financing farms was not always the same; but its characteristic features during these years of confidence can be simply described. In some cases, especially when the Great Farm is concerned, contracts are advertised by official statements that Commissioners will attend the customs-house on specified days for the purpose of receiving tenders, or by a public notice posted in the Exchange.[1] Lombard Street gossip, however, is swifter of foot than decisions in Whitehall, and, in the first golden shower on a thirsty land—eight grants of farms in just over eighteen months and rumours of more to come[2]—a formal notification of prospective blessings is hardly required. Bargains are in the air. Influential notabilities angle for them. Promoters get wind of them, and organise their syndicates. Competition, which at this period is keen, results in some overbidding to the public advantage; but there is a natural reluctance to spoil a good thing by offering a price which will impair its attractions. The struggle of rival concessionaires is often, therefore, less an affair of the mutual cutting of economic throats, than of claims and counter-claims, followed, once the ritual teeth-gnashing is over, by a compromise

---

[1] *Cal. S.P.D. 1603-10*, no. 134, statement by Lord Treasurer Dorset that the King has resolved to farm all his customs, and has appointed Commissioners to attend the customs-house three times a week to receive contracts. See also Hist. MSS. Comm., *Cranfield Papers*, pp. 101, 291; Notestein, Relf and Simpson, *Commons' Debates, 1621*, vol. v, p. 300; Dietz, *op. cit.* p. 358.

[2] The eight grants in question were (*a*) the silk duties (continued 15 May 1603 to Cecil and leased by him to a syndicate of merchants 30 July 1603); (*b*) sweet wines (August 1603, to Earl of Southampton); (*c*) French and Rhenish wines (continued 18 October 1603, for four years to Sir John Swinnerton); (*d*) sea coals (27 January 1604, to Sir Thos. Bludder); (*e*) currants (7 April 1604, to Earl of Suffolk, sublet by him 27 October 1604 to a syndicate); (*f*) tobacco (29 October 1604, to two nominees of a group of merchants); (*g*) patent to issue licences to sell wines by retail (8 December 1604, to Earl of Nottingham and Lord Howard of Effingham, sublet by them to a syndicate 22 December 1604); (*h*) Great Farm of the customs (leased to a syndicate from 24 December 1604, lease sealed 6 February 1605). The similar grants made between the end of 1604 and May 1608, some of them arising out of those already made, were (*a*) duties on logwood, etc. (9 December 1605, to Earl of Dunbar); (*b*) increased rates of duty on silk (1606, leased by Cecil to a syndicate); (*c*) increased imposition on logwood, etc. (grant to a syndicate, with Ingram as collector 21 September 1607); (*d*) duties on imported and home-produced starch (to Earl of Northampton, 15 March 1608, leased by him to a syndicate, 14 May 1608); (*e*) duties on French and Rhenish wines (grant in reversion to nominees of Earl of Devon, 1606, on expiration of Swinnerton's lease in 1607; lease acquired by a syndicate of merchants, Michaelmas 1607).

beneficial to all concerned, and accompanied at times by arts of the kind employed, in Mr Belloc's unjustly forgotten satire, to float the M'korio Delta Company in the adventurous days when Lord Lambeth was still Mr Barnett.

A tame peer, a Mar, a Dunbar, a Harington, or even, on occasion, one so eminent as Northampton himself, can be mobilised to work the *coulisses*. Ground-bait may be dropped in the form of some unobtrusive service to a Minister or a loan to his daughter.[1] Intruders are bought off with the offer of shares, or bluffed with the threat of reprisals in their special fields, or reminded of irregularities in the last grant secured by them, the exposure of which they would not enjoy. It is always bad policy to leave an enemy in the rear. So an unsuccessful candidate for one farm may be appeased with another; or alternatively, as in 1605 and 1625 in the case of the Great Farm, and in 1613 in that of the lease of the Irish customs, when Ingram and Cranfield were for once antagonists, a fusion of interests may be arranged, which enables consolation prizes to be provided for the disappointed parties in the shape of a place in the partnership. Once the concession has been secured and the necessary formalities completed, the shares and fractions of shares—a one-fifth part of one-quarter plus one-eighth and so on—into which it is divided become a marketable asset. Part of them are retained by the original subscribers, part unloaded on a wider circle of capitalists, who hold or resell as suits them. Naturally, when the thing looks good and the economic weather is propitious, there is a scramble; not a little backstairs work in getting in on the ground-floor; much speculative dealing; all the symptoms in short of the riot of infectious credulity today described as a stock exchange boom. The day was to come when, with economic collapse and sharpened political divisions, the bottom fell out of this exciting, brilliant, vulgar little world. But the atmosphere, while it lasted, was intoxicating.

'The Court...a kind of lottery...the City of London...always a fit receptable for such whose prodigalities and wastes have made them instruments of debaucheries.'[2] In negotiating with Ministers the capitalists involved in the larger undertakings were in the position of professionals bargaining with amateurs. Such a situation, as Cranfield's experience reveals, was not without its dangers. It was

[1] E.g. Hist. MSS. Comm., *Cranfield Papers*, pp. 152–3.
[2] Arthur Wilson, 'The Life and Reign of King James', in *A Complete History of England* (1706), vol. II, pp. 663 and 674.

partly, indeed, a belated realisation of the need for an independent expert, 'who could, and honestly might, discover the cunning craft of the cozening merchant',[1] which, at a moment when two important contracts were about to fall in, prompted his appointment as economic adviser to the Government. It is not the least of the merits of his papers to reveal, behind official policies and the results set out in customs accounts, the interplay of personalities and interests which left its mark on both. The picture which emerges is less that of the mere squalid conspiracy between bureaucratic corruption and capitalist greed denounced by the Puritan severity of Wilson than of a body of social conventions analogous to those which, in some countries, sanction graft and squeeze today, but which require, nevertheless, that in spite of such concessions to human frailty, the public ends of the service in question shall not be too habitually or too grossly ignored. It is of Ministers whose solicitude for the revenue is not expected to preclude a dignified curiosity as to perquisites for themselves, surrounded by concession-hunters versed in that aristocratic weakness and quick to play upon it. Nor must it be assumed that the vices castigated by critics affected all branches of the system to the same extent. Farms differed greatly in financial importance, and varying degrees of scrupulousness and irresponsibility, competence and inefficiency, were shown by the dozen or so different groups which during most of James' reign were concerned with their administration. The most instructive course, therefore, is to glance at a handful of specimens illustrating the manner in which some of the particular concerns in which Cranfield was interested worked.

The keystone of the edifice was, of course, the Great Farm. Financially, it stood in a class by itself. After the revision of the terms forced on the patentees by the revelations of a rival in 1607, the income derived from it amounted to over half the receipts from the customs, and accounted in 1609 for approximately a quarter of the total ordinary revenue, rising by 1620-1 to a slightly higher figure. The role of the potentates controlling the Great Farm was correspondingly important, and, partly as a result of their financial services to the Crown, their relations with the Government were close. On the externals of its history it is needless to dwell. It is

---

[1] 'Aulicus Coquinariae', in *The Secret History of the Court of James I*, ed. Sir Walter Scott (1811), vol. II, p. 253. The probable author of the paper is stated in the Introduction to it to have been William Sanderson, who is thought to have had access to material belonging to Goodman.

sufficient to note the striking rise between February 1605, when the first lease was signed, and December 1624, when the third expired, in the income yielded by it;[1] the continuance in command, in spite of fierce attacks, of the same group of business notabilities for sixteen years on end; and finally, when two of the leading patentees fell on evil days, the accession of equally or more distinguished capitalists to the helm.[2] It happens, however, that, partly owing to the on-slaught made in 1612, with Cranfield's support, on the alleged mis-management of the farm,[3] but, still more, as a result of the evidence given by its official spokesmen twelve years later, on an occasion when Cranfield himself was in the dock, our information on the administration of the Great Farm is less jejune than in the case of most of the humbler members of the family. The second of these episodes, which offers us for once an inside view, belongs, of course, to a later chapter of its history. It is probable, however, that apart from the political issues touched on below, the account of farming methods and problems given in 1624 would in essentials have been valid at an earlier date.

Space does not permit a recapitulation of the story told the Lords; but the tale unfolded in the *Journals* of the House makes livelier reading than some of the more august proceedings recorded in them. The legal formalities involved, from the Letters Patent to the Big Four acting for the partnership and responsible to the Crown for the rent, to the approval by the Treasurer of the security offered by them, pending which the King's Remembrancer cannot issue the warrant to give the grant effect, proved in 1622, for reasons later explained, of more than ordinary importance, but must not now detain us. A second issue, the inevitably recurrent question of the effect on farming prospects of the economic climate obtaining at the moment when a particular concern is launched, was at the date in question acute. It is illustrated by the disastrous repercussions on the concession of the collapse of trade in 1620–1; by the consequent

---

[1] The rent of £112,400 payable from 24 December 1604 was raised by agreement to £120,000 in 1607, from which date to 1611 it stood at that figure. It was £136,226 for the years 1611–14, £140,000 in 1614–21 and was increased to £160,000 in 1621, at which date another farm, previously separate, that of silks, lawns and cambrics, was included in the Great Farm.

[2] Francis Jones and Nicholas Salter, the two original patentees of 1604, and William Garway, the head of a rival group merged with theirs in 1605, were the heads of the Great Farm down to 1621. Their successors were Sir John Wolstenholme, Henry Garway (son of Sir William Garway), Abraham Jacob and Maurice Abbott.

[3] Hist. MSS. Comm., *Cranfield Papers*, pp. 290–6.

decision of Cranfield to induce his old ally, Ingram, to organise a rival syndicate which would bid the rent up, in order to mobilise the competition which, as eighteen months before he had foreseen, the depression of the early 1620's had knocked on the head; and finally, by the sudden revival of business confidence on the news that, in the August of 1623, the long awaited East India Fleet is at last safely home. A third phase of the affair, the division of the farm into shares, and their allotment by the patentees was, of course, common form;[1] but, if ever—which may be doubted—that contentious business went on wheels, on this occasion it did not, nor did general approbation greet the decisions reached. The refusal of the patentees to accept as partners the Treasurer's nominees, for the reason that the abominable Sir Arthur will inevitably be among them; the struggle of some disappointed investors to get in; the determination of some successful ones to get out, on the ground that the future of the farm looks none too bright, and that the disposition of the directing potentates to treat shareholders as ciphers savours too much of a dictatorship for their associates to feel at ease; the delight of the Chancellor of the Exchequer at the terms on which, just at the right moment, his shares have been sold; the angry denial by the patentees that his chief, the Lord Treasurer, in spite of the latter's allegations, holds any shares to sell[2]—all this, with a wealth of confirmatory facts and possibly some fictions, is unrolled before the reader's eyes. The background of political tension against which, in May 1624, the dull details were exposed, was of course, abnormal. But the cross-currents of conflicting business interests, personal loyalties and antipathies, and unpredictable economic changes, amid which the magnates of the Great Farm had to steer, were, it may be suspected, less the exception than the rule. The account given by them of farming problems and procedure is the more convincing because merely incidental to the charge of corruption on which their testimony was sought.

Cranfield owned a share in the Great Farm from its start in December 1604, as one of the syndicate to which the first contract

---

[1] As Dr R. Ashton points out ('Revenue Farming under the Early Stuarts', in *Econ. Hist. Rev.*, 2nd series, vol. VIII, no. 3 (April 1956) p. 320, n. 3) the division of the farm into thirty-two parts did not necessarily involve the existence of thirty-two partners. The practice of sub-dividing parts made it possible for the number of persons holding them to exceed that figure; while, conversely, the engrossing of parts by individuals might cause the number of shareholders to fall below it.

[2] See below, pp. 258–60.

had been let, and four years later, in January 1609, added another
to it.[1] He bought them, not to resell, but as an investment, on which,
in his opinion, he did well, and which he continued to hold till, at
least, the eve of his entry into public life. Compared with that
majestic organisation the lesser farms were minnows to a whale.
Several of them, in particular those concerned with currants and
French and Rhenish wines, were, on their humbler level, important
to the Exchequer; but, apart from their financial disparity, they
differed from the Great Farm in two significant respects. In the
first place, handling as they did the duties on single commodities,
they were exposed to acuter uncertainties on the side both
of demand and of supply, and promised, therefore, less security
than the broader-based, more comprehensive and more stable
institution. In the second place, unlike the latter, whose directorate
invariably consisted of well-known personalities, combining eminence
in business with official experience, the minor farms were granted,
with few exceptions, to noblemen and courtiers whom the King
desired to favour, and were then sublet by them to syndicates of
capitalist under-farmers, in return for a rake-off to the patentees.
For both reasons, it was the opportunities offered by the fluctuating
fortunes of these smaller undertakings which specially appealed to
the speculator with an eye to audacious deals.

The adventures of silk are a case in point. On the death of the
Queen, the duties granted by her in 1602 to two men of straw, in
trust for the Secretary of State, automatically lapse. The City pricks
up its ears and sniffs the wind. Massam, who has the entrée,
hastens to write to Cecil that there is much talk on Change of the
future of the farm; warns him that his agents have a bad name with
business; and urges—by way of frustrating the odious under-
farmers' plan for stepping into their noble patron's shoes—the
appointment of a collector to act instead of them. Cecil coquets

---

[1] Hist. MSS. Comm., *Cranfield Papers*, p. 101, gives some particulars of these two
investments. In December 1604 Cranfield acquired, as a member of the syndicate, a one
forty-eighth share, and states that the net profit received from it for the year 1605 was
£619. 4s. The price paid for the share is not stated. On 14 January 1609 he bought from
Thos. Ivatts, presumably a fellow shareholder, a one sixty-fourth share ('one-half of one
thirty-second part'), including all the profits made on it for the two years preceding
Christmas 1608, as well as those to be made during the three years following that date,
the sum paid to Ivatts being £900. *Ibid.* p. 348, under the heading '1611, July 16.
A Calculation of my estate', gives the profit received from the Great Farm for the two
years ending Christmas 1611 as £400. *Ibid.* p. 310, includes among moneys received
by Cranfield between 15 April and 16 October 1612 'profit of the Great Farm £300'.

with the suggestion, and waits on events, as, in a rising market, he can well afford to do. In the meantime Massam and Ingram organise their syndicate, only to find that a rival group is in the field.

To discourse unto you [groans the former to Cranfield], of Mr Venn his coming to me into the country, of his seeking to undermine me in our suit, of my answers and denials made to him, of his opening our suit in part, as namely that we went about farming the custom of linen and jean fustians and had used the Earl of Mar in our suit, of his former proceeding with others in the same suit and that they had trod in our steps, ... of that and 100 things else passed in conference between us I have not had time to write; it would require a whole day.

Venn was an angry man. Massam and Cranfield, he complained, had let loose against him, to back a suit which was also his, no less a person than a lifelong intimate of the King, the Earl of Mar. They must compromise or fight. If allotted a quarter share in the partnership, he will throw over his present associates and divulge their plans; if not, he will join with Wolstenholme to outbid it. On Massam's advice, Venn is bought off with his quarter share; but Cranfield gets his own back. He does not join the syndicate, but having purchased from Hare and Venn in December 1604, a 'one-sixth part of what they paid Mr Ingram for his one-eighth part', he resells it to them ten months later—'Allmighty God be praised' —at a figure put by him at not far short of three times the initial price. Nor is that all. The *coup* is hardly through when a turn of the wheel makes silk once more a magnet. The tariff of November 1604 had brought a substantial rise in duties. Silk happens—as such things will happen—to be among the articles most affected by it. Hard pressed for cash, Salisbury decides in 1606 not to raise the rent of the existing farmers, but to sell the addition to the duties for a lump sum down of £3200 odd. So a second silk concession comes on to the market, and a second group, with Hare and Co. as the principal partner, and Massam, Duncombe and Cranfield each taking a fifth, is formed to exploit it. Six years later, by 1612, the partners have received their capital back, plus 10% interest, plus a modest profit.[1]

Apart from the initial City gossip and high words behind the scenes, the silk affair was managed with decorous unobtrusiveness. Occasions arose when the assistance, not only of individual Ministers, but of the State, required to be invoked. The starch lobby and dye-woods racket—if terms so profane may be employed—reveal the

[1] Hist. MSS. Comm., *Cranfield Papers*, pp. 57-9, 69-70, 122-3, 125, 347.

arts employed to set the august machine in motion.[1] In a scarcity economy, where foodstuffs were apt to be in short supply, the control of starch-making, which competed for cereals with more urgent demands, had something to be said for it, and would presumably, in similar circumstances, be in force today. Since the industry was predominantly a domestic one, carried on in every farmhouse, regulation was unpopular. Since it would involve the restriction of production to licensed undertakings, it appealed to the few firms specialising in the trade, who, while confident of themselves securing licences, were delighted at the prospective suppression of their humbler rivals. The last patent granted to an individual had been revoked in 1601. On the subsequent establishment of a Starch-makers Company, its charter had been pronounced by the judges to be invalid, unless confirmed by Parliament.

It is on Parliament, therefore, that the manufacturers, together with the financiers who see money in a starch farm, first train their guns. In March 1607 a bill for the regulation of starch-making is introduced, with two acquaintances of Cranfield, Sir Edward Greville, himself an assiduous, though unsuccessful, manufacturer, and the well-known wit, Richard Martin, an intimate friend and adviser of Cranfield, as tellers for the Ayes. The House will have none of it.[2] The course which remains is to work the Executive. Ingram and Cranfield—'no loss but certain gain without hazard'— press for a dose of that sovereign cordial, the appointment of a Control Commission. The Council, one of whose leading members, the Earl of Northampton, was to do well out of the business,[3] gives them all, and more than all, they ask. It prohibits the use of wheat in the manufacture of starch; restricts the production of the latter to authorised places; imposes duties both on the imported article and on starch produced at home, which are duly granted to Northampton, and makes Ingram, who has done most to engineer the affair, the officer to collect them. Finally, it appoints, not one Commission, but three, to execute the programme, with Cranfield and his associates in

[1] Hist. MSS. Comm., *Cranfield Papers*, pp. 154–8 and *Var. Coll.* vol. VIII (*Temple Newsam MSS.*); W. Hyde Price, *The English Patents of Monopoly* (1906), pp. 15–16, 37–8. [2] *C.J.* vol. I, 24 May 1607.

[3] *Cal. S.P.D. 1603–10*, p. 412 (14 March 1607), demise by King to Northampton of duty of 10s. per cwt. on imported starch and 5s. per cwt. on starch made in England, on condition of payment of one-fourth of revenue received; *ibid.* XXXII, no. 48 (14 May 1607), letter from Northampton to Salisbury stating that he has let the imposition on starch granted him by the King to Ingram, Dalby and others.

force on two of them. As the same group farm Northampton's grant, they come out on velvet. The second string to Cranfield's bow—his financial transactions with the wretched Greville,[1] who snatched at starch-making as a life buoy, only to find it sink under him like a stone—belongs to the less edifying side of his activities as a banker. It may properly be relegated to that forbidding context.

Of the international aspects of the dye-woods speculation something has been said above; but the London end of the business is not without instruction. Its promoters discreetly by-passed the House of Commons, but it conformed, in other respects, to the standard pattern. The import of foreign woods had been prohibited on technical grounds—they did not yield fast dyes—with the exception of small quantities brought in under licence, the farm of the duties on which had been granted to a courtly nonentity then Master of the Household, the Earl of Dunbar. A sudden rise in the demand for them, caused by the invention of a process for fixing the dyes, made the possibility of cornering supplies and securing the farm of the duties attractive to financiers. The first step is to organise a ring; and here the energumen in chief is Cranfield's fellow-mercer, Thomas Dalby.

At present [writes the former to Ingram], there is not 150 tons of all four sorts [*sc.* dye-woods] in London. Mr Dalby and myself have already bought half, and will buy the rest before Saturday. If for yourself, Mr Massam, Mr Dalby and myself, in equal fourths, you could farm the imposition of these woods at £2000 *per annum*, or, rather than fail, at £2500, it would prove the best match that ever you made. There is but one maim in the business. The old patentees have 300 to 400 tons of logwood, which will serve the kingdom for a year. We will take it off their hands at a reasonable price, which must be done before they know our pretensions. Assure my Lord Salisbury there shall be no monopoly that shall cause a general clamour, and it shall be no more scandal to the undertakers than the imposts on wines or currants, nor so much.

It might easily not have been 'so much'. As appeared a few years later, when Cranfield himself was holding up shocked hands, the wine farm[2] stank, and currants, thanks to Mr Bate, are in all the

---

[1] See below, pp. 17.

[2] I.e. the farm of French and Rhenish wines, held by Sir John Swinnerton in the later years of Elizabeth. Shortly before the expiry of the lease, the Earl of Devonshire obtained it for seven years, in the name of two nominees, and at once conveyed it to a syndicate headed by William Garway and Salter, who succeeded to it in spite of an offer of increased rent by Swinnerton. In 1613 there was a renewed struggle between the latter and the syndicate: for the details see Hist. MSS. Comm., *Cranfield Papers.*

books today. But Cranfield knew, or thought ke knew, his man: 'in my opinion the project will be very pleasing to that great lord, and the service you do him in it most acceptable'. The second essential, as his words suggest, was to square the Government. Ingram's past services to Cecil in connection with silk marked him out for that congenial task. The result showed that Cranfield's confidence in ministerial pliability, which at first sight seems exaggerated, was not misplaced. A new scale of duties is issued. Ingram, once again, is appointed to the collectorship, an office which he resigns—in return, of course, for suitable compensation—a few months later. Six of the seven patentees who, in July 1608, undertake the farm, are persons associated with Cranfield in his other speculations. He himself, though it is not quite clear that he became a farmer, has a series of subsidiary deals in the purchase and sale of dye-woods on his hands for the next three years. It is not, it seems, till 1614 that his interests in the article are finally wound up.[1]

Cranfield's association with currants and tobacco was unenlivened by similar strokes of diplomatic guile. Half his investment in the farm of the latter was sold within a month, the remainder being held for another fourteen years, while he continued to feel a sufficient interest in the former, his first farming venture, to join a syndicate headed by Swinnerton, which, on the death of Salisbury in 1612, made an abortive bid for the farm.[2] The rapidity with which, in some cases, shares changed hands arouses curiosity as to the extent of the market which dealt in them and the dimensions of the class to which investment and speculation in farms appealed. Analogous transactions in the shares of commercial companies and public loans seems to have been a well-established practice in the Low Countries. The *rentes* of the Paris Hotel de Ville were a favourite investment of the French *bourgeoisie*. In the prosperous little principality of Liège, as a recent historian of its economic life has told us, State *rentes* were half a century earlier widely held. 'Tax-farming,' he writes, 'which triumphed in the last two decades of the sixteenth

pp. 299–309. For Cranfield's views on the sharp practice of the farmers, see *ibid.* pp. 301–2, 305–6.

[1] *Ibid.* pp. 146–50.

[2] For the farm of currants see *ibid.* pp. 68–9 and for the tobacco farm, *ibid.* pp. 130–1, 310. Cranfield bought a one-eighth share in the former on 23 November 1604 for £179. 15s. and a one-tenth share in the latter on 24 December 1606 for £200. In October 1621 he gives £500 as the value of his then interest in the tobacco farm (*Cranfield MSS.* no. 6844).

century, provided opportunities for speculation on a scale previously unknown;...financial capitalism entered on a new era.'[1] Is there reason to think that the ripples set in motion by the English customs-farms spread equally far?

The remoter ramifications of such operations as those of Cranfield and his associates are difficult to trace. If his papers contain any convincing evidence of a wide distribution of shares in farms among the general public, it has not come the present writer's way. Individual cases[2] occur in which a provincial notability invests in the farm of a local industry, or is moved to risk his savings in a speculation launched in London; but the march of progress, which was to produce in due course an institution to assist him, had not yet done its perfect work. A stock-market was in its infancy, and transactions by outsiders were, as far as our present knowledge goes, a rare exception. The impression left by Cranfield's papers is that, while it was common in business circles for an individual to deal in the shares, as he did himself, of half-a-dozen or more concerns, the layman hardly came into the picture. Such a statement, however, tells less than half the story. Financial contacts between the public and the City, and, through the City, with the needs of an impecunious Government, could be established in more ways than one. If the link which consisted in the purchase by an investor of a share in a farm was, outside the world of business, too infrequent to count, that forged by the initiative of the farmers themselves in borrowing from the public was of increasing importance.

Its significance became apparent a generation later, towards the close of Cranfield's life. In the *cause célèbre* of 1641, with the brood of reports, memoranda and petitions engendered by it, much dirty linen was washed, and some surprising facts emerged. The practice of the financiers arraigned by Parliament had been, it appeared, when called on by the Crown for loans, not merely to rely on their

---

[1] Jean Lejeune, *La Formation du Capitalisme moderne dans la Principauté de Liège au XVIᵉ siècle*, 1939, pp. 95–103, 123–4. For the Netherlands, see Violet Barbour, *Capitalism in Amsterdam in the Seventeenth Century*, 1950, ch. IV, and for the French *rentes*, Germain Martin, *L'Histoire du Crédit en France sous le Règne de Louis XIV* (1913) especially pp. 21–5.

[2] E.g. a bequest to parties named by the ninth son of the Earl of Northumberland (Baron Percy of Alnwick) in 1643 of '£1000 in the hands of the Coal Farmers' (will in Hist. MSS. Comm., Exhibition of documents in private archives, 1951); sale by Cranfield and other farmers of Irish Customs of one-tenth share of £300 to James Craig of Castle Craig, Ireland (*Cranfield MSS.* no. 4251, 6 December 1613). In each case the local connection is obvious.

own resources but to borrow a substantial part of the funds to be advanced. The sums due from them to their creditors, who included well-known country gentlemen, as well as business men and the relics of both, had been raised, it is suggested by Mr Harper in his valuable study of the episode,[1] partly in the form of loans secured on the incoming customs, partly by deposits accepted from merchants to cover future liabilities for the payment of duties, partly by the sale of assignments on the customs revenue in the shape of tallies which circulated in the open market. But—and this for our present purpose is the significant point—the procedure revealed by the explosion of the 1640's was by no means a novelty. On the contrary, it was the continuance, if with enlarged dimensions, of methods long familiar. It was naturally in the case of the syndicate administering the Great Farm of the customs that the practice developed earliest and on the most imposing scale. It was the normal procedure, as Dr Ashton[2] tells us, for a substantial part of the resources used to finance its larger transactions with the Crown to consist of funds raised by it in the City, the farmers making their profit on the difference between the rates at which they borrowed and re-lent. Confronted with overdrafts in thirteen out of the twenty-two years of James' reign, as well as with sudden demands for loans, like the £120,000 supplied in 1607, where else, indeed, can it turn except to savings stagnating or fructifying in the pockets of the public? That, by the admission of both parties to the sharp little controversy which arose in 1612 as to the renewal of the farm, is what, in fact, it does. That they have mobilised torpid wealth by 'taking up upon their credits, almost every year, twenty or thirty thousand pounds for His Majesty's service' is not the least of the achievements claimed by the indignant farmers. That, with large sums of public money in their hands, they ought to have been ashamed to do anything of the kind, is the reply made to their pretensions by the most formidable of their critics.[3]

Cranfield's retort was uttered at a moment when the first intensive phase of his career as a speculator was drawing to its close. He had been fortunate in his season. The era of unrestricted opportunity, in which he floated upwards, was not destined to last. In the middle and later years of James, and still more under his successor, farms

---

[1] Harper, *Public Borrowing*, ch. v.
[2] R. Ashton, *Government Borrowing*, chs. v and vi.
[3] Hist. MSS. Comm., *Cranfield Papers*, pp. 292, 295 (October 1612).

were increasingly grouped and let in blocks, or leased as in 1632 to the syndicate already holding the greatest of them. The lay element in their management diminished; the professional increased. Such developments may well have meant a more effective service. Their result, however, was to reduce the number of prizes offered for competition, and thus to circumscribe the field of manœuvre over which the enterprising privateer could deploy his arts at will. In the glad confident morning when Cranfield girt his loins to enter the lists, neither of these inhibiting contributions to administrative efficiency, which later he himself did something to promote, was yet in sight. It was the moment when the abstruse science of company-promoting—

> We'll take in citizens, commoners and aldermen
> To bear the charge, and blow them off again,
> Like so many dead flies, when it is carried.

was about to be expounded by the ingenious Meercraft.[1] A glittering handful of concessions is flung, with gay profusion, on a hungry market. Business is buoyant; salutes the announcement of the most imposing of them as one more proof that the bleak years of the depression have at last run their course; and demonstrates its enthusiasm by organising three competing syndicates to intrigue and scramble for it. Cranfield, a sanguine opportunist, is not backward in the race. To trace in detail his successive operations would be tedious. It is sufficient to say that, apart from his other speculations, he acquired between November 1604, when he began the game with currants, and the autumn of 1608, shares in eight farms; that, in 1609, he increased his investment in the Great Farm by the purchase of a one sixty-fourth share in addition to the one forty-eighth share bought in 1604; and that, in the next four years he picked up three collectorships, as well as shares in two further farms.[2]

---

[1] Ben Jonson, *The Devil is an Ass* (1616), Act II, i.

[2] The eight farms were: 1604, currants, silk, the Great Farm; 1605, farm of wine licences; 1606, improved rates on silk, tobacco; 1607, dye-woods; 1608, starch. It is not clear that Cranfield was a farmer of the logwood duties, but he was concerned with the establishment of the farm and was engaged in speculations made possible by it. He sold his share in the silk farm, which was bought 22 December 1604, on 28 October 1605, while retaining till 1612 or longer his interest in the farm of the increase of the duties on silk. The collectorships were those of the imposition on velvets, silks, etc. (Hist. MSS. Comm., *Cranfield Papers*, pp. 269–70, 16 July 1612), that on sweet wines (*Cranfield MSS.*, nos. 4228–9), and the additional 3*d*. imposed in 1613 on goods exported

It is not possible to state the market-value of Cranfield's holdings in these ventures. We know the sums originally invested, but not, in most cases, the price at which at different dates the shares acquired were sold; nor can it be assumed that those not mentioned as disposed of were, in fact, retained. It is clear, however, that from the latter part of 1604 this branch of his activities greatly increased, and that, unlike his export business, it survived, if with a tempered exuberance, his entry on official life. Some notes on his financial position in October 1620, when he had been for rather more than seven years a servant of the Crown, put the value of his interests in various farms as in the region of £16,000;[1] and just over a year later, when he sat, as Lord Treasurer, in the seats of the mighty, a last belated deal showed that the hand which had manipulated silk and tobacco had not lost its cunning. But the controversy occasioned by the terms on which, in January 1622, he acquired the sugar duties—£2000 rent for a lease promptly sublet for £6000 and later sold for £12,000—is not here in place. It belongs rather to his ministerial, than to his business, career.[2]

6. THE DEALS IN CROWN LANDS

Cranfield's first contact with the properties later to be described as 'the public patrimony' was unexciting. It arose from his purchase in April 1605 of the Receivership of Crown revenues in Somerset and Dorset. To judge by his accounts, the profits of the office, which he retained for eight years, were inconsiderable; but it had its compensations. Apart from the addition to his working capital made, pending their transfer to the Exchequer, by the sums collected, it had a further advantage. It gave him an insight into the technicalities of an intricate and important part of the financial system which was to prove of value when he flew at higher game.

The opportunity to use his experience was not slow to arrive. In the year when he became Receiver, the second phase of the royal

---

or imported by foreign merchants (Dietz, *op. cit.* pp. 372–3, 377). He had also acquired by July 1611 a share in the impost on sweet wines (Hist. MSS. Comm., *Cranfield Papers*, p. 347). For the Irish Customs, see *ibid.* p. 257, *Cranfield MSS.*, nos. 4133, 4184, 4794, 6143, 6335, and Dietz, *op. cit.* pp. 434–5.

[1] *Cranfield MSS.* no. 6844.

[2] For the sugar farm see below p. 251, n. 2, and Dietz, *English Public Finance*, pp. 357–8.

landslide begun under the Queen was already in the offing. It opened on a low note. The estates in question included a miscellaneous mass of small and scattered properties, at once expensive to manage and not too remunerative. The Exchequer, under Dorset, decided to get rid of them; and, from 1605 onwards, it was at work capitalising rectories, parsonages, tithes, free chapels and chantries —the débris of the Reformation—by offering them for sale.[1] Salisbury, Dorset's successor, was no friend to a plan which met present liabilities by the sacrifice of future income; but the financial situation forced his hand. At Michaelmas 1606 the debt was 30%, and in May 1608, when his reign at the Treasury opened, over 40%, above the figure commonly given for that left by the Queen.[2] With interest at 10%, a Finance Minister could hardly let so grave a problem slide. On James' accession, an indenture approved by Parliament had scheduled the royal properties and annexed them inalienably to the Crown. A new instrument of May 1608 removed large blocks of land from the list, though adding to it some others, and, as far as the former were concerned, untied the Lord Treasurer's hands by entrusting the disposal of them to him and the Chancellor of the Exchequer.[3] A few months later action on it began.

The plan adopted was a frontal attack, with large reserves thrown in. The traditional expedient of sales by special Commissions was continued, and brought in, between 1605 and 1614, just over £180,000; but a procedure more audacious and less dilatory was held to be essential. The mobilisation of the financial resources of the City appeared to provide it. Instead of dealing piecemeal with a multitude of individual purchasers, not a few of whom would require time to pay, the Government sold wholesale and, whenever possible, for cash down. It disposed of a further batch of rectories, tithes and chantries, some four hundred mills, with the lands attached to them, and hundreds of manors in every corner of the country, to a value not far short of half-a-million, to syndicates of London capitalists, few in number, but containing the men who counted. These 'Contractors', as they were called, kept such plums as pleased them, and unloaded the remainder on a market consisting partly of business magnates like themselves, partly of middlemen on the alert to squeeze in, partly of country gentlemen, well-to-do trades-

---

[1] Hist. MSS. Comm., *Cranfield Papers*, p. 210.
[2] For the debt at the dates mentioned see Dietz, *op. cit.* p. 121, and above p. 142.
[3] Hist. MSS. Comm., *Cranfield Papers*, p. 181, and Dietz, *op. cit.* p. 106.

men and, here and there, as the properties disintegrated, handfuls of obscure villagers.

The chance for the speculator was alluring. Cranfield, with whom alone we are concerned, followed the fashion in company with familiar names. Not only his usual associates, Ingram, John and Daniel Cooper, Hare and Venn, Richard Croshaw and others, but such occasional allies as Sir William Ryder, Sir John Bennett, James Cullimore, William and Robert Angell and Martin Freeman took a hand with him in his venture. A list compiled by him in November 1609 of eligible properties in some fourteen counties[1] suggests that he took the business seriously. His financial interest in it, though not comparable with that of an Eldred, a Hicks, or an Ingram, was not a trifle. He was one of six partners who subscribed £32,000 in 1607 for the purchase of rectories and chantries; acquired, as the creditor of a partner, a share in a second group handling similar properties; and was leader of one of the eight syndicates which together put through, in June 1609, a deal to the value of £67,000, making himself responsible for £2300 out of the £11,000 put up by the group headed by him. The Government, though by parting with capital it had reduced its debt to the lowest point since James' accession, was still out of its depth, and appealed in December 1609 to the capitalists with whom it was in treaty to keep it afloat. Three of the leading Contractors flew to the rescue. Cranfield's contribution to the loan of £30,000 advanced by them was just under £1000.

These repeated conversions of land into cash involved a drain on liquid resources. Not a few of the transactions were financed with borrowed money. Cranfield, like other speculators, had to take that course. He secured £600 odd on loan from the Chamber of London —the City Treasury—and something over £1100 from individuals of standing in the City, including the celebrated Thomas Mun, who lent, like a gentleman, at 1% below the legal rate, an ex-Lady Mayoress, who did the same, and a former Lord Mayor, who insisted on the maximum of 10%;[2] but the strain was severe. It was

---

[1] *Cranfield MSS.* no. 3673. The properties consisted of twenty-two manors in twelve counties, plus lands only in one of them, and of lands, tenements and messuages in two others.

[2] *Cranfield MSS.* no. 3700 contains the entry, 'to the Chamberlain of London [bound] in £800 for the payment of £624 upon the 22 day of June, 1610', and refers to a counter-bond given by two leading contractors, Eldred and Whitmore. Payment of that amount into the Chamber of London is referred to in *MSS.* no. 3740, and appears

possibly as a result of it that, in February 1611, he wound up his connection with the partnership led by him. He sold to it his share, roughly one-quarter, in the lands not yet disposed of by it, receiving in part-payment a manor in Yorkshire, and retaining such properties as had already been allotted to him.[1] Complaints of the exorbitant profits made by the Contractors were voiced in the Parliament of 1614; but the financial results of their operations as a whole are an intricate problem, and a verdict on them, if possible at all, must be expressed with reserve. Cranfield himself, to judge by the evidence of those of his transactions on which we have light, did not fare too badly. An account presented when the work of the principal syndicate in which he was interested was almost completed put at £6600 its receipts from sales of land bought by it for £5471, and at £4435 its prospective receipts from sales of land bought for £4013 and not yet fully paid for by those to whom it sold them, a net return of £11,035 for a total outlay of £9484. His own estimate of the dividend on his quarter share was just over 16%.[2]

The fate of the lands in half-a-dozen different counties, the disposal of which he handled himself, is less easily summarised. It is a story partly of substantial sales, partly of properties divided and re-divided into morsels digestible by land-hungry, but impecunious, peasants and craftsmen. The Yorkshire lands are quickly bid for, at a price which, Cranfield calculates, will yield him a profit of 21%. Most of the manor of Wellington in Somerset goes on less attractive, but not unsatisfactory, terms to Lord Chief Justice Popham, who already held part of it on lease from the Crown, and to half-a-dozen smaller buyers. The lands in the Isle of Wight drift away in little lots, largely acquired, it is probable, by the sitting tenants. Those of the defunct monastery of Dunkeswell in Devonshire go much the

in his ledger under 17 June (£300) and 25 June (£324). The ledger (f. 212) also has entries of £209. 10s. borrowed at 9% from Thomas Mun of London, merchant, £418 from Lady Slanye at the same rate, and £528. 3s. 4d. from Sir John Spencer, Kt. and Alderman, at 10% on 24 June.

[1] *Ibid.* no. 3678 (8 September 1610), a note by Cranfield on an account by William Angell of the same date relating to the sale of Crown lands, contains the first reference to his intention to wind up his connection with the syndicate. His action on it is recorded in *ibid.* no. 3677 (6 February 1611), memorandum of sale by Cranfield to William and Robert Angell (who did the business of the syndicate) of his quarter of all such lands as are still unsold by it, taking in part-payment certain lands specified in the memorandum. It should be noted that Cranfield continued to hold other properties bought by him from the Crown independently of the syndicate, and that these were sold by him piecemeal over the next ten years.

[2] *Ibid.* no. 3675 (endorsed '1611' in later hand).

same way. Originally bought from the Crown on 29 March 1610 by two leading contractors, Eldred and Whitmore; sold by them on 30 March to another Londoner, one Paddon, an official in the Exchequer; resold the same day, with the exception of some 170 acres, by Paddon to Cranfield, they hang on the latter's hands, a slowly wasting asset, for the best part of eight years, while a shoal of voracious minnows—a handful of yeomen, a potter at Dunkeswell, a weaver at Hemyok, a linen-draper at Honiton, another shopkeeper at Tiverton—nibble them piecemeal away. We may leave him disposing, in 1618, of the remnants of the carcase of St Mary's Abbey to a tallow-chandler in London.[1]

7. 'PUTTING OUT MONEY FOR GAIN'

By the time when Cranfield threw the sanguine Mr Downer these thrice-gnawed bones to pick, his epic age of speculation lay behind him. On the purposes to which he applied the profits yielded by it, we have only inference to guide us; but there was another of his many activities which also expanded during this phase of his career, and whose growth, it is probable, they helped to foster. The part played by credit in the economy of the day is now an old story. It is clear that individuals in every walk of life—peasants and craftsmen, shopkeepers and merchants, substantial landowners, mining and manufacturing entrepreneurs, not to mention political dignitaries—found the purveyor of accommodation a necessary servant, and, on occasion, a remorseless master. Thanks to Professor Judges, Dr Richards[2] and their successors, we can observe emerging from a

---

[1] *Ibid.* no. 3728 gives the cost of the three-quarters of the manor of Tibthorpe (Yorks) purchased by Cranfield, of the farm of Bottleburne, and of the remaining quarter of the manor on which he held an option, as £852 odd, and the price offered him for them as £1034. His ledger shows that between 30 June 1610 and 21 February 1611 he sold to Popham land to the value of £1066 odd, and smaller parcels to a number of other buyers. The essential facts as to Dunkeswell are given in *ibid.* nos. 6007 (30 March 1610, indenture of sale by Paddon to Cranfield), 4113 (9 February 1613, list of thirty-seven tenants and rents totalling about £234), 4417 (11 February 1613, commission from Cranfield to a local personage, one Palfrey, to sell the land to such of the sitting tenants as will give for it not less than 6½ years' purchase, and, failing them, to other buyers), 4493, 4994, 4987, 4747 (sales to local people, as above), 4898 (29 June 1618, sale of remains of land, apparently about 80 acres, plus tithes, etc., to John Downer for £35, plus an annual payment of £7 odd).

[2] A. V. Judges, 'Money, Finance and Banking from the Renaissance to the Eighteenth Century', in *European Civilisation*, ed. E. Eyre, vol. v, pp. 401–99; R. D. Richards, *The Early History of Banking in England* (1929).

chaos of unsystematised chaffering small groups of specialists, each with its own distinctive technique for meeting the requirements and exploiting the necessities of different categories of clients. 'I have been a doer in this world these thirty winters', remarks the merchant in Wilson's *Dialogue*, 'and yet never found I better or more assured gain than by putting out my money for gain,...the easiest and best trade that could be in the world.'[1] Cranfield soared to heights beyond the vision of the pedestrian Gromelgayner; but he acted on the latter's maxim. Remembered by posterity as a merchant-prince turned statesman, to not a few of his contemporaries he was primarily a money-lender.

Judged by the customers with whom he dealt, his transactions were of two main kinds. Neither was novel, but both appear to have been lucrative, and one offered advantages not merely economic. The practice of entrusting to a successful business man, of a standing to command confidence, cash to be repaid on demand and, in the meantime, re-lent, has, as Professor Unwin long ago showed,[2] a lengthy history behind it. The question of interest is not that of the origins of so obvious a procedure, but of its relative importance at different periods. Limits to its extension continued to be set in Cranfield's day both by the reluctance of the timorous possessor of a surplus to 'put his money into unknown hands' and by the absence, when he plucked up his courage, of signposts to direct his faltering steps. Neither condition, when the seventeenth century closed, was wholly a thing of the past; both, when it opened, were in retreat. Hoarding did not abdicate; but, for two generations before the Civil War, its empire was thought by shrewd heads to be contracting. At least by the later years of Elizabeth, not only the professionals, such as brokers, scriveners and notaries, whose exploits are in all the books, but a growing body of enterprising tradesmen, were providing an alternative which the prudent *rentier*, whether capitalist or landowner, increasingly preferred to the strong-box and plate cupboard. The multiplication of practitioners who, while retaining their traditional designations, abandoned trade for finance or combined the two, was a natural result. Viscount Campden, the silk-mercer, who owed his peerage to his fortune, and no small part of his fortune to his proficiency in borrowing at

---

[1] Thomas Wilson, *A Discourse upon Usury* (1572), ed. R. H. Tawney (1925), p. 249.
[2] 'London Tradesmen and their Creditors', in *Finance and Trade under Edward III*, ed. George Unwin (1918).

one rate and lending at another, was merely the most eminent of a small galaxy of shopkeepers, who had achieved a less spectacular success by their exercise of the art.

Cranfield's incursion into this fashionable field began, in the orthodox manner, as an adjunct to his other interests. Not all the operations resulting from it are easy to unravel; but, at any rate from 1605, they are sufficiently systematic and continuous to justify Professor Newton's description of him as 'ready to accept loans... comparable with the deposits of modern banks and to pay out the money as directed'.[1] The clients with whom this branch of his business is done include friends and relations, like Thomas Coryat, Richard Martin of the Temple, Cranfield's cousin, Sir Edward Randall, and his tedious father-in-law, Richard Sheppard; business associates of the type of Ingram, Massam, Hare and Venn; and finally individuals with whom he had few, if any, personal connections, ranging from magnates of the City, such as Sir Francis Jones, a leading figure in the Great Farm, Sir John Swinnerton, another farmer, Sir Thomas Bennett, Sir William Craven and Sir William Courteen, to a miscellaneous collection of tradesmen, a sprinkling of country gentlemen, and now and then a yeoman. He receives deposits from them; honours orders to pay—in effect, though the form was not standardised, cheques—in favour of the drawer or of a third party; makes advances; discounts bills; changes money; and takes charge of valuables or consigns them to the keeping of a trusted goldsmith. These unspectacular operations, the bulk of which greased, in effect, the wheels of domestic enterprise with surpluses accruing from foreign trade and successful speculations at home, were the backbone of his financial business. Their continuity and scale are of some interest to the historian of banking; and to allow them to be overshadowed by the pathological episodes in Cranfield's money-lending career is to falsify perspectives. It must be confessed, however, that the transactions, which, because of the length, and sometimes the heat, of the correspondence engendered by them, are apt to arrest the reader's eye, are of a less constructive, though possibly a more profitable, type.

Convincing evidence of the relative movements of commercial and landed incomes is still to seek. There is something, however, to be said for the view that, while the tendency of both was upwards, the former were the more elastic, and reaped the gains of a rising

---

[1] Hist. MSS. Comm., *Cranfield Papers*, pp. 67–8.

price level more quickly than the latter. Of the efforts of some land-owners to neutralise the time-lag by curtailing domestic expenditure, rationalising estate-management, developing neglected assets such as minerals and timber, and securing subsidies, in the shape of patents, offices and other profitable privileges from the Crown, this is not the place to speak. Some—perhaps most—of them succeeded; but not all the unfortunates possessed the qualities, or the means, or the influence, required to employ such expedients with effect. The City, which thrives on the economic conditions, and some-times the personal habits, that bring the victims low, has its own methods of ascertaining how long they can last, and watches with interested curiosity their gambols and capers. Sooner or later they trot off to be shorn. Their first experience of the operation is rarely their last.

'The ways to enrich', remarks Bacon, 'be many, and most of them foul.'[1] It cannot be said that all Cranfield's transactions were in that respect beyond reproach. It is possible that some of those to which Bacon's stricture seems at first sight to apply were in reality advances to facilitate reproductive expenditure, which would yield in due season a return; but, apart from the already-mentioned loans to his friends and fellow business men, the purpose, when it can be determined, of most of the remainder appears to have been different. It was the relief of the necessities of borrowers confronted by an emergency and often already on or near the rocks. A principal part of the science required in such matters has been described as the discretion to discern when to soap and when to bully. If so, Cranfield's proficiency in the second was among his less engaging traits. Some of his loans are of trifling sums; others of large; others, again, begin on a low note, but, with renewals and 10% interest, swell portentously. With some of his clients he plays touch and go; others, like Sir Richard Preston, later Lord Dingwall and Earl of Desmond, he keeps in tow for the best part of twenty years. The security for some of his advances is note of hand: for others plate and jewels; for others a patent or an insurance policy taken out on the borrower's life, the premium being duly entered in the prudent creditor's account; but the basis of most of his larger transactions with this class of customer is land.

The procedure, with minor variations, is throughout much the same—loans; more loans; mortgages; foreclosure or sale to Cran-

[1] Bacon, *Essays*, 'Of Riches'.

field, followed either by resale, or, if he decides to hold the property acquired, by an inquiry into methods of making the most of it. Sir Edward Greville, one of his partners in the starch farm, hopes to reduce his debts by producing that article behind the new tariff; he succeeds only in increasing them. Cranfield, who has financed him to the tune of just under £1300, takes a mortgage on a property bought by Greville from the Contractors for Crown Lands, which, in default of early repayment, is to vest in his creditor. The debtor's liabilities, so far from diminishing, continue to mount. Cranfield gets the parsonages; Greville, a few months later, is attached for other debts due to the Crown.[1] In a desperate attempt to clear his feet, Sir Richard Gargrave, the ne'er-do-well son of the Speaker of Elizabeth's first House of Commons, sells his park near Wakefield to Cranfield. The transaction is hardly over when he is running up fresh debts, with the result that the rest of his lands fall piecemeal into Cranfield's hands, and that almost a decade later the embittered prodigal is appealing to his alleged spoiler—then a prince in Israel —to discharge arrears of payment allegedly long overdue.[2] The latter's Yorkshire agents discover that the owner of a neighbouring estate, one Peter Frobisher, nephew and heir of the famous explorer, is near the end of his tether. His land, they report, can be got cheap —'he knoweth not what it is'— especially if a would-be purchaser will pave the way with a few judicious loans, and, above all, induce him to mortgage, which 'will make work for him for ever'. The flies are thrown and taken. The manor—Frobisher Hall, coal-mines and tithes—is duly landed.[3] The Earl of Sussex—a peer with a pleasing gift for polite invective—'You have the advantage of me .... You have both the money and lands in your hands. If others troubled me for lands that I have sold so much as you do, I should be in evil case'—shows more fight. The point at issue—Cranfield's refusal, after buying a property from the Earl, to complete the payments for it or release the seller from an outstanding debt, unless the latter's heir will bind himself, on attaining his majority, to confirm the sale—is referred to arbitration. Cranfield, to judge by

---

[1] Hist. MSS. Comm., *Cranfield Papers*, pp. 144, 154, 156–8, 208–9, 216.

[2] *Ibid.* pp. 161–70, 173, 179. Gargrave alleged in a letter of 1621 or 1622 that Cranfield had undertaken to pay him £2500 for Wakefield, of which, at the date of the letter, only £1664 had been paid. Against this must be set an acquittance of 29 June 1608 by Sir Richard Gargrave of John Cooper and Daniel Cooper, the nominees of Cranfield, for £2000 paid for the Old Park of Wakefield.

[3] *Ibid.* pp. 191–7, 204–7, 260.

a heart-broken letter addressed to him four years later by the Countess, does not emerge the loser.[1]

Such examples of the bloodless conquests of the City must not, of course, be made the basis of generalisations purporting to embrace all members, or most, of the classes concerned. They illustrate one type, but only one and not the most important, of the transactions in which a financial magnate thought it worth while to engage, and one species, not more, of the clients resorting to him. Cranfield's dealings with the veteran of the Armada, still in his dotage Lord High Admiral, the Earl of Nottingham, and his heir Lord Howard of Effingham, belong in part to the same category, They are marked, however, by features—in particular Cranfield's combination of the roles of creditor and farmer—sufficiently distinctive to deserve a passing word.

Among the concessions which brightened the opening years of James, the patent, once held by Raleigh, to license retailers of wines had an important place. Conferred early in December 1604, in spite of parliamentary protests, on Nottingham and his son, it had been leased by them a fortnight later to a syndicate consisting in the first instance of Fearne, the irrepressible Ingram and Cullimore, but subsequently enlarged, in March of the following year, by the inclusion of Cranfield and his old associates, Hare, Venn and Massam. The Wine Office, as it was called, was a considerable affair. Controlling, in theory, from its headquarters near Charing Cross the retail trade in wine throughout England and Wales, and collecting rents and fines from a hundred and fifty or more licensees, it appears to have been regarded by investors as a sound concern. The two leading associates, Fearne and Ingram, prudently retained a five-eighths interest in it, the remaining three-eighths being divided between the five other partners. The three-fortieths share acquired by Cranfield for £710 odd is described by the editor of his papers as a profitable venture. Since six months later, in September 1605, he increased his stake in the business, by buying, at a price which by then had risen, another one-fortieth, in the shape—to quote the contemporary

---

[1] The occasion of the dealings of the Earl of Sussex with Cranfield was his sale to the latter for £4200 of his manor of Shering in Essex, for which he received £1200 on 13 September 1614, and recognisances for the payment of three further instalments of £1000 each (*Cranfield MSS.* nos. 4281, 4292). For his complaints of Cranfield's failure to pay, see *ibid.* nos. 4623, 4455, 4456, and for the arbitrator's award no. 4612 (7 April 1616). The last letter on the subject, in 1620 (no. 1074), is a piteous appeal from the Countess.

fractions—of a fifth of a half of a one-quarter share, which Ingram in that month decided to sell, it would appear that Cranfield thought the same.[1]

These small investments, some £960 odd in all, were opening gambits. To the noble patentees the annual £3000, for which the farm had been let by them, was a flea-bite. Amply endowed with lands and offices though such aristocrats might be, they 'were often', in the words of Professor Newton, 'hard put to it to find cash for their day to day expenditure'. The Earl of Nottingham and Lord Howard of Effingham appear to have been a case in point. What they require, and at times, it seems, require at once, is lump sums down. One expedient by which they obtain them is the sale of successive fragments of the rent, in the form of annuities, to the members of the syndicate which pays it. The Wine Office, being held a safe concern, annuities on it are in demand. The partners, therefore, not only buy and sell between themselves, but can unload them at a profit on a wider public.[2] The results for Nottingham and his son are two. Their immediate necessities are relieved by the conversion of instalments of rent into capital payments, which they can spend as income. Their revenue from the farm is progressively reduced, from £3000 to £1000, in less than four years. In the meantime, they raise the wind by borrowing, and, here again, it is the not reluctant farmers to whom they turn. Lands may be mortgaged for a variety of different objects, some constructive, some the reverse. It is impossible to judge, without fuller evidence than at present we possess, whether the majority of Lord Howard of Effingham's transactions with Cranfield were as imprudent as some of them, at first sight, seem to have been; but the financial dependence for a decade or more of the former on the latter is hardly open to dispute. A succession of small loans comes first; then the sale of the lease of

[1] On this patent and the subsequent arrangements, see Hist. MSS. Comm., *Cranfield Papers*, pp. 75–100. For the allotment in March 1605 of the shares between the seven parties, and for the profits and Cranfield's purchase of another share for £253. 10s. in September 1605, see *ibid*. pp. 96–7, and *Cranfield MSS*. no. 354, with Professor Newton's comments. The latter states that Cranfield's share of the profits in the year 1605 was £455. 16s. 6d. As a result of parliamentary criticism, the grant to the Howards was revoked in July 1614, and the issue of licences resumed by the Crown. This step, however, did not end Cranfield's control of the Office, as Letters Patent of 7 November 1614 granted to him the Receivership of fines for the issue of licences. He continued to derive an income from the Office for at least another seven years. In October 1621 he put the value of his interest in the Wine Licences and Office at £3400 (*Cranfield MSS*. no. 6844).

[2] For the traffic in annuities, see Hist. MSS. Comm., *Cranfield Papers*, pp. 92–7.

the castle and park of Donnington, which Cranfield buys for £288, plus a loan of £1000 gratis for six months, and resells the same year for £1700—'gotten by this bargain for which Allmighty God be praised, £1411'; then the mortgage, followed by the sale to Cranfield, of the manor of Speenhamland; then the mortgage of the Barnstaple property, through the good offices of Cranfield, to his friend, Richard Croshaw, the goldsmith; then a request that the mortgage shall be increased; then a plea for a further loan and an offer of the sale of further lands.[1]

There are passages in Cranfield's correspondence—'if ever your heart could have remorse of any you have bought land of...then for God's love requite me for my love so much as to lend me £5'; 'my daughter's children are like to want the estate...I have had forty journeys about it...now it is dead, except you revive it'; 'you are a great lord...at your pleasure your lordship may oppress me'—which make piteous reading. Letters so happily unconscious of possible catastrophes to come as those of William Lord Howard cannot properly be numbered with them. Cranfield was not of the anglers so squeamish as to find Walton's counsel to pike-fishers—'use your frog tenderly, as though you loved him, that he may live the longer'—too realistic to act on; but, in dealing with the Howards, he seems to have had few occasions for the iron hand. It ought not to be forgotten, in reading his transactions with these and other feeble victims, game hardly worthy of his bow and spear, that, if at times inhuman in exploiting the follies of the weak, he was equally intrepid, when the hour came, in challenging the strong.

[1] Hist. MSS. Comm., *Cranfield Papers*, pp. 152, 216–17, 347, and *Cranfield MSS.* no. 2177.

PART II

CRANFIELD AS MINISTER

CHAPTER V

THE OPENING YEARS

I. THE COMMERCIAL EXPERT

Cranfield's banking and customs-farming interests were not dropped when, in July 1613, he entered the service of the Crown; but they took henceforward a second place. The stages in his ascent need not be more than mentioned. The principal paths to an official career were patronage, patrimony and purchase. He approached it by the first.

As a member of the syndicate which undertook in 1608 the farm of the duties on starch, and later as a Contractor for Crown Lands, he had been of some small assistance to the statesman who, on Salisbury's death, became the leading figure on the Council and the Commission for the Treasury.[1] It is not surprising that, in the crisis resulting in 1612 from the embargo on English textiles imposed by the Spanish Netherlands, Northampton, then Lord Privy Seal, should have had recourse to one whom he already knew as 'a merchant ...more witty and of better judgment in those mysteries than any',[2] or that, later in the same year, he should have referred to him the technicalities involved in the struggle of competing syndicates for two important farms.[3] The client more than justified his patron's expectations. Convinced by his knowledge of 'the Archduke's countries' with which he had himself done business, that its Government dared not risk a rupture with its most important market, he recommended retaliatory prohibitions on its exports to England. His advice on the second problem was equally trenchant. By way of supporting the group favoured by Northampton, he exposed in a series of devastating memoranda 'the omissions and deceits' of its rival, the existing farmers; called their bluff with the assertion that if, as they threatened, they threw up their contract, there would be no lack of eligible concessionaires to take their place; and

---

[1] Hist. MSS. Comm., *Cranfield Papers, 1551–1612* (*MSS. of Lord Sackville*, vol. I), pp. 154–6, 265–6. The group of Contractors for Crown lands with which Cranfield was associated had obtained on lease lands in Greenwich. He facilitated the acquisition by Northampton of part of them for his new foundation, Trinity Hospital.

[2] *Ibid.* p. 274. [3] *Ibid.* pp. 282–96, 299–309.

succeeded, by his own account, in forcing a substantial improvement in their bid.[1]

Such an achievement was of a kind to move the hearts of kings. James, who already knew its author as Northampton's protégé, was duly impressed.[2] A planned revolution in the character of the greatest of English exports was simmering behind the scenes. Commercial politics enjoyed, therefore, a vogue in unexpected places; while finance, if not yet the nightmare that it was shortly to become, made ominous noises. The appointment in July 1613 as Surveyor-General of the Customs of a figure prominent in the City, who was also acceptable at Court, was, in such circumstances, a more realistic response to the exigencies of the day than most of the previous innovations of the reign. Replacing four surveyorships suppressed in 1604 at the instance of the farmers on the pretext that the abandonment of direct administration had made them superfluous, the office conferred on its holder unprecedented powers of initiative and control.[3] Its attraction for the Crown was the addition to the customs receipts expected to result from a firmer hand at the helm. Cranfield himself took a more ambitious view of the possibilities of his post. He regarded it, not merely as a means of eradicating administrative abuses unforeseen when, nine years before,

---

[1] *Cranfield MSS.* no. 4463. Cranfield reminds the King of the farmers' threat to throw up their lease of the Great Farm, 'upon which untrue allegation I did so order that business (with the assistance of Sir John Swinnerton and other friends) that the farmers became humble suitors to continue that farm, and advanced to His Majesty £10,000 *per annum* by way of an increase.'

[2] Cranfield's services were rewarded by the grant to him, 18 October 1612, of a pension of £150 a year for life (Hist. MSS. Comm., *Cranfield Papers*, p. 296).

[3] *Cranfield MSS.* no. 4182, May 1614: Note by Cranfield on his office. To the statement of the farmers that four out of five surveyorships had been suppressed in order to save £1700 a year to the King, he replies that the real purpose of their abolition was that 'they might not take notice of the excessive gain the farmers made of the King per year', and to the allegation of loss to the customs officers through the reversion to farming that 'in the truth they lost nothing but their deceits'. On his office of Surveyor-General he writes that 'there was never so ample power given to any Surveyor before'. The suggestion that the post should be created appears to have originated with Cranfield himself; see *ibid.* no. 4143, July 1613, draft for a petition by Cranfield to the King, which states that 'the concealing of the true value of his Majesty's customs by his late officers, now become farmers...hath stirred in me a desire to do his Majesty an acceptable piece of service by reforming so great an abuse', and that, in order to be successful, he must be made Surveyor-General of his Majesty's Customs. The warrant appointing him (*ibid.* no. 4553), gives as a reason for the post the fact that, owing to the 'negligence and unfaithfulness in the offices of his customs, he [*sc.* the King] hath not been truly informed of the yearly value of the same... whereby some of those who obtained lease of the said customs shortly after His Majesty coming to the Crown have greatly enriched themselves'.

the reversion to farming had taken place, but as an instrument to be employed for the purpose of rationalising the tariff, stiffening English commercial policy, and stopping some, at least, of the holes through which the royal revenue leaked away.

The hostility of a section of London business, which complained to the House of an alleged increase in vexatious fees, was the first obstacle to be overcome.[1] Having weathered that initial storm, the new Surveyor-General could boast that within two years of his appointment, by August 1615, he had increased the Crown's ordinary income by some £30,000 a year.[2] Even more important was the connection formed by him with one who was to exercise a decisive influence on his career. Among the lands bestowed on Villiers to support his recently acquired Viscountcy was a property, the manor of Sherborne, which he desired to exchange on favourable terms for another estate. Cranfield, who had already had a hand in Villiers' business affairs, was requested by Bacon, then Solicitor-General, to assist in re-valuing Sherborne, with the result that the figure put on it was substantially increased. With that service he combined a second, which only one personally acquainted with the new Viscount and with business sentiment in London could have rendered with success. He addressed to him a letter of confidential, but emphatic, admonitions on the danger that a financial intrigue set on foot by his brother, Sir Edward, would bring the wrath of the City both on them and on the King.[3] He found in the favourite a second, and

---

[1] For details see *ibid.* nos. 4178 (September 1613) and 4175, 4182, 4324, 4345, 6576 (all 1614). The essential facts appear to have been as follows: (*a*) In July 1606, the farmers had agreed with Lord Treasurer Dorset and the Chancellor of the Exchequer to allow merchants an abatement of 5% on all duties collected for the next two years. (*b*) Under Cranfield's terms of appointment, he was granted a salary of £200 a year, plus the right to collect a fee of 4*d.* per bill or warrant. (*c*) In 1614, some sixty odd merchants signed a petition to the House of Commons complaining of the fees charged by customs officers in London, alleging them to be illegal, and on 6 May Cranfield, then himself an M.P., was ordered by the House to submit his patent to the Committee for Privileges (*C.J.* vol. I, p. 476). (*d*) His reply to the alleged grievances was that the fees paid him by the merchants—some £400 a year—were derisory compared with the value of the 5% abatement which, with other allowances, brought the rebates granted them up to £15,000 or £20,000 a year; that the abatement was continued purely as an act of grace, which could at the royal pleasure be revoked; and that, though nominally a concession by the farmers, it was in fact paid by the King, since, as a result of it, the customs were leased at a lower figure than otherwise they would have fetched.

[2] *Ibid.* no. 4463 (August 1615).

[3] For Villiers' Viscountcy (August 1615) and his wish to exchange Sherborne see Gardiner, *History of England, 1603–1642*, vol. III, pp. 30–1; for Cranfield's intervention in Villiers' business affairs, R. Davies, *The Greatest House at Chelsey* (1914), pp. 112–13

more powerful, patron, though one destined in the end to destroy him; and, from that date to his final fall in May 1624 he went, with occasional setbacks, from strength to strength, becoming in November 1616, a Master of Requests; in 1618, Master of the Great Wardrobe; in 1619, Master of the Court of Wards and Liveries and Chief Commissioner of the Navy; in 1620, a Privy Councillor; in 1621, Baron Cranfield and Lord Treasurer; and in 1622, Earl of Middlesex. The Committees and Commissions on which he played an active, and often a leading, part were not few. He sat for Hythe in the Parliament of 1614, and for Arundel in that of 1621. In the former, he rarely opened his lips. In the latter, he was prominent, first in the Commons and then in the Lords, as a spokesman for the Crown.

It was, therefore, as a successful merchant, with a head for business politics, that Cranfield entered the service of the State. Financial reform, which was later to make and break him, attracted his attention from the start;[1] but his rise from official to statesman was neither swift nor foreshadowed by his first three years of public life. During that initial phase of his career he played the important, but subordinate, role of a commercial adviser, on whose experience of the City the Government relied to supply technical guidance on all matters, whether foreign or domestic, relevant to policies affecting trade.

The two major issues first to confront him have been treated too fully in the book of Professor Friis[2] to require here to be discussed at length. In the manœuvres which heralded the Crown's capitu-

---

(letter from Villiers to Cranfield), and J. Spedding, *The Letters and Life of Francis Bacon*, vol. VI, p.116; and for Cranfield's warning letter *Cranfield MSS*. no. 1531 (26 October 1616, Sir Lionel Cranfield to Lord Villiers. Sir Edward Villiers had apparently been offered money by the farmers to induce the Crown to stop an action for a sum, put by Cranfield at £30,000, brought by a group of merchants against them, and had attempted to enlist his brother's influence with the King. Cranfield points out that the case is 'the common talk of Westminster and the City', and that interference with the course of justice will gravely compromise both Lord Villiers and the King.

[1] E.g. *ibid*. no. 4074 (July 1613).

[2] Friis, *Alderman Cockayne's Project and the Cloth Trade* (1927). The issues in question related to the cloth trade and to impositions. Decisive action on the former was taken by the Proclamation of 23 July 1614, which prohibited the export after 2 November of undyed and undressed cloth. Cranfield, though apparently not consulted in advance as to that policy, was a close observer of its results. See, in addition to returns of cloth exports, communications received from Merchant Adventurers in Hamburg and London (*Cranfield MSS*. nos. 4557–9, all in 1615), as well as letters and memoranda by himself, e.g. *ibid*. nos. 4556 (7 January 1616, suggestions for a Commission), 4578 4 September 1616, action against the Dutch), 4580 (2 November 1616, names of fourteen Commissioners), 4579 (9 November 1616, letter to Villiers reporting resolutions passed

lation to the insidious Cockayne, the Surveyor-General, though, in view of his office, the obvious consultant, appears to have had no hand. Regarding the company-promoter's mare's-nest, with its glittering prospectus, as a favourite child—*mon coup à moi*—and incited by Bacon,[1] a prophet of smooth things, to hurry down the primrose path, the King was not disposed to court destructive criticism. Cranfield, on his side, with his career still to make, was not sufficiently well established to venture to volunteer it. As all went from bad to worse, he was summoned—too late—to attend the Council in his capacity of economic expert; conducted a damning investigation into the new Company's failure to ship in any quantity the dyed and dressed cloths the encouragement of whose export had been the pretext for its charter; and secured the appointment of a Commission of leading business figures, the conclusions of which confirmed his own. As a loyal Merchant Adventurer, he could hardly be expected to love his Company's pampered rival; but his political conscience was also up in arms. The project, he wrote, had been launched amid 'a glorious show of public good, with profit to his Majesty'. What had come of it all? Its author—'all public good by protestation, but in truth malice and greed'—had cleared a handsome profit by buying cloth at knock-down prices from manufacturers who found their former markets closed; but the greatest of English industries, and all dependent on it, 'the clothiers, the gentry, the cloth-workers and dyers', not to mention the 'old merchants' whose business was in ruins, had been sacrificed to a mirage. 'The making of cloth is impaired with certainty for the hope to gain dyeing and dressing, which in respect of that is but a shadow.' Whether there is truth in Professor Friis' suggestion that it was Cranfield who finally, in the tranquillising air of Newmarket, brought the King to reason, we cannot say. The rumour current in London that he and Towerson, the Merchant Adventurers' deputy, were to be knocked on the head, as the principal assassins of the life-giving plan, by the exasperated cloth-workers was, at least, well invented.[2]

at a meeting of the Old Company attended by Cranfield 'upon his Majesty's Service'), 4570 (1616, answers to interrogatories concerning the practices of the New or King's Merchant Adventurers).

[1] J. Spedding, *op. cit.* vol. v, pp. 170–2. Bacon later changed his views and, 'after some private speech with Sir Lionel Cranfield', advised the King as to the procedure to be adopted in breaking with the new Merchant Adventurers' Company (*ibid.* pp. 236–8, 256–9).

[2] For Cranfield's visit to Newmarket, see Friis, *op. cit.* p. 356, and for the rumour of a projected attack on him, *S.P.D. Jas. I*, xc, no. 147 (29 March 1617).

The royal essay in economic *Machtpolitik* was not quickly forgotten. Long after James had been gathered to his fathers, the Merchant Adventurers continued to point to his fatal flirtation with Cockayne as the fountain-head of all their later woes.[1] Even in 1641 an experienced business man, while expressing sympathy with the desire to develop the finishing trade, could remind the Long Parliament of the classical example of governmental ineptitude offered by the measures taken with that laudable object a quarter of a century before.[2] The immediate consequences of the episode for Cranfield's career were important. Shortly after entering office, in the year which saw cloth exports reach their peak, and when the future fiasco was still little more than a cloud on the horizon, he had forecast, for other reasons, rough weather to come. The principal grounds for his despondency had then been two. The first was the rise in the cost of English exports caused partly by impositions—'a burden to all English merchants, and especially to the Merchant Adventurers'—but still more by the tightness of money and stiffer interest rates resulting from the pressure on the market of large-scale Government borrowing and sales of land. The second disquieting factor had its source abroad. It consisted in a change against this country in the terms of trade.[3] In the past, he argued, doubtless with his own business in mind, foreign merchants had sold their silks and satins against English cloths and kerseys shipped to the Company's continental depots, with the result that the English exporter obtained not only—an important consideration—quick returns, but also good prices, since the foreign buyer had an interest in pushing the sales of the wares purchased by him, and could squeeze the native consumer with an efficiency beyond the English factor's art. The conversion since that day of customers into competitors had made those happy harmonies a thing of the past. No longer content to wait for the English Merchant Adventurer to pick up their wares when he marketed his own, continental firms were increasingly abandoning a passive for

---

[1] *S.P.D. Chas. I*, CCLXXVII, nos. 124, 124(I) (November 1634). Cockayne's New Company is alleged to have reduced cloth exports in two years from 90,000 to 40,000 pieces, and the latitude subsequently allowed interlopers to have prevented a more than partial recovery.

[2] Henry Robinson, *England's Safety, in Trades Encrease, most humbly presented to the High Court of Parliament* (1641).

[3] The unfavourable balance of trade is ascribed, not only to 'the great quantity we receive', but to 'the great price we pay more than we were accustomed, whereas the commodities of the kingdom do not increase either in the one way or the other but rather decline in both'.

an active trade. They preferred now to sell through factors of their own in London; fleeced the English consumer by price-rings; and were remitted their ill-gotten gains, not as previously, in the form of English manufactures, but in specie or by bill. The consequences to be expected were, he thought, a decline in English commodity exports and an outflow of bullion.[1] When, in the spring of 1615, the Council took alarm at the collapse of cloth shipments, it had ordered, possibly at Cranfield's instance, a statistical investigation of the balance of trade. The reports by him and Wolstenholme, which reached it in July, though reassuring on the past, were disquieting for the future. They suggested that pessimism in high places might be only too well founded.[2]

The cure for the first of the ailments diagnosed by Cranfield was a policy destined later, though for different reasons, to become his central theme, but on which discretion forbad a raw recruit to public life to state the brutal truth. It was that the Crown, instead of competing against private business for capital in short supply, should live within its means. But what was the remedy for the second? The traditional prophylactic against 'the over-balancing of the kingdom with foreign commodities' consisted in the antiquated system of exchange controls known, for the mystification of posterity, as the Statutes of Employment.[3] At once the theorist's delight and the administrator's despair, the policies in question were as difficult to enforce as edifying to invoke. The over-driven customs officials in the provinces, where innumerable tiny cargoes were unloaded at a multitude of small and scattered ports, uttered sceptical groans at the impossibilities demanded of them by 'empiricks apter to pry into customers' books...than to spell and judge of them'.[4] Objections

---

[1] *Cranfield MSS.* nos. 4022, 4023 (both September 1614).

[2] *Ibid.* 4532 (25 March 1615, copy of paper given by Cranfield to the Lord Chancellor on 15 March) states his views on the effects of the unfavourable balance of trade and his remedies for it. Nos. 4540 and 4541 (June 1) give the estimates of imports and exports in 1612 and 1613 made by Cranfield and Wolstenholme respectively. No. 4354 (7 June) contains Cranfield's criticisms on Wolstenholme's conclusions. His objection to (among other points) the years chosen for investigation as being 'great years outward in some respects, and not like to be durable' illustrates his pessimistic view of the commercial future. See also Friis, *op. cit.* pp. 207, 212–14.

[3] The Acts requiring importers, native and alien, to export English wares to the value of their sales in England.

[4] *Cranfield MSS.* no. 4176 (n.d.). The paper is introduced with the statement that it is the work of 'the customers of Kent', composed when, in 7 Jas., 'the late L. Treasurer Salisbury, born in hand of great sums that might be drawn from strangers by the Law of Employment', made a similar attempt to enforce an impracticable system. That the

of that pedestrian order left the potentates in London cold. Already, on receipt of its experts' figures, the Council had appointed a committee, which included Cranfield, to review expedients for arresting the alleged drain of bullion. Six months later, undeterred by the perennial objurgations of the men on the job at doctrinaires in Whitehall, it brought into action the whole rusty battery of embargoes on sales by foreign importers for cash, against bills, and to other foreigners as suspect as themselves.[1]

Even when embellished by the new invention—its author's special boast—of an additional surtax of 3*d*. in the pound on alien imports and exports[2], the time-honoured repertory was obviously small beer. Cranfield, an enthusiast for sterling protection policies, was all applause; but he himself had larger ends in view, and he welcomed the ritual incantations partly as a curtain-raiser to more audacious schemes. An appreciation of the importance of quantitative data—a trait more characteristic of the next generation than of his own—had led him some years before to launch an investigation into the character of English foreign trade, designed, not only to yield global figures of imports and exports, but to facilitate a detailed classification of the commodities composing them.

The purpose of his inquiries had been practical.[3] Convinced that, with the balance of payments against it, the country was in danger of bleeding to death, he was bent on a rationalisation of the tariff

author was not the only provincial customer combining a grievance with a lively style is shown by a spirited memorial (*ibid*. no. 4177, April 1614) from the customers of the out-ports to the King, protesting against their condemnation by public opinion as extortioners. The real criminals, they remark, are the farmers, who 'love customs and subsidies as mice do cheese, whilst the customers... like bears tied to stakes...[are] fit for nothing but basting and beating'.

[1] *Acts of the Privy Council, 1615–16*, pp. 272–3, 354–5 (23 July and 19 December 1615). The Council blames the officers for the fact that the Statutes of Employment 'have been of late times so coldly and ineffectually executed'. It orders the enforcement of 'the plain and short articles' mentioned above.

[2] *Cranfield MSS*. no. 2376. The 3*d*. surtax had been invented, apparently in 1613, by Cranfield, who was entrusted with its collection (Dietz, *English Public Finance, 1558–1641* (1932), p. 377). *Cranfield MSS*. no. 4667 (25 October 1616) shows that it was later granted to Lord Villiers.

[3] *Ibid*. no. 4179 (June 1613), 'Concerning my book to show the King the true state of trade of the several ports of his kingdom'. The author states that a view has been taken of all the customs books of the several ports of the realm to show what goods, wares and merchandise have been exported, distinguishing their nature, quantity, and quality, and that the same has been done for the imports, distinguishing their place of origin. *Ibid*. no. 4363 (1614) consists of a tabulated list (without values or quantities) of articles exported and imported. The different kinds of exports, including re-exports, number 106, and of imports 212, or, with subdivisions (six sorts of wool, four sorts of hemp, etc.), 270.

which would shift the main burden of duties from exports to imports; substitute for flat rates a graduated scale pressing heavily on luxuries, but lightly on necessaries and raw materials; and, while yielding a larger revenue, do so without raising the legal issue of the Crown's right to impose, which had proved, in the last Parliament, the rock of offence. His own preoccupations remained in 1615 still primarily commercial; but the Government's financial embarrassments, which came to a head in the autumn of that year, were grist to his mill. It was a moment when James' advisers were torn between the expediency on fiscal grounds of a renewed appeal to the House and political alarm at the explosion for which the inevitable debate on impositions would fire the train. In such an atmosphere the news of proposals on the stocks which, in addition to laying that vociferous spectre, might make the vital branch of the revenue bedevilled by it at once less obnoxious to the Commons and more profitable to the King was manna from Heaven. Suffolk, the Lord Treasurer, who had reasons of his own for fearing light, was hostile; but the majority of the Council, without pretending to grasp the technicalities of the proposed reforms, were not, it seems, disposed to look a gift horse in the mouth. The Surveyor-General's hints of a reconciling formula appear to have been received by them with a sigh of relief.[1]

The array of clamorous interests which even a modest tinkering with tariffs brings into the field is today an old story, and was not a new one then. Thanks to their constitutional celebrity, the ingredients added to the Jacobean cauldron by law and politics need not be more than mentioned. The root of the matter, as far as those aspects of it were concerned, was simple. It was that different elements in the revenue collected at the ports, though similar in their economic effects, did not stand on the same legal footing, and that the famous decision of the Court of Exchequer, which had smoothed the way for the conversion in 1608 of an exceptional expedient into one of the State's financial stand-bys, so far from allaying controversy, had inflamed it. The situation, therefore, when Cranfield took the work in hand was one in which, as in a later and more celebrated case, the fiscal merits or demerits of the taxation in question were overshadowed by the political issue of the title to

---

[1] For a full report of the discussion at the Council, 24–28 September 1615, see Spedding, *op. cit.* vol. v, pp. 194–207. The 'project delivered to his Majesty by Sir Lionel Cranfield', as Sir Thomas Lake called it, was among the numerous proposals advanced.

impose it. His retort to the challenge was a characteristically sanguine attempt to change the venue. He thought, to judge by his papers, that problems insoluble in isolation might prove less intractable if handled *en bloc*, and that, with luck, one well-aimed stone might bring down several unpleasant birds at once. Hence his strategy for winding up the guerilla war of the last seven years was neither retreat nor negotiations, but an attack on the broadest possible front.

His plan, the principles of which had been put on paper six months before,[1] was intricate in detail, but simple in design. Salisbury had proceeded by adding to the standard customs duty of 5% another 5% in the shape of impositions, and then, alarmed by the storm, had attempted to allay it, not by varying the rates, but by a hasty and wholesale removal of the detested surtax, at an annual cost to the Exchequer of close on £20,000, from two thirds of the articles first made subject to it. Cranfield's policy was the opposite. In the first place, he intended to handle impositions and customs duties together, as the different species of a single genus which to the economist they were. The majority of the former were to be abolished, but, in order to compensate for the loss, a considerable proportion of the latter, which aroused less odium, were to be substantially increased. Secondly, since the aim of the reformer was expansion abroad and protection at home, his hand was to fall more heavily on imports than exports, on only three[2] of which—two of them minerals of national importance—were impositions to continue to be charged. Thirdly, he anticipated the orthodoxy of a later age by proposing the substitution for low rates on a wide range of articles of higher duties on a smaller number. Impositions were, therefore, to be removed from over 240 of the 260 odd commodities, including all the raw materials, still subject to them. In the case of a small

[1] By, at least, 1613, Cranfield had been emphatic as to the necessity for 'the taking away the scandal of the new impositions, yet to continue his Majesty's revenue' (*Cranfield MSS.* no. 4177). His programme underwent elaboration in the course of the next two years. *Ibid.* no. 4532, sets out the three main types of argument, commercial, social and fiscal, in favour of it. By stimulating exports and reducing imports, the rearrangement of duties will correct the unfavourable balance of trade and check the outflow of bullion. By increasing duties on luxury imports and diminishing them on necessaries and raw materials, it will relieve the poorer consumers. Finally, it will augment the yield of the tariff to the Crown: 'upon those superfluities there may be a great revenue raised to the King, with a particular profit to his people, and a general good to the state of the kingdom.' See also Friis, *op. cit.* pp. 193–212.

[2] Bays, tin and lead.

group of luxury products, both impositions and customs were to be increased by as much as one-third. A third category of wares was to be relieved of impositions, but to pay higher customs. A fourth was to continue to pay both, at the same rate as before.[1] Finally two ancient scandals were brought to book. Official undervaluations and fraudulent declarations had hitherto been winked at. Henceforward, both groups of offenders were to get their deserts.[2] The political harvest of the measures would, their author held, be as rewarding as the economic. In addition to rescuing the Exchequer, gratifying export interests and appeasing consumers, they would cause irritating minutiae and legal technicalities to be forgotten in general satisfaction at the solid advantages of a comprehensive settlement.

The Surveyor-General's programme anticipated in some respects the proposals for a selective and graduated tariff later to be advanced in a more comprehensive form during the interregnum by such business economists as Robinson, Maddison and Violet;[3] but in its own day it fell, it seems, on stony ground. Supported on the Council by the King's Secretary, Lake, and accorded the compliment of barbed applause by Bacon, it was referred by the Crown to a committee composed of representatives of London business and customs officials,[4] only, after receiving their endorsement, unexpectedly to slip from sight, partly, it is to be presumed, as a result of the King's refusal, in the teeth of the Council's advice, to risk a Parliament. Some authorities have held that the proposals were, nevertheless, brought into operation by executive action, but convincing evidence

[1] Stated summarily, the general result, when currants, tobacco and wines are included in the picture, is that impositions were to be abolished on all but seventeen commodities, fourteen imports and three exports; that they were to be increased on five and remain unchanged on twelve; and that customs were to be increased on twenty-seven commodities. But see also Friis, *op. cit.* pp. 206–12.

[2] *Cranfield MSS.* no. 4137, which states that to rate all kinds of merchandise at their full value will increase the customs revenue by one-fifth, if not one-fourth, and demands the execution of the law against 'all merchants that deceive his Majesty of his customs'.

[3] See, for example, M. P. Ashley, *Financial and Commercial Policy under the Cromwellian Protectorate* (1934), pp. 11, 21, 27–31; W. K. Jordan, *Men of Substance* (1942), pp. 232–3, 363–4.

[4] For Sir Thomas Lake see J. Spedding, *op. cit.* vol. v, pp. 195–9; D. H. Willson, *The Privy Councillors in the House of Commons, 1604–1629* (Univ. of Minnesota Press, 1940), p. 36; Friis, *op. cit.* pp. 208–9; for Bacon, Spedding, *loc. cit.*; and for the personnel and terms of reference of the committee, *A.P.C. 1615–16*, p. 366. The Council instructed them 'to certify their opinions what alterations may be made in the Book of Rates', and to take as their starting-point the plans prepared, on the Council's order, by Cranfield.

to that effect seems to be still to seek.[1] If, however, a verdict on the consequences, if any, for public policy of Cranfield's earliest essay in fiscal reform must remain in suspense, its significance as a turning-point in his career is beyond dispute. Establishing his reputation as a financial expert, and opening doors into spheres more illustrious than the supervision of the customs service, the first of his abortive battles on the stricken field of impositions raised him as high as the last was to bring him low. It launched him on the course which culminated, six years later, with his appointment as Lord High Treasurer.

2. 'THE MANOR OF ENGLAND'

A discussion of the causes which made financial anaemia, not a feature peculiar to the England of the early Stuarts, but, except in the business Mecca of the United Netherlands, a malady afflicting most leading States of the day,[2] cannot here be attempted. But Finance Ministers, more than most men, must play to the score. Before, therefore, turning to the issues which increasingly occupied Cranfield during the remainder of his career, a few brief words on two preliminary points may not be out of place. The first of the topics in question is the nature of the system—if such it can be called—which the Stuarts and their advisers had to work; the second the special difficulties besetting it at the time when, first in a subordinate capacity and then as the official head, the new broom from the City took the task in hand.

[1] The objections to the view in question are partly negative, partly positive. The former consist in the absence of direct evidence, e.g. in the *A.P.C.* or the *Port Books*, indicating a change in the scale of duties charged in or shortly after 1615. Examples of the latter are passages in Cranfield's papers implying that the reforms proposed by him neither have been nor are likely in the near future to be given effect, e.g. *Cranfield MSS.* no. 4461 (probably near the end of 1615), 'For the imposition, considering the king's present estate, there is no hope that they [*sc.* the merchants] should have their ease in it, but hereafter, when it shall be a fit time, they shall be ever sure to have his furtherance in this or any other thing for their good', and *ibid.* no. 2230 (1616), 'The most ready and speedy way for payment of the debts...by mending the Book of Rates, and taking away many of the small and unprofitable (but yet offensive) impositions, by increasing the impositions upon other wares of greater worth, serving for delicacy, luxury and excess ....When all or some of these things before mentioned shall be begun and doing, as namely...the amending of the Book of Rates, the reforming of the Impositions, etc. ..there will be required a Parliament.' I am indebted to Mrs Millard for calling my attention to the first of these quotations.

[2] 'At the end of the sixteenth century and in the early seventeenth none of the greater western European States was financially sound' (Sir E. Barker and others (eds.), *The European Inheritance* (1954), vol. II, p. 132).

Richelieu,[1] while admonishing his master on the prudence of fiscal self-restraint, could remind him that, in the last resort, he rendered his involved accounts to Heaven alone. That agreeable condition was, however, the exception, not the rule; and in most parts of Europe the hereditary revenues of rulers were combined with taxes granted by estates. To us, who know the denouement, the distinction between the ordinary and extraordinary budgets, which was the English version of the same general scheme, has at times an air of unreality, as of a fiction wearing thin; but behind the conservative ritual of accounting lay issues which cut deep. Inextricably interwoven with venerable conceptions of the nature of the partnership between King and people, the division of responsibilities between an Executive assumed to command, in normal times, the means to pay its way and a Parliament supposedly alert, at moments of emergency, to fly to the rescue was among the *arcana imperii* which, till sovereignty itself was in question, it was unthinkable to dispute. Under the resulting dualism part of the Crown's revenue was received by it, in theory, regularly and of course year by year, from sources legally its own; part must be negotiated, as and when required, with an independent and increasingly unfriendly power. The latter caused most political stir, and bulks largest in our books. Financially the former dwarfed it. Since the ordinary receipts were the normal annual stand-by, their preponderance over the exceptional and intermittent additions to them made by parliamentary grants was, on any extensive survey, in the nature of things.[2]

The role of the ordinary account as the fiscal keystone is the crucial commonplace from which all incursions into the maze of Stuart finance must start. It dictated four-fifths of the routine tasks of the ministers concerned: determined the form assumed by threatened breakdowns; and fixed the mould into which, with few exceptions, projects of reform should run. A modern Government has in mind the total annual output as the source from which the

---

[1] Richelieu, *Testament Politique*, ed. Louis André (1947), p. 434.

[2] The lay subsidies, together with tenths and fifteenths, received by James from 1603 to 1621 (including those granted 43 Elizabeth and collected in the next reign) totalled £913,430 (*Cranfield MSS*. no. 6924, October 1621). The ordinary revenue for the only five years of that period for which figures appear to be available (1604-5, *c.* 1609, 1615-16, *c.* 1618, 1620-1) averaged approximately £446,000 a year (*Add. MSS.* 36969; *S.P.D. Jas. I*, XLVIII, no. 45; *Lans. MSS.* 16, no. 52, ff. 113 seq.; *Add. MSS.* 11598; *Cranfield MSS*. no. 6894). It should be added that the figures of the ordinary revenue are sometimes rather in the nature of estimates by contemporaries than statements of recorded facts.

requirements of the State are to be supplied. Its Stuart predecessors, in the absence of extraordinary measures, tapped only the limited fraction of the national income derived from the shrinking body of proprietary and semi-proprietary rights owned by the Crown; a low scale of customs duties annexed to it for life, together with, after 1608, the recent remunerative, but contentious, addition to them known as impositions; and a miscellaneous mass of minor items, of which the most profitable consisted, at the accession of James, of ecclesiastical first-fruits and tenths. The former thinks of insolvency, if it thinks of it at all, in terms, not of unpaid accounts, but of a national product insufficient to meet essential needs. The latter, whatever the increase in the total output, did not, except through a possible rise in the yield of the tariff, gain directly from it; while, if its expenditure outran its receipts, however prosperous the country, it was at once in distress. Only a sale of capital assets in the shape of land, or a loan, or the difficult political operation of a parliamentary grant, increasingly accompanied by criticisms and demands obnoxious to the ruler, could keep it off the rocks.

Given these conditions, the scope of financial policy was correspondingly circumscribed. They caused it to conform with the pattern depicted by the late Professor W. R. Scott,[1] when, citing the Elizabethan phrase 'the manor of England', he describes the Tudor administration of the ordinary revenue as in principle an enlarged version of the management of a private estate. The validity of the comparison was not affected by the change of dynasty. There are occasions, it is true, in the later years of James when issues of a kind familiar today in States supported by annual taxation—the need, for example, to adjust fiscal burdens to the national capacity to bear them, their equitable apportionment between different classes, and the reaction of the demands of the Exchequer on enterprise and investment—figure prominently in debate; but the traditional and still predominant preoccupations of a Stuart finance minister are different. They are those less of a financial statesman than of a prudent steward or bursar. His immediate, most continuous and most urgent task is not taxation, one large block of which is outside his control, while another consists of customs let for terms of years, and only intermittently, when the lease is about to fall in, a burning question. It is to avoid the necessity for a recourse to it.

[1] Scott, *The Constitution and Finance of English, Scottish and Irish Joint-Stock Companies to 1720*, vol. III, p. 487.

It is so to administer the ordinary budget as to ensure that outgoings are covered by receipts, without, save at moments of exceptional stress, an appeal either to the City for loans or to Parliament for grants. What, in the opening decade of the seventeenth century, were the principal impediments to the achievement of that aim?

A striking memorandum by Bacon[1] impressed on his master a commonplace already hinted by Raleigh and stated by Cranfield in blunter terms. It was that a financial system of the English type could be made to work only if the ordinary receipts of the Crown, though in theory the King's to use as he pleased, were treated as in effect a trust-fund, public claims on which were given an unquestioned priority over personal predilections and private demands. The doctrineless sagacity of the Queen, without enunciating that principle, had during much of her reign acted on it. For fifteen years or so preceding the rupture with Spain, and again from 1590 to 1602, she had contrived, with Burleigh at her elbow till his death in 1598, not only to balance the ordinary revenue and expenditure, but to carry a small surplus to the extraordinary account.[2] The prophet of a Free Monarchy threw the maxim to the winds. His insolvency was not gradual, or intermittent, or for manageable sums. It was immediate, continuous and gross.

Providence has arranged, for the mingled exasperation and entertainment of mankind, that the combination of sage and financial moron shall be a not uncommon type. James' place in that engaging gallery seemed for long secure. It is proper that additions to our knowledge of the economic background of his age should cause the verdict to be reconsidered; but a rebound from traditional strictures on Stuart fiscal follies to a view which classes their first author among those on whom the tower of Siloam fell, as the unoffending victim of impersonal forces beyond human control, over-shoots the mark. The economic and political significance of the great depreciation, the exonerating factor commonly invoked, is not, of course, in dispute. On the one hand, as explained above, a substantial block of the royal revenue was composed of payments not easily readjusted to keep pace with the changing realities of economic life, with the result that, in the event of rising prices, its real value fell. On the

---

[1] Spedding, *op. cit.* vol. V, pp. 187–8, where Bacon speaks of the necessity of treating part, at least, of the ordinary revenue as an 'inviolate' fund 'for the discharge of such debts as touch the life-blood of the state'; Oldys and Birch, *The Works of Sir Walter Raleigh*, vol. VIII, pp. 193–4; *Cranfield MSS.* no. 2330.

[2] Scott, *op. cit.* vol. III, pp. 497–8, 499, 501–3, 507–8.

other, it was precisely that contingency which for more than half a century had been for the Crown, as for other landowners, an important fact. A satisfactory index-number remains to be constructed; but on the evidence of those most often cited, James appears to have inherited the nemesis of an advance in the price level amounting between his predecessor's accession and his own, to approximately 50 %.[1]

It is proper to emphasise that, in such conditions, the management of the ordinary account was inevitably, if not yet a desperate, an exacting and unhopeful, task. Two considerations, however, make it difficult for an observer of the financial crisis of James' early years to see in the continuance of the price revolution the villain of the piece. The first is the rapidity with which, on the advent of the new regime, the royal outlay mounts. The financial statistics of the period must not be pressed too hard; but, unless those at our disposal are wholly off the mark, the ordinary expenditure did not merely climb by unspectacular, if continuous, degrees, but bounded

[1] The two index-numbers in question are those of G. Wiebe, *Zur Geschichte der Preisrevolution des xvi und xvii Jahrhunderts* (1895), pp. 374-6, and of D. Knoop and J. P. Jones, 'Masons' Wages in Medieval England', in *Economic History*, vol. II, no. 8 (January 1933). Wiebe's number is based on Rogers' prices of seventy-nine articles, reduced to grams of silver, with the result that it measures the purchasing power of silver at different dates rather than that of coin of the realm. That of Knoop and Jones is based on the prices of twelve foodstuffs calculated from Steffen's ten-yearly average, which also owed its materials to Rogers. The results here relevant are three:

(*a*) Both index numbers show a rise of roughly 50% between the decades 1551–60 and 1593–1602, a figure which Sir John Clapham, *A Concise Economic History of Britain* (1949), p. 187, also accepts.

(*b*) Both show the rise to have been particularly precipitate in the last decade of the sixteenth century, but the degree of abruptness is not the same in each. Wiebe's number for 1593–1602 is 22%, and that of Knoop and Jones 37%, above the level of 1583–92.

(*c*) According to both, the first two decades of the seventeenth century were a period when the ascending curve of prices somewhat flattened out. On Wiebe's figures, the index-number for 1603–12 is 3%, and for 1613–22 5%, above the level of 1593–1602. The corresponding figures of Knoop and Jones are 7% and 15%.

It should be noted, as Mr J. D. Gould has been good enough to remind me, that, apart from other defects, Rogers' figures, on which those given above are based, are heavily weighted with grain prices, and that, as a consequence, they exaggerate the rise of prices at a period of bad harvests, such as the years 1593–1602. It is probable, he thinks, that, had a different periodisation been adopted, the rise in prices in the last decade of Elizabeth would have appeared less sensational, and in the early years of James more pronounced, than under Rogers' division into periods they do. It remains a question, however, whether, even so, the rise in prices which he ascribes (*Econ. Hist. Rev.*, 2nd series, vol. II, no. 1, Aug. 1954, p. 86) to the first half of James' reign can have been on a sufficient scale to be regarded as the decisive factor in the formidable increase of royal expenditure which had taken place by *c*. 1609.

upwards with an impetus which established it, in the course of little more than half a decade, on a wholly novel plane. Whatever view may be taken of the admittedly uncertain price history of the reign, no one would suggest that it opened with a rise in the price level of over 50% in six to seven years. It is, however, an advance of that order of magnitude in the Crown's disbursements of which, it seems, a student of its financial embarrassments must take account.[1] Nor, in the second place, though allowance must be made for the King's expensive family, is the principal cause of that surprising increase a matter for doubt. It was not primarily the rising cost of functions which no Government can evade. For the last four or five years of the reign when, as a result of the European breakdown, English rearmament was slowly gathering way, the plea of inexorable necessities, though not the whole truth, is to the point. For the peaceful first two-thirds or so it is a myth. Down approximately to 1620 the swollen charges crippling the Crown are not in the main, if Ireland be excepted, incurred for austere affairs of State. An analysis of the items composing them shows them in 1609 to have been predominantly the price of royal concessions to hypertrophied appetites for luxury, bounty, and display[2]. In his later years, when the mischief had been

---

[1] The best account of expenditure in the closing years of Elizabeth is still that given by Scott, in *The Constitution and Finance of English, Scottish and Irish Joint-Stock Companies to 1720*, vol. III, division xv, particularly pp. 507–9 and 517. *Cotton MSS.* Titus B. IV, ff. 285b–293b, on which he relies, contains a return of the average annual issues for the five years 1598–1603, but does not distinguish between ordinary and extraordinary expenditure. In estimating the latter, Scott allows 'the usual ordinary provision for the Navy, Ordnance, and Ireland', and a few minor items, and treats in each case expenditure in excess of that figure as extraordinary. His conclusion is that 'the whole ordinary expenditure from 1598 to 1603 may be taken to have averaged £225,000 a year'. It is possible that the latter figure is too low, and that one in the region of £300,000 might be nearer the mark. Even so, as the ordinary expenditure *c*. 1609 is estimated at approximately £500,000 (*S.P.D. Jas. I*, XLVIII, no. 45), the rapidity of its growth in the six years following 1603 would remain impressive.

[2] The ordinary expenditure on defence and diplomatic services (Navy, Ordnance and Armoury, Castles and Forts, Ambassadors) was estimated *c*. 1609 (see *S.P.D. Jas. I*, *loc. cit.*) at 4% above the average of 1598 to 1603, as given by Scott; while, if the expenditure on Ireland (some of it possibly extraordinary) and on the English forces in the Netherlands be included, the rise was approximately 12%. The increase during the same period in the outlay on the Household, Wardrobe, Chamber, and Privy Purse, together with that on the gentlemen pensioners, Office of Works, and the payments variously described as fees, salaries, perpetuities, annuities and pensions, was on an altogether different scale. The expenditure on these objects was by 1609 put at more than double the average annual charge incurred on account of them in the last five years of the Queen. It may be noted that, of the total addition made during the six years ending 1609 to the ordinary expenditure, more than half was due to the expansion of two items, the Household with its adjuncts, and fees, annuities and pensions. For

done, some inkling of that truth appears to have penetrated to the King; but, during the formative youth of the regime, when its style and standards became fixed, both the fact and its significance continued, to judge by his conduct, to elude him. The monarchy, in short, does not fight a losing battle against a remorseless tide of rising prices. Before it can be submerged by the advancing flood it is well on the way to drown itself.

Seen in a longer perspective than the reign which formed the setting of Cranfield's work, the story, no doubt, is different. Some branches of the revenue were obsolescent, while others were doubtfully worth the annoyance occasioned by them. As Salisbury had not been slow to grasp, without some up-to-date and permanent addition to the ordinary receipts no ritual appeals to the maxim that the King should live of his own could enable that venerable anachronism to continue to speak with a convincing voice; nor, if the revenue side of the traditional system crumbled, could it be expected that the Crown's exclusive control of the ordinary expenditure would for long survive its fall. A discussion of these remoter issues, however, is not now in place. On a short view, which alone is relevant here, the conclusion urged, not only by the critics, but on occasion by friends, of the regime, is difficult to resist. It is that, granted the importance of augmenting the revenue of the Crown—a truism which Cranfield was not likely to dispute—the immediate cause of its difficulties lay nearer home. It consisted less in the inadequacy of its resources, insufficient though they were, than in the failure to husband and use them for what they were worth.

Such a verdict, though correct, tells less than half the truth. 'The Queen', wrote one who saw her methods at close quarters, 'was never profuse in the delivering out of her treasure, but paid many, and most of her servants, part with money and the rest with grace...we have not many precedents of her liberality or of any large donations to particular men.'[1] It is a commonplace that her successor represented, in those respects, the opposite extreme. It is equally pertinent, however, to recall that, if the King's fiscal propensities were suicidal, influential groups among his loving subjects

Cranfield's remarks on a similar comparison of certain heads of revenue and expenditure in the last years of the Queen and 1620–1, see *Cranfield MSS.* no. 7887, printed below as no. 3 in App. at end of volume.

[1] Sir Robert Naunton, *Fragmenta Regalia, or Observations on the late Queen Elizabeth* (1642), pp. 7, 29 (quoted Scott, *op. cit.* vol. III, p. 498).

conspired to egg the royal spendthrift on, and that to ascribe to the personal idiosyncrasies of the ruler a prodigality which the habits of the fashionable world in a period of inflation had made less an individual vice than a social institution is to mistake the bubble for the stream. James did not originate a new style in extravagance; he flattered, fostered by his example and too frequently financed a fashion in polite circles already all the rage. The significant fact, in short, is not that the parvenu from hyperborean squalor found the milk and honey of his new domains too much for his none too steady head. It is the alacrity with which high society in London, from courtiers in Whitehall to plutocrats in the City, exploited his patronage and purse for orgies of its own. On that point—the plunge into 'debauchery and riot' which followed, in particular, the peace with Spain—the Puritan Wilson and the supposedly Romanising Goodman expressed in almost identical language the same alarm. The indignant rejoinder of Raleigh's honest justice to the noble plunderer of the Crown, in answer to the latter's cynical 'shall we hinder ourselves of £50,000 per annum to save the King £20,000?'; Jonson's morality play on the idolatry of our Lady Pecunia—'the Venus of the time and State'—and between the two the scandalous, but unanswerable, Tom Tell-Truth's irreverent derision of 'pilots [who] nowadays know no other route than that of their own fortunes, according to which they tack and untack all public affairs'—these and similar utterances hit, in their different ways, the same nail on the head.[1] To such observers the financial *débâcle* was not merely financial. It was a particular case of a more general collapse of public *morale*.

The economic factors which comments of that order overlooked are too obvious to state. The consequences, however, of the frailties pilloried by the moralists were not of a kind to be lightly dismissed. The conspicuous, though not, of course, exclusive, part played in the embarrassments of the régime by laxity and corruption both strengthened the conviction reiterated by Cranfield that, given the will, recovery was not beyond the wit of man, and caused economy measures to overshadow revenue policies in programmes of reform.

[1] Arthur Wilson, 'The Life and Reign of King James I', in *A Complete History of England* (1719), vol. II, p. 703; Goodman, *The Court of King James the First*, vol. I, p. 199 and *passim*; Oldys and Birch, *The Works of Sir Walter Raleigh*, vol. VIII, p. 218; Jonson, *The Staple of News*, Act II, scene i, and L. C. Knights, *Drama and Society in the Age of Jonson* (1937), pp. 218–23; *Harl. Misc.* vol. III, pp. 423–42; *Tom Tell-Truth, a Free Discourse touching the Manners of the Times, directed to his Majestie* (probably 1622).

The partnership in prodigality between the King and the beneficiaries of his munificence meant that such measures, in order to
succeed, must defeat, not only royal inertia, but the resentment of
his entourage, as well as the hostility of more widely ramifying
interests hopeful of pickings from the extravagance of King and
Court alike. It caused attempts at amendment, therefore, to have an
even rougher passage than would have been their lot had James' personal foibles been the only obstacle to be overcome. But, whatever
the view taken of the responsibility for the financial breakdown, its
practical effect in the shape of continuous deficits and of a debt
which, after being reduced in 1609 by heavy sales of land to manageable dimensions, trebled in the course of the next three years and
was to rise by a further 70% at the end of another six,[1] was not
open to dispute. In the middle years of James, the time when a
modest credit balance on the ordinary account had been the rule
was not yet remote. Could not a similar equilibrium again be
achieved?

3. A BUSINESS DIAGNOSIS

The Council of September 1615, whose provisional blessing had
encouraged Cranfield's hopes of an amended tariff, had been convened with more important aims in view. Summoned at a crisis in
order to consider 'the establishing of the King's estate', it had
discussed the financial problem at length in a series of animated
sessions, of which an unusually full report survives.[2] The majority
of members had favoured a recourse to another Parliament; but
two facts were plain. It was certain that the hope for a grant to
cancel royal debts would remain a mirage unless backed by a convincing demonstration that the culprit had already taken steps to
mend his ways. It was equally indisputable that, in the absence of
economies to balance the ordinary account, the embarrassments
which occasioned his appeal for funds would inevitably recur. The
Council's political recommendations had, therefore, been prudently
accompanied by a list of financial and economic reforms,[3] designed

---

[1] For the figures, see Dietz, *English Public Finance*, pp. 125–6, 149–50. The debt,
as given by him, was £597,000 in May 1608, when Salisbury became Treasurer;
£160,000 in 1609; £500,000 at his death in 1612; and between £800,000 and £900,000
in 1618. The annual deficit is thought to have averaged, from 1612 to 1618, about £50,000.

[2] Spedding, *The Letters and Life of Francis Bacon*, vol. v, pp. 194–207.

[3] *Ibid.* (pp. 206–7). The recommendations numbered seventeen. Those specifically
concerned with finance (pp. 206–7) were: (1) 'stay of gifts', (2) 'reducing of expenditure
by abatement (in Ireland, the Navy, the Household and the Wardrobe) to the proportion

to appease the House of Commons, if it met, and to keep the Crown afloat, if it did not. Bacon had deplored the paralysis of a ruler disabled by poverty from 'exercising not only the political part of his office... but the very economic, by setting himself out of interest, making provision beforehand, taking things at just prices and the like',[1] precautions hitherto quite beyond the means of James. It was with the laudable object of ending that scandal that the programme of the Council had been planned.

It was planned, and put on paper, but did not march. Like other authoritarian regimes, conciliar government required a firm hand in command. Stuart administrative energy, as represented by James and the officers trusted by him, was as weak as Tudor had been strong; while among the King's less repulsive pleasures patronage and sport held a prominent place. It is not surprising, therefore, that economy proposals which included, in addition to other objectionable features, a cut in pensions and the sale of a batch of royal forests should, save for a few trivialities, have hung long in the wind. Actually, it was not till after the lapse of over fifteen months, in January 1617, that the attempt to act on them began. The only remarkable feature to modern eyes of the timid moves then made is that safeguards so elementary had not, as a matter of course, been in operation long before. The first was the announcement of a decision to ration the spending departments by fixing maximum outlays, to instruct the officials concerned to adjust their estimates to them, and to order them to treat assignments on the revenue in favour of private persons, not as gifts, but as loans to be repaid.[2] A month later two further concessions to the principle of central control directed that allocations of funds to different services should be made in accordance with a scheme of priorities, and that they should be based, not on the inflated quantities and prices of estimating officers, but on the assumption that only the indispensable minima were ordered and that cash was paid.[3]

---

of the revenue', (3) 'remove of grievances in general, (4) 'imposition in special', (12) 'Parks, Forests, and Chaces', and (17) 'assurance that money given should be converted to public uses'. But several others of the topics mentioned had a bearing on questions of finance, e.g. (6) 'importation and exportation', (7) 'the matter of employment' (i.e. of enforcing the Statutes of Employment), (9) 'a justification of his Majesty's expenditure', (14) 'matter of monies', and (16) 'execution of the law against strangers'.

[1] *Ibid.* p. 26. The words occur in a draft by Bacon of a speech to be delivered by the King to the Parliament of 1614.   [2] *S.P.D. Jas. I*, xc, no. 44.

[3] *Ibid.* no. 71 (*c.* February 1617), 'A sum of the King's business touching the repairs of his estate'. The document deals with various other topics besides those mentioned above.

These belated essays in the obvious were well enough in their way; but the translation of principles into practice was not a trifling task. The Council itself was a body too august for the detailed drudgery of reform. The departmental officials, who alone knew the facts, could neither be ignored nor left to work their not improbably obstructive wills alone. There were offices, again, whose future raised delicate issues of royal dignity and convenience. The King must be induced to look with not too unfriendly eyes on changes affecting their scale and organisation. Finally, the Court, particularly its buying departments, was an important market. The contraction of the demand of these centres of conspicuous waste was only too likely to add to the protests of the genteel supernumeraries hitherto supported by them a formidable outcry from London tradesmen up in arms. Thus the lions in the path were neither few nor somnolent. An unusual combination of administrative experience, familiarity with the tricks of trade, personal tact and toughness would be needed to placate or circumvent them.

Professor Willson remarks that, while in 1615 the Council had come 'much closer to reality than before', such subsequent reforms as were effected were the work of officials, not of 'the Council as a whole'.[1] It was inevitable that, as the idea of an economy campaign slowly gathered way, the officer with functions most nearly approaching those of an economic adviser to the Government should find his work and opportunities increased. It would, perhaps, be credulous to accept Cranfield's estimates of the value of the services already rendered by him.[2] Apart from his success in deflating the demands of customs farmers and his suggestion of a surtax on the export of high-quality textiles, which anticipated the plan later embodied in the so-called praetermitted customs of 1619, his contributions to financial policy, which was hardly yet his sphere, had not been impressive. Some of them, indeed, were remarkable principally for the almost comic contrast between the Pactolus of his golden forecasts and the slender trickle which they caused to dribble in.[3] It is

---

[1] H. Willson, *op. cit.* pp. 39–40.

[2] *Cranfield MSS.* nos. 4069 (June 1613), 4321 (October 1614), 446 (August 1615). The claim contained in the last to have increased the annual revenue by £33,000, plus a capital sum of £16,000, is based on Cranfield's success in securing improved terms from customs farmers, and may well be justified. The words with which it concludes —'and, that which crowns his service, he hath raised all this justly, without clamour and by advancing the public good'—are characteristic.

[3] *Ibid.* no. 4463 (August 1615). Cranfield points to a revenue of £3000 from the additional 3*d.* on the imports and exports of foreign merchants, and states that the tax

clear, however, that his achievements, whatever the discount to be put on his account of them, were regarded by 1616 as sufficiently distinguished to open prospects of a career more brilliant than that of the head of the customs service. It was not till November of that year, with his appointment as one of the four Masters of Requests, that official promotion came his way; but, before that modest eminence was reached, he was hailed by the discerning as a power behind the scenes. Gossip asserted that it was only the repugnance for a parvenu felt by the Lord Treasurer—who, it may be remarked in passing, had more cogent grounds for dreading a business expert at his elbow—that had caused Cranfield to miss the under-treasurer-ship, and that, even so, the King relied on him for financial advice.[1] If the last rumour was correct, it was probably the omnipotent Villiers who opened royal doors; but Cranfield's early memoranda, as well as the language used by him in the farming controversy of 1612, prove that the fiscal dilemmas of the Crown had occupied his mind before the task of grappling with them came his way. The former, some of them suitable for circulation to colleagues, others, to judge by their uncourtly vehemence, reflections for his private eye, are for two reasons instructive. They offer, in the first place, an independent-minded business man's diagnosis of the fiscal maladies of the regime, and state the remedies by which, during that first sanguine phase, he feels reasonably confident that its health can be restored. They reveal, in the second, the decline of his initial optimism caused by a reluctant realisation that even an increase in the resources at the disposal of the Crown will leave the apparently unending battle with interests bent on plundering it still to win.

'The general received opinion'—so the first of his financial papers begins—'is that the King's bounty hath caused, not only his own, but his subjects' poverty.' That view, Cranfield insists, is a popular delusion. Writing about the same date, Raleigh remarked that it was the agreeable English habit to ascribe the alleged impoverishment of the nation to the inhuman rapacity of Scottish adventurers in bleeding the Crown, but that, in reality, for every much-advertised pound extorted by these obnoxious aliens, gentlemanly English

on new buildings will yield 'a great sum of money...being estimated at £100,000'. Six years later, in 1621, the former still yielded only £3000 (*ibid*. no. 6894, 6 October 1621); while the yield of the latter from 1615 to the end of 1619 was £8000 odd (*ibid*. no. 6753, 24 February 1620), or something under £2000 a year.

[1] N. B. McClure, *Letters of John Chamberlain*, vol. II, p. 39 (23 November 1616), and Goodman, *op. cit.* vol. I, p. 307.

blood-suckers contrive discreetly to pocket ten.[1] Cranfield goes further. Lavish gifts and grants, he agrees, though not the most important cause of royal embarrassments, are undoubtedly one factor in them; but 'admitting the King's bounty to his subjects and their liberalities to him, it is notwithstanding impossible that the King's gifts to his people, or the people's gifts to the King, should impoverish them both, because what one loseth the other gaineth'. If, in short, the King chooses to confer on private persons, whether Scots or English, resources which he might have spent on himself, how do these internal transfers prejudice his subjects?

Overtaxation—the conventional reply—to replenish empty coffers? Overtaxation, Cranfield retorts, is the most unplausible of mare's-nests. 'There are not one hundred men in the whole kingdom whose estates have been weakened to the value of £100 a man by subsidies, loans or gifts in his Majesty's...reign, which is such a trifle as it is not worth mentioning.' And why should every minute deduction from the income of the well-to-do be regarded as an outrage, as though their luxuries were sacred, and the State should be content to take the leavings which these favourites of fortune are good enough to spare?

A gentleman of a £1000 per annum is rated in the subsidy at £20 land, which pays £4. Admit the same gentleman to spend in his house one tun of French wine yearly, for which he was accustomed to pay within these twelve years at highest £16, he now pays for the like £24. So in this one particular he pays to the King of France, and sends it in money yearly, £8, which is as much as he pays to the King, his sovereign, for two subsidies....In every suit of satin which he makes for himself, he pays at least half a subsidy in price more than formerly, and in every gown of satin he makes for his wife and daughter a whole subsidy (in price only) more than accustomed. Then look what quantities of wines, etc. we spend by excess more than formerly, and what quantities of silks, etc. we put in the apparel both of men and women more than heretofore, and how often we have new by continual alteration of fashions, and it cannot but

---

[1] *The Prerogative of Parliaments*, in Oldys and Birch, *op. cit.* vol. VIII, p. 194: 'there is not a penny given to that nation [*sc.* the Scots] be it for service or otherwise, but is spread all over the kingdom; yea, they gather notes, and take copies of all the privy-seals and warrants his Majesty hath given for money for the Scots, that they may shew them in Parliament; but of his Majesty's gifts to the English there is no bruit, though they may be ten times as much as the Scots.' The date of composition of Raleigh's book, which was first published in 1628, seems to be uncertain. Professor J. W. Allen, *English Political Thought, 1603–1644* (1938), p. 65, ante-dates it in placing it between 1605 and 1610. The *D.N.B.* on internal evidence puts it after April 1615.

appear to those who have but common understanding that King and people are hereby impoverished, and the treasure of the Kingdom herein consumed. I mention but these two particulars, one of each kind, by way of illustration; but all the rest are in the same predicament, which if I should particularise, it would appear that in general, from the highest to the lowest, every man in quality and price, even in foreign commodities, spends now yearly more than in the last Queen's reign the value of five or six subsidies.'

In such circumstances complaints of poverty caused by taxation are grotesque. 'That which impoverishes the people is their excess, not only in diet, but in wines, tobacco, fruits, silks and such like foreign commodities.' Before preaching parsimony to the Crown, the critics would do well to set an example of austerity themselves. In reality, the crucial issue lies in a region remote from the fictions popularised by propagandists. It is a question less of means than of management.

The true ground and cause of the King's want hath proceeded from the misgoverning His Majesty's revenue as well in receipt as in payment; in receipt, because the King hath wanted one third of his due by farms, etc; in payment, because the King hath paid one third more than was needful in all his expenses. To improve his Majesty's revenue by the reformation of this...will be without difficulty or danger. For all men well affected to their King and country grieve that the King should be deceived of his own, and be thereby constrained, for support of his royal estate, to make supply upon his subjects by projects, etc.

It is here, therefore, with the administrative problem, that reform must begin.

The first essential is full and exact knowledge. Precise information must be produced to show what the total revenue of the Crown would be, if relieved of existing deductions from and charges on it. An analysis is required of the grants by which its receipts have been reduced, of the beneficiaries profiting by them, and of the consideration, if any, paid for these excessive and too frequent gifts. A similarly searching investigation must be made into expenditure. It must show the quantity, quality and price of all wares bought to the order of the Crown; must indicate possible savings under each head; and must examine the economies to be effected by an intelligent use of rights of composition and purveyance. Even if such inquiries do not, as Cranfield is convinced that they will, increase the income of the Crown and reduce its outlay, their effect on public opinion will more than repay the trouble involved. 'There is a double partition wall between his Majesty and his subjects, the one in the impositions, the other in the general opinion of the people that the King's wants and their poverty hath been caused by the King's bounty only, and that, if they should supply him, it would be spent by that means, and so impoverish them more and not help him.' Suspicion, Cranfield holds, will yield to light. Once the financial realities are public property, malcontents will be silenced, and Parliament may open its purse.[1]

Five years later the author would hardly have written with equal indulgence of royal prodigality; nor, it is probable, would he have expressed the same degree of confidence that the reforms required could be effected 'without difficulty or danger'; but, on one point his convictions remained throughout unchanged. His insistence that the key to solvency is rational administration, and the condition of administrative efficiency a grasp of the relevant economic facts, is characteristic. It recurs from Cranfield's first financial paper to one of his last, addressed, long after James had quitted the scene, to the unattending ears of Charles.[2] The same note—the all-importance of a judicious 'government of the revenue'—is struck in some jottings[3] put together by him in 1615, in order to show that the income of the Crown had increased, and should, if wisely husbanded, be adequate to the demands upon it. The character of the particular steps which prudent management would involve was, of course, a different question. Principles—a short way with parasitic grantees; the resumption, 'by a fair course of justice, without strain of power', of public revenues now in private hands; business methods in the allocation of contracts and the conduct of departments—had been formulated; but the all-important details remained to be worked out. A memorandum produced in the same year by Ingram, which found its way into Cranfield's hands, made some suggestions to the point. In addition to hints, apparently ignored by those responsible, for the better conduct of Exchequer business, it urged an examination of the costs, allowances and deductions charged by all officers—farmers, receivers-general, sheriffs, escheators, and others—concerned with the collection of revenue; a similar scrutiny of recent advances in official fees; and a comparison of existing departmental expenditures with those of the later years of Elizabeth. Dis-

---

[1] *Cranfield MSS.* no. 4074 (July 1613).
[2] *Ibid.* no. 8218 (*c.* 1637); see below, pp. 293–5.
[3] *Ibid.* no. 4458 (January(?) 1615).

afforestation and the business management of Crown estates were among the measures proposed. Finally, as already mentioned, it advised that, instead of leasing the customs, the Crown should return to the former system of direct administration, and that in no case should it in future grant concessions of the kind for a term exceeding five years.[1] To the last recommendation Cranfield does not refer, but a subsequent memorandum by him owes something, perhaps, to the remainder of his friend's ideas. It was written apparently in the year which the locusts devoured between the pious resolutions of the Council convened in September 1615 and the first faint stirrings of a will to act.

The tone of the document enables the reader to understand the animosities excited by its author. It is one of genuine alarm on public grounds, combined with an exasperated impatience, which usually, at this period, Cranfield contrives to control, but which here is unconcealed. 'The King's estate in a consumption or fever hectic'; 'so great and dangerous a consumption which might in time ruin the State'; courtiers, 'as Barnard saith, *importuni ut accipiant, inquieti donec accipient, ingrati ubi acceperint*'; 'mature consideration and speedy execution'; '*rerum occasiones tarditatem nostram et ignaviam non expectant*'—such are some of the aphorisms punctuating the paper. Key-words, intelligible enough to those accustomed to the writer's style, take the place of argument. Logical arrangement there is none; but the sense is plain. The first necessity is, of course, a balanced ordinary account. That once established, the King must at last determine to maintain it, by 'keeping inviolate'—Bacon's word—his ordinary receipts. Given the will, the achievement is not beyond the wit of man. On the expenditure side, all further grants and pensions, whether foreign or domestic, must cease at once. The outlay on Ireland, on the United Provinces and on half-a-dozen departments, which Cranfield lists, must be drastically cut. The Crown's relations with contractors and purveyors must be put once for all on a strict business footing. Sinecures, such as fees for the nominal guardianship of ruined castles, forts and houses, must be abolished. Recently created offices—jobs for genteel unemployables —must be strictly scrutinized. Lavish gifts and grants, squeezed from the Crown by 'false suggestions, vulgar considerations... fraud and deception', must be brought before the courts and, when voidable, cancelled. The nauseous tribe of profiteers who have

---

[1] *Ibid.* no. 4462.

grown fat on speculations in Crown lands, dealings in leasehold reversions, the plunder of royal forests, the hunt for questionable titles and the whole unsavoury catalogue 'of shifts and bargains' for which these unsleeping sharks are perpetually on the watch, must be brought to book. If proved to have swindled the Crown, they must be compelled to disgorge.[1]

When Cranfield wrote of policies to increase the royal revenue, some of the measures in his mind would today more naturally be described as reductions in expenditure than as additions to income. An important group of them took the form of action to abolish or curtail the charges for the benefit of favoured individuals deducted from rents or the proceeds of taxation before the sums in question reached the Exchequer, and thus to cause the Crown's net receipts to approximate more nearly to the total which the public paid. He was also concerned, however, not merely to make the most of existing sources of revenue, but to mobilise new; and here his recommendations, if as well-intentioned and specific as those on the economies to be affected, seem to lack the latter's cutting edge. The first recourse, in a similar emergency, of a modern Chancellor of the Exchequer would presumably be additional taxation. It is characteristic of the contrast between the financial system of Cranfield's day and our own that, except in connection with his abortive project for a rationalised tariff, such a possibility hardly seems at this stage even to cross his mind. Direct taxes are the province of Parliament; his business is to ensure that the Crown exploits to the full the resources at its own command. It owns, in the first place, a mass of property, some potentially profitable, some mere lumber. It should at once get rid of the latter and develop the former. It should sell in fee-farm such outlying forests, parks and chases as the royal sportsman will not miss; land recently reclaimed from the sea, to which the King has a title; superfluous castles and ancient houses not worth their keep; non-parochial tithes, and reversions of dubious value. It should modernise the remainder, enclosing and improving commons and

---

[1] *Cranfield MSS.* no. 2330 (1616). I am indebted to Professor C. R. Cheney for informing me of the source of Cranfield's quotation from St Bernard. It is the *De Consideratione*, lib. IV, c. 2, f. 774 in Migne, *S. Bernardi Opera Omnia*, Paris, 1879. The *De Consideratione* was dedicated to Pope Eugenius III; and the parasitic courtiers denounced in it were presumably Romans who sponged on the papal *curia*. *Cranfield MS.* 2330 is in Cranfield's hand throughout and is endorsed by him *Maiestas imperii salutis tutela: Quintus Curtius.* I have failed to find in Quintus Curtius or elsewhere the source of these words or of the sentence, *Rerum occasiones* etc., cited above.

enfranchising copyhold and customary lands, with a view to future fee-farm sales of them as well; disposing of worthless timber for what it will fetch, and leasing coppices and underwoods. There are also, in the second place, assets of a more questionable kind, of which something may, perhaps, be made. The Crown owns the Mineral and Battery works; is financially interested in the glass, starch and tobacco patents, as well as in Sir Hugh Middleton's water company; has not yet wholly despaired of the Royal Company of Merchant Adventurers; and has sunk money in the Yorkshire alum monopoly. Confronted by a crisis, Cranfield, sceptical of 'projects' though he usually is, is not above enrolling some of these unpromising recruits. A third, and more important, addition to the revenue is to be expected from 'the balancing of exportation and importation' and 'the amending of the book of rates', his views on which he has already explained. It is primarily, however, not methods of increasing income, but the necessity for economies, suggested by the earliest of his recurrent comparisons between expenditure under the Queen and in the present reign, which is the burden of his theme. Crushed by debts resulting, not, as is maliciously alleged, from James' prodigality to wastrels, but from the ministerial mismanagement of his affairs, 'the King payeth usury to his own subjects, and sometimes for his own money'. If an intolerable situation is to be ended, economies on a scale beyond anything yet attempted must be ruthlessly enforced.

CHAPTER VI

THE ECONOMY CAMPAIGN

I. DEPARTMENTAL RETRENCHMENT AND REFORM

At the time when the last of the above-mentioned papers was composed, its author had barely three years of official life behind him. It was not to be expected, for all his reputation for business *expertise*, that his views on major matters of financial policy, the interests touched by which were legion, should carry all before them. On the other hand, the case for drastic economies, already admitted by the Council, had been further reinforced by the logic of financial facts. If retrenchment was to be more than a phrase, it was obviously with an attack on the departmental extravagances of the Government—'waste in the offices', as Cranfield wrote—that the unpleasant process must begin.

Given the acceptance of that platitude, the chief candidates for deflation—though he took the trouble to list them—virtually designated themselves. Contemporary figures, needless to say, leave much to be desired; but in 1617, the year which most concerns us, the expenditure on the Household is depicted as well over twice, and the expenditure on the Wardrobe approximately three times, that of the last years of the Queen; while substantial debts were owed by both. Together they were thought to absorb not far short of a quarter of the gross ordinary revenue.[1] Nor did these august offenders stand alone. The financial and technical mismanagement of the Navy caused alarm. The inefficiency and corruption of its small adjunct, the Ordnance Office, was a recurrent scandal. The achievement of the oft-announced aim of reducing the charges of the Irish establishment still seemed remote. The problems presented by the Exchequer, if of a different order, were in some respects more grave. It was responsible for the receipt and disbursement of

---

[1] The expenditure on the Household is given as £29,452, 'on the medium of the last five years of Queen Elizabeth' (*Cranfield MSS.* no. 7887), and £85,500 in 1617 (Dietz, *English Public Finance, 1558–1641*, p. 108). That on the Wardrobe is stated to have averaged £9845 from 1598 to 1603 (*Cotton MSS.*, Titus, B. IV, ff. 285b–293b), and to have been in 1617 in the region of £30,000 (*A.P.C. 1616–17*, p. 402). The debt on the Household at midsummer 1618 was put at £19,566, and on the Wardrobe at £69,000 (*Cranfield MSS.* no. 6987).

the largest block of revenue. Ugly rumours were afloat of laxity bordering on malversation in the control of both.

The impression made by it all was heightened by the even more alarming figures of deficits and debt.[1] The result, if language so modern may be pardoned, was an economy and administrative reform campaign combined. It was a three years' effort, launched with the approval of the King and supported intermittently by Buckingham, in which members of the Council, leading officials, and a few well-known business men, with Cranfield as expert and go-between, co-operated in the overhaul of the organisation and finance of a series of departments, with the object of setting the Crown on its financial feet.

The Offices to which the royal eyes were most easily directed were naturally the two first; and of these the Household, as the heaviest spender, was the more urgent case. When, therefore, economy becomes the fashion, it is with that expensive prodigal that the start is made. On its functions and organisation, which had altered little, save in scale, since the death of the Queen, the work of Miss Woodworth[2] makes it needless to dwell. It is sufficient to remind the reader that the Court included, in addition to the royal family, a considerable body of officials, other privileged notabilities, and the retainers and servants of both, together with menials, wives and children, all of whom were entitled to meals and some other necessaries at the King's expense, in accordance with scales laid down by an approved 'Book of Diet' and 'Bouche of Court', specifying nicely graded menus and allowances of bread, beer, wine, fuel and light, appropriate to the varying conditions of different categories of consumers. The operative, as distinct from the ornamental, organ which supplied their needs consisted of the so-called 'Household below Stairs', controlled by the hierarchy of majestic dignitaries, with the Lord Steward at the head, who composed with their assistants the Board of Green Cloth; organised in some twenty sub-departments; negotiating contracts for provisions with the counties and despatching purveyors as required. The machine in question had as its principal function to purchase, store and prepare the provender to satisfy a mass demand which annually attracted to Whitehall over 2000 oxen and veals, 13,000 odd sheep

---

[1] For the figures see above, p. 142, n. 1.
[2] Allegra Woodworth, 'Purveyance for the Royal Household in the reign of Queen Elizabeth', in *Trans. American Philosophical Society*, vol. xxv, pt I, December 1945.

and lambs, and nearly 19,000 dozen hens and chickens, not to mention cartloads of grain and dairy produce.[1] The mixed multitude for which it catered was inflated under James, partly as a result of the larger and less select Court countenanced by him, partly by the virtual impossibility of excluding the unauthorised intruders described by an uncharitable pen as hungry 'hang-bys, whole families of poor people, especially Scots', who, 'as poor people do always flock to a common,...did...flock here only for diet'.[2]

The expansive propensities of the Household had given Burleigh sleepless nights. On the advent of the new regime, the reforms introduced by a Commission under his leadership appointed in 1591[3] had gone with the wind. By 1617 the expenditure to be cut was not the £30,000 or so of the Queen's last year, but more than twice that figure. The January order of the Council, rationing departmental outlay, had sounded a warning note. It is not, however, till late in October of that year that a letter from Buckingham to Bacon provides convincing evidence that action is on the way. Cranfield, it states, has seen the King 'about his own business', on which he had already conferred with the writer. James has directed that further conversations on the subject shall take place between them, and particularly desires that all matters relating to it shall be treated by Bacon as strictly confidential.[4]

The reference to Cranfield is something of a landmark. It signalises the beginning of his career as an administrative reformer, and throws light on the personalities at work behind the scenes. At this period, it is evident, he was co-operating with Bacon, with whom he subsequently fell out; while Buckingham, who later threw them both to the wolves, was not above lending a helping hand with James. The Chancellor's allusions to Cranfield are, on occasion, slightly patronising; but, once administrative reorganisation is the order of the day, Cranfield, as Bacon realises, becomes the indispensable man. He has the entrée to the King, who permits him to offer advice, not merely on financial technicalities, but on issues of

[1] *Cranfield MSS.* no. 4801 (1618), where figures are given.

[2] Goodman, *The Court of James I*, vol. I, pp. 320–1.

[3] Woodworth, *op. cit.* pp. 14–16. Dietz, *op. cit.* pp. 417–20, gives earlier examples of Burghley's attempts to reduce expenditure.

[4] Spedding, *op. cit.* vol. VI, p. 269 (26 October 1617). Further references to the start of the attempt at departmental reform are contained in the *Fortescue Papers*, ed. S. R. Gardiner; Camden Society, N.S. (1871) No. XIV, pp. 30–2 (Lake to Buckingham, 14 November 1617); No. XV, p. 33 (same to same, 21 November 1617).

general policy.[1] His contacts in the City and Whitehall enable him to mobilise allies representing the union of commercial with official experience required to plan and execute reforms. When, as in October, he falls ill, business must be postponed till he is fit to play his part.[2] When obstacles are encountered, it is he who turns their flank.

The corporate solidarity of the Household, which impressed observers, made the office a difficult nut to crack. It involved the 'inconvenience that every man should hide and conceal each other's faults'; that, in the absence of deliberate efforts to fortify *morale*, 'there should be a kind of conspiracy and combination to cozen and cheat their master'; and that the life of the innovator was made a burden, since 'they that are before, and they that come behind, like so many wasps, shall encounter him'.[3] Some six years before, a rash employee had advanced a plan by which the department could reduce its outlay by approximately a third. The fury of his colleagues had compelled the wretched man's dismissal; nor is it to be supposed that when, in 1615, equally unanimous opposition prevented the appointment of Ingram as Cofferer, the hostility to that astute reprobate was due to ethical fervour alone.[4] Departmental reactions to the Government's new economy programme ran true to form. The Council informs the King that, in accordance with his orders of 14 November, it has notified the officers of the Green Cloth of the decision to reduce the expenditure of the Household to a maximum of £50,000, and has instructed them to produce within a fortnight a plan to that effect. The functionaries concerned reply with noises of deprecation. They 'pretend difficulties in the contriving of so great a work, and an incapacity in themselves to accomplish or to judge of the convenience of many retrenchments'. Explanations by the Board that no more is asked than a provisional draft—'to propound a scheme hypothetically'—are altogether impotent to restore their shattered nerves.[5]

In the paralysis threatened by 'the declining and tergiversation

---

[1] *Cranfield MSS.* no. 4847 (a memorial to the King, probably composed in the autumn of 1617); see below, pp. 281–2.

[2] Letters of Lord Keeper (Bacon) to Buckingham, 19 and 20 November 1617 (Spedding, *op. cit.* vol. VI, pp. 275–6).

[3] Goodman, *op. cit.* vol. I, pp. 254–6.

[4] *S.P.D. Jas. I*, LXIII, nos. 22–4, April(?) 1611 (Morgan Coleman to Salisbury). For Ingram, see McClure, *Letters of John Chamberlain*, vol. I, pp. 584 and 588.

[5] *A.P.C. 1616–17*, pp. 271–2 (17 November 1617).

of the inferior officers',[1] the brutal man of action intervenes to cut the knot. 'Sir Lionel Cranfield's proposition'[2]—to use Buckingham's phrase—is approved by James; and the Lord Keeper is instructed, after further consultation with its author, to put it in the form of a communication to the Council, to be signed by the King. The letter, as drafted by Bacon, was addressed to the Board, but was intended, no doubt, to be a polite ultimatum to the recalcitrant officials. The difficulties which have arisen in the Household, it remarks, are a particular case of a general problem which, unless promptly handled, will recur whenever economies are proposed, with the result of frustrating the whole policy of reform. The subordinate officials, who alone possess the knowledge to propose specific changes, are deterred by self-interest or fear from proposing them; while it is out of the question for the Board as a whole to spend time on a mass of administrative technicalities. The King has reached the conclusion, therefore, that the task must be attacked from a different angle. He has decided that the detailed investigations required—'the mechanick and laborious part of the business'— shall be devolved on a sub-Commission in the nature of a departmental committee, and instructs the Council to forward a list of Exchequer, Custom-house and Audit officials, from whom he will select the members to compose it. The sub-Commission is to meet regularly, to take evidence from such officers of different grades as may be deemed expedient, to work under the direction of the Council, and to prepare plans to be considered by it.[3] The Council replies by sending the names, and, fortified by the royal mandate, brings the departmental trade union temporarily to heel. It reports that, in response to peremptory orders, the officers of the Household will have ready by the date assigned alternative proposals for reducing expenditure to the prescribed maximum; that, in addition, it has arranged for some pensions to be temporarily suspended and others to be cut by a third; and, finally, that the authorities of the Wardrobe have consented to a diminution of its costs.[4] It may be remarked, in passing, that the token reduction promised by the elegant trifler who held the Mastership of the last department was in the nature of a gesture. It left the charges of his expensive

[1] Lord Keeper to Buckingham, 19 November 1617 (Spedding, *op. cit.* vol. VI, p. 275).

[2] Buckingham to Lord Keeper, 19 November 1617 (*ibid.* pp. 275-6).

[3] Lord Keeper to Buckingham, 27 November 1617, enclosing draft of sub-Commission (*ibid.* pp. 279-81).

[4] *A.P.C. 1616-17*, pp. 399-400 (5 December 1617).

office at almost three times the figure which had sufficed under the Queen.

The expedient of a sub-Commission appears to have been a success. Bacon, who from October 1617 to January 1618 was in constant correspondence on the subject with Buckingham, had emphasised that the new organ must take its orders from the Council, and that its work must be supplementary to that of the latter, not a substitute for it. His advice was followed, and the efforts of both in the cause of economy proceeded together. Cranfield, who was at home in matters of the kind, and who saw the official world with business eyes, supplied the dynamic. He plays a leading part on the sub-Commission; nominates, in conjunction with Bacon, its other members, mostly old acquaintances in the official world, but including a leading business man and customs expert, Sir John Wolstenholme;[1] drafts memoranda for it, and periodically reports its proceedings to the King.[2] Rumours of reform had naturally encouraged gossip as to methods of cutting costs. Will economy best be served by curtailing the list of persons entitled to free diets, or by reducing the number of courses supplied, or, as Bacon desired, by amalgamating tables, or by abolishing some outright?[3] One cause of inflated charges consisted in a custom which, since the salaries of officials were perpetually in arrears, condoned, by way of compensation, the retention by them of undefined quantities of the articles supplied; another, in the long credits which tradesmen were compelled to allow; a third, in the fact that the superfluous foodstuffs and crockery, instead of being sold, were simply thrown away. Was it not conceivable that savings might be effected by the punctual payment of employees and tradesmen, and that a market could be found for surplus stores? Such questions were obviously pertinent, but they touched only the fringe. To see the problem as the experts saw it, one must turn to the dossier assembled by Cranfield.

On 7 April 1618, the report of the sub-Commission had been duly presented. The Council declared that it contained 'apparent and demonstrative grounds of reason' that there might be saved about

---

[1] The other members included Sir Richard Weston, two auditors of the Prests, Sir Francis Gofton and Sir Richard Sutton, Cranfield's brother-in-law, John Osborne, Lord Treasurer's Remembrancer, and William Pitt, also of the Exchequer.

[2] *Cranfield MSS.* no. M. 991 (introductory note by A. P. Newton). The instructions to the sub-Commission were signed by the King, 2 December 1617.

[3] Lord Keeper Bacon to Buckingham, 19 and 22 November 1617 (Spedding, *op. cit.* vol. VI, pp. 275, 276-7).

£22,000 a year, 'without diminishing either diet or dish'.[1] It accordingly referred it, together with some suggestions produced by a Household dignitary, to a committee of five of its number, who summoned the not unwilling Cranfield to give evidence before them. The sub-Commission, among other things, had gone at some length into the delicate question of meals, including in its scheme for the future regimen of the Household an elaborate collection of menus, differentiated for 'flesh-days' and 'fish-days', and graded from the diets appropriate to the potentates entitled to ten courses to the underlings required to make the most of a plebeian two.[2] If the officers dissent, the Council remarks, the burden of proof must rest on them. The indignant department is not slow to take up the challenge.

The story of the ensuing paper-war is told in Cranfield's notes. Statistics of expenditure and consumption had been compiled for 1616, the year chosen by consent as the basis for calculation. The sub-Commission argue that they prove that the Household can be handsomely run for £55,560, and that, therefore, £22,000 odd can be saved on the £77,630 actually spent. The officials retort that the latter sum is the indispensable minimum, and that the suggested economies are moonshine. Cranfield, after demolishing their figures, observes consolingly that their arithmetical errors are not surprising, since, the more they spend, the more they pocket. 'The officers' gain had hitherto been made by his Majesty's loss...as, for example, in every tun of wine their fee is 30 gallons [and] in every quarter of wheat in the privy bakehouse 4 bushels.' According to the Cofferer's account, the outlay on beer and ale in the preceding year was £9882; the figures of amounts consumed show that, at current prices, the expenditure should have been less than half that sum, or £4344. A comparison of departmental calculations of the mutton and beef required to feed the Household with the Knight Marshall's figure of sheep and oxen actually bought shows that 1248 more sheep and 132 more oxen were purchased than found their way down courtly throats. In what secluded corner, Cranfield politely inquires, have these bashful flocks and herds contrived to secrete themselves? Strong in technical experience, the officials counter-attack with an ironical request to be informed of the names of tradesmen who will supply beer, ale and poultry, and buy remainder hides, tallow and wheat, at the prices specified by their critics. The sub-Commission

[1] A.P.C. 1618–19, p. 98 (7 April 1618).　　[2] Cranfield MSS. no. 4729.

reply that the King and Council did not appoint them 'as under-takers when the purse is not at their command', but 'to show how his Majesty might be eased in his charge', and that, 'if the officers will do their duty', the economies suggested can undoubtedly be made.

We leave Cranfield administering *coups de grâce* to clerks of the Lord Privy Seal abridged of their diet, gentlemen ushers indignant at the board-wages allowed them, officers of His Majesty's Chamber grumbling at their rations of bread and wine, and serjeants of the pantry for equally cogent reasons up in arms.[1] Chamberlain, who detested him as a plebeian upstart, rubs genteel hands at the thought that 'the late Commission of the reforming the Household, wherein he was more forward, and (as they say) more insolent and sawcie than any of the rest', has caused the vulgar *arriviste* to be 'little beloved in the Citie and less in the Courte', and deduces from that gratifying odium that, 'when all is done, it will come to nothing, but fall to the ground, as such things use to do that are undertaken by unskilful men and out of theyre own element, and against so many well backt adversaries'.[2] He was right on the first point, but wrong on the last. It was all very well for Cranfield, in answer to the remonstrances of Goodman at 'the abridgement of diet and allowances at Court', to reply that 'he had not abridged them one farthing, but only their stealings and thieveries, and that yet still they had such an overplus and surplusage as no three kings in Christendom had the like'.[3] In reality, his role as a reformer earned him bitter enemies, and, not being a simpleton, he can have expected nothing else. The fact remains that, on this occasion, he brought the ship to port, and that a Stuart, for once, did not let an honest servant down. On 1 June 1618 James inaugurated, at least on paper, the new regime, by signing the regulations for the management of the Household drafted by the sub-Commission.

The reform of the Household had been planned, not as an isolated episode, but as the opening of a fresh financial chapter. It was natural, therefore, that in the summer of 1618, when the labour devoted to it showed signs of bearing fruit, two other spending departments, both prominent in Cranfield's papers, should come under review. Fulke Greville, the Chancellor of the Exchequer, to whom, on account of his previous experience as Treasurer of the Navy,

[1] *Ibid.* nos. 4741, 4742, 4740, 4743, 4745, 4839, 4840, 4756.
[2] McClure, *op. cit.* vol. II, pp. 149–50.   [3] Goodman, *op. cit.* vol. I, p. 320.

the Council early in June referred the thorny problem of 'the better direction of a course for the husbanding and ordering of the Navy',[1] decided to rely on the now well-tried instrument of sub-Commissioners. Eight of the twelve members of the Commission for the Navy, appointed on 21 June,[2] consisted of the group of high officials and business men who, during the past six months, had worked together on the Household, the additions consisting of a leading commercial magnate, Sir Thomas Smythe, and three experts, John Coke, later Secretary of State, who had started his career as an associate of Greville in the Navy Department at Deptford; a well-known naval architect, William Burrell, Master of the Shipwrights Company; and a certain Thomas Norreys. In addition to its investigations into navy finance and personnel, the Commission employed its own staff of six shipwrights to make an exhaustive survey of every ship in the fleet, in order to produce a convincing return of the number fit for active service, of the cripples capable of being restored at reasonable cost, and of the corpses—not a mere handful—nominally on the strength, but rotten beyond the possibility of repair.[3] Aided—thanks, presumably, to Greville—by precise and practical instructions from a sub-committee of the Council, the work went forward with almost disconcerting speed and efficiency. The chief credit for the result belongs to Coke; but the influence in high quarters wielded by Cranfield, who had in August received through Buckingham assurances of royal support, made him an invaluable ally; and his papers show that he did not shirk his share of the detailed drudgery which a Commission that means business entails. On 29 September a report,[4] drafted by Coke but with emendations by Cranfield, was presented by the latter, as spokesman for his colleagues, to a meeting of the Council held in the presence of the King at Hampton Court.[5]

Mr Oppenheim's valuable study of naval administration makes it needless to dwell at length on the scandals disclosed by the Commission and its proposals for ending them.[6] To the recommendations

---

[1] *A.P.C. 1618–19*, p. 157 (4 June 1618), and A. P. Newton, note on *Cranfield MSS.* no. 4852.

[2] *A.P.C. 1618–19*, p. 179. The Commission did, and, as the instructions given it show, was intended to do, much more than merely investigate scandals. The best account of its work is still that contained in M. Oppenheim, *A History of the Administration of the Royal Navy and of Merchant Shipping in Relation to the Navy* (1896).

[3] *Cranfield MSS.* no. 4855.

[4] *Ibid.* nos. 4858 (draft report) and 6156 (summary).

[5] *A.P.C. 1618–19*, p. 263, and *S.P.D. Jas. I*, CL, nos. 1, 2 and 3.

[6] M. Oppenheim, *op. cit.* pp. 194–6.

summarised by the amiable Coke, a wrathful dove, Cranfield adds some characteristically caustic comments. 'The two royal ships... at Woolwich fit for nothing but firewood'; 'the King shall now know that ships are not immortal'; 'dead pays for men, for dead ships, for ordnance'; 'a captain allowed 200 men; when he goes to sea, he leaves 50, 60 or 100 men behind him, and yet hath victuals and charge for the full number'; 'there is above £10,000 worth of cordage received lately which is not serviceable'; 'a new office erected at Woolwich called the keeper of the store, charge certain to his Majesty £78 *per annum*, and not the value of 40/- under his charge'; 'two gulfs, receiving in of provisions and delivering out: a great question which is the greater: both extraordinary'—such explosions[1] illustrate the qualities which made their author a salutary, but unpopular, tonic. Though his business conscience revolted at a service honeycombed with peculation, bribery and waste, he was sufficiently human to be more concerned to create a navy which could sail and fight than merely to save money. The Commission's plan[2] was designed, 'by conjuring and driving away the spirits of ships long dead', by strictly controlling the allocation and execution of contracts, and by sacking a mob of parasitic supernumeraries—'a rabble of loose people trusted in the ships'[3]—to attain both ends at once. Its programme, as he expounded it, was simple and audacious. It was, first, to build two ships a year and re-condition two, and thus to provide at the end of five years a force '3050 tons more than the navy of Queen Elizabeth, when it was greatest and flourished most, and 6240 tons more than now'; second, to maintain it in a condition for action 'at two or three days' warning'; third, to reduce the annual expenditure on it, not by sacrificing efficiency, but by pruning waste. He estimated that, were the Commission's proposals given effect, the annual cost of the Navy during the next five years would be, instead of the existing £57,700 odd, just over £30,000, and that at the end of that period, when re-equipment had been completed, and only maintenance and repairs would be needed, it would amount to slightly less than £20,000.[4]

Here again, as in the case of the Household, the interests threatened by reform did not capitulate without a struggle. Early in November,

---

[1] *Cranfield MSS.* nos. 4856, 4855.   [2] *Ibid.* no. 6156.
[3] Hist. MSS. Comm., *MSS. of the Earl Cowper*, vol. I, p. 101 (draft of letter from Coke to Buckingham, 1618).   [4] *Cranfield MSS.* no. 4855.

the Council, after further interviews with the Commissioners and officers concerned, delivered its verdict. It showed its confidence in the Commission by re-establishing it on a permanent basis as a Board responsible for the administration of the Navy. Cranfield was appointed Chief Commissioner, in February 1619, but by that time he had other fish to fry. Called to the Mastership of the Great .Wardrobe in September 1618, he found himself involved, this time single-handed, in a labyrinth similar in kind, if smaller in dimensions, to that from which he had recently emerged. The minister preceding him, Lord Hay, later Earl of Carlisle, who held the Mastership from 1612 to 1617, had been an expensive Scottish aristocrat, who made enough out of the post to be consoled, on his retirement, with a bonus of £20,000, but who had left to unsupervised underlings duties too like work to be worthy of him. His omission to produce accounts for his last two years of office makes the figures for his later days a matter of conjecture; but his expenditure during the first four years of his term had averaged not far short of twice his predecessor's, and over four times that of the later years of the Queen.[1] The fantastic prices charged by purveyors to the Crown; the long credits on which insolvency compelled its buyers to insist; the mounting arrears annually carried forward; the impenetrable mysteries of Wardrobe accounting—'wardrobe lists, wardrobe measures, wardrobe allowances and payments'[2]—all this was an old story.

Cranfield's attack on the jungle was marked by a brutal simplicity. In accordance with the maxim ascribed to him by Goodman— 'the King shall pay no more than other men do, and he shall pay ready money, and, if we cannot have it in one place, we will have it in another'[3]—he insisted on competitive tenders; scrutinised quality with an indecently vigilant eye; standardised where he could; paid cash down; and, to the annoyance[4] of some of his subordinates, short-circuited the profitable meanderings of the time-honoured routine with an ungentlemanly contempt for official formalities which was later, in the hour of his eclipse, to be remembered

---

[1] *Cranfield MSS.* no. 6543 (September 1618). Hay's expenditure for the four years 1612–13 to 1615–16 averaged £48,034 odd. It is fair to remember, however, that in the first of them the marriage of Princess Elizabeth raised wardrobe expenditure to £65,999 odd.

[2] Goodman, *The Court of James I*, vol. I, p. 309.

[3] Goodman, *op. cit.* vol. I, pp. 309–10.

[4] See, e.g. *Cranfield MSS.* no. 6367, which contains the complaints of the under-clerk of the Wardrobe at Cranfield's divergence from the ancient course of Wardrobe accounting.

against him. Judged by results, his brusqueness worked, and the royal gratitude conveyed to him in December by Buckingham[1] was deserved. Pressed to economise, his predecessor had consented, with the air of one reluctantly risking a rash concession, to cut the annual expenditure of the Wardrobe to £28,000.[2] Cranfield undertook to manage the office at a cost not exceeding £20,000, on condition that he retained the savings made below that figure, and then, if Professor Dietz's figures are correct, ran it during the three years 1618–19 to 1620–1 on an annual average outlay of £13,000 odd.[3] The charge that he did well out of his speculation was, therefore, well-founded, but was less than half the truth. He pocketed between £6000 and £7000 a year for himself by saving the Crown an annual £8000.

2. THE COMMISSION FOR THE TREASURY

Of the financial significance of these reforms something is said below. Before their fruits could be reaped, a more formidable issue, which touched not merely particular spending departments, but the Crown's finances as a whole, had stepped on to the stage. After a period of partial eclipse by the cluster of Courts erected by the early Tudors for the management of their augmented land revenues, a renovated Exchequer had again come into its own. It had absorbed in the 1550's three of Henry's short-lived creations; reluctantly and with growls, had made room in its venerable precincts for officials versed in the indecently expeditious techniques invented by those innovating organs; and, in the later years of Elizabeth, had incorporated the small Office of Alienations.[4] About one-tenth of the total gross revenue continued to be received by two minor finance departments, the Court of Wards and the Duchy of Lancaster, which had survived the Marian concentration, and the former of which was to play an important role in the financial history of the next reign;

---

[1] *Ibid.* no. 167 (10 December 1618) Buckingham to Cranfield: 'I have acquainted his Majesty with your letter, who is very well pleased with the account you give there in of the proceeding in his business, and with your exceeding care of abating his charge in all things where it may be well done.'

[2] *A.P.C. 1616–17*, p. 402 (7 December 1617).

[3] Dietz, *op. cit.* p. 405, gives Cranfield's annual expenditure for the three years Michaelmas to Michaelmas 1618–19, 1619–20, 1620–1 as £15,810, £12,232 and £11,964.

[4] M. S. Guiseppi, *Guide to the Public Records*, vol. I, pp. 73–5, 117–19, 258; M. D. George, 'The Origin of the Declared Account' in *E.H.R.* vol. XXI (1916), pp. 41–58; G. R. Elton, *The Tudor Revolution in Government* (1953), especially pp. 241 and 256 *seq.*

but, with those exceptions, the Exchequer reigned alone. Enlivened till the days of Lord Treasurer Juxon[1] by a departmental civil war, in which pugnacious officials performed miracles of joyful casuistry in disproving the need for each other's existence, it was little troubled by external rivals.

Among the improvements pressed by Bacon on an uninterested King was the necessity 'to bring all accounts to one purse in the Exchequer'.[2] In that matter, as in others, he wrote before his time. The exigencies of an age weak in communications and transfer facilities made it natural that the revenues of the Crown, like the rents of other substantial landowners, should be forwarded to London, not as raised, but after the subtraction from them of fees, allowances and other costs of collection, as well as of local liabilities, such as customary subscriptions to schools and charities. More important, the system of inter-departmental transfers known as assignments meant that half the income of the Court of Wards and nine-tenths of that of the Duchy of Lancaster was paid by them direct to the Household, Wardrobe and Chamber, without being passed through a central account, and that their contributions to the Exchequer were correspondingly reduced. The charges, also called assignments, which grew portentously under James, imposed on particular branches of the revenue in favour of privileged notabilities, made further and less justifiable inroads on gross receipts. As a consequence, the balance reaching the Treasury—'the clear and ready money paid into the Receipt of the Exchequer'—might be less than half the total raised.[3]

It remains true, nevertheless, that, in spite of limitations on its domain, the Exchequer occupied a position of unique prestige and power. With an imposing tradition behind it; responsible for

[1] George, *op. cit.* p. 53.

[2] Spedding, *op. cit.* vol. VII, p. 149 (Letter to Buckingham, 29 November 1620).

[3] *Cranfield MSS.* no. 6894, headed 'My Lord President of the Council his book about his Majesty's Revenue the 6th October, 1621'. This gives 'the whole annual revenue' as £485,804, and the part of it yearly paid 'in clear and ready money, into Receipt of the Exchequer to be disposed of to furnish and supply his Majesty's occasions' as £208,474. The latter figure, it may be remarked in passing, is substantially less than the true net revenue. The deductions from the gross revenue by which it was reached included departmental assignments of £148,000 odd; and, as the writer's object was to show the free money actually paid into the Exchequer, that procedure was, for his purpose, a reasonable one. Such departmental assignments, however, were employed for public purposes, to defray expenditure which, in their absence, must have been met from other sources. They were, therefore, part of the revenue.

the two great blocks of revenue supplied by the Customs and Receivers-General, as well as for numerous minor items; confronting the frailties of financial man with a labyrinthine procedure of checks and controls, the famous 'course of the Exchequer', whose majestic convolutions were the pride of its officials, it was not, indeed, the largest, but the most important and dignified of public offices, and its head, the Lord High Treasurer, was conventionally regarded as the leading minister of the Crown. It was this august department— 'the quintessence of all invention..., so perfect in all points that the best wittes cannot find what to add or take away in any particular without injury to the whole'[1]—which, in the summer of 1618, found itself in the dock.

The events of that year, though precipitated by a scandal, were not a bolt from the blue. They must be seen against a background of deepening scepticism as to the quality of the higher direction of the financial system. Abuse of the bureaucracy is not a recently invented pastime, and contemporary criticisms are, doubtless, to be read with a grain of salt. As far as the Exchequer was concerned, the targets of attack were two. It was asserted, on the one hand, that departmental inefficiency in collecting the revenue deprived the Crown of income which it ought to have received, and, on the other, that laxity, or worse, in controlling disbursements resulted in the waste or actual malversation of public funds. Incompetent or dishonest local officers—to summarise the first indictment[2]—accept gratuities to turn a blind eye on defaulters, and, by mendacious affidavits, 'swear the King out of his revenues'. Overworked, and rarely remaining long enough in office to master the intricacies of individual claims and liabilities, their superiors inevitably neglect their financial responsibilities. Summonses to pay are not despatched by the department at the proper date. Dilatory pleas, fraudulent conveyances, erroneous inquisitions, instead of being followed by the appropriate legal action, are allowed to pass unchallenged. Since no register of bonds and recognisances is preserved, merchants can engage with impunity in the export of prohibited wares, relying on the complaisance of port officers, who 'can lend them certificates to save their bonds, in case they should be questioned'. The end of the consequent ever-lengthening list of arrears, unless determined action

---

[1] *Cotton MSS.*, Titus, B. IV, ff. 1–6 (*temp.* James I), quoted by George, *op. cit.* p. 54.
[2] *S.P.D. Chas. I.* XIV, no. 4 (1625), a paper based on the experience of the later years of James.

is taken to bring the defaulters to book, must be 'an irrecoverable consumption'.[1]

If methods of revenue collection were susceptible of improvement, the control of disbursements also, it was argued, left something to be desired. Precise information as to faults and frauds occurring in the day-to-day routine is, for obvious reasons, scarce; but the comments of observers in touch with the department, and the correctives applied on occasions when its lapses came to light, convey hints of the weaknesses which were apt to spring a leak. Ingram had few financial tricks to learn, and the rules for the management of the office communicated by him to a relative of the Treasurer, who had sought his advice, are of a devastating simplicity. The Treasurer must stop once for all the practice by which funds due to the Crown are diverted, with official connivance, before reaching the Exchequer, into private pockets, yet entered, nevertheless, as paid into the Receipt; and when, as in the case of grants, royal authority is alleged, must satisfy himself that a *bona fide* warrant in fact exists. In the matter of issues he must keep himself posted on liabilities falling due; must determine in advance, week by week, the order in which they are to be met; must prevent irregularities on the part of the tellers by communicating in writing his decisions to the particular individual by whom payment will be made; and must insist on an exact compliance with his instructions. He must refuse to sanction issues in the absence of cash in hand to pay them; must imitate the good example set by Burghley and Dorset in keeping a record of all orders drawn on him; and must regularly scrutinise the register of assignments, to know what demands have been met and what are still to meet.[1]

The dazzling obviousness of such precautions was a comment on the mental and moral ailments which caused a regimen so self-evident to be prescribed.[2] Mere laxity, however, was not the gravest charge. The Exchequer contained able and conscientious officials, without whose assistance the reforms associated with the name of Cranfield could not have been planned or put in force. But the Howard gang at the head of it would have turned a nunnery into a den of thieves. It would be unfair to hold against a department

---

[1] *Cranfield MSS.* no. 4662 (1615).

[2] Spedding, *op. cit.* vol. VII, pp. 59–61, contains extracts from a contemporary report, which gives a good idea of the various forms which corruption in the Exchequer could take.

staffed by mortal men the depredations of Suffolk, his unspeakable wife, and her creature of the Audit Office, the 'what d'ye lack?' Bingley of Bacon's speech. If, however, allegations of dishonesty and peculation—Crown lands under-rented, sharp practice by customs-farmers condoned, salaries provided for keepers of ruined castles and non-existent parks, influential creditors, with inducements to offer, paid out of their turn—ought not to be made the basis of a general indictment, neither can they be ignored. The characteristic vice of the age was venality. Public opinion, if shocked by glaring scandals, looked with indulgence on squeeze, backsheesh, graft— the acceptance by underpaid and unpensioned *ronds de cuir* and their superiors of the propitiatory offerings politely known as 'gratifications'—as in similar circumstances it would today. It is difficult to think of a department against which colourable charges of peculation were not brought. It would have been surprising if the Exchequer had escaped them.

'His Majesty', wrote a courtier in the spring of 1618 to a friend at the Hague, 'is now preparing an exact examination and censure of the abuses in the Exchequer, which in all men's opinion are likely to prove very foul.'[1] The revelations of the inquiry into the Household had strengthened the suspicion that public resources were, not merely mismanaged, but plundered. Rumour had long pointed to two notorious figures at the Exchequer as the leading racketeers,[2] and the withdrawal of royal protection from the Treasurer, whom even James[3] had recognised for a blockhead, but whom he had hitherto contrived to regard as less knave than fool, untied the critics' hands. The Council's first step was to take stock of the financial situation. On 26 March, in order 'that his Majesty may see his clear receipts', it instructed the Exchequer and the two minor finance departments of the Wards and the Duchy to produce a return of the revenue for the year ending Michaelmas 1617, together with a statement of deductions from it.[4] A heavy liability, and one which offered a golden opportunity for dishonest officers to conspire with courtly mendicants to rob the Crown, consisted of the pension list. A month later that question was taken up, with the result that a Commission, headed by the Chancellor of the Exchequer—Fulke Greville, an

---

[1] *S.P.D. Jas. I*, CXVI, no. 91 (Murray to Carleton, 28 March 1618).

[2] *Ibid.* XC, nos. 25 and 26 (Chamberlain to Carleton, 18 January, and Sherburn to same, 21 January 1617); *ibid.* XCVI, no. 74 (Harwood to same, 25 March 1618).

[3] Goodman, *The Court of James I*, vol. I, p. 290.

[4] *A.P.C. 1618–19*, p. 84 (26 March 1618).

honest man on bad terms with his chief—produced a report to the Council whose principal recommendations James was induced, at least on paper, to accept.[1] A few characteristic jottings by Cranfield—'gratitude of the King for securing his own estate and the honour of his country...great gifts exhaust the King's treasure and overthrow his own work, shut the people's hands...the King's inclination to thrive'[2]—suggest the atmosphere of the time; but it was not till after midsummer that matters came to a head. Denounced for illegal exactions by a former employee, Suffolk was at last removed from office on 19 July, while his fellow-criminal, Bingley, the under-Treasurer, was sent to gaol.[3] For the next two-and-a-half years the Treasury was in Commission.

The reform of other departments had proved that mere re-organisation was not, by itself, enough. It was necessary to accompany it by an infusion of new blood to replace officials wedded to the old regime. In the case of the Exchequer, events had cleared the ground. Given the mediocrity of most of James' Councils, the Board which now took charge was not too badly manned. Including, as it did, in addition to two leading ecclesiastics, the Lord Chancellor, the Lord Chief Justice, the Chancellor of the Exchequer, a former holder of that office, now Master of the Rolls, and the Secretary of State, its *personnel* was not, with one exception, brilliant; but it represented a respectable array of legal and official *expertise*. Bacon, its most active member—'treasure...is now the *summa summarum*'—was at pains, as his letters to Buckingham show, to keep the King in tow.[4] It was not till early in the following year, when he became a Privy Councillor, that Cranfield was added to the Commission; but, as the adviser on whom it principally relied, he bore the main burden from the start. An earlier Commission for the Treasury appointed five years before, on Salisbury's death, had set a bad example by exploiting every artifice, however trivial or vicious, for raising the wind which the ambiguities of the prerogative allowed.[5] If its successor of 1618, while not wholly avoiding similar futilities, devoted its main energies to more fundamental tasks, it was largely, it may be suspected, to Cranfield's combination of

---

[1] *S.P.D. Jas. I*, XCVII, nos. 19 (24 April 1618).
[2] *Cranfield MSS.* no. 4872 (May 1618).
[3] Spedding, *op. cit.* vol. VII, pp. 1–3.
[4] *Ibid.* vol. VI, pp. 378–9 (Lord Chancellor to Buckingham, 25 November 1618).
[5] For examples, see Dietz, *op. cit.* pp. 172–3, 177–9.

realism, expert knowledge and reforming zeal that the welcome change was due.

The scandals which occasioned the Commission's appointment determined its initial task. The details of its orders of 24 July for the management of the Exchequer[1]—in essence a much elaborated version of Ingram's earlier admonitions[2]—need not detain us. Technicalities apart, their intention is plain. To ensure by means of classified returns that liabilities in respect of debts, assignments and pensions were accurately known; to enforce exact compliance with a prescribed routine; to define with precision the duties of different grades in the official hierarchy; to establish an effective chain of command from the Commission downwards—such were the objectives sought. Given an efficient central machine, the remaining problems obviously fell under two main heads. The first was the establishment of arrangements ensuring the receipt by the local officers, and despatch by them to London, of every penny due. The second was the continuance of the attack on extravagance and waste.

The land revenue derived from the Receivers-General was put in 1618 at approximately one sixth of the gross ordinary income;[3] but the system under which it was collected was notoriously a sieve. At the end of its first months of office, in April 1619, an attempt[4] was made by the Commission to stop the holes. The plan adopted was to prescribe an administrative routine, with which every officer, central and local, must henceforward comply. Stewards and bailiffs of Crown manors are ordered to prepare up-to-date and accurate rentals and to forward them, together with the rolls of courts held during the preceding year and particulars of heriots, fines, waifs and strays and other casualties, to the auditors responsible for the counties concerned. These officials, on their side, are to check the items in question by reference to the court rolls; are to be scrupulous in recording both new or increased rents and reductions caused by sales; and, in general, are to ensure that the 'true annual revenue may be known, how it riseth or falleth year by year'. Finally, debtors in arrears with payments and officers behind with work are impartially brought to book. On the one hand, Receivers are instructed to show in their annual declarations such liabilities of bailiffs and collectors as remain undischarged. On the other the departmental

---

[1] Spedding, *op. cit.* vol. VI, pp. 317–19.
[2] See above, pp. 148–9 and 166.   [3] *Add. MSS.* 11598.
[4] *S.P.D. Jas. I,* CVII, no. 57 (20 April 1619).

torpor—'Exchequer men will be Exchequer men still'[1]—which leaves Receivers' accounts unchecked till they are three years out of date, is given a jolt. Officials, it is drily remarked, do not serve the Crown for nought. They may reasonably be required to do their work to time. Nor, key position though the land-revenue was, could minor branches of the income be ignored. The Commission for the Treasury intervenes to settle difficulties, apparently of a personal character, in the Office of Alienations; attempts to improve the management of the Mint; and, since recusancy has its fiscal side, labours to introduce a new *modus vivendi*, at once less oppressive to the suspect minority and more profitable to the Crown.[2] In its treatment of the single most important source of revenue, the tariff, it showed, with one possible exception, more caution than dash. Here, no doubt, it followed the advice of Cranfield, who, with the depression looming up, thought the moment inopportune, not only for the issue of a new Book of Rates, but for opening negotiations to re-let the Great Farm on better terms. Some minor farms, it is true, were due for treatment, and conditions were arranged on which, on the expiry of existing leases, new contracts should be made. But bargaining of the kind was Cranfield's long suit, and an account of his proceedings in that sphere may conveniently be postponed.

Efforts to increase the revenue could not quickly yield their fruits. The question was how best, in the meantime, by immediate and trenchant operations on the other side of the account, to enable the regime to struggle on. The economy policies of the Commission followed well-worn paths. Staffs in the land-revenue and customs services, as well as in certain other departments, are cut. Defalcations, including fees and other charges of collection, subtracted from gross receipts percentages ranging from 7·3 in the case of the Receivers-General and 8·6 in that of the Great Farm of the customs to more than 9·0 on the farm of French wines and on the impositions, 13·0 on the tobacco farm and over 22 on that of coals.[3] Experienced observers, including Cranfield and Ingram, had long denounced

---

[1] Spedding, *op. cit.* vol. VII, pp. 73–4 (Bacon to Buckingham, 20 January 1619).

[2] *Ibid.* p. 86; *S.P.D. Jas. I*, CXLI, no. 78; *ibid.* CXV, nos. 9, 10, 31, 32.

[3] The figures of defalcations are taken from *Cranfield MSS.* no. 6339 (27 August 1619), and, with one exception, those of the gross receipts from which they were deducted from *ibid.* no. 6128 (1618). For the impositions, I have used the average of the figures for the three years 1617–19 given by Dietz, *The Receipts and Issues of the Exchequer during the Reigns of James I and Charles I*, p. 141. For reference to a review of defalcations by the Treasury Commission, see Spedding, *op. cit.* vol. VII, pp. 86–7.

such deductions as exorbitant. Now an attempt is made to bring the extortioners to heel. The wisdom of the Commissioners' decision to deal drastically with at least some categories of grants and pensions is equally beyond dispute. Unfortunately, it is frustrated by the mingled recklessness and pliability of James, who leaves the assault on a major scandal of the regime to heighten, at a later stage, the unpopularity of his stony-hearted minister. Two other reforms meet a better fate.

Inheriting the legacy of the departmental economies launched in the preceding year, the Commission acts on that example; and, here again, it is Cranfield on whom the load descends. The Ordnance Office had for a generation been attacked as a hotbed of corruption. Projects advanced in the later years of the Queen[1] for cleaning the sink had languished under her successor, whose extravagances did not include so crude a luxury as arms, and then, in the financial crisis of the reign, again came to the front. Incompetence and dishonesty had by that time done their work. Combined with inadequate assignments, they had by 1616 brought the departmental debt to close on £14,000; and, while the Lieutenant of the Ordnance lined, or sought to line, his pockets, his subordinates went unpaid.[2] In a period of outspoken reports, that of the Commission appointed in November 1619 with Cranfield, backed by Smythe and Wolstenholme, at its head, is more than ordinarily scathing.[3] The dismissal of parasitic supernumaries planted on the Office; a rational division of duties between the staff retained; the suppression of the pickings politely termed allowances; savings on superfluous stores, at present scandalously wasted—such were the chief proposals made. Combined with the transference from profiteering contractors to the Crown of the manufacture of the indispensable saltpetre, they would, it was argued, both increase efficiency and reduce by more than three quarters the annual cost to the State.

Except for the unhappy officials, who continue to besiege Cranfield with appeals for arrears of pay, the regimen prescribed appears, at least temporarily, to have improved the patient's health; and to Coke, on all that concerned the Navy at once a fanatic and an

---

[1] E.g. *S.P.D. Eliz.* CCLXII, no. 105 (3 April 1597); CCLXVIII, no. 13 (July (?) 1598); CCLXXVI, no. 40 (1600?).

[2] *S.P.D. Jas. I*, LXXXVII, no. 82 (30 June 1616).

[3] *Ibid.* CXVII, no. 54 (3 November 1620) and *S.P.D., Addendum, 1580–1625*, XLI, no. 97 (? 1618).

expert, the report of 1620 remained the bible of reform.[1] In the meantime a second and less constructive task had descended on its author. The royal spendthrift had claims as well as liabilities, and if as a debtor he was ill at ease, his position as a creditor was not a bed of roses. A Commission had accordingly been appointed in 1619 under the chairmanship of Cranfield, to report on debts owed, not only by, but to, the Crown.[2] There could be no question, of course, of recovering more than a minute fraction of the million odd estimated by the Commission to be due; and the proposal of the Crown's officials to sell general pardons to defaulters at the modest price of £6. 13s. 4d. per head does not suggest that they thought the attempt to recover arrears a gold-mine to the State.[3] It may well be true, nevertheless, that the Commission's revelations were not wholly wasted. They made it possible for conspicuous defaulters to be brought to book, as some, in fact, were; while the meagre sum extracted from the General Pardon, for which its labours were intended to pave the way, was, in a day of small things, not to be despised. More important, the mere existence of such a body had the salutary effect of acting mildly *in terrorem*. The investigations[4] launched by its indefatigable chairman set officials re-examining their books; warned tax-payers and tenants of a possible time-limit to arrears; and, by reminding all three of an authority which could call them to account, impeded, if it did not prevent, the extension of the area of evasion. It must be confessed, however, that much of this part of Cranfield's work consisted in locking stable doors after the steeds had flown.

Must the same depressing verdict be pronounced on the remainder of the Commission's labours? Of the consequences of its slowly maturing revenue measures, in particular those relating to land, it is

[1] *Cranfield MSS.* no. 7122 (28 July 1621); Hist. MSS. Comm., *MSS. of the Earl Cowper*, vol. I, p. 112 (letter of Coke to Buckingham, 16 July 1624).

[2] *Cranfield MSS.* no. 6286: Order of the Lords Commissioners for the Treasury, 23 July 1619. The Commission was composed of officials and business men in about equal proportions. Seven of the fourteen had already served on Commissions concerned with other financial matters.

[3] *Cranfield MSS.* no. 7624 (1621, before 12 December), 'Two points to be mentioned in the Proclamation which is to go out before the Pardon', and *S.P.D. Chas. I*, XIV, no. 4 (1625), which states that 'the subject of late years hath had the...favour to be disburthened of above £500,000 in separate and recoverable debts'.

[4] *Ibid.* no. 6989 (30 July 1621): 'A Note of several Books of debts owing to his Majesty delivered to the Lord Treasurer.' Of the total, £592,313 was due from the Lord Treasurer's Remembrancer; £222,796 from the King's Remembrancer; and £228,087 from the Clerk of the Pipe. More than half the debt ante-dated the Armada.

hardly possible to speak. On the whole, however, with one crucial exception, the principal economies urged by Cranfield were, thanks largely to his efforts, given effect. The resulting reduction of departmental charges by £60,000 to £70,000 deserved the commendations bestowed on it by the King.[1] The gravest defeat of the Commission was its rout on the issue of grants and pensions. The proposal originally put by it to James, when the economy drive began, had been that, subject to such special exemptions as he might make for the benefit of foreign potentates, a few trusted servants and a handful of Privy Councillors, he should announce a general cut in pensions of not less than one-third. James' rejection of the plan of a wholesale reduction, and his insistence that the case of every pensioner should be considered individually by the Council, were admirably calculated to ensure that action should be smothered by an eternity of debate.[2] A second and not less significant saving, on which the Commission might have had something pertinent to say, was excluded from its purview as *ultra vires*. It was that to which Cranfield had referred when, three years before, he included in his list of necessary economies 'abatement in Ireland'. The Irish problem was held, however, too grave to be entrusted to a subordinate organ; and Bacon, on proposing to Buckingham in October 1620 that the King should order the Commission for the Treasury to prepare a plan to ensure that Ireland should pay its way, received the answer that James had already referred the subject to the consideration of the Master of the Court of Wards. Not the least momentous episode of the two and a half years for which the Commission sat was one of which no mention has yet been made. It was the appointment to the office specified by the King of the already over-burdened Cranfield.[3]

---

[1] Notestein, Relf and Simpson, *Commons Debates, 1621*, vols. II, pp. 8–9, IV, p. 4 and V, p. 448. As the editors point out, there are discrepancies between the figures given in different reports. The conclusions suggested by them is that the reduction of expenditure on the Household may be put at £18,000; on the Navy at £25,000; and on the Office of Ordnance at £20,000. The savings on the Wardrobe (see above, p. 163) appear not to be mentioned in any of the Reports.

[2] *Fortescue Papers*, Camden Soc., N.S. vol. I, No. XV, p. 35 (Lake to Buckingham, 17 November 1621).

[3] Cranfield, while retaining his other offices, became Master on 5 January 1619 (*Cranfield MSS.*, no. 6706, Letters Patent appointing Sir Lionel Cranfield Master of the Court of Wards and Liveries). It may be added that the Commission for the Treasury ceased to exist in December 1620, with the appointment of Montagu as Lord Treasurer.

3. CRANFIELD AS MASTER OF THE COURT OF WARDS

The causes which combined to make the Court of Wards and Liveries at once unpopular and important need no lengthy explanation. Writing in the early years of Elizabeth, her Secretary of State had hinted discreet doubts of the justification for arrangements which permitted 'a freeman and gentleman to be bought and sold like an horse or an ox';[1] and more than one of the ambassadors accredited by Venice to her successors held up shocked hands in polite amazement at a barbarity unknown in other civilised nations.[2] The blow to personal dignity and family pride was aggravated by the consciousness of economic loss. Falling capriciously, as it did, on certain lands and sparing others, the cumbrous and antiquated taxation known as the feudal incidents did not only diminish their owners' income. It also—a point of some importance when prices were rising and land changing hands—depreciated the capital value of the property subject to it. 'Free socage; it cannot be found that any heir of this land was ever ward' is among the attractions of an estate; 'no inconvenience, save that it is *in capite*', damps the prospective buyer; while the rumour that a would-be seller had done fealty causes a prudent agent to advise his principal to hold his hand, 'since fealty must necessarily prove a wardship, which, I perceive, you like not'.[3] Such utterances leave no doubt that land burdened with the obnoxious dues was a security at which the circumspect investor was prone to look askance. They belong to a somewhat later date; but before the issue entered politics under James, sentiment and interest were already up in arms. Resentment had become, by the 1580's, sufficiently widespread to prompt the leading figure among Catholic missionaries to England to include the suppression of the vexatious anachronism in his catalogue of blessings awaiting a heretical people restored to the true faith.[4]

[1] Sir Thomas Smith, *De Republica Anglorum*, ed. L. Alston, p. 120.

[2] Barozzi and Berchet (eds.), *Le Relazioni...degli Ambasciatori Veneziani nel secolo decimo settimo, Serie IV, Inghilterra*, pp. 37 (Nicolo Molin, 1607, 'questa insupportabile gravezza'); 100, 105–6 (Marcantonio Correr, 1611, 'legge molto barbara...gravezza non introdotta sotto altro principe nel mondo'); 315 (Vincendo Gussoni, 1635, 'desolazione e rovina alle facoltà e sostanze di chi ha l'infortunio di rimanere per la morte del padre in età pupillare').

[3] Hist. MSS. Comm., *MSS. of the Earl of Egmont*, vol. I, pp. 85, 112, 138.

[4] *The Letters and Memorials of Cardinal Allen (1532–94)*, hist. intr. by T. F. Knox, (1882), p. 304. I am indebted to Dr J. Hurstfield for calling my attention to this passage.

The conditions which sharpened the dislike of the system also heightened the significance of the revenue derived from it. To Governments grappling with intractable accounts, the vice of existing arrangements was neither the social irritation nor the economic injury occasioned by them. It was their deplorable deficiencies as a financial engine. During his thirty-seven years as Master of the Wards, the laborious and careful Burghley, though he attempted to check evasion by legislation,[1] appears to have deliberately refrained from raising the prices charged for Wardships.[2] It was not, in fact, till the financial crisis of the Queen's last difficult decade that the question was taken up in earnest. The story from that date falls into three chapters. The first was an essay in administrative reform. Future developments lend some interest to the gossip—described by the correspondent retailing it as too good to be true—that the Government was coquetting with the idea of surrendering the feudal incidents in return for annual payments from the lands subject to them.[3] The rumour proved a mare's nest; but when in May 1599 Robert Cecil succeeded[4] his father as Master, matters began to move. He tightened administration; issued a new code of Instructions for the guidance of local officers; and was alleged to have doubled payments for Wardships.[5] The ensuing improvement in the receipts of the Court does not appear to have been maintained; but it was sufficient, it seems, to cause alarm. The second phase, which opened with the inclusion of tenures among the grievances[6] formulated, four days after James' first Parliament met, on 23 March 1604, was partly, it may be suspected, the result of that small, but unpopular, success. Behind the legal technicalities and financial higgling of the next seven years lay

---

[1] E.g. *L.J.* 28 November 1585: An Act to provide remedy against fraudulent means used to defeat Wardships, Liveries and Primer Seisins.

[2] J. Hurstfield, 'Lord Burghley as Master of the Court of Wards, 1561–98', in *Trans. R.H.S.*, 4th ser., vol. XXXI (1949), p. 113 ('Burghley deliberately kept the price at a fairly low level'), and *Econ. Hist. Rev.* vol. VIII, no. I, p. 60 ('Burghley had been anxious to increase the number of wardships discovered for the Crown, but not to raise their prices'). The turning-point in the financial history of the Court occurred, in Dr Hurstfield's view, with the accession to the Mastership of Robert Cecil in 1599.

[3] McClure, *Letters of John Chamberlain* vol. I, p. 48 (Chamberlain to Carleton, 20 October 1598).

[4] After the office had been vacant for over nine months.

[5] *S.P.D. Eliz.* CCLXIV, nos. 43–5, 1600 (new Instructions and tightening of administration): XXIV, no. 65, 1606(?) (higher rates for wardships).

[6] Hist. MSS. Comm., *MSS. of the Duke of Buccleugh*, vol. III, p. 80 (speech of Sir Robert Wroth).

principles[1] which cut deep, but a discussion of which is not here in place. The important point for our purpose is the sequel. The break-down of negotiations in which each party, it seems, over-played its hand once more changed the situation. In 1611 administration, not policy, again becomes the capital pre-occupation, which, for the next thirty years, it was to remain. Such attention as is given to the subject of the Court of Wards is devoted, not to reconstructing the machine, but to tightening its screws and driving it at higher pressure.

Cranfield held the office of Master for just over five years, from January 1619, till his fall in May 1624. The rise in the department's receipts under a succession of heads of whom none, save Salisbury, had been outstanding, suggested that its financial possibilities were not yet exhausted. Given the assumption, which events were to confirm, of reserves still to tap, it was natural that the victor in hard-fought battles with lethargic officials and grasping customs-farmers should be hailed as the Moses best qualified to strike ampler streams from the rock. The position to which he succeeded was not a sinecure. Of the feuds distracting the office, and the irregularities of its way-ward local agents, something is said below. These administrative difficulties apart, the Master was confronted by a permanent and even more intractable problem. It had its source in the conflict of functions inherent in an institution at once fiduciary and fiscal, which also, since it had prizes to bestow, offered an alluring target to interests alert to snatch them.

'His Majesty', Bacon had written, 'is *pater pupillarum* where there is any tenure by knight service of himself, which extendeth almost to all the great families...of the kingdom; and therefore, being a representative father, his purpose is to imitate and approach as near as may be to the duties and offices of a natural father.' The Master of the Court of Wards, who acted for the Crown, was in theory, therefore, a trustee, concerned with 'the good education, well bestowing in marriage, and preservation of the houses, woods, lands and estates of the wards'.[2] He was also, however, the head of an important revenue department. As such, he was under an obligation so to conduct it as not merely to protect the interests of the minors whom the death of a tenant brought within his jurisdiction, but

[1] *S.P.D. Jas. I*, XXIV, no. 65, 1606(?). For the suggestion that the Great Contract meant 'a ready passage to a democracy', see *Lans. MSS.*, 19, ff. 23–36 and Goodman, *The Court of James I*, vol. I, pp. 40–4.

[2] 'A Frame of Declaration for the Master of the Wards' (*Works of Lord Bacon*, vol. I, p. 486).

also to secure the maximum income for the Crown, and for that purpose to consider the prices offered for a wardship as well as the welfare of the ward. Charges of systematic callousness brought against the Court ought, perhaps, to be discounted. Its rules for the protection of minors were, on paper, strict, and if not in advance of the opinion of the age, were not noticeably behind it. An orator in the House might appeal 'to the original right of all men by the law of God and nature that children should be brought up by their parents and next of kin';[1] but not all of Sandys' audience were in a position to cast stones. Pillars of propriety trafficked in wardships; nor were cases unknown in which landlords exercised over their tenants powers of a kind denounced by them as outrageous when used against themselves.[2] The fact remains that the results of arrangements which submitted the intimacies of family life to the rigours of the economic calculus were too often the reverse of edifying. The instructions given to the Master required him to take 'a special care that our just and reasonable revenue may be raised without diverting the same to others, and that nevertheless our tenants may be moderately charged and our wards may be educated in religion'.[3] Profits and humanity did not always agree.

In some, perhaps many, cases the Court appointed as guardian the widowed mother or other relative of the ward. In others, connections or friends anxious to save a child from unsympathetic strangers were exposed to the competition of rivals to whom the object of their affection was primarily an investment, to be bought, sold and assigned like any other piece of property, and who might include speculators in treaty for half-a-dozen such prizes at once.[4] 'I would think her dearly bought for £400 at the uttermost'; 'you may have the wardship and lease for £900, and I doubt not but you shall double the money'; 'in regard that the child is very sickly, and that my trouble

---

[1] *C.J.* 26 May 1604 (speech of Sir Edwyn Sandys).

[2] E.g. W. S. Baddeley, *A Cotteswold Manor* (1907), pp. 174-9, where particulars are given of a dispute at Painswick between lord and tenants on the subject of wardship. Henry Jerningham, the lord, claimed wardship up to the age of 21 on the death of a copyhold tenant. The tenants asserted that, by custom, the wardship belonged, not to the lord, but to the next of kin.

[3] *Add. MSS.* 11765, ff. 44-5: Instructions for the Master of our Wards and Liveries, etc. The document refers to other Instructions, apparently of 11 December 1618, in which the words quoted above occur.

[4] The transactions of Sir Philip Percivall, feodary and escheator for the County of Limerick, are a classical example (Hist. MSS. Comm., *MSS. of the Earl of Egmont*, vol. I, *passim*, and p. 113 for a note of grants from the Court of Wards comprising seven cases of heirs in which he is interested).

and expenses have been extraordinary, I humbly crave at your hands to forbear £100'; 'I find...the mother thereof to be my earnest competitor, suggesting many things altogether untrue to withhold the same [*sc.* the wardship of her daughter] from me, and thereby to procure it to herself, which if your honourable Lordship do not help to prevent...I shall hardly be able to free my poor estate or to make any due satisfaction to Sir Francis's so many creditors'; 'the Earl of Montgomery hath lately gotten divers good suits as...the wardship of the young Lord Dormer, which is like to prove a matter of great value'[1]—such utterances have the ring of the horse-market. To regard all guardians as ogres would, no doubt, be absurd; but it was to be expected that an unscrupulous minority would spend capital as income, fell timber, stint expenditure on the education of the ward, and on occasion seek to manœuvre him or her into marriage with an impecunious relative or monied undesirable. It was hardly less inevitable that the Court should at times play into their hands. Theoretically guardian-in-chief, it was in fact an interested party. Its officers were aware that negligence or favouritism had in the past caused wardships to be disposed of on terms below their market value. Faced by the duty of weighing the interests of individuals against the requirements of the State, they could hardly be blamed if, at periods of financial stress, they permitted the necessities of Leviathan to tip the scales.

Cranfield's correspondence shows that a fair share of these routine dilemmas came his way. With their appeals for the conversion of military tenures into socage, requests for rewards for the discovery of concealments, and above all, demands by notabilities, from the insatiable Buckingham downwards, clamouring for the bestowal of wardships on favoured nominees, the letters received by him reveal the snares besetting high financial office.[2] His insistence that the interests of the State—the necessity, for 'the King's service, to continue competition for securing good composition'[3]—must come first, did not make him beloved, and throws some doubts on Goodman's eulogy of his single-minded solicitude for the welfare of wards.[4] In the circumstances of the time, however, a Master was to be judged less by his adroitness in manipulating the small change

---

[1] Hist. MSS. Comm., *Salisbury MSS.*, vols. III, pp. 324–5, and IV, pp. 345, 352–3, 597; *idem. Middleton MSS.* p. 620; Birch, *The Court and Times of James I*, 7 December 1616.

[2] E.g. *Cranfield MSS.*, nos. 811, 821 (military tenure and socage), 427 (concealments) 56, 180, 187, 430, 1068, 8877, 8895 (wardships).

[3] *Ibid.* no. 438.   [4] Goodman, *op. cit.* vol. I, p. 311.

of official hack-work than by his energy in tuning up a lax, but potentially remunerative, department. Here Cranfield's reforming zeal found full scope and left its mark. Orders to local officers for prompt remittance of monies due; pressure on the Crown's defaulting debtors to clear off arrears; renewed consideration of the possible substitution of lump payments for the trifle irregularly dribbling in by way of respite for homage; possible improvements in the receipts from fines on alienations; a review of the formidable list of annuities charged on the income of a hard-pressed office— such measures, the natural reaction of a man of affairs dismayed by bureaucratic torpor, were in line with the short way already taken by him with other branches of the public service, and do not call for special notice. The more significant issues were of two main kinds. The first related to the department's local agents, the second to its central machinery.

The deficiencies of the Court's provincial officers had long been an old story. The feodaries, in whose 'faithful certification of the wards...the improvement of the revenue now solely resteth',[1] occupied a key position. Not only did the receipts forwarded by them account for between a third and a half of the departmental income, but it was on them that devolved the duty of ascertaining in their different counties the extent, value and tenure of the real property of all persons holding land from the Crown at the date of their decease; of preventing the evasions known as 'concealments'; of ensuring that reliable returns were made to the Court; of administering the lands of minors and idiots, and of transferring the payments derived from them to London. The work might in some areas be light; in others, where feudal tenures were thicker on the ground, it was heavy. The status and remuneration of the officers in question were not, unfortunately, commensurate with their responsibilities as 'the eyes and hands of the Court'. Purchasing their posts, expected to be equally expert in grappling with manorial archives and in bullying juries, exposed to aristocratic pressure from above and popular suspicion from below, they led, if busy or conscientious, a life of care. It is not surprising that too often they should have yielded to the temptation to supplement derisory fees with bribes for under-assessment.

The second problem, if it attracted less attention, was not less grave. Shortly after his appointment, Cranfield appears to have

---

[1] *S.P.D. Chas. I*, XLIV, no. 2 (1626 ?).

decided that the procedure of the Court required to be overhauled. By way, perhaps, of strengthening his hands, he set on foot a survey of abuses to be corrected, and gave the investigator access to confidential papers. The resulting report[1] was a cheerless study in corruption and disorder. Its author, who, if not himself an official, obviously wrote with inside knowledge, alleged that misdemeanours revealed by him three years before had been hushed up by the then Master for fear of public scandal; that, six months before Cranfield entered office, a sum of £15,000 due to the Crown was detained by the Receiver; and that the department was distracted by internal feuds between the auditors and their superiors. If the Court's contribution to the revenue was disappointing, the reasons he remarked, were not far to seek. The Attorney, who conducts himself 'as though the King had neither Master nor any other officer', and his clerk, feather their nests by issuing orders in chambers at 20s. apiece to stay the issue of process for the recovery of debts due to the Crown. Action by the auditors to get in money is paralysed by the refusal of the clerk to notify to them the names and addresses of feodaries, lessees and sureties. Collusion between him and the sheriffs results in the latter seizing for debts running into hundreds of pounds lands worth a few shillings, while the former draws leases at low annual rents, with the result that the King must wait interminably for his money, 'if he get it in at all'. Were business properly conducted, and no stay of process granted save in open court or by order of the Master, 'the King's revenues would be greater, the Auditors' troubles less, and the Attorney and his clerk the poorer'. It is possible that the anonymous author, who writes as one with old scores to pay off, painted too dark a picture; but subsequent complaints[2] from an experienced official of the Attorney's misbehaviour lend some colour to it. The indictment of malpractices at headquarters, combined with the notorious shortcomings of the Court's provincial agents, provided a *prima facie* case for action. The conventional remedy for both diseases consisted in the issue of a new and more stringent code of procedure for the guidance of the Master and Council of the Court. Cranfield, after some hesitation, decides another application of it.

---

[1] *Cranfield MSS.* no. 4845 (1620): 'Means to remedy abuses and to increase the King's revenue in the Court of Wards and Liveries.'

[2] *Ibid.* no. 6890 (27 November 1622), Mr Auditor Curle to the Lord Treasurer; Goodman, *op. cit.* vol. I, pp. 310–11.

The last preceding series of Instructions, those of 11 December 1618,[1] had been concocted with some care. The product of conferences between the Attorney-General, the two Chief Justices and the three leading officers of the Court, they had been designed as a final solution of problems acute since, at least, 1610.[2] Bacon, who had played an active part in preparing them, wrote of them to Buckingham in glowing terms as involving a possible addition to the Court's revenue of £10,000 to £20,000,[3] an impressive advance on the average of the current receipts for the three preceding years. The instrument from which these results were expected was barely two months old when Cranfield entered office. It was partly, perhaps, a wish to give fair trial to so recent an essay in reform which caused the new Master to allow more than two years to elapse before attempting a revision of his own. In the course of 1621 he suggested to the King a review of the existing Instructions, and secured from him an order in October of that year authorising the preparation of an amended version after consultation with the officials.[4] It was not, however, till 21 August of the following year that the fruits of his labour saw the light.

The new Instructions,[5] for all the storm that they raised, were on paper little more than an austere edition of a familiar scripture. After a preamble of ritual lamentation at the injury inflicted on wards by their consignment to irresponsible or avaricious guardians, they formulated directions to be observed by the Court; renewed the effort to exorcise jobbery in the grant of wardships; and insisted that lessees of wards' lands should be charged the full competitive rent. Their novel features, in so far as such can be said to have been possessed by them, were, perhaps, two. The first consisted in the heightened stringency of the rules laid down for the procedure of the regional officers on whose competence and honesty all, in the last resort, depended; the second in the increased number of matters reserved for central decision. A permanent obstacle to the effective enforcement of royal rights was the reluctance of juries of small landowners to injure honest men by making true returns. Now, since no frontal attack could shake them, their flank was to be turned. Henceforward they were to be consulted only in the last resort,

---

[1] *Cal. S.P.D. Jas. I, 1611–18*, p. 601.
[2] Spedding, vol. VI, p. 377, and *S.P.D. Jas. I*, CLXV, no. 1.
[3] Spedding, *op. cit.* vol. VI, p. 446.   [4] *Cranfield MSS.* no. 5075.
[5] A Commission with Instructions and Directions...to the Master and Council of the Court of Wards...for compounding for Wards, Idiots and Lunaticks (*B.M.*, E. 80 (3)).

when inquiry from more promising sources drew a blank. On the death of a tenant, the feodary was to inspect the property or otherwise inform himself about it, to consult the relevant records, to frame the highest possible estimate of its value, and not till documentary evidence had failed, to empanel a jury. In no case was a nil return to be made within one year of the late owner's death,[1] unless the local officials had first notified the Court and received its instructions. In no case, again, was the value returned to be less than that specified in any previous survey since the Court's establishment, unless the cause of the reduction was expressly stated, in which case it would be for the Court itself to determine whether the lower figure was justified or not. In order that its freedom of decision should not be compromised by commitments made without its sanction, the feodary was forbidden to inform interested parties of the estimate which he put on an estate, or to accept any fee from them for his services in valuing it. Candidates for wardships were to declare on oath that they had offered no bribe to officers of the Court, and officers that they had received none.

The case for a measure of house-cleaning seems today overwhelming, and Cranfield may well have thought the same; but the principal object of the Instructions leaped to the eye. It was, in the first place, to caulk the cracks through which existing revenues leaked away; in the second, by insisting on competitive tenders, to increase future receipts. Both aims were resented; neither could be concealed. A high official of the Court, Sir Walter Pye, the Attorney, with whom Cranfield discussed his plans before they left the stocks, applauded the prospective additions to the income of the Crown, but warned him that the intention to extract heavier payments from the public must on no account be divulged.[2] 'The directions for setting higher values upon the subject's lands'[3] was the blunt description of the new regime given by another officer. The steward of an important block of properties in Sussex, an antiquary of some note, had recently excused the omission from his account of them of full details as to tenures with the remark that 'the escheators and feodaries of these times have Argus eyes for peering'.[4] The Master's admonitions

---

[1] In the technical phraseology of the document, 'that no office be found within one year of the death of an ancestor against us'.

[2] *Cranfield MSS.* no. 431 (1 March 1622).

[3] *Harl. MSS.* 6809, no. 18, f. 62 (1622 ?).

[4] *The Booke of John Rowe*, ed. Walter H. Godfrey, Sussex Record Soc., vol. XXXIV, pp. 136–7.

were resented as designed to make that repulsive vigilance a professional or civic virtue. Nor was Cranfield's insistence that the transactions of the Court with applicants for wardships should be based on sound commercial principles, and that its local representatives should toe the business line, the sole count against him. His hand was heavy, not only in the provinces, but at headquarters in London. A lifelong admirer, Bishop Goodman,[1] observed that the Court in the past had been dominated by its Attorneys, who managed its business with an eye to pickings for themselves, and that the new minister had earned public gratitude by a concentration of the authority which put these rapacious functionaries in their place. The Master's colleagues and subordinates saw his centralising zeal in a less flattering light. They accused their imperious chief, not only of monopolising power, but of abusing it.

Fleetwood, the Court's Receiver, who in 1618 had earned Bacon's commendations by his part in preparing the Instructions of that year, was particularly bitter. His indictment appears to have seen the light in the spring of 1624, when the arrogant colossus was tottering to his fall;[2] and the charges contained in it may more appropriately, therefore, be considered in the context of the impeachment.[3] Here it is sufficient to note that the financial results of Cranfield's Mastership appear to have been those which he was appointed to attain. The revenue of the Court, depending, as it did, upon necessarily irregular payments, fluctuated from year to year; and inferences from its movement to the efficiency of new brooms are for that reason precarious. All that can be said is that the shocks administered by him set a new advance in motion, the impetus of which was not exhausted at his fall. The Department's contribution to the total ordinary revenue was not, it is true, sufficient for an upward movement in its income to convert the financial debility of the State into robust health. Even so, in the circumstances of the time, the increase during Cranfield's Mastership of over a quarter in the current receipts of the Court was an achievement not to be despised.[4]

---

[1] Goodman, *op. cit.* vol. I, pp. 310–11.

[2] *S.P.D. Jas. I*, CLXV, no. 1: 'Information of Sir Miles Fleetwood against the Lord Treasurer touching the Court of Wards' (date in *Calendar* 10 May 1624).

[3] See below, pp. 255–7.

[4] The Court's current receipts, exclusive of arrears, appear to have averaged for the six years beginning 1613–14 £29,300, and for the next six, which ended in 1624–5, just over £37,700 (Court of Wards: *Rec. Gen.'s Accounts*).

CHAPTER VII

CRANFIELD IN COMMAND

I. THE PARLIAMENT OF 1621

A verdict on this phase of the unpopular reformer's career is best deferred till his financial work has been surveyed as a whole. In the meantime, before his first two years as a Minister had run their course, the second shock of the European earthquake had changed, not only the continental, but the English, landscape. The Spanish military occupation of the hereditary territories of James' son-in-law did not shake the King's neutrality on the Bohemian question; but the effect on English politics was immediate and profound. Accepted as inevitable within a month of the arrival of the news in London, the Parliament which met on 30 January 1621 voted with alacrity[1] a fraction of the sum required, in the words of a member, as 'supply against Spinola in the Palatinate'.[2] It then resumed the already opened inquisition into domestic problems which was to be its principal preoccupation during the ensuing months.

Save for a sterile two months in 1614, a decade had elapsed since the Commons last met. The issues which, in the intervening years had piled up against the dam were not a trifle. Abuses in the administration of justice, from jurisdictional conflicts between an innovating Chancery and the Common Law to exorbitant fees; the proliferating crop of 'protections'—in effect *moratoria*—to debtors against creditors; the unsavoury tricks of informers; the multiplication of superfluous, and not always edifying, justices of the peace, defaced one corner of the long unweeded garden. The further inflation, by the creation of new offices, of public services already deemed too large, choked another. Economic grievances—grants to patentees, monopolists and nosers-out of 'concealed' lands;

---

[1] The bill granting two subsidies (about £140,000) was read a second time on 7 March, and received the royal assent on 22 March (Notestein, Relf and Simpson, *Commons Debates, 1621*, vol. II, pp. 177, 257). Subsidies were rarely voted so early in the session. The value of a subsidy was put by members at £71,000 (*ibid.* vols. V, pp. 224, 409 and VI, p. 208). Gardiner, *History of England, 1603–1642*, vol. IV, p. 32, puts the value of two subsidies at about £160,000.

[2] *Proceedings and Debates of the House of Commons in 1621* (Oxford, 1765), vol. I p. 36 (Sir John Jephson, 23 February).

recent additions to the tariff and the surreptitious extortions of
the myrmidons collecting them; a mischievous interference with
fishing, and even more mischievous neglect; the export of wool and
import of Irish cattle; the injury caused to provincial business by the
export cartels of the capital—tainted a third and fourth. Over all, an
offence which smelt to Heaven, hung the blight of the criminal indulgence shown to Papists.

With the assembling of Parliament, these and allied scandals, not
to mention the small change of drunkenness, profane swearing and
Sunday dancing, came into their own. The House of Commons,
while forgetting neither international affairs nor the cause of true
religion, rose to the occasion. In the four months preceding its
reluctant adjournment on 4 June, it had given over fifty-two bills,
some of them trifling, but some of imposing trenchancy and scope,
their second reading, and still had another forty or so on the stocks.[1]
An adventitious factor, to which the speech from the throne had
made a passing reference, but which has received less attention from
historians than its importance deserves, heightened the sense of
urgency with which the House set about its work. Like some of its
modern analogues, the Great Depression of the early 1620's was an
event in political, as well as in economic, history. It had cast
sufficient shadows before to evoke administrative action in the
preceding year. It was not, however, till the gathering of members
at Westminster caused grazier, cereal farmer and textile exporter
to cap each other's tales of falling prices, unsold cattle, corn and
wool, and contracting foreign markets, that the dimensions and
significance of the collapse became apparent.

The note of emergency born of the crisis is conspicuous in the
first session, and, even in the second, when other issues hold the
floor, finds from time to time a voice. 'All grievances in the kingdom
are trifles, compared with the decay of trade.' 'The opening of our
trade, advancement of our home commodities and the increase of
commerce between man and man—these things are the most
weighty causes of the Parliament.' 'Poverty and want pinch the
kingdom..., and what are bills against drunkenness and for
keeping the Sabbath to remedy these wants?' 'We have sat here
these thirteen weeks, and have had several meetings for trade, and
yet are no nearer good success than we were at first.' 'For the ports,

---

[1] Notestein, Relf and Simpson, *Commons Debates*, vol. VII, pp. 300–7, which gives a
list of bills at different stages in June 1621.

they are decayed and looms decrease...I had rather be a ploughman than a merchant.' 'Our trade is decayed, and the letters and remedies of the Privy Council have wrought no good effects at all.' 'That which will content the country is not only bills...they look to have...some ease of trade as well as a few bills.'[1] These sentiments are voiced, not—with one exception—by the wild men from the out-ports, to whom the City was a plutocratic Babylon and the Merchant Adventurers Company a gang of brigands, but by responsible leaders of moderate opinion. The note of exasperated alarm sounded in them has a distant resemblance to the American mood of October 1929. It is not, perhaps, surprising that the proceedings of the House should have included legislative efforts at an economic new deal.

Cranfield, who sat in the Commons for Arundel till, in July, his peerage took him to the Lords,[2] was not of the ministers to whom Parliament was a word of fear. Observing economic trends and the reaction of London business to them—'the City undone; the trade of the kingdom lost; the merchants, to use their own term, "bought and sold"'[3]—he had long foreseen rough weather when the Commons met; but he remained convinced that for financial, if for no other, reasons the Government must face the storm. An acquaintance, such as few could boast, with the fiscal maladies of the regime had forced him to the conclusion that, as later he wrote, additional revenue on a scale which only subsidies could supply was the most 'honourable, just and certain cure'.[4] Hence, on joining the Council in January 1620, he had worked with the group which pressed a Parliament on James. Later, when all went awry, he did his unavailing best to avert a dissolution.

He played, while Parliament sat, a dual role. Sick of the corruption in high places by which his best-laid plans were wrecked, and with a business man's dislike of the disturbance of the settled course of trade by an executive at the mercy of feather-headed favourites, he found among his fellow-members an outlook which, in some

---

[1] The first three quotations are from Sir Edwyn Sandys, 29 and 31 May (*Proceedings and Debates...in 1621*, vol. II, pp. 121–2, 137, 141); the fourth from Sir Robert Crane, 30 May (*ibid.* p. 128); the fifth from John Delbridge, 31 May (Notestein, Relf and Simpson, *op. cit.* vol. III, p. 373); the two last from Sir Robert Phelips, 26 November and 15 December (*Proceedings and Debates...in 1621*, vol. II, pp. 212, 234).

[2] Cranfield was created Baron Cranfield of Cranfield on 9 July 1621.

[3] *Cranfield MSS.* no. 6774 (November 1619). See Appendix, I.

[4] *Ibid.* no. 6770.

respects, differed little from his own. The House, on its side, took him seriously. His success in the City and his administrative achievements gave him a standing which, merely as a minister, he would hardly have enjoyed. The opening speech[1] in which he defined the principal concerns of the moment as religion, justice, trade and patents, struck the right note, and made some stir. The alacrity with which he invited scrutiny of the methods of his own department[2] produced a good impression. His attitude on informers, on bills of conformity, on the fees of officers, on the need to define the jurisdiction of different courts, and on Floyd's case—though, on the last, he was, perhaps, too humane—was all that could be desired.[3] His peculiar qualifications made it natural that he should be voted into the chair of the Committee on Money, and play a prominent part in that on Trade.[4] His activities were not confined to these specialist spheres; but it was primarily, doubtless, his services as an economic expert which earned him the commendations of respected members of the House.

Against these successes there are failures to be set. Not all the latter were Cranfield's fault. Professor Notestein, in a brilliant essay, has depicted the process by which in the course of barely half a century, the House created a committee system, evolved an experienced and semi-permanent leadership, and thus prepared the way for the transference of the political initiative from the representatives of the Crown to the spokesman of the Commons.[5] When Cranfield for the second time entered Parliament, the transition was far from complete, but it was on the way. Its effect in complicating the tasks of ministers needs no emphasis. The King, reluctant to recognise that, in this region, the realities of power were slipping from his grasp, expected them, as in the past, to dominate the House with

---

[1] Notestein, Relf and Simpson, *op. cit.* vol. II, p. 44 (8 February). Chamberlain reports the good impression made by Cranfield's speech (McClure, *Letters of John Chamberlain*, vol. II, p. 345).

[2] Notestein, Relf and Simpson, *loc. cit.*

[3] *Ibid.* vols. III, pp. 20-1 (informers); II, pp. 223, 226-7 (bills of conformity); II, pp. 89-90, and III, pp. 23-4 (jurisdiction of courts); III, p. 127 (Floyd's case). Cranfield, like Sir E. Sandys, was against whipping Floyd.

[4] More than one committee dealt with money and trade. Cranfield appears normally to have acted as chairman of the Committee on Money, and Sir Edwyn Sandys of that on Trade. On occasion, however, we hear of a sub-committee 'for matter of trade and money', e.g. on 21 April, when Sandys presided (*ibid.* vol. III, p. 45). On 17 April Cranfield reported for the Committee on Trade (*ibid.* vol. II, p. 396). Apparently he had undertaken this business during the recess.

[5] Wallace Notestein, *The Winning of the Initiative by the House of Commons* (1926).

the authority which his confidence conferred; to repress its encroachments on spheres—in the language of today 'reserved subjects'—traditionally his own; to keep him informed, not only of the state of parliamentary opinion, but of the conduct and demeanour of individual members; and, if not, like their Elizabethan predecessors, to initiate legislation, at least to eliminate from it provisions repugnant to him. Such functions were not easily reconciled with the assumptions on which, by 1621, the House had learned to act. 'We about the chair', Cranfield once remarked, 'have a heavy burden, for we are questioned for all things in the House of the King.'[1] The truth is that the small group of Privy Councillors in the House of Commons, on paper nine, but in practice not more than six, were confronted in fact, if not in form, with the problems inseparable from a dual allegiance. Their first duty was to the King; but the House increasingly resented the conduct which that obligation entailed.

Cranfield was not a political thinker. Ingenious and resourceful in his own administrative field, he was conventional to the point of platitude outside it. Co-operation—'supplies and grievances going hand in hand'[2]—is his well-worn and unhelpful formula of salvation. Employed from time to time, though less often, it seems, than Calvert, the Secretary of State, to signify the royal pleasure to the House, and, more rarely, to represent its wishes to the King, he temporarily finds conciliation his unaccustomed role. His line in Parliament is to depict both it and the Crown as equally the victims of fraudulent officials; to magnify royal concessions; to put a favourable construction on communications entrusted to him by James; to report, if his own account may be accepted, the proceedings of members in a not less sympathetic light; and to endeavour to head debate off dangerous ground. If his success was modest, and diminished as the sessions advanced, the reason was not merely the natural suspicion felt by the House of one who rose from its sittings to recount them to the King.[3] It was also the personality of the reporter.

Whatever Cranfield's gifts, the virtues of the peace-maker were not among them. The truculence which had stood him in good stead in fighting business rivals and brow-beating officials was a weapon

---

[1] Notestein, Relf and Simpson, *op. cit.* vol. III, p. 135 (2 May).

[2] *Ibid.* vol. II, p. 22 (5 February).

[3] *Ibid.* vols. II, p. 411 (Sir Edward Cecil), III, p. 376 (Sir Edwin Sandys).

liable in Parliament to cut his hands. Not only did he quarrel—no difficult feat—with Sir Edward Coke, and, more surprising, extract an apology from him, but he also fell out with his principal colleague on the Committee for Trade, Sir Edwin Sandys, who told him bluntly that the greatest, on entering the House, 'must lay down his greatness at the door'.[1] The brusque superciliousness with which, on the strength of statistical information not accessible to private members, he snubbed a leading spokesman of the western out-ports, which, in his calmer moments, he desired to placate, was gratuitously rude.[2] His denunciation of 'Bills of Conformity' granted by the Chancery in favour of insolvent debtors hardly deserves Gardiner's reproach;[3] but the violence of his attack on Bacon, a fellow Privy Councillor, at whom the shaft was aimed, was politically inept, as well as indecent. His admonition to members that they might later be questioned for words spoken in the House invited trouble.[4] The letter in which one of his oldest friends, Ingram, the member for Appleby, implored him, for his own sake, to moderate his language, was unquestionably to the point.[5] It is not surprising that, before the session ended, he was shouted down.[6]

These unhappy idiosyncrasies weakened Cranfield's influence. His position, however, as the leading business expert in Parliament continued, when economic grievances and policy were the order of the day, to give him weight. On topics within that large and contentious sphere, there were, of course, cross-currents in the House. Wool-growers, middlemen and manufacturers did not always see eye to eye. The proposed prohibition of corn imports was welcomed by the cereal-farming areas, but alarmed Devonshire and London, which depended on imported grain, as well as the northern textile districts, whose kerseys shipped to Baltic markets were paid for in rye, and who argued in language later famous, 'no imports, no exports'. The Bill for free trade in cloth between Wales and England was supported by the Welsh producers, but alarmed Shrewsbury, whose Drapers' Company had hitherto sought to dominate the market. The long-standing feud between the provincial ports and the corporate capitalism of the metropolis flared up in some lively scenes.[7]

---

[1] *Ibid.* vol. III, p. 376. [2] *Ibid.* vol. III, pp. 363, 373.

[3] Gardiner, *History of England, 1603–1642*, vol. IV, p. 57.

[4] Notestein, Relf and Simpson, *op. cit.* vols. II, p. 416, III, pp. 392–3.

[5] *Ibid.* vol. III, p. 358, n. 19. [6] *Ibid.* vol. III, p. 346.

[7] The references in debate to the above topics are numerous. The following are a small selection from them: (a) Wool: Notestein, Relf and Simpson, *op. cit.* vols. II,

But, if the House was not the block of indignant unanimity sometimes depicted, it remains true, nevertheless, that on certain crucial
issues the majority of members quickly found a common mind.
Monopolies conferred by the executive; other patents, often then
described by the same name, such as those creating offices to register,
license, search and seal; the recent surtax on exported textiles
known by the awkward title of the pretermitted customs; impositions, a venerable grievance, levied by the Crown; now and then
extraordinary impositions levied by a charterd company, are cases
in point. In spite of Coke's reiterated 'freedom is the soul of trade',
to describe the mentality of the House as anti-restrictionist would
be an anachronism. Unquestionably, however, its hostility to
capricious intervention in business by the Crown and parties privileged by it was more violent and vocal than in any previous Parliament. The tenour of its debates, and the bills given a second reading,
are conclusive on that point.

Cranfield, if he did not share that outlook, felt some sympathy
with it. His dislike of patents was unconcealed. The 'fair pretences'[1]
by which, as a Master of Requests, he had seen charlatans wheedle
grants had nauseated him. The Cockayne fiasco had left him sceptical
of grandiose strokes of economic state-craft. He had laboured for
financial reasons to increase the revenue from the tariff; but he
admitted the burdens on exporters, and it was partly through his
influence that some recently imposed charges were later reduced.
Speaking on the chartered companies for foreign commerce, he
took the line that they must stand or fall by their public utility, and
by that alone.[2] The fury with which the agreeably intemperate
Mr Neale of Dartmouth let fly at the fatuity of the proposal to seek
light on the causes of the decay of trade by examining the Merchant
Adventurers, who are 'the most principal decayers of trade by the
great impositions they set on it', can hardly have pleased him; but
he left the defence of his company to the astute members for the City,
three out of four of whom were connected with it. Possibly he

pp. 75–9, 214–7, IV, pp. 95–8, 150–2. (*b*) Corn imports: *ibid.* vols. II, pp. 177–8, III,
pp. 280–3, IV, p. 357. (*c*) Welsh wool and Shrewsbury: *ibid.* vols. II, pp. 214–15, IV,
p. 150, VII, pp. 70–5; see also T. C. Mendenhall, *The Shrewsbury Drapers and the Welsh
Wool Trade in the XVI and XVII Centuries* (1953), chs. V–VII. (*d*) Complaints against
companies: Notestein, Relf and Simpson, *op. cit.* vols. III, pp. 105–6, IV, pp. 175–7,
271–2, V, pp. 162–3; *Proceedings and Debates...in 1621*, vol. I, pp. 320–30, where
Neale of Dartmouth lets himself go.

[1] Notestein, Relf and Simpson, *op. cit.* vol. II, p. 90.   [2] *Ibid.* vol. II, p. 89.

reflected that he had done, in his day, some interloping himself, and that the Crown was, in any case, unlikely to let so financially convenient an organisation down.[1]

His contribution to the debates on the depression emphasised two points. It was natural that the first feature to strike landowners unable to find purchasers for their produce or to get in rents should be, in the words of one of them, 'the want and scarcity of coin'.[2] Cranfield's angle of approach was different. In memoranda written shortly after his entry into public life, he had ascribed, in the conventional language of the day, the commercial difficulties of the country to the 'over-balancing' of trade, caused by the excess of unrequited imports, and recommended measures which, by diminishing their volume and ensuring that payment was made for them in goods, would diminish the supposedly mischievous outflow of bullion.[3] Seven years later his outlook was the same. Whether in an age of national bi-metallisms, currency depreciations, exchange competition and irregularly working mints, export controls on specie were as irrational as till recently they seemed, need not here be discussed. The classical case against restrictionism was to be stated by one whose commerce consisted in importing from India the produce of the Spice Islands; re-exporting part of it via London to continental markets; and settling his Eastern debts with funds reaching England from Spain, Genoa or Amsterdam in return for English textiles or oriental wares. It is unlikely that Cranfield was disposed to credit Mun's improbable doctrine that merchants, if they cast their coin upon the waters, would find it after many days, and that the forces which, when English prices were high, took specie out, would, when they fell, bring it in, with, in the language of the time, 'a duck in its mouth'. His own experience had been at the opposite pole. His business at Middelburg and Stade had consisted, in effect, in the sale of English woollens against Italian luxury fabrics. The symptoms that the former customers were turning to new-fangled arrangements, under which they sold their silks and satins through their own agents in

---

[1] If he did so reflect, he was right. See *Proceedings and Debates...in 1621*, vol. II, p. 16: 'His Majesty saith further that the Company of Merchant Adventurers have been with him, for that we seek to abridge them of what they have granted by their charter. He would have us meddle with abuses, but not with what belongs to the King and State.'

[2] *Ibid.* vol. I, p. 16.

[3] *Cranfield MSS.* nos. 4022 and 4023 (September 1614), 4532 (March 1615). See above, pp. 128–9.

London, filled him with dismay. Holding such views, he put, in his report from the Committee on Money, 'the unequal balancing of trade' at the head of his list of evils to be cured. 'The want of money', he retorted to a member who rehearsed the miseries resulting from it, 'is because trade is sick, and, as long as trade is sick, we shall be in want of money.'[1] He held, in short, that the fundamental fact was the collapse of textile exports. Not only domestic causes, but foreign tariffs and the political break-down of central Europe, had conspired to produce it.

The crisis, thus envisaged, was unquestionably grave. If Cranfield, in the second place, was less alarmed than other leading figures in the House, the reason was partly a more intimate familiarity with commerce and commercial policies than most of them could boast. With memories of earlier slumps and booms behind him, he saw existing distresses in perspective, and was immune to the emotions which wrung from a member the agonised cry that, rather than face his constituents without remedies in his hand, 'I wish I were in Heaven'.[2] Official information and a statistical turn of mind helped him to keep his head. He dismissed as a mare's nest allegations of a mercantile marine in ruins. To the piteous stories of the members from some western ports he replied by observing drily that the figures told a different tale. A return, which he offered to show them, proved that their trade had doubled since the Queen's time, and that, while their exports were now down, their imports were up.[3] That un-balance—trade 'great', but not 'good'—was regrettable on public grounds, but it did not look like destitution.

It is possible that Cranfield's public utterances were more sanguine than his private views. As a minister concerned for public order, and conscious that the two subsidies voted were a flea-bite to the Crown's actual needs, he may well have thought that political exigencies required him to affect more confidence than he felt. Some notes for a speech in Parliament, apparently drafted by

---

[1] Notestein, Relf and Simpson, *op. cit.* vol. VI, p. 296. For two instructive analyses of contemporary views, see J. D. Gould, 'The Trade Depression of the Early 1620's', in *Econ. Hist. Rev.*, 2nd series, vol. VII, no. 1, Aug. 1954, and B. E. Supple, 'Currency and Commerce in the Early Sevententh Century', *ibid.* vol. X, no. 2, December 1954. Both authors are disposed to take more seriously than has hitherto been the fashion contemporary complaints of the shortage of money.

[2] Notestein, Relf and Simpson, *op. cit.* vol. III, p. 344. The speaker was John Delbridge, member for Barnstaple.

[3] *Ibid.* vol. III, pp. 363, 373.

him in November, convey that impression. Their theme is the ingratitude which, because 'wool and corn, by reason of plenty and some foreign accidents [have] these two years fallen in price, and trade by like foreign occasions somewhat declined', forgets the cornucopia of blessings showered on the nation since the accession of the King. Religion flourishing; justice never better administered; universities and schools at the height of their vigour; Scotland at last a firm friend; Ireland turned from a liability to an asset; trade, staple commodities and land all advanced, till two years ago, one-third in value—such was the picture.[1] His discourse delivered at the opening of its second session was more restrained in tone, but similar in substance. Combining an admission of royal extravagances and official misdemeanours with an account of the aggravation of financial difficulties by the affairs of the Palatinate, he argued that the nation's long prosperity had left it with ample means to overcome the crisis.[2] So unplausible an optimism deepened gloom.[3]

'Let the burgesses of the out-ports', Cranfield had declared on the last day of the first session, 'make never so much haste into the country, there will be order taken, before they come home, for their ease and liberty of free trade.'[4] The legislative sterility of the preceding four months was partially compensated by the administrative activity of the Council; but the measures[5] adopted by it, in which he played an active part, needed time for their effects to show. It is

---

[1] *Cranfield MSS*. no. 7495; notes in Cranfield's hand, endorsed 'Paper for Parliament', printed Notestein, Relf and Simpson, *Commons Debates, 1621*, vol. VII, pp. 617–19, and dated by them 20 November 1621. For the remainder of this passage, see above, p. 18.

[2] *Ibid.* vol. III, pp. 424–6, 21 Nov. 1621.

[3] McClure, *Letters of John Chamberlain*, vol. II, p. 410 (24 November 1621). Most members of Parliament, Chamberlain remarks, 'knew the realm was never so bare and poor since he was born'.

[4] *Proceedings and Debates...in 1621*, vol. II, pp. 166–8 (4 June).

[5] A proclamation of 10 July 1621 revoked eighteen patents, and left the parties aggrieved to take legal proceedings in the case of seventeen more (Hyde Price, *English Patents of Monopoly* (1906), pp. 166–8). The other steps taken are conveniently summarised by Notestein, Relf and Simpson, *op. cit.* vol. III, pp. 415–16. They included among others (*a*) pressure on the Merchant Adventurers which induced them, at the instance of Cranfield, to admit (11 June) the out-ports to trade in the new draperies on the same terms as themselves, (*b*) the withdrawal by the Council of a previous order restricting to Oswestry the trade in Welsh cottons, (*c*) the resumption of negotiations between the East India Company and the Dutch, (*d*) action by the Council on a letter of 21 June from the King urging consideration of the scarcity of money, excess of imports over exports, exportation of wool, extraordinary charges at the ports and decay of trade. By way of dealing with the depression, the Council brought into existence several Committees. On 11 September it invited each of twenty ports to advise it on the decay of

not surprising, therefore, that when, on 20 November, Parliament reassembled, members should have spoken slightingly of their futility, and that the House should have taken up its programme of reform at the point where, four months before, it had laid it down. In the meantime, a shift in the distribution of ministerial offices had taken place. The most significant changes had been three. Within a fortnight of the adjournment, Williams had become Lord Keeper. Two and a half months later, at the end of September, Montagu had been succeeded by Cranfield as Lord Treasurer,[1] with, after the lapse of a few weeks, Weston, in place of Greville, now Lord Brooke, as Chancellor of the Exchequer.

2. EXCHEQUER PROBLEMS

Bacon, an active member of the Commission for the Treasury, had applauded its achievements, but deplored, as a nightmare of procrastination, the protracted deliberations required to produce them.[2] Urging the King to substitute an individual head for the labyrinthine intricacies of collective control, he had pleaded the necessity for a minister with the nerve to take the initiative in reform, act on his own responsibility and force the pace. Montagu, who in 1620 had invested £20,000 in the purchase of the office, appears to have had some leanings towards the light;[3] but the masterful energies demanded by the impatient sage—'invention, and stirring, and assiduity, and pursuit, with edifying one thing upon another'—were not his line.

Cranfield, for whom after nine months he was retired to make room, possessed by general consent these unpleasant indispensables, not merely in abundance, but to excess. The eight years which had elapsed since his appointment to his first official post had seen a sensational advance both in his private fortunes and in his standing

trade and scarcity of coin. On 14 October a Committee of the Council was ordered to review the evidence thus obtained. On 2 November, it appointed a Committee including fourteen M.P.'s, seven leading merchants (four of them M.P.'s) and three well-known customs officers (one of them an M.P.) and the Clerk (see Friis, *Alderman Cockayne's Project*, ch. VI). Action was also taken with regard to abuses in courts, informers and the excessive number of J.P.'s.

[1] *Handbook of British Chronology*, by F. M. Powicke, assisted by Charles Johnson and W. J. Harte (1939), p. 86, gives the dates of Cranfield's Treasurership as 29 September 1621 to 25 April 1624.

[2] J. Spedding, *op. cit.* vol. VII, pp. 85–90.

[3] See the reference to his papers, in Dietz, *English Public Finance*, p. 932.

in the public eye. The summaries[1] left by him of his financial position at different dates are in the nature rather of an annotated record of milestones passed than of precise and exhaustive statements; but the speed and continuity of the ascent depicted by them can have left the aspiring pilgrim few grounds for discontent. It is not merely that, by his own account, the net value of his assets increased over threefold between 1611 and 1620. Equally, or more, significant was the addition to the range of his interests made by the offices which favour in high places brought his way; by the expansion not only of the number, but, still more, of the scale, of his money-lending operations; and by his success in broadening the foundations of his position as a substantial landowner, which it had long been one of his ambitions to attain. Some of his largest territorial acquisitions came to him, it is true, somewhat later, between 1620 and 1624;[2] but already, at the first date, his real property could be put by him at something over a third of his total wealth. While, in short, his profits as an exporter had been by no means to be despised, they were not comparable in his case with the rewards of public life.

The complaint that 'the times allow anything to be done for money'[3] is in most ages common form. In few societies has it had more convincing evidence to cite than in the England of James I; and Cranfield's modest fortune, though far from classing him among the leviathans, was sufficient to make him, in the eyes of envious rivals, a competitor for advancement 'many thousands strong'.[4] It is probable, however, that, in the summer of 1621, his experience and record of achievement temporarily counted for more than his command of cash. 'A notable stirring man',[5] he had already over-hauled several government departments, had coached the Treasury

---

[1] E.g. Hist. MSS. Comm., *Cranfield Papers, 1551–1612*, pp. 28 (10 March 1599), 111 (31 December 1606), 346–50 (16 July 1611); *Cranfield MSS.* nos. 4076 (January 1612), 6844 (11 October 1620). The last of these give his total assets as approximately £90,000, including land and houses in London to the value of £11,760, and in Herts, Essex, Yorkshire and the Isle of Wight to that of £26,200.

[2] In August 1622, he values the lands recently acquired by him in Gloucestershire at £4000 and his Irish lands, also apparently a recent acquisition, at £4500 (*Cranfield MSS.* no. 8208). In February 1623, on the death of the Dowager Lady Sherley, he completed the process of acquiring the extensive Sherley estates in Sussex (Hist. MSS. Comm., *Cranfield Papers, 1551–1612*, p. xxv). Finally, during his Lord Treasurership, he bought from the Crown, presumably for sentimental reasons, the small manor of Cranfield in Bedfordshire (*ibid.* p. 26).

[3] *S.P.D. Jas. I*, xcv, no. 28, 31 January 1618.

[4] *Ibid.* xcv, no. 28.

[5] J. Howell, *Familiar Letters* (1903), vol. I, sect. III, Letter I, p. 156.

Commission from the start, and had joined it as a member on becoming a Privy Counsellor in January 1620. His promotion in the autumn of the following year, to the highest post in the service of the Crown may have been prompted, as Gardiner suggests[1], by his success, qualified though it was, in handling during five contentious months the Lower House; but it is difficult not to see it also as a characteristic stroke by Buckingham, whose dependence on an expensive patronage system to maintain his power made friends at the source of supplies important to him, and who may have counted on a protégé, recently married to a connection[2], to hold the purse-strings loose. If so, jobbery and merit for once went hand in hand. The truth was that Cranfield's record spoke for itself. The Lord Keeper, a sycophantic fox later his opponent, did not exaggerate too grossly when, in administering the oath of office, he quoted Hector's famous
                                    ...*Si Pergama dextra*
          Defendi possent...

and told the new Treasurer: 'You were stated in this place by the voice of the people, before you understood the pleasure of the King.'[3]

The Exchequer of the early Stuarts had a stormy past behind it; but, save for an occasional outrageous scandal, such as that of the nauseous Suffolk, the sensational chapters in its history were few. Cranfield's regime, too short for the health of the State, and too long for his own, may fairly be numbered among them. The place in the public eye of an office conferring an informal primacy among members of the Council, and held in a not distant past by the acknowledged leaders of national life, focused attention upon him. Together with the other posts which he continued to retain, it made him the natural target of communications—projects, petitions, remonstrances and complaints—of a kind today addressed to one or other of a dozen different ministries or unloaded on the Press. It is not surprising, therefore, that during the concluding phase of his political career, his papers should include a mass of miscellaneous business, ranging from international affairs, the reform of the Government of Ireland, economic policy towards Virginia, and commercial diplomacy to peasant grievances at home, civil service wrangles, and the sorrows of an aristocratic recusant persecuted by the malicious

---

[1] Gardiner, *History of England, 1603–1642*, vol. IV, p. 140.
[2] On 29 December 1619, Cranfield had married, as his second wife, Ann Brett, a cousin of Buckingham's mother, Lady Villiers.
[3] J. Hacket, *Scrinia Reserata* (1693), pp. 103–4.

zeal of Puritan justices, remotely connected, if at all, with the special duties of his new position. It was, however, as the financial navigator whom 'the King, in his piercing judgment, finds best apt to do him service',[1] that Cranfield had been summoned to take the helm. It is primarily, therefore, by the verdict on his efforts to steer a water-logged vessel through economic reefs that his reputation as Treasurer must stand or fall. How does he envisage his task?

'The first thing to be done is to know the true cause of his Majesty's wants. That known...the supplying of them will be effected without great difficulty.'[2] The conclusion did not long retain its sanguine gloss; but the premise was characteristic. Cranfield was of the administrators, in his day not a host, whose executive efficiency owed as much to care in diagnosis as to energy in action. It had long been his practice, before formulating a policy, to assemble a dossier of information on the dimensions and character of the problems concerned. Confronted by the tasks now devolving on him, it is to that familiar procedure that he instinctively recurs. Already in July, when a personal letter from Buckingham first gave him the news of his prospective promotion, he had used the breathing-space of the parliamentary recess to draft a skeleton return,[3] speci-fying the heads under which he desired material on the subject of the Crown's revenue, expenditure and debts to be collected and presented. Later, he enlarges his demands. Experience had con-vinced him that the roots of the crisis lay deep, and that, though palliatives had their use, only a fundamental change of regimen, which would vest in the Treasurer powers of control and veto hitherto denied him, could effect a cure. How more effectually convert colleagues and King to the acceptance of the drastic discipline required than by displaying the financial maladies of the regime, not as a passing weakness, but as a wasting disease—to use his own

---

[1] McClure, *op. cit.* vol. II, p. 399 (Chamberlain to Carleton, 13 October 1621). In view of Chamberlain's dislike of Cranfield, the words 'piercing judgment' have a slightly ironical sound.

[2] *Cranfield MSS.* no. 7500 (1621?), Notes in Cranfield's hand, apparently for a speech in Parliament. For a brief account of some features of the financial situation at the date when Cranfield became Lord Treasurer, see Appendices 2 and 3.

[3] *Ibid.* no. 6776 (July 1621): 'A balance of the King's estate to be made from Michael-mas next.' The return was to contain a statement classifying under the appropriate heads (*a*) the revenue, certain and casual, (*b*) expenditure, ordinary and extraordinary, (*c*) the various categories of debt, distinguishing between loans borrowed, arrears due for annuities, outstanding liabilities of individual departments, and anticipations upon the revenue of future years. Finally, it was to state in detail, giving names and amounts, the sums owed by private persons to the King.

word, a 'consumption'—progressively undermining health since the dynasty's accession? Once in command, therefore, he calls for comparative figures showing expenditure in the later years of the great Queen and the first decade of her successor, as well as in 1620–1.[1] Finally, thus armed, he sets to work himself, analysing in a series of papers the causes of present disorders, and discussing methods of grappling with them. Both the views advanced by him and the evidence on which they purport to be based, must be read, of course, with due reserve. If, in the following pages, the statistical data supplied him by his department, and his deductions from them, are quoted at some length, the reason is not that either can be accepted as beyond reproach. It is merely that together they reveal the materials on which the reformer worked and the conclusions to which the facts, as he knew them, seemed to him to point.

His starting-point is a question in our day rarely posed, but inevitable in his. It relates, not to the financial standing of the Government, but to the quality of the departmental organisation serving it. 'The more I look into the King's estate', he writes within a fortnight of entering office, 'the more cause I have to be troubled... I have...not to reform one particular, as in the Household, Navy, Wardrobe, etc....Every particular, as well of his Majesty's receipts, as of payments, hath been carried with so much disadvantage to the King as, until your Lordship see all, you will not believe that any men should be so careless and unfaithful.'[2] It is needless to add to the examples already given of the abuses by which King and public were robbed. It may be remarked, however, that an even graver evil than these specific, and often petty, misdemeanours by underpaid officials, consisted in the vice inseparable from arrangements under which, while large blocks of the ordinary revenue moved slowly, if at all, expenditure was only too easily increased by the caprices of a ruler notorious even among crowned heads for his

---

[1] *Cranfield MSS.* no. 541 (3 May 1622), Lord Treasurer to Sir Francis Gofton (one of the Auditors of the Prests): 'I find there is much difference in many branches of his Majesty's ordinary receipts and issues between the present time and those in the late reign of Queen Elizabeth.' He accordingly requests 'a certificate of the state of those accounts in the total receipts and disbursements as they fell out in the 30th year of Queen Elizabeth the 40th year of her reign, the 8th year of his Majesty and the last year, making one paper of the receipt and another of the issues, and distributing either of them into four columns'. Some of the information required had already been put together, shortly after he entered office. See, e.g. *ibid.* nos. 6987 and 7887.

[2] Goodman, *The Court of James I*, vol. II, pp. 207–9 (Cranfield to Buckingham, 12 October 1621).

indifference to prudential maxims concerning cloth and coats. A finance minister had no choice but to play to that depressing score. He must adapt himself to a situation in which the scope for financial strategy was small, and the importance of tactical efficiency overwhelmingly great. Cranfield's preoccupations reflect the priorities dictated by these unfriendly facts. The injurious reactions on the revenue of the depression in trade were only too obvious, and he more than once refers to them;[1] but the main burden of his argument is not, as at the moment when he became Treasurer it might well have been, the adverse set of economic tides. It is the commonplace necessity of ensuring that the Exchequer lays its hand on every penny of income due, and spends every penny on the service of the State.

If the deficiencies of the departmental machine were the Treasurer's first anxiety, the financial situation, in the second place, as revealed in the accounts prepared by it, was not calculated to allay alarm.[2] Wages and salaries in arrears; a vicious circle of deficits and debts, with, as a consequence of the resultant growth of two of 'the three cankers of his Majesty's estate, defalcations, anticipations and interest',[3] more deficits and debts to come; a service demoralised by the consciousness that economies effected by 'the care and providence of officers' will be stultified by recklessness in regions beyond their control, and that additions to the revenue will be dissipated as soon as made—such was the picture. Nor was that the worst. The two encouraging features revealed by Cranfield's survey of the preceding twenty years were the increases in the income yielded, first, and most conspicuously, by the tariff, and second, on a humbler scale, by the Court of Wards. For the rest, his conviction of the gravity of the regime's disorders was deepened by his glance at the history behind them. The financial débâcle was not, it was evident, an unpredictable disaster; on the contrary, it was the logical climax of a prolonged mismanagement, to some of whose inevitable consequences attention had repeatedly been drawn, and which, while permitting, since Elizabeth's closing years, a reduction of approximately one-third in the revenue from Crown estates, and of one-half in that from five other sources, had inflated nine heads of expenditure two and a half times.[4] Given a continuance of such conditions—

---

[1] E.g. *Cranfield MSS.* no. 6774, November 1619 (see Appendix, 1), and no. 6770, October 1621 (references to 'the want of money in the Kingdom; the great dearth; the state of trade').   [2] See Appendix 2.

[3] *Cranfield MSS.* no. 7887.   [4] See Appendix 3.

given, in Cranfield's words 'the decay of the Prince's ordinary revenue and increase of the ordinary charge'—did not the achievement of a balanced budget pass the wit of man?

Deficits and debts were no novelty; but the Treasurer's retort to the courtly triflers, who proclaimed that the State had nothing to fear from a continuance of burdens borne so long, was only too convincing. It was, in effect, that the world had changed, and that the follies of yesterday were the crimes of today. The Crown, in the first place, could no longer count on the reluctant auxiliaries whom, in the last resort, it had hitherto invoked. It had postponed an appeal to Parliament as long as it dared, nor had it been enthusiastic in wooing the City; but it had had till yesterday some grounds for believing that, in the last resort, it could fall back on both. Now those much-enduring cocks would no longer fight. To expect that, in the absence of drastic reforms, further grants would be added by the House to those already made, or that the City, with the interest on its last loan in arrears, would unbutton its pocket, was to cry for the moon. The second, and more alarming fact—'the present lamentable state of Christendom'[1]—was even less within the Government's control. During the peaceful interlude of James's earlier years, the Extraordinary account had played an unobtrusive role. Now, as the international crisis deepened, it crept from its corner, making frightful faces. The additional cost of the Palatinate business had been put by Cranfield in October 1621 at £162,000, the equivalent of the two subsidies just voted and already more than half spent. The main load of military expenditure, which the soldiers on the Council of War had put at five to six times that figure, was still to come.[2]

3. POSSIBILITIES AND PLANS

Faced by similar embarrassments, a Chancellor of a later age would presumably have cut expenditure, increased taxation, and funded such part of the floating debt as he could not hope in the near future to repay. The third member of the classical trinity was to remain a

[1] *Cranfield MSS.* no. 6770.

[2] *Ibid.* The items composing the total are given as (1) the Palatinate, £130,000 per year, (2) the Queen of Bohemia, £12,000 per year, (3) ambassadors, packets and other extraordinary charges incident to the business of the Palatinate, at the least or by estimate £20,000. Gardiner, *History of England*, vol. IV, p. 31, gives £900,000 a year as the estimate of the Council of War in its report of 13 February 1621. The same figure was given by Digby in his speech of 21 November in Parliament (Notestein, Relf and Simpson, *op. cit.* vol. III, p. 423).

mirage till half a century after Cranfield's death. The mass of short-term obligations, maturing at awkward moments, was a finance minister's nightmare; but it was one which no regime lacking the confidence of business could hope to dispel. The English division of financial powers between Crown and Parliament did not make the second course the open road which in the two neighbouring absolutisms it had become; but it left the door ajar. Something in the way of additional indirect taxation had recently been done, and there remained, Cranfield thought, something more to do. The first expedient, an economy campaign, would hit too many and too powerful interests to be described as the line of least resistance; but the savings promised by it were beyond dispute. Polite society might gnash its teeth; but the State would be nearer solvency, and, outside Court circles, the public would applaud.

We can observe the Treasurer weighing the alternatives, scrutinising the proposals submitted by his officials,[1] and, with the aid of his predecessor, Montagu, whom on occasion he calls into counsel, sifting the wheat from the chaff. Devaluation, and a change in the ratio of English and foreign currencies? Specious; but likely, on any but the shortest view, to do more harm than good. A veto on the payment of pensions? Already once attempted, and followed by a storm which caused the Council to retreat. The sale of Crown estates? The most eligible have already gone, and most of the remainder are let on long leases. Besides, alienations mean a diminished annual revenue, and leave the plain man asking whether, when Crown property has melted, he will not be called on to foot the bill. The conversion of lands into rents by granting them in fee-farm? Little cash in this, and much possible damage to the monarchy's prestige. A reduction in the cost to the Exchequer of the Irish administration? By all means; the Government has on three occasions investigated the problem, and is now sitting on it again. In addition to the last proposal, four others—disafforestation and sales of Crown timber; the strict enforcement of pecuniary penalties for encroachments on royal manors; less lavish hospitality to foreign embassies; and, above all, a temporary 'cutting-off of all bounty and magnificence'—receive an unqualified blessing.[2]

---

[1] *Cranfield MSS.* no. 6898 (8 October 1621): 'Considerations from Sir Francis Gofton and Sir Richard Sutton about his Majesty's estate.'

[2] *S.P.D. Jas. I*, CXXIII, no. 79 (October (?) 1621): 'Notes of plans suggested for relief of the King's Estate.' Cranfield describes the document as a selection from 'heads collected between my late Lord Treasurer Mandeville and myself'.

On certain of these issues Cranfield remained immovable. He refused to the end to play tricks with the currency.[1] He stubbornly resisted suggestions that the King should live on capital by disposing of his estates as, not only economic lunacy, but fatal to the political authority of the Crown.[2] In spite of the unhappy precedent of former failures, he intended, as his subsequent proceedings show, to fight his battle with the pensions racket through. The principal difference between the conclusions agreed with his predecessor and the programme expounded in his confidential papers is one which the reader familiar with his temperament will note without surprise. It consists in the uncompromising trenchancy of the policies which, when following his own bent, he feels moved to press. Whether his earlier proposal[3] of a cut of approximately one-quarter in twenty-two heads of outlay was meant to be taken *au pied de la lettre*, we cannot say; but undoubtedly his plans both for increasing the revenue and for reducing expenditure were marked by an audacity of which no one else had yet ventured to dream.

His demand for a capital levy is a case in point. Elizabeth, he argued, when grappling with the crisis of her closing years, had resorted to extraordinary expedients. Faced by an emergency not less grave, the King should do the same, and do it, not like her, by alienating Crown property, but by recovering from the beneficiaries of his bounty some small proportion of the fortunes conferred on them by him. A tax to the amount of one year's income should be imposed on all persons in enjoyment of pensions, fees, gifts of land and offices and all other grants in England, Scotland or Ireland bestowed by the King since his accession. Not only nobles and wealthy notabilities conspicuously backward in meeting their obligations, but even humble secretaries of officers of State, if in receipt of more than £20 a year, are to be swept into the net. The proceeds must be carried to the Extraordinary account, and used to meet the exceptional demands now descending upon it.[4] The economy measures contemplated are hardly less drastic. On the one hand, all Government departments must undergo the house-cleaning which had set the Household, Navy and Wardrobe temporarily, at least, to rights. Staffs must be cut, and sinecures, such as the

---

[1] Goodman, *The Court of James I*, vol. I, pp. 316–17.

[2] *Ibid.* vol. I, p. 322.   [3] *Cranfield MSS.* no. 6775 (July 1621).

[4] *Ibid.* no. 6770. An analogous, but less comprehensive, proposal for a fine of one or two years' fee of all offices held by letters patent is made in *ibid.* no. 7887, where it is suggested that the sum raised should be employed to meet the extraordinary expenditure.

guardianship of decayed or non-existent castles and forts, suppressed. It is essential, on the other, not only to curtail current outlay, but to arrest for good the fortune-hunters' plunder of royal assets, by which, with its own connivance, the Crown's position has been undermined. An absolute veto must be imposed, as by the so-called 'Book of Bounty'[1] in theory it long has been, on the alienation of the Crown's revenues, whether derived from land or from other sources. The preposterous practice of not only granting pensions, but permitting them to develop into perpetuities enjoyed by a succession of parties other than their first recipient, must cease. Both they, and—if functionless offices are inevitable—such offices as well, must expire with the death of the original grantee.[2]

Such reforms had all the reason on their side, and all the influence against them. The problem was to make the patient take the pill. Strict Treasury control with himself as controller-in-chief, would, Cranfield was convinced, do more than half the job. But how secure consent to a dictatorship of the Exchequer from a King wedded to his patronage and a Council basking in its beams? More than ordinary guile in broaching that repulsive innovation was obviously the first essential; and tact, its sponsor is aware, is not his longest suit. The master of system and method rises to the occasion. Accustomed, before acting, to commit his plans to paper, he adds to the draft of his proposals a recipe for simulated diffidence designed to ensure that, when they come to be expounded, the deficiencies of a too aggressive nature shall be neutralised by diplomatic art. He must bridle, he reminds himself, his fatal impetuosity; must be careful to hold his fire till his fellow-councillors have either stated their ideas or—more probably—shown by their silence that they have none to state; and must then introduce his scheme with words of modest deprecation—'not properly mine, but the necessity of the

---

[1] The 'Book of Bounty' had originated as an attempt on the part of Salisbury to check James' extravagance. It had been drawn up in 1608, and printed in 1611. A second edition appeared in 1619. It gave a list of twelve 'special things which we expressly command that no suitor presume to move us, being matters either contrary to our laws, or such principal profits of our Crown and settled revenue as are fit to be wholly reserved to our own use, until our estate be repaired'. The list included monopolies, rents, lands, leases in possession or reversion; all lands entailed upon the Crown; customs and impositions; licences to import or export commodities prohibited by law; profits arising out of our tenures, alienations and fines levied on recoveries, assarts and defective titles, as well as other matters. It also expressly laid down, 'no new pensions to be granted'. A reprint is given by Notestein, Relf and Simpson, *op. cit.* vol. VII, pp. 491–6.

[2] *Cranfield MSS.* nos. 6770, 7887. The proposals made in these documents, though differently worded, come to much the same.

times, and his Majesty's affairs, and the duties of my office, make me the proposer"[1]—so surprising in the speaker as to strike his colleagues dumb. Later, more than one attempt was made to reduce his principles to practice. The reception accorded such efforts suggests that his plans for a precautionary barrage had not been otiose.

Cranfield's central thesis—the keystone of his programme—was simplicity itself. It was the necessity that, in future, the Treasurer, not his royal master, should be the arbiter with whom decisions on requests involving expenditure would rest. Burghley, 'the screen',[2] in Bacon's phrase, between grant-grabbers and Queen, had left no successor to play the same essential role. As a consequence, those daughters of the horse-leech, petitioners and projectors, had had their way with James. The result—since 'to move the King to give now is to move the King to make himself miserable'[3]—had been cruel to him and ruinous to the country. In future, if Cranfield's procedural improvement be adopted, no project and no petition for a grant will receive royal approval, unless first submitted to the Treasurer, who, after considering the costs involved and the funds available to meet them, will at his discretion endorse, amend or reject it. The advantages of even so modest a measure of Treasury control will not be small. Expert advice will shelter the King from the torrent of demands and appeals, intrigues and disputes, at present afflicting him. The knowledge that suits addressed to the Crown must run the gauntlet of a critical scrutiny by official eyes will of itself halve their number. The gains, direct and indirect, to the Exchequer will be substantial. On the one hand, the financial liabilities, which most projects, however plausible, and all grants, entail, will at last be kept within bounds. On the other, the revival of political *moral* by austerity in high places will be a tonic to the revenue. Deprived of the hitherto unanswerable excuse that money voted to the King is a gift to genteel wastrels, Parliament and public may at last feel moved to come to the rescue.

4. THE TREASURER IN ACTION

There are conditions in which realism requires that the maxim *l'économique prime la politique* should be reversed. Cranfield's conception of a bridge of mutual confidence between King and people

---

[1] *Cranfield MSS.* no. 6770. [2] Spedding, *op. cit.* vol. VII, pp. 89–90.
[3] *Cranfield MSS.* no. 6770.

built by the reconciling hands of an impeccable Exchequer paid tribute to that truism. Odious in principle to the classes whose scope for loot it curtailed, the structure was to collapse before completed, and to bury the architect in its ruins. At the start, however, before the hunt was up, all went, if not well, at least better than, in view of the patient's condition, could reasonably have been hoped. The burdens of office—'not a quiet hour day or night'[1]— were not a trifle; but the first desperate months of Cranfield's term at the Exchequer, when emergency expedients were the order of the day and panic won him allies later to turn and rend him, may well have been its least unhappy phase. His credit in London and continental banking circles stood higher than the Government's. He used it to extract from a group of City acquaintances a small loan to meet military expenses in Germany, and contrived, by skilful exchange operations at Amsterdam, to transmit for employment in the Palatinate Dutch currency to the amount of twice the usual figure.[2] On the immediate economy and revenue measures required, he entered office with his mind made up. The dissipation of the Crown's scanty resources in unearned gifts to individuals had always exasperated him; while, as chairman of the Commission on debts due to and from the Crown, he had acquired a familiarity with the tax-evaders' arts which left him little to learn. He dealt, in his initial fortnight, with both subjects at once.

In the first place, he fired his opening round as Treasurer in the long and losing anti-pensions campaign touched on more at length below. He reissued an order temporarily suspending further payments pending an investigation into the justification, if any, existing for them; followed it up with a personal appeal to Buckingham to make the King understand the impossibility of refusing to honour old claims if, in accordance with his usual practice, he countenanced new; and concluded by imploring his patron to ensure that the prevalent abuse of sanctioning the transfer of the rights in question from party to party should be ended for good.[3] In the second place, he at once set to work to bring defaulting debtors, whether tax-payers, occupants of 'concealed lands', or withholders of payments due on

---

[1] *Ibid.* no. 2415 (19 October 1621), Sir Henry Fane to the Lord Treasurer. The letter also quotes Buckingham as saying that 'the King's estate was so desperate as he thought it could not prosper in any hands but your lordship's'.

[2] *A.P.C. 1621–3*, pp. 92–3 and 99–100 (Nov. 24 and 12 December 1621); Goodman, *The Court of James I*, vol. II, pp. 210–18 (Cranfield to Buckingham, 4 December 1621).

[3] Goodman, *op. cit.* vol. II, pp. 207–9 (Cranfield to Buckingham, 12 October 1621).

feudal tenures, to a long-delayed account.[1] Finally, he launched yet another attack, in addition to that set on foot by the Commission for the Treasury, on exorbitant deductions, in the shape of allowances and defalcations, from gross receipts, which depleted the revenues reaching the Exchequer.[2] As a result of it all, he could report in December that the crisis of two months before, if not yet a thing of the past, was no longer out of hand. Current expenditure had been met without borrowings and anticipations. Salaries and wages had for once been promptly paid. Money had been found for ambassadors, posts, munitions and forts, as well as, amid not unreasonable grumbles from the Treasurer, James' favourite foreign sycophant, the Duke of Holstein. The debt had not been reduced, but neither had it been increased.[3]

The Treasurer's initial *tour de force* might dazzle amateurs, enchanted by the prospect of a few unharassed months before them. Delivered from the Council's suggestion—'that damnable overture', as Cranfield had called it—that, in order to meet current expenses, the Crown jewels should be pawned, the King was in transports at the expeditious miracles worked;[4] but no one knew better than the magician how short a way his conjuring went. Financial history has a dullness all its own. The immediate and crucial problem was, as always, to balance the ordinary account. The conventional gambits were well known, and it would be cruel to weary the reader with the details of the game. Cuts in official salaries and expense accounts; the sale of such costly liabilities as ruined forts; vigilance in insisting that supernumerary posts, instead of being prolonged by reversions, should on the death of the grantee, automatically lapse[5] —all this was as much the common form of economy campaigns as were the Treasurer's efforts to put a more cheerful face on the other side of the account. Himself an old hand in manipulating customs-

---

[1] Goodman, *op. cit.* vol. II, pp. 207-9; J. Hacket, *Scrinia Reserata*, pp. 204-5.

[2] For returns to some of these inquiries see *Cranfield MSS.* e.g. nos. 6942 (October 1621, Office of the Pipe), 7225 (October 22, new impositions), 7223 (29 October, pretermitted customs), 7226 (22 March 1622, great customs).

[3] Goodman, *op. cit.* vol. II, pp. 210-18 (Cranfield to Buckingham, 4 December 1621).

[4] *Cranfield MSS.* no. 2462 (7 December 1621), Buckingham to Lord Treasurer: 'Have shown your letter to the King, he was exceedingly pleased with it, and holdeth it for a great mystery that, whereas at Hampton Court there was talk of pawning jewels only for his removal, now without any such step he is removed, and his servants paid, and yet money remaining'.

[5] *S.P.D. Jas. I*, CXXX, no. 136 (May (?) 1622): Notes of points to be represented to the Council for the reduction of the King's expenses.

farms, he knew too much of the tricks of the trade to succumb to the wiles of the capitalists tendering for them. He scraps the contract for the largest single concession, which his more pliable fellow-councillors had been disposed to accept; screws up the rent; rejects the syndicate's demand for the usual seven years' term, on the ground that, if the economic weather improves, the Crown must be free to bargain for better conditions at the end of three, and handles with equal decision two other farms.[1] The reconstruction of the impositions had been among his earliest projects of reform. Here, since the subject is political gunpowder, he walks warily; but he contrives, in an evil day for himself, to add three new duties,[2] two of them later to be incorporated in a new edition of the Book of Rates. To him, as to most substantial landowners, disputed titles and concealments were an old story. His papers show him engaged in constant communications with the Commission appointed to ferret out these abuses, and, since there is money in compositions with detected offenders, driving the investigators hard.[3] The plunder of Crown forests by neighbouring landowners had long been a scandal. He arranges that the Crown shall entrust him and the Chancellor of

[1] Cranfield's scope in dealing during his Treasurership with the customs-farms was limited by the fact that four of them (coal, currants, French wines and sweet wines) had been relet in 1620. He negotiated in December 1621 new contracts for the great farm, silk farm and tobacco farm. The two former, which he merged, he let for £160,000, as compared with the previous rents of £140,000 and £16,000, stipulating that the contracts should be breakable at the end of three years, in the too sanguine expectation that the cessation of 'the general wars in Christendom' would enable the Crown to secure better terms than in 1621 it could obtain. The increase in rent—only £4000—was a trifle; but it must be compared with the decrease of £10,000 which James had been warned by other advisers to expect. Cranfield also re-let the tobacco farm for £8000, claiming that the figure was £2000 more than the Council, when negotiating with the farmers, had been able to secure, and that the limitation of imports of Spanish tobacco, on which he had insisted, would create such a scarcity as to enable the next year's rent to be doubled (Goodman, *op. cit.* vol. II, pp. 210–18, Cranfield to Buckingham, 4 December 1621).

[2] The principal changes in the impositions were a doubling of the duty on French and Spanish wines, as addition of 10% to the duty on imported hops; and an increase of 9d. in the pound in the surtax on imports and exports by alien merchants (*A.P.C. 1621–3*, pp. 114, 115, 123, and 326, 10, 12, and 26 January and 30 September 1622). See also Dietz, *English Public Finance 1558–1641*, pp. 195, 374). The new edition of the Book of Rates, though printed, was held back for political reasons (see below, p. 242, n. 3) and was apparently never published.

[3] *Cranfield MSS.* no. 7121 ('A brief of the Commission for defective titles, as it is now to be renewed, allowed of by the Lord Treasurer and the Chancellor of the Exchequer, which was before in two Commissions') states the personnel of the Commission and specifies its functions at considerable length. The endorsement states that it was approved 'by the last Lord Treasurer' i.e. Mandeville.

the Exchequer with the task of making these properties more nearly a paying proposition; sets on foot the disafforestation of some, while insisting that encroachers on others shall discharge in full the fines due; and, anticipating appeals to the all-powerful Buckingham, beseeches him not to favour his clients to the prejudice of the King.[1]

No one, it seems, could see the Exchequer from within without feeling impelled to tune up the machine. Cranfield, as prompter to the Treasury Commission, had helped to get the task attempted once. With the issue of a new set of regulations for the guidance of officers in collecting the revenue,[2] he tries his hand at it again. In most matters of the kind, though he brought to them a dash and drive which put his predecessors to shame, he was treading beaten paths. If in a remoter, more important and much-debated field, discussion was at last converted into action, it is principally to him that such small credit as is due belongs. The condition of Ireland,[3] as a colony exploited by English capital and adventurers and simmering with revolt, made it a liability rather than an asset to the English Crown. When, in 1618, financial reform had become the topic of the day, the subjects suggested as ripe for treatment had included Ireland,[4] the cost of whose administration exceeded the revenue derived from it, and which it was hoped to make 'self-supporting' in the idiomatic Anglo-Saxon sense of supporting, not only herself, but English troops and officials as well. It is not clear that Cranfield had visited the country; but, as a farmer of the Irish customs, a member of the Commission appointed in 1616 to establish a staple system to control the export of Irish wool, and a speculator in Irish land, he had views, nevertheless, on its financial future. In one of his earliest memoranda on finance, he had noted the problem

---

[1] *Cranfield MSS.* no. 305 (20 October 1622): Letter from Treasurer to Buckingham, informing him that the King has given commission to Cranfield and the Chancellor to improve some of his remote forests, chases and waste grounds, both for the increase of the yearly revenue and to raise some money towards the supply of his pressing and manifold occasions. The Treasurer states that much Crown land has been wrongfully encroached on, and begs Buckingham not to countenance the suit for pardon of one of the offenders. *Ibid.* nos. 7753–4 (16 August 1622): Privy Seal to the Treasurer and under-Treasurer referring to a Commission of 12 April 1622 for disafforestation of six forests. There are many other papers on the disafforestation of particular forests, including correspondence between the Treasurer and John Pym, one of the Commissioners for the disafforestation of Blackmore and Pewsham, Wilts.

[2] *S.P.D. Jas. I*, CXXXI (14 June 1622).

[3] For the brief account here given of Cranfield's Irish policy I am principally indebted to Mr V. H. Treadwell.

[4] *S.P.D. Jas. I*, XCVII, no. 91 (March 1618).

as one with which the Government should grapple; and later references show that his interest in it was maintained. Shortly before taking charge of the Exchequer, he had assured Buckingham that the annual liability of £20,000 imposed on it by Ireland should and could without great difficulty be extinguished.[1]

Bacon in the preceding year had suggested a Commission; and the first idea of the Council, when, in the summer of 1621, it recurred to that suggestion, was an inquiry into the Ulster plantation. Cranfield took a broader view. Anxious though he was to arrest the drain on the English Exchequer, he recognised in the English regime in Ireland the vices of torpor, inefficiency and corruption which he had fought at home, and valued financial reform less as an end in itself than as a step towards raising the level of Irish public life. He was convinced, therefore, that fruitful results could be expected only from an investigation which, instead of being restricted to a single topic, produced a report embracing, in addition to the plantation policy, religion, recusancy, public finance and other topics, on the treatment of which a general settlement must depend; and the Council, after some hesitation, accepted that view. It was a moment when, immersed, as he was, in the state of the English finances, the effects of the depression, and the problems of a not too tractable Parliament, Cranfield was carrying too large a load, and it is not surprising that he paid the price in a breakdown before the year was out. He insisted, nevertheless, on adding Ireland to his other burdens. It was he who, in effect, drafted the Commission's terms of reference, who nominated, subject to the King's approval, its chairman and leading members and who finally, after further delays, got it safely embarked in the latter part of March 1622 for its scene of operations.[2] He owed much to the help of two public-spirited and expert associates, Sir Dudley Norton, secretary of state for Ireland, and Sir Francis Blundell, James' secretary for Irish affairs. Buckingham, on the other hand, appears to have been indifferent, and later hostile. His heart was apparently set on the more lucrative project of an Irish Court of Wards, in place of the existing Commission, with either himself, or a creature of his own, as Master, and the prospect of larger pickings in the shape of wardships. It is not

---

[1] Goodman, *op. cit.* vol. II, pp. 205–7 (28 July 1621), Cranfield to Buckingham.

[2] For the report of the Commission of 1622, see *Add. MSS.* 4756. That document, a summary of which was kindly lent me by Professor T. W. Moody, gives the excess of English expenditure (£70,000 odd) on Ireland over receipts as roughly £24,000.

surprising that the comparatively enlightened Irish policy of Cranfield, though it appears temporarily to have reduced the costs of Ireland to the English Exchequer, did not long survive his patron's return from Spain.

Few of these economies, and none of the additions to the revenue, could yield their fruits at once. Not only so, but it was a question whether, even when they matured, they would do more than meet the worst arrears of the debt, while leaving the situation which produced it as intractable as before. The benevolence launched in January 1622, did something to relax the strain.[1] It went better than the talk of passive resistance had caused to be expected; but it was slow to dribble in, and its political costs were high. Cranfield's reflections when, in the summer of that year, he surveys the ground lost and won, suggest a mood of despair foreign to his sanguine temper. In the three months since Easter, the ordinary expenditure, he writes, has amounted to £70,000, and the extraordinary to £80,000. Two principal branches of the ordinary revenue, the customs-farms and impositions, are too heavily charged with anticipations for the contributions made by them to be other than minute. The one substantial block of revenue has been the £63,000 received from the last subsidy, of which another £17,000 still remains to come. Not only, however, is the deficit on the last three months in the region of £86,000, but other liabilities, on account of ambassadors, the secret service, the navy, Ireland, diplomatic missions, interest on the City Corporation's loan of 1617—due at Christmas, but still unpaid—and other smaller items have, in the meantime, piled up to the tune of £98,000. 'What we have paid more than we have received', writes the unhappy minister, 'hath been made by the strictest means we could use to get in debts. And there are now to be satisfied all these payments, which are so pressing as I know not how to defer them, nor yet how to pay them at the present time.'[2] It seems possible that Cranfield overstated, formidable though they were, the inroads on the revenue made by anticipations, and underestimated the elasticity of the yield of part, at least, of the tariff. Even so, the prospect confronting him after nine months of office was grim. What was to be done?

The Treasurer's first reply to that question, which was given in

---

[1] Dietz, *English Public Finance*, p. 194, puts the yield of the benevolence at £105,489 in 1622 and £10,492 in 1623, a total equivalent to slightly more than three-quarters of the two subsidies granted in 1621.   [2] *Cranfield MSS.* no. 8231 (July 1622).

August, did not lack audacity. It was to admit that, for the moment, the Government was at the end of its financial tether, and to declare a moratorium in its favour by a temporary veto on all payments from the Exchequer.[1] His second reaction was equally characteristic. By way of arming himself for the battles which he saw before him, he resorted to his usual expedient of assembling a dossier of information. He instructed his officials to produce comparative figures of expenditure—though not, unfortunately, of revenue as well—for three recent years: 1618-19, when the Treasury Commission had begun its work; 1620-1, the period of Montagu's nine months' Treasurership; and his own opening chapter of 1621-2. The resulting returns[2] are not free from discrepancies; but they offer, at least, an indication of the scale and character of the perplexities afflicting him.

Their first and most significant feature leaps to the eye. The fundamental fact is no longer, as earlier in the reign, the reckless indulgence of the ruler in the expensive delights of domestic improvidence and display. These extravagances, it is true, continue, if in an attenuated form; but, though not negligible evils, they are now overshadowed by graver issues. The new and alarming aspect of the situation confronting a finance minister is the inflation and distortion of the ordinary expenditure caused by the reactions set in motion by the European war.[3] As the effects of the Bohemian

[1] *S.P.D. Jas. I*, CXXXII, no. 92 (10 August 1622, Locke to Carleton).

[2] These returns are contained in *Cranfield MSS*. nos. 7906-8, all dated 29 September 1622. No. 7906 gives 'the ordinary annual payments according to the balance made in 1619' and compares them with the sums paid for the year ending at Michaelmas 1622, distinguishing between the ordinary expenditure and 'the excesses upon the heads of the ordinary'. No. 7907 is a duplicate, in a slightly different form, of no. 7906. No. 7908 sets out 'the last two years' disbursements compared together'. It gives not only the ordinary expenditure and excesses upon the ordinary, but also the extraordinary expenditure, for the years 1620-1 and 1621-2. It appears, as already stated, that not all the ordinary expenditure is covered by these returns, Hence, while useful comparisons may be made between the totals of the three years concerned (1618-19, 1620-1, 1621-2), the figures of the aggregate ordinary outlay given by them are not comparable with those given for *c*. 1618 (*Add. MSS*. 11398), for 1620-1 (Hist. MSS. Comm., *Fourth Report*, pt I, App., p. 281, and for 1622-3 (*S.P.D. Jas. I*, CLVIII, no. 59).

[3] By, at any rate, the later years of James the partition between the ordinary and extraordinary expenditure was in practice wearing somewhat thin. An emergency, of course, causes the extraordinaries to bound up; but its effect is not confined to them. It also means that certain services maintained, in normal times, on a modest scale, from the Crown's ordinary revenue, are correspondingly enlarged. The increased costs, which their expansion involves, are extraordinary, in the literal sense of being occasioned by a special crisis. In fact, however, in the papers prepared for Cranfield, additions of this kind to the ordinary expenditure, e.g. for ambassadors, the secret service, the navy and the ordnance office, appear at times in the ordinary account.

revolution spread, they produce, in the first place, diplomatic activity on a formidable scale; a stream of missions, staged, staffed and adorned, for reasons of prestige, with the ostentatious disregard of economic realities parallelled, for the same motives, in our own day by the international banquets of poverty-stricken States; additional brigades of secret service agents; and an expanded postal service. They involve, in the second place, if not a rush, at least a slide into rearmament, in England affecting, above all, of course, the Navy, and also such minor departments as the Ordnance Office and the Armoury. The result was that, while the cost of the foreign and defence services debited to the ordinary account in 1618–19 had been respectively £16,400 and £42,600 odd, the corresponding figures in 1620–1 were £58,900, and £64,000, and in 1621–2, £79,900 and £98,800.

The virtual trebling of expenditure under these heads more than wiped out the savings effected on other items. It meant that at the end of the three years in question the ordinary expenditure of the Exchequer, including the additions to it—'the excesses upon the heads of the ordinary'—made as a result of the European crisis, was, in comparison with that of 1618–19, some 40% up.[1] Nor was that all. The condition of the extraordinary account was equally cheerless. It showed in 1621–2 an outlay not far short of twice that of the preceding year,[2] and unlikely, in view of the international situation, to be held at its existing level. It was brutal facts of this order which caused the Treasurer, when besieged by piteous appeals for grants and gifts, to darken yet further his reputation for a churlish misanthropy by hardening his heart. The essentials, as he saw them, were two. The first, in the absence of liberal grants from a Parliament unlikely to make them, and of which, in any case, the King at the moment would not hear, was to snatch such trifles in the way of additional income as he could, and, above all, to cut domestic

---

[1] The following table shows the ordinary expenditure in the three years 1618–19, 1620–1 and 1621–2, as given in *Cranfield MSS.* nos. 7906, and 7908:

	1618–19 £	1620–1 £	1621–2 £
Ordinary expenditure	310,459	278,495	277,308
Excesses upon the heads of the ordinary		106,640	154,633
Total	310,459	385,135	431,941

[2] The Extraordinaries amounted in 1621–2 to £176,171 as against £90,628 in 1620–1 (*ibid.* no. 7908).

expenditure to the bone. The second was to resist adventurous policies involving the assumption of costly liabilities abroad, except when plainly inevitable on grounds of national interest.

5. THE PENSIONS ISSUE

In the autumn of 1622, therefore, the war on two fronts, by which since his promotion to the Treasurership Cranfield had been faced, though not yet lost, was still far from won. In the matter of revenue he proceeded on lines already laid down. Gossip[1] depicted him as revolving sensational schemes for raising the wind, including the capital levy of which he had once been rash enough to write. In reality, the limitations on the fiscal powers of the Crown, which precluded it from tapping by direct taxation the increasing wealth of the country, allowed a Treasurer no large repertory of policies from which to choose. Middlesex, as he must now be called,[2] had already set on foot action designed to increase the receipts from the land revenue, the tariff, and the Court of Wards. These steps having been taken, he could do no more than throw his formidable administrative energy into the strict enforcement[3] of the measures concerned, and, for the rest, allow them time to produce their results, as in due course the two latter, it seems, did. A drastic economy policy, from which probably he hoped more, was not less of a necessity than at the moment, when, four years before, he had first put his shoulder to the wheel; but, if equally urgent, it was more difficult to apply.

As recently as 1618 it had been easy to point to frills to cut. Since then the movement launched in the autumn of the preceding year to put the Crown's establishments on something more nearly resembling a business footing had begun to yield its fruits. The reduction between 1618 and 1622, by not far short of one-fifth,[4] of

---

[1] *S.P.D. Jas. I*, CXXXIII, no. 59 (26 October 1622, Chamberlain to Carleton) lists several proposals, among them the demand for a year's salary from all officers of the Government and from courtiers and nobles.

[2] Cranfield had been created Earl of Middlesex on 16 September 1622.

[3] *Cranfield MSS.* no. 656 (10 June 1623), a warrant from the Lord Treasurer and Chancellor of the Exchequer, illustrating the action taken to compel defaulting sheriffs and other accountants to pay overdue arrears. *Ibid.* no. 8565 (15 October 1623), shows the Treasurer obtaining the royal permission to print, not, indeed, a new Book of Rates, but a new edition of the existing Book, incorporating recent additions, from the pretermitted customs of 1619 to the new duties of 1622 on wines.

[4] Actually 17%, on a comparison of the figures for 1618-19 in *Cranfield MSS.* nos. 7906-7 with those for 1621 in no. 7908. For James's estimate, in his speech to the Parliament of 1621, see p. 173 and App. no. 4.

the costs of the principal departments concerned was, in itself, a ground for satisfaction; but obviously it did not facilitate further advances along the same lines. It was natural, nevertheless, that, noting the sums still spent in 1621-2 on the Household, Wardrobe and Chamber, a hard-pressed Treasurer, who had seen these august institutions at close quarters, should ask himself whether a further instalment of his earlier curative treatment might not be overdue. The result of his meditations on that point was the appointment towards the end of 1622 of a Committee, apparently composed of Privy Councillors, to consider the possibilities of another dose of Household reform.[1] A second target was offered by a more formidable quarry. It consisted in an abuse, long Cranfield's *bête noire*, to which most previous projects of reform had alluded, but with which discretion had forbidden their authors to come to grips. While other domestic extravagances had shown a gratifying, if modest, decline, the sums absorbed by the beneficiaries of royal bounty had, at a time when England was in the throes of a depression and the Continent ablaze, continued actually to increase. The order temporarily withholding the accustomed largesse had evoked indignant growls,[2] but had now spent its force. Had not the moment come to deal the hydra-headed monster the *coup de grâce*?

'Pensions and annuities', 'annuities and fees', 'perpetuities, fees and annuities'—to cite a small selection of the expressions employed[3] —were a heterogeneous family. Their common characteristic was their source in a grant by the Crown, entitling the recipient to monies from public funds; but, that feature apart, they belonged to a variety of different types. Contemporary usage described by the word pension, not only the deferred pay or provision for the contingencies of life suggested by it today, but a mixed multitude

---

[1] McClure, *op. cit.* vol. II, p. 468 (21 December 1622, Chamberlain to Carleton). The allusion in *Cranfield MSS.* no. 7191 to the economies effected as a result of 'the late settling of the provision for the Household by way of composition for a reduction of charges' may, perhaps, refer to the Committee's work.

[2] E.g. *ibid.* no. 2460 (14 November 1621, The Earl of Nottingham to the Lord Treasurer): 'I do understand that your Lordship hath made a stay of all pensions till such time as you be well informed of the state of them.' The Earl then recites his former services, states that he 'cannot spend £200 in all the world', and begs that payment of his pensions be resumed.

[3] The word 'perpetuities' refers to grants not limited to a specific term of years, and in some cases, if not all, transferable by the original grantee to a third party by way of gift or sale. 'Fee' normally means an old-established salary for an office. A grant in addition to a fee was often a method of adjusting the salary to changed conditions, e.g. an advance in prices.

of payments, resembling each other in their legal origin, but differing widely in the reasons which caused them to be made. The term was applied to incomes as diverse as the remuneration of official posts, supplementary grants augmenting it, compensation for proprietary rights surrendered to the State, and annuities bought from the Crown as a speculation or investment, as well as to gifts to individuals bestowed on grounds too tenuous to define. The last—the functionless gratuities—made most public stir; but the view that the royal pension list was composed of them alone is an illusion. It also included items in whose absence the work of government could not have been carried on.

To attempt a logical classification of drafts on an account in which the public liabilities of the Crown and the private munificence of the King were inextricably intertwined would be an anachronism. The distinction of most importance to a minister bent on reform, if difficult to enforce in practice, was in principle plain. It was between payments for services rendered and financial favours conferred as an act of royal grace on influential notabilities whom the King desired to conciliate, or on dependents, associates and friends, whom, like Ahasuerus, he delighted to honour. The value of the grants in question, whatever their objectives, depended, of course, not merely on the nominal sums conveyed, but on their prospective duration and the solidity of the assets behind them. Judged by their financial backing, they fell into two distinct types, though the line of division cannot be sharply drawn. One considerable block consisted of assignments on different branches of the revenue for the benefit of privileged grantees, to whom the monies in question were paid before the balance of the total collected was transferred to the Exchequer. These 'deductions at the source' were not a trifle. Varying from 1% on the receipts from the farm of French and Rhenish wines to a third in the case of the Alienations Office and over half in that of the silk farm, they amounted, in 1620-1, under eleven heads of income, to just over one-tenth of the gross receipts.[1] A second, individually less impressive, but collectively more considerable, group of pensions was paid by the Exchequer on receipt

---

[1] *Cranfield MSS.* no. 6894 (6 October 1621), where the deductions by way of pensions (as distinct from departmental assignments and defalcations) are entered under the rubric: 'How much of the said annual revenue is assigned and paid in annuities and pensions, the money never coming into the Exchequer.' The sources of revenue listed here as charged with pensions number eleven. For the pretermitted customs and the charges on them see below, note 2, p. 216 and App. no. 2.

of a privy seal or other authorisation, from the funds from time to time at its disposal.[1] To describe the former type, which included the most imposing payments, as gilt-edged securities would be to exaggerate; but, when charged on a reliable source of income, for example the Great Farm or the Court of Wards, such pensions were, perhaps, as near an approach to that desirable category as the regime could offer. It is not surprising that when, in 1618, the farm of a new duty was in the wind, there should have been a rush to get a finger in the pie, by securing a grant on its receipts.[2] Pensions of the latter kind were less well secured. Being liable, when bad times or unexpected calls reduced the State's resources, to dwindle or run dry, these more speculative claims were a principal source of the stream of petitions, lamentations and reproaches dinned into the much enduring ears of officials, ministers and King.

The disquieting feature of the situation was not merely the trite contrast, by that time ancient history, between the parsimony of Elizabeth and the prodigality of her successor, which had evoked the Treasurer's acid comment that, on the average of the Queen's last five years, the cost of nine heads of outlay under her was exceeded in his day by the pensions bill alone.[3] The more formidable fact was that, in this form of indulgence, James in his dotage rivalled, or outdid, the prodigies of his prime. It was, in short, the continued increase of an expensive and unpopular largesse, against which, since his first entry into public life, Cranfield had repeatedly protested, and which now, in the reign's unhappy close, when other extravagances had, at least, been pruned, continued amid distress at home and war abroad unashamedly to swell. We do not know the proportions in which expenditure labelled 'pensions, annuities and fees' was divided between necessary or defensible payments to public servants and provender for the royal menagerie of genteel beggars. Justice requires that the former should be borne in mind; but in holding that the cost of the latter was not a bagatelle,

[1] The significance of the distinction may be illustrated by a letter from the Earl of Nottingham to the Treasurer (*ibid.* no. 2460, 14 November 1621). The Earl states that, on giving up the Admiralty, he had been granted by the King £200 to be paid out of the Great Customs, 'for I desired it should not be paid out of the Exchequer, because I thought there were some there that did not befriend me, so that some stay might be made of it'.

[2] The largest grantees planted on the farm of the pretermitted customs were the Marquis of Hamilton (£2500) and Sir George Goring (£2000). For the attitude of the City to these grants, see Dietz, *English Public Finance*, pp. 373–4.

[3] See, e.g. *Cranfield MSS.* no. 7887.

Cranfield, like Raleigh[1] before him, shared a common, if sometimes exaggerated, view. The bill for both together was put in 1618–19 at just under £63,000. Two years later, in 1620–1, it was thought to be 16% up. Then, after the suspending order of September of that year, it was either, as one set of figures indicates, stabilised at the higher level, or as suggested by another, again on the rise.[2] A second and more determined onslaught on the Blatant Beast was obviously not the path of prudence. It is to Middlesex's credit that he decided to face the monster's teeth and claws.

His views on the expedients to employ had passed through several phases. He had considered whether grants obtained by misrepresentation should not be tested in the courts; had urged that pensions should be made non-transferable during the life, and non-renewable at the death, of the first grantee, on the ground that, in that event, the evil, instead of, as too often, being 'immortal', would in time abolish itself; and when, on learning of his prospective promotion to the Treasurership, he returned to the problem, had suggested a cut in the pensions bill of roughly one-third.[3] Now, after fifteen months of office, he chose a more audacious course. The key position was obvious. The cause of the malady was the unending flow of grants. The sole effective remedy, it seemed, was to turn off the tap, and thus to arrest the fatal stream, not merely in detail, as and when particular concessions were brought to his attention, but at the source. Control, since it implied the possibility of a veto on royal bounty, required, in order to produce results, that the King should first be brought to heel. The policy adopted by Middlesex, therefore, was that expounded by him a year before in a paper on which he had not hitherto ventured to act, but the substance of which was now embodied in a royal declaration issued on 7 October 1622.[4] In future, it was announced, no grant relating to the revenues of Ireland and to customs and impositions in England; no grant of

---

[1] Raleigh, 'The Prerogative of Parliaments', in Oldys and Birch, *The Works of Sir Walter Raleigh*, vol. VIII, pp. 193–5.

[2] *Cranfield MSS*. nos. 7906 and 7908 (29 September 1622), give the following figures of expenditure on perpetuities, fees and annuities: 1618–19, £62,895; 1620–1, £74,136; 1621–2, £73,839. Another paper of the same date (*ibid*. no. 7389), states that, allowing for diminutions caused by death, surrenders and determinations, the net increase between Michaelmas 1621 and Michaelmas 1622 was only £4,472. Figures kindly shown me by Mr G. Hammersley of the sums paid in grants between Michaelmas 1618–19 and Michaelmas 1622–3, though differing somewhat from those here given, support the view of an increase in the later years of James.

[3] *Cranfield MSS*. no. 6775 (July 1621).   [4] *S.P.D. Jas. I*, CXXXIII, no. 41.

Exchequer lands, pensions and allowances; and, finally, none involving lands owned by the Duchy of Lancaster, was to be legally valid, unless first approved by the Treasurer, Chancellor of the Exchequer and other officers concerned, and, in the case of Duchy lands, by the Chancellor of the Duchy. Deprived of its opportunities, the unsavoury business of personal solicitation, jobbery and intrigue would, it was argued, automatically cease. The majority of demands for bounty would be strangled at birth. The minority which continued to reach the royal ear would be stamped with the seal of an official *imprimatur*.

The merits of this decorous substitution of minister for monarch, as the fountain of such attenuated blessings as should in future flow, were greater than its chances of success. Buckingham had saluted its author's opening strokes with the remark that 'hitherto the King had been sharked upon by all men and that now the tables must be turned'; while James had imposed a twelve months' veto on demands by Buckingham involving further charges on the revenue, and the Prince, it was alleged, had combined with both in a self-denying ordinance to refer all petitions for grants to the judgment of the Treasurer.[1] Detested by the Court, but for a time encouraged by the approval of its master and the favourite, Middlesex appears to have counted on a continued disposition in high places to see his struggle with embittered gratuity-hunters through. The subsequent discovery that, once the fears of an immediate breakdown were removed, none of his supposed allies was of the metal to back an unpopular cause on public grounds alone, seems to have taken him by surprise.

'The Marquis', observed a contemporary, was 'in courtesy more luxuriant than was fit for his place; not willing to deny a suit, but prone to gratify all strangers, especially if any of his kindred brought them in their hand; and was far more apt to believe them that asked him a favour than those that would persuade him it was not to be granted.'[2] His appeals on behalf of hungry clients, begun within two months of Cranfield's entry into office, and during the ensuing year a rising flood,[3] should have taught the Treasurer what to expect. The truth is that grants were for Buckingham a piece of patronage too convenient to forego. It was not to be supposed that a self-denying ordinance put into the mouth of James by one whom he

---

[1] *Cranfield MSS*. nos. 22, 2415.   [2] J. Hackett, *Scrinia Reserata*, p. 107.
[3] E.g. *Cranfield MSS*. nos. 2417, 2571, 7708, 8711, 8718, 2459.

regarded as a creature of his own would cause the adventurer to mend his expensive ways; and reproachful reminders from his protégé[1] that his demands were not only ruinous to the Exchequer but in flagrant contradiction with principles laid down by Buckingham himself, fell on stony ground. The ambitions of the favourite were only less fatal than the futility of the aged and unhappy King. James did not conceal his disgust at the parasites who plagued him. He respected Middlesex and promised him that, during Buckingham's absence, no new concessions should pass;[2] but his practice was as incorrigible as his professions were fair. The mingled imperiousness and pathos of his letters[3] to his formidable minister reveal him still wedded, at the end of his reign, to the financial frivolities in which it had begun. While the generals sell the pass, their subordinate continues to fight his guns, indecently regardless of the eminence of the heads on which his barrage falls. Alleging 'the over-ruling necessities of the King',[4] he snubs an influential peer with a blunt refusal to entertain his suit; spins out negotiations; displays an ingenuity in referring an applicant to half-a-dozen other sources of supply which wrings from the unhappy knight the anguished cry, 'how many varieties of delay your Lordship has found to torment me, the Giver of all doth know';[5] interposes obstacles to personal interviews between petitioners and the king; and cuts down such claims as he consents to consider with a scrupulous conscientiousness at once maddening and beyond reproach. When at last brought to bay, he insists on the time-consuming formality of a special warrant as the necessary condition of approving a grant; and then, to crown all, surrounds the concession with a barbed wire entanglement of technical limitations nicely calculated to deprive it of more than half its charms.[6]

What effects, if any, these labours produced, it is impossible to say. The lynch-pin of Middlesex's policy had been the ban of 7 October imposed on acts of royal bounty not sanctioned by himself

---

[1] *Cabala*, pp. 266–7 (Earl of Middlesex to Duke of Buckingham, n.d.).

[2] Goodman, *op. cit.* vol. II, pp. 267–9.

[3] *Cal. S.P.D.* for the first six months of 1623 contains summaries of many such letters. CLXIV, no. 39, is an extreme example, though the sum involved was in that case trifling.

[4] *Cranfield MSS.* no. 8742 (24 November 1622, Lord Treasurer to Earl of Exeter).

[5] *Ibid.* no. 1105 (1 June 1622, Sir George Chaworth to Lord Treasurer).

[6] *Ibid.* no. 1128 (1 March 1623, Lord Treasurer to Sir Thomas Coventry, Attorney-General).

or his department. The resentment aroused in the quarters most directly affected by so sinister a lengthening of the bureaucratic arm was immediate and sustained. Within a week of the odious order's issue, the Lord Deputy of Ireland was protesting to the Council the disastrous results which he expected from the block of Irish pensions, some of which represented not gratuities, but compensation for lands surrendered in furtherance of the official plantation programme.[1] English exasperation, if less easily canalised, was equally acute. It is not a chance that later, when the offender's days were numbered, Fleetwood, by way of mobilising in Parliament the mass resentment required to bring him down, should have prefaced his exposure of abuses in the Court of Wards by a more general indictment of the presumption which insisted that the last word on grants should rest with minister,[2] not King. In the intervening eighteen months, the victims of the Treasurer's vigilance paid by their indignant outcries a tribute to his success. Evidence on a scale to permit a general statement as to the results of his campaign is still to seek. It seems clear, however, that such victories as he won left the essentials of the situation unchanged. Alarming and exasperating to individuals, they lacked the consistency and force to overthrow a system connived at by the very powers in whose interest his attacks on it were launched. In reality, only an impossible divorce between James and his entourage, accompanied by an equally improbable change of heart in members of the Council, could have served the reformer's turn. As things were, the courtly Philistines who plundered the master were too many for the man. Complaints[3] of rebuffs inflicted by Middlesex on Buckingham's impecunious friends pursued the all-powerful patron even to Madrid; but another correspondent tells a different tale. It is that the Treasurer's reforming whirlwind has proved a six months' wonder, and that, now that the storm has passed, the old game of grab goes on as merrily as before. 'By importunity men are growing to do their business. The King is much disgusted with it.'[4]

---

[1] *Cal. S.P. Ireland, 1615–25*, no. 959 (14 October 1622).
[2] See below, p. 240, n. 2.
[3] Goodman, *The Court of James I*, vol. II, pp. 302–3 (1 August 1623, R. Turpyn to Buckingham).
[4] *Ibid.* pp. 267–9 (29 March 1623, Toby Matthews to Buckingham).

6. THE CRISIS IN FOREIGN AFFAIRS

'The Lord Treasurer', wrote in January 1623 an unfriendly observer, 'still stands as right as ever he did, though he were much lifted at, and many complaints and petitions made against him.'[1] The ensuing twelve months saw the climax and the close of the constructive phase of the reformer's labours. Six years divided Cranfield's initial onslaught on departmental waste from his final battles against favourite and prince for economy and peace. His financial policy during that period had followed varying lines, but its overriding aim had been throughout the same. Its purpose has been an improvement in the ordinary account sufficient to enable the Crown to approach a critical House of Commons, not as a self-made mendicant imploring relief, but with the assurance of a solvent and respected partner. The only statement which we possess of the ordinary revenue and expenditure in the twelve months ending Michaelmas 1623, suggests that in his last full year at the Exchequer that objective was on the way to be achieved. It is possible that the surplus shown by it was fictitious, and that a diminished deficit would be nearer the truth. If, however, an approach had been made, as on either view it had, towards a regime which, apart from special emergencies, paid, or nearly paid, its way, the principal explanation of that happier condition was not far to seek. In consisted in expenditure reduced and revenues increased in departments of the national economy whose improvement since, seven years before, in 1617, he was summoned to the rescue, Cranfield had made his special aim.[2]

---

[1] McClure, *Letters of John Chamberlain*, vol. II, p. 471 (4 January 1623, Chamberlain to Carleton).

[2] *S.P.D. Jas. I*, CLVIII, no. 59 (revenue and expenditure 1622–3). The illusion of a favourable balance was so easy to create that suspicion may be pardoned. It should be noted, however, that Gardiner, *History of England, 1603–1642*, vol. V, p. 229, refers to Middlesex as 'the Minister who had built up a surplus out of a deficit by the unremitting labour of years'. The more recent verdict of Professor A. P. Newton is substantially the same: 'Middlesex, aided by the dogged labours of men like Weston, Pye and Gofton, had by the middle of 1623 succeeded in making the Exchequer solvent for the first time for many years' (Paper on 'Cranfield as Treasurer' by A. P. Newton, among those in box marked nos. 1100–99). A comparison of *S.P.D. Jas. I*, CLVII, no. 59, with *Add. MSS.* 11598, which states the revenue and expenditure *c.* 1618, gives a rough idea of the changes by which the deficit at the earlier date of £15,000 odd had been replaced by a surplus of just under £36,000 at the later. The most striking were, on the revenue side, the increased income from the tariff (Customs and Impositions), and the Court of Wards, and on the side of expenditure, the decreased cost of the Household, including the Royal family, and its adjuncts (Great Wardrobe and Robes, Chamber, Privy Purse and New Year Gifts) and Ireland.

Apart, therefore—a formidable exception—from extraordinary liabilities, the State's financial health seemed somewhat on the mend. The obvious prescription, in such conditions, was the mixture as before. The Treasurer acted on that maxim;[1] but it is probable that his earlier operations had depleted his repertory of reforms, and, even had his quiver remained full, he could hardly have resisted the necessities imposing a change of targets. The truth is that the circumstances of the moment made it inevitable that efforts, however desirable, to improve the Crown's ordinary account should take a second place. In 1623, even more than in the three preceding years, domestic policy in general, and fiscal policy in particular, were overshadowed by perplexities born of the widening ramifications of the international crisis. It is not surprising that, during this last chapter of his official career, the Treasurer's interests and activities should reveal a corresponding change of front. His hope had been to restore to the Crown the freedom of manœuvre which only financial stability could confer. The extraordinary demands now descending on the Exchequer made that ambition a mirage. During the remainder of his term of office, therefore, the former leader of assaults on the strongholds of established torpor and greed is thrown on the defensive. His chief preoccupation is not, as hitherto, to conduct a planned advance towards a more orderly, efficient and reputable financial system. It is to hold, under overwhelming pressure, a crumbling line.

One obvious weakness of the financial techniques, and indeed of the economies, of the day consisted in the difficulty experienced by them in mobilising resources to meet an emergency. The three traditional English stand-bys had been accumulated reserves, the support of the City, and a compliant Parliament. The Queen, in the crisis of the eighties, had relied on all at once. Her successor, without cash, credit or good will, could count on none. The annual expenditure involved in the half-hearted defence of the Palatinate,

---

[1] With the exception of his struggle to cut pensions and increase the land revenue, the measures in question were mostly small beer. They included the already mentioned committee to effect further economies in the Household, intensified efforts to make the Commission for Defective Titles a useful fiscal instrument (*Cranfield MSS.*, no. 1121, 14 November 1622); the prosecution of the long-discussed project to induce the shareholders in the New River Company to sell their holdings to the Crown (*ibid.* nos. 1008, 2422, 621, 1177); the appointment of a Commission to survey fortifications, with instructions either to make them of some military value or to scrap them outright (*ibid.* no. 1163, 30 Aug. 1623, and McClure, *op. cit.* vol. II, pp. 513–14); and, of course, recurrent attempts to prevent tax evasion by influential personages.

subsidies to its exiled rulers, and the inevitable crop of diplomatic missions, may have been, it seems, in the region of £80,000, to which should be added part of the cost of naval rearmament and the trifle paid as interest on the Danish loan.[1] Judged even by the standards of the time, the total—not much more than half the sum despatched to the Netherlands in the pre-Armada year—was not alarming; but it sufficed to carry an already floundering regime out of its depth, and justified the fear that a wave of new demands would sink it.

In February 1623, the fatality came, from a quarter which few could have foreseen. The political imbecilities of the amateur diplomacy of Buckingham and Charles are so imposing as to dwarf its less spectacular financial results. The latter, however, were on a scale to count. Eight years were to elapse before the fiscal legacy of the Spanish escapade was finally wound up. Its total cost cannot be precisely stated; but—to ignore the expensive incidentals—two items alone, the Prince's outlay in Spain and the cost of the armada mobilised for several months on end to escort the truants home, together ran to a figure which put the Government's German liabilities in the shade.[2] The leading actors in the farce appear to have viewed their adventure not merely as a brilliant political stroke, but as a joy-ride to be conducted regardless of expense. It is not surprising that financially it was a disaster.

The Treasurer, it appears, was not consulted as to that, or any other, aspect of the new departure in foreign policy; but it was

---

[1] *Cranfield MSS.* no. 6890 (1624), 'Paper concerning the extra-ordinary expenditure and the satisfying thereof', and the statements of Middlesex and Weston to Parliament in early March 1624 (*S.P.D. Jas. I*, CLX, no. 30) give the extraordinary expenditure for the period, roughly 4½ years, since Michaelmas 1619. The former puts the figure for the defence of the Palatinate at £172,388, that for 'Ambassadors extraordinary and others sent abroad' at £145,763, and 'for the expense of the King and Queen of Bohemia and other their necessaries' at £30,300, a total of £348,450, or approximately £77,000 per year. (These figures somewhat exaggerate the German expenses of the Government, as they include all extraordinary diplomatic charges.) The sum paid as interest on the Danish loan is given at £5000. The extraordinary naval expenses are not stated, but Cranfield's paper remarks that during the last five years 'all the ships have been repaired and ten new built, besides building of docks and new magazines'.

[2] *Hist. MSS. Comm., Fourth Report*, pt I, App., pp. 276–7, gives the total of the Prince's disbursements in Spain as £44,477. *Cranfield MSS.* no. 7890 puts the cost of the naval squadron to escort him home at £52,226. In addition, Buckingham was alleged to have spent in Spain £28,000 odd of his own, part of which was subsequently repaid to his executors (Dietz, *English Public Finance*, p. 197). The £50,000 borrowed by Cottington appears to have been repaid in 1631 (*ibid*). The subsidiaries—messengers, presents for ambassadors, jewels for the Infanta etc.—seem to be incalculable.

inevitably he who stood the racket. Everything, from the £50,000 borrowed at the start by Cottington, a reluctant bear-leader, and the £10,000 which, shortly after his arrival in Madrid, Buckingham requests Middlesex to have available on demand,[1] to Charles' instruction, five months later, on the eve of his return, to put £30,000 at his disposal for parting presents and travelling expenses,[2] ultimately comes back on the Exchequer and its unhappy head. To Middlesex the excursion in search of a wife was neither a romantic venture nor a diplomatic *coup*. It was a rash speculation, whose only too probable failure would be a disaster both for the State and for himself, but which might conceivably, given exceptional skill and luck, yield handsome dividends. Viewing the transaction with business eyes, he is torn between horror at the desperate straits—'I was never put to such a plunge for money'[3]—to which its initial costs have reduced him; dismay at the inevitable consequential demands; and a fading hope that the gilt-edged bride, with a dowry put by rumour at £600,000, may in the end make the game worth the outrageously expensive candle.

The Treasurer's letters to his patron[4]—letters couched in terms of a feverish anxiety markedly in contrast with the writer's usual self-possessed and sanguine tone—ring the changes on these themes. He for his part, he protests, is doing his utmost, to the point of mortgaging his land and jeopardising 'an estate and credit' acquired by thirty years of labour, to 'keep things alive until we may be supplied by you'; but his efforts will be fruitless unless Buckingham, on his side, will face the brutal truth that 'compliments [are] of no

---

[1] Buckingham to Cranfield, 18 March 1623, printed in R. Davies, *The Greatest House at Chelsey* (1914), pp. 122–245.

[2] *Cranfield MSS.* no. 2454 (18 August 1623), Charles to Lord Treasurer. Thanks him for paying bills of exchange for £12,000 upon Mr Alexander Stafford. Is about to return to England. Needs money for presents, gifts and expenses of journey. Asks Lord Treasurer immediately to put £30,000 in the hands of Stafford. Informs him that a further £2400 has been charged on Stafford by Charles' order.

[3] *Harl. MSS.* 2454 (30 March 1623, Middlesex to Buckingham).

[4] For the passages cited below see in particular *Harl. MSS.* 1581, ff. 93–7 (letters from Middlesex to Buckingham, 30 March, 8 April, 3 May 1623); *Egerton MSS.* 2595, f. 183 (letter from Middlesex to Earl of Carlisle, then on his way to Spain, 30 March), and 1525, f. 26 (letter of Middlesex to Sir Anthony Ashley, 26 July). Other correspondence between Middlesex and Buckingham is printed in E. Lodge, *Portraits of Illustrious Personages of Great Britain*, vol. IV, and R. Davies, *op. cit.* I am indebted to the kindness of Mr Paul Johnson, of the University of Minnesota, for some of these references, as also for showing me his transcripts from the *Harl.* and *Egerton MSS.*

value in comparison with money' and base his conduct on it. The essentials are three. The impecunious pilgrims must cut their expenses to the bone. Charles must somehow be induced to refrain from pacifying his creditors by drawing bills for Middlesex, with an empty Exchequer behind him, to meet as best he can. Above all, cash—'I know not whether the necessity or the expectation of it be the greatest'—must be remitted from Spain, and since preparations for the marriage are already eating money, remitted, if not, as Middlesex would have preferred, in the form of an immediate instalment, at least as soon as the Infanta is on the way. 'I beseech your Lordship to take especial care to bring as much of the portion in money with the fleet as is possible. I dare not write how much it will concern the King.' The question of the jointure caused Middlesex some perplexity. Reluctant to provide it in real property, for fear that to do so would reveal to unfriendly eyes 'the miserable condition of his Majesty's estate in land', he hoped that, if a reasonable income were assured to the Princess, the decision as to the revenue on which it should be secured might be left to the English Government. Here again, however, his first concern was speed. He fell, it must be confessed, below his usual reasonable self in hinting, as at times he does, that the harness, or part of it, might be handed over before the contract to buy the mare was through; but he was a man driven beyond endurance. The concluding words of the last letter of the series—'I hope your Grace will not forget the portion; I have not had so much as one comfortable word in any letter concerning it'—are a cry from the heart.

In approaching a vain, pigeon-witted egoist, these unwonted exhibitions of emotion were, perhaps, the proper card to play; but the other side of the story, which is contained in the record of the Treasurer's battles in Whitehall, does not suggest that he sought to heighten his appeal by a recital of fictitious woes. The impression left by it is of a Sisyphus condemned, under the shadow of impending disaster, to roll uphill, not a rock, but a mountain of pebbles. Dunned for official salaries in arrears,[1] and with debts to the Crown's creditors piling up, he is obliged not only to find money for new liabilities at a moment when, as he writes to a colleague, he is 'overwhelmed with the cares...which the necessities already known will bring upon us',[2]

---

[1] *S.P.D. Jas. I*, CXXXIV, no. 38; CXXXVIII, no. 510; CXXXIX, no. 5.
[2] Quoted from letter of Middlesex to Secretary Conway, Dietz, *English Public Finance*, p. 200.

but also, in the hope of restraining extravagance, to add to his responsibilities for financial strategy duties of a kind today entrusted to junior clerks.

It is a comment on a capacity for work which even his enemies admired, as well as on the strains which the administrative system of the day imposed, that the Treasurer should have found it necessary to toil daily at his desk, personally checking, querying and revising the minutiae of expenditure. The minimum dietary allowance compatible with the dignity of the new envoy from Spain; the manning and provisioning of the squadron detailed to escort the tardy princess; the new chapel—the foundation stone of which was prematurely laid in May, possibly with some suppressed smiles, by Gondomar himself—designed 'with great state and costliness' by Inigo Jones to ensure that the Catholic bride should, during her sojourn in the heretical wilderness, continue to enjoy the consolations of her Faith—such matters[1] had doubtless their importance; but the spectacle of the chief Finance Minister of the Crown, who is also Master of the Court of Wards and a member of the hard-worked Commission for Spanish Affairs, devoting at a critical moment his personal attention to official hack-work, gives ground for surprise. The heavier such extraordinary demands, the greater the necessity for rigour in the management of the ordinary account; but, here too, the pressure on the parsimonious Treasurer is intense. As though timed to aggravate embarrassments already grim, there are symptoms —one cannot say proofs—of an increased liveliness on the always unquiet aristocratic poverty front. Encouraged, perhaps, by the spectacular preparations for orgies of royal hospitality, the unceasing whimper of the Court—Give! Give!—becomes, if anything, more insistent than before. The King, who stands to lose most by concessions, is the first to press his officer to make them.

'Sick at heart with these extraordinary charges, when the King is ill able to meet his ordinary expenditure; cannot hold out unless some extraordinary supply be thought of or some large sums come in from Spain with the fleet'— such, in the spring of 1623, is Middlesex's lament to his not too co-operative colleague, the Secretary of State.[2] Informed in July by Buckingham that all

---

[1] *S.P.D. Jas. I*, CXLV, no. 49 (28 May 1623, diet of Spanish envoy and victualling of ships); CXLIII, no. 60 (24 April 1623, manning and victualling of ships, see also no. 80); McClure, *Letters of John Chamberlain*, vol. II, pp. 494, 500 (chapel for princess).

[2] *S.P.D. Jas. I*, CXLIII, no. 60 (24 April 1623).

difficulties had been overcome, and that the signature of the marriage
contract was a matter of days, he replied to the illusionist's optimism
by redoubling his adjurations, not only to hurry home himself, but,
above all things, to bring the auriferous Lady and her treasure with
him.[1] The arrival in London, seven weeks later, of Charles did not
end the negotiations for a treaty, for which the English Ambassador
at Madrid continued to labour; but it meant that, during the three
months' unedifying epilogue which preceded Bristol's recall,[2] the
former enthusiasts for the match were now, dowry or no dowry,[3]
its bitterest opponents. Middlesex was not a simpleton to be deceived by diplomatic suavities as to mere postponement. He must
quickly have realised that, though a polite convention might require
the game to go on, the Exchequer's stake in it, which mattered most
to him, had been irretrievably lost.

Had that been all, the blow to a harassed finance minister would
have been severe. The anxieties[4] tormenting him during nine
difficult months had been, at least, alleviated by the reflection that, as
his patron's last letter had suggested, the spell to exorcise the fiscal
spectre might at any moment come to hand. By the autumn it was
evident that, while the costs of the quest for El Dorado remained to
be met, the prize which, by rescuing the Crown from its financial
duress, was to make amends for all had gone the way of other will-o'-
the-wisps. Nor was that negative misfortune the worst. The Treasurer
may not have shared his master's passion for peace; but he knew,
with a precision beyond the wit of James, the inability of the English
State to finance a war. It had been hoped, though for different
reasons, by both that, if not a cessation, at least a restriction, of
hostilities might be one of the few redeeming features of the Prince's
and his companion's compromising sojourn among castles in Spain.

---

[1] R. Davies, *The Greatest House at Chelsey* (Buckingham to Middlesex, 8 July 1623);
Harl. MSS. 1581, f. 97 (Middlesex to Buckingham, 13 August 1623).

[2] Bristol had agreed to the marriage ceremony taking place on 29 November. He
received, on 26 November, an order from James to postpone it, and was recalled, in
partial disgrace, on 30 December (Gardiner, *History of England, 1603–1642*, vol. v,
pp. 152–9).

[3] James, of course, had larger ends in view; but his solicitude as to the dowry is shown
by his letter of 13 November to Bristol, insisting that the whole sum be paid in cash
down (*ibid.* pp. 133, 145).

[4] The debt in May 1624, was put at £1,000,000 (Dietz, *English Public Finance*,
p. 271), and was presumably between that figure and £750,000 in the preceding autumn.
The estimated deficit for the coming year, 1623–4, was £160,000. Even, therefore,
if the ordinary account for the year ending Michaelmas 1623 was satisfactory, the future
prospect was not bright.

The discovery that, if the disappointed travellers had their way, the opposite result would follow, was a shock to the King and a portent to his officer. It is a question, nevertheless whether, even so, that 'most tenacious Minister',[1] as the Venetian ambassador had called him, realised that not only the financial harvest of his labours but his political existence was at stake. His enlightenment on that point was not long delayed.

[1] *Cal. S.P. Ven. 1621-3*, no. 699, pp. 524-5 (16 December 1622).

PART III

THE FALL OF MIDDLESEX

CHAPTER VIII

THE IMPEACHMENT

I. THE BREAK WITH BUCKINGHAM

'All Treasurers', the King later told the Lords, 'if they do good service to their masters, must be generally hated.'[1] Given a system under which the management of the ordinary account was the province of the Crown, it was inevitable that financial discontents should be focused on the minister appointed by it, and equally unavoidable, in view of the range and complexity of the interests on which his activities impinged, that occasions for friction should recur. At periods when the embarrassments of the Exchequer caused Governments to turn the screw, or when a depression made fiscal burdens more than ordinarily vexatious, these occasions increased.

Confronted, like Middlesex, by both contingencies at once, even a Solon might have left a trail of animosities behind him. Sneers from supercilious fellow-councillors and groans from officials harried in their tranquil Edens were, of course, to be expected.[2] Unfortunately, the Treasurer's ravages had not been confined to spheres too elevated to fear or too humble to resent them. His affection for the City and desire to placate it were, doubtless, genuine; but whispered allegations that he used his inside knowledge of its ways to the disadvantage of his former friends were not easily disproved.[3] Accompanied by hectorings of its powerful customs-farming interests, a surtax on its principal export, and an additional imposition on a profitable import, was it probable that his protests of solicitude for the nurse of his fortunes would be accepted as sincere? The shareholders of the Virginia Company included more than a sprinkling of men of influence and wealth. Were truculence to its spokesman

---

[1] *L.J.* vol. III, p. 344, 7 May 1624, Lord Keeper's report of the King's speech to the Lords on 5 May.

[2] See, for example, J. Hacket, *Scrinia Reserata*, pp. 104–5, for the 'dry laughter' at the Treasurer's proposal with regard to the disposal of the fees of persons taking out a pardon. For the annoyance caused by him to officers in the Household, Wardrobe, and Court of Wards, see above, pp. 155–9, 162, 182–3.

[3] J. Howell, *Familiar Letters* (1903), vol. I, sect. II, letter XII, p. 118.

and threats to its charter the way to win their hearts?[1] Could a House
of landowners be expected to view with friendly eyes a Master who
boasted that he had raised the price of wardships? Or naval officers
a Chief Commissioner of the Navy who insisted that they earn their
pay or go? Or tradesmen grown fat on the custom of the court a
skinflint one of whose first reforms had been to cut their bills?
Or courtiers a Harpagon inexorably hostile to their pickings and
contemptuous of themselves?

It might, perhaps, have been anticipated that, if powerful adversaries looked at him askance, the reformer's economy campaign
would win him friends in quarters hurt both in pocket and in conscience by the laxity and corruption which were the targets of his
attack. Middlesex himself did not share that illusion. He was
conscious, on the contrary, that, while enemies in high places would
rub their hands at his failure, the critics of the regime were not
eager for his success. Desiring before all things a Parliament, the
opponents of the Court, he wrote,[2] saw in the Crown's necessities
the best security that its summons could not be long delayed, and
were less than enthusiastic at the Treasurer's efforts to relieve the
embarrassments which hastened its approach. His talk of retirement,
and his outburst, 'Since I accepted the staff, I have led such a life
as my very enemies pity me...I never desired to quit the world,
with all the fooleries in it, till now',[3] voiced, perhaps, a passing mood.
Undoubtedly, however, in his last year of office, isolation was his lot.

That chink in his armour had its importance. It meant that,
when he needed allies most, he looked for them in vain. But to
make too much of the dispersed, heterogeneous enmities surrounding
him would be an error. The significant fact, on a long view, had
been, not that the interests hit by him had growled, but that hitherto
they had growled in vain. The blow which felled him came from
a more exalted quarter. It was of the nature of a society in which
patronage was the avenue to advancement, that the client, when
himself a power, might still have much to hope and fear from the
greater power which had raised him. Apart from his own talents,

---

[1] For an occasion on which Nicholas Ferrer, counsel and later deputy-governor of
the Virginia Company, stated the Company's case before the Council and 'the Lord
Treasurer with violent passion often interrupted him', see P. Peckard, D.D., *Memoirs
of the Life of Mr. Nicholas Ferrer* (1790) pp. 121, 124-5, 141-2; and W. F. Craven,
The Dissolution of the Virginia Company, pp. 318-21.

[2] *Harl. MSS.* 1581, f. 95 (Middlesex to Buckingham, 8 April 1623).

[3] *Cabala*, pp. 266-7 (same to same).

Middlesex had owed his career to two influences, the favour of James and the favour of Buckingham. The King, in his senile, helpless way, remained his friend. The Duke became his implacable foe. The alliance thus dissolved had served both the parties to it well. Then, as long after, though in a different guise, personal relations were the warp and woof of English public life. An *arriviste* from the City might serve the Crown as a specialist in affairs beneath the ambition or above the capacity of aristocratic rivals; but, without influence to lend him wings, he was less likely to soar than to endure 'the spurns that patient merit of the unworthy takes'. Supported by the Grand Vizier who administered the whole vast patronage of his royal master, Cranfield had found few doors closed, and had travelled in a decade fast and far. The advantage of the connection to his backer, if less obvious, had not been small. Buckingham was not content with the privileges and perquisites of a favourite; he demanded the realities of power as well. To satisfy that ambition, he required, not merely a monopoly of the royal ear, but creatures of his own, on whose loyalty he could count, in key positions in the State. A protégé of the calibre of Middlesex, domineering to others, but docile to himself, and an acknowledged master of the mysteries of finance, was a gift from the gods.

The future of the favourite depended on the future of the regime. A concern for its fiscal stability had made it his interest, as well as the King's, to support the expert's essays in departmental reform. The encouragement thus given had had an unexpected sequel in the blessing bestowed by Buckingham on the personal bond created by the marriage between their author, whom he regarded as his henchman, and his kinswoman, Anne Brett. The client becomes for a time 'my cousin', for whom he not only secures a peerage, but honours by acting as godfather[1] to his son. Unfortunately, as intimacy increased, confidence had cooled. Constitutionally incapable of distinguishing between public interests and his own, Buckingham needed funds to keep his *claque* in tune, and had expected his creature, the Treasurer, to supply them. He discovered, to his chagrin, that he had mistaken his man. Middlesex was no purist; but, like others who, in private, are lax, he revealed, where his work as a specialist was concerned, an unexpectedly pugnacious

---

[1] McClure, *Letters of John Chamberlain*, vol. II, p. 418 (4 January 1622). For Buckingham's influence in 'mediating' Cranfield's peerage, see the latter's letter of thanks of 4 July 1621, and Buckingham's reply, in R. Davies, *The Greatest House at Chelsey*, pp. 113–14.

conscience. Determined, for his own sake and the State's, to make such a success as was possible of his staggering task, he felt the professional's exasperation at impediments erected by the recurrent cry for cash of a politically all-powerful, but incurably shiftless and irresponsible, amateur. Whether Buckingham's annoyance at grants blocked, pensions whittled down, and the Mastership of the Irish Wards,[1] on which his heart was set, inexplicably delayed, was aggravated, as the wiseacres averred, by suspicions that Middlesex had a rival favourite[2] up his sleeve, we do not know. It is clear, at any rate, that before the former donned his false beard for Madrid, relations between him and his stiff-necked kinsman were not what they had been. During his absence from England, kind friends on both sides made haste to blow the flame. The Duke was warned that the thankless recipient of his favours was plotting mischief behind his back; the Treasurer, that his benefactor's mind was poisoned against him.[3]

Goodman, who knew Middlesex well, told him later that his capital blunder had been to keep the Prince, when in Spain, short of funds.[4] The Treasurer's reply that the charge of niggardliness

[1] R Davies, *The Greatest House at Chelsey*, pp. 121–2 (Buckingham to Middlesex, 14 November 1622).

[2] Arthur Brett, Cranfield's brother-in-law. Chamberlain refers to him on 22 June 1622 as having recently been made a groom of the bedchamber, and later, on 10 April 1624, as 'a new idol', which the Treasurer had attempted to set up. Buckingham took Brett seriously enough to see, before leaving for Spain, that he was shipped off to travel on the Continent. After Cranfield's fall, the wretched youth, who would 'do anything to become prime courtier again', found himself in July 1624, temporarily committed to the Fleet (see McClure, *op. cit.* vol. II, pp. 442, 479, 553, 560, 571, 580, and Gardiner, *History of England, 1603–42*, vol. V, p. 220). He appears to have been nothing worse than a fool, and ended as Henrietta Maria's agent at Rome (Gardiner, *op. cit.* vol. VIII, pp. 138, 144).

[3] *Harl. MSS.* 1581, ff. 93–4, Middlesex to Buckingham, 30 March 1623: 'I assure your Lordship that the evil spirits that were very active at Christmas to divide your Lordship and me are not yet quiet, but have been more busy than ever since your departure'; Davies, *op. cit.* p. 127, citing letter of 9 May to Middlesex from Sir George Goring at Madrid, in which the writer states that it had been reported 'that the Duke should have had many ill offices done him of late by some great men, of whom your Lordship was one in a high kind'. On the action ascribed to Laud in reporting to the absent Buckingham the alleged complicity of Cranfield and Williams in a plot against him, see P. Heylin, *Cyprianus Anglicanus* (1671), p. 107.

[4] Goodman, *The Court of James I*, vol. I, pp. 227–9. Goodman was in two minds as to the statement ascribed to Cranfield 'that the voyage [*sc.* to Spain] was foolishly undertaken and maintained with prodigality'. He remarks that it was quite in keeping with the character of Cranfield, 'as open-hearted a man as ever I knew, who did not desire to cover the nakedness of his thoughts'. On the other hand, he points out that no charge of making such a statement was subsequently brought against him, as, had he used the words in question, it probably would have been.

was refuted by Charles's own expense accounts, with which a much-tried Exchequer was only too familiar, was doubtless true enough; but it answered the form, rather than the substance, of the Bishop's reproach. Even when accompanied by reluctant assurances that debts would be duly paid, sermons on economy in the manner of a guardian admonishing two wayward undergraduates were not calculated to please. Less unteachable spendthrifts than the heir-apparent and the Duke might pardonably have felt indisposed, once their travels were over, to court further counsels of prudence from the same censorious lips. Had, however, such irritations been all, the quarrel might have ended with the correspondence which had sharpened its edge. In fact, since issues more profound were at stake, it had only begun.

Buckingham and Charles returned from Madrid in the mood of the disappointed suitor who demonstrates the depth of his devotion by cutting the ungrateful loved one's throat. Both, with the former, no doubt, in command, were bent on a full-dress war with Spain, preceded by a Parliament to dissolve the treaties and—so the innocents assumed—to foot the bill. The discovery that the Treasurer, who would have to find the funds, dismissed their diplomatic revolution as hare-brained megalomania, and was opposed, not only for financial reasons, but on grounds of principle, to the whole brilliant international transformation scene in which their vanity had cast them for the leading parts, converted mere annoyance with an elderly obstructionist into active indignation. Further sterile exchanges between London, Madrid and the ex-Elector combined with the hesitations tormenting the unhappy James to postpone the prompt decisions on which the incendiaries' hearts were set; but at the end of the year, with the signature of the warrant for the issue of writs for a new Parliament, the crisis came.

Middlesex was far from the insular-minded Philistine, indifferent to his country's responsibilities and prestige abroad, depicted by his critics; nor, to judge by his record, was he a fanatic for appeasement.[1] It was he, after all, not Buckingham or Charles, who had done most, next to Coke, to make the long-neglected navy an effective fighting

---

[1] See above, p. 123 and App. no. 1, for Cranfield's advice to the Government in 1612 to tell the Archduke to have his tariff war if he dared, and to see whether England or the Spanish Netherlands tired first; and later, in 1619, his fury at the rumours, possibly unfounded, that the government had approved 'the damnable proposition' to capitulate to the Dutch in the East—'to sell the Adventurers and consequently the trade of the East Indies to the Hollanders' (*Cranfield MSS.* no. 6774, November 1619).

force;[1] and a memorandum in his hand, written, apparently, on the eve of the close of his public career, shows him, for all his championship of peace, concerting measures for crippling the old enemy to be put in force should the need for them occur.[2] It was necessary, however, to Buckingham's plans that the Privy Councillors composing the Commission for Spanish affairs should be, if not cordial, at least acquiescent, and that Middlesex neither was nor would pretend to be. He remained, in fact, the most conspicuous, as well as the least placable, of the lions in the path. Not only had he uttered a disloyal growl that Princes, like common persons, might on occasion be required to sacrifice private predilections to public needs, but at meetings of the Commission he had voted the Duke's proposals down, and subsequently, when blandishments or threats had brought his fellow-heretics to heel, he had remained unmoved by both.[3] The Treasurer's reputation, the importance of his office, and, above all, the confidence still reposed in him by the King, made his obduracy an obstacle too grave to be merely ignored. At some date between 16 February, when Parliament opened, and the end of March, it was decided to destroy him.[4]

[1] See above, p. 161.

[2] *Cranfield MSS.* no. 8436, 1624 (?), memorandum endorsed by Middlesex 'of great importance; to be done without the loss of an hour, so far as possible'. The steps specified include (a) pressure on France and the States to make no peace or truce with Spain, (b) munitions and other naval stores to be put at once on an active service footing; the selling of oaks fit for ships to be stopped forthwith, (c) Spanish rearmament to be paralysed by cutting off supplies of powder, masts, tar, etc. shipped to Spain from Hamburg, Lübeck and other Hanseatic ports, (d) careful consideration to be given to the methods to be employed, i.e. whether to seize the merchantmen in transit, or to blockade the ports at which they lade, or to attempt a deal with the Hanse towns to divert the freights to English ports.

[3] For Middlesex's remark that it was the duty of the Prince to marry the Infanta 'for reason of state and the good that would thence redound to Christendom', see Gardiner, *The History of England, 1603–1642*, vol. v, p. 229, and for the meetings of the Commission, *ibid.* pp. 176–8, and D. H. Willson, *The Privy Councillors in the House of Commons, 1604–1629* (1940), pp. 162–3.

[4] Two further points have been mentioned as relevant to Buckingham's decision to crush the Treasurer. They are (a) the return to England in March 1624, of Middlesex's brother-in-law, Arthur Brett, the Duke's hypothetical rival (b) the rumour that Middlesex had supplied the Spanish Ambassadors with part of the information used in their charge that Buckingham was conspiring against the King. The second of these suggestions seems difficult to reconcile with the dates. The first symptoms of the prospective attack of the House of Commons on the Treasurer occur on 2 April, in Sandys' report from the Committee for Trade, and the first proposal to impeach him is made on 8 April (*C.J.* vol. I, pp. 752–3, 759). Lafuentes did not see James on the subject of the alleged conspiracy till 20 April, nor did James bring the matter before the Privy Council till 2 May (Gardiner, *op. cit.* vol. v, pp. 233–30).

The salient features of the political background, against which subsequent events must be seen, were two. The first was the increasing eclipse of James. 'The King', reported in July the Venetian Ambassador, 'has always detested business, and now hates it more than ever.'[1] James, who profoundly distrusted the policies favoured by his heir, had struggled earlier in the year to retain control, only to find that a planned isolation made his belated efforts to assert himself vain. Charles was not reluctant to spare his father's failing powers by ruling before he reigned; nor, with Buckingham at his elbow, was he fastidious in his choice of means. Interpreting, for the enlightenment of Parliament and nation, pronouncements from the throne; harmonising by additions and glosses the royal intentions with their own; schooling ministers and officials to look for guidance and advancement to the rising sun, Prince and Duke conducted affairs almost in the manner of a Council of Regency wielding in an interregnum the powers of the Crown, and, while humouring the King, did not scruple to forward in his name designs repugnant to him. The assurance with which they acted was heightened by a second factor, whose tonic influence neither was again to know. The Parliament, whose summons was the signal that a new course had been set, was as welcome to the politically minded public as distasteful to the King. Thus the steersmen were conscious of favouring winds behind them.

The early months of 1624 were the moment of Charles' brief honeymoon of popularity. The enthusiasm of a people rejoicing at its deliverance from a Catholic Queen was undimmed by the knowledge that negotiations to provide it with a substitute of the same detested creed would shortly be on foot; and the favourite's militant diplomacy, as yet undeflated by events, made the ogre of tomorrow the idol of today.[2] What more dramatic move could be made to confirm the authority of the new regime than, by extinguishing at a stroke the most prominent critic of its policies, 'to strike terror into others, that they might not attempt the like'?[3] And how more

---

[1] *Cal. S.P. Ven. 1622–25*, 6 July 1624. For James' practical seclusion from business earlier in the year see McClure, *Letters of John Chamberlain*, vol. II, p. 522 (31 January 1624); and for the strained relations between him and Charles, Hist. MSS. Comm., *Supp. Report on MSS. of Earls of Mar and Kellie*, p. 201 (22 May 1624, letter of Kellie to Mar).

[2] *Cabala*, pp. 90–3 and 217–22, where Buckingham is stated (p. 219) to have been praised in Parliament as 'the redeemer of his country'. See also Willson, *op. cit.* pp. 160 *seq.*

[3] Goodman, *op. cit.* vol. I, p. 227.

convincingly demonstrate that the offender fell, not as the victim of a personal vendetta, but as an enemy of the people, than by relying for his liquidation on the verdict of a Parliament indignant at the sink of sordid avarice and peculation long masked by hypocritical pretensions of reforming zeal, but now, by its investigations, at last dragged to light?

We do not know by whom the word impeachment was first pronounced. It is difficult, however, to resist the evidence that Buckingham and Charles, if they did not prompt the plan, quickly made it their own, and, once resolved on it, left little to chance. The relations established by them with the popular leaders in both Houses, which caused it to be said that the Duke and 'all his party' were working against Middlesex; the encouragement given to the latter's official colleagues and subordinates to recall his past misdeeds; the lightning conversions which induced witnesses called in his defence to testify against him, 'as if they had been corrupted to do him mischief'; the blunt refusal of individual Peers, whose support for the Treasurer was begged by the King, to 'adventure upon the frowns of the Prince and Duke'[1]—these and the other manœuvres analysed by Professor Willson[2] bear the marks of design. They suggest that Middlesex's influential adversaries did not spare their efforts to prepare the ground for the parliamentary attack and to ensure its success. The popular description of the case, as 'the Prince's undertaking'[3] does less than justice to the dominating influence on Charles of his indefatigable tutor; but, that omission apart, it hits the nail on the head. If, on 12 May, the Treasurer was declared guilty of 'bribery, extortion, oppression, wrong and deceipts',[4] it was partly to these preliminary labours that the denouement was due.

2. THE ATTACK IN THE COMMONS

The evidence held to justify that verdict is best studied in the *Journals* of the Upper House. The proceedings which culminated in it had

---

[1] Hacket, *Scrinia Reserata*, pp. 190–2.   [2] Willson, *op. cit.* pp. 163–7.

[3] Hacket, *op. cit.* pp. 189–90. The words come from the report made by Williams to the King, who had instructed him to secure supporters for the Treasurer in the House of Lords. Williams, by his own account, had attempted the task and found it hopeless. 'The Prince', he stated, 'is the main champion that encounters the Treasurer.' Hence the King must choose between sacrificing his 'old and perhaps innocent servant' and discrediting his son. As on a later, and more famous, occasion, Williams recommended the easiest course: 'necessity must excuse you from inconstancy or cruelty'.

[4] *L.J.* vol. III, p. 382, 12 May 1624.

begun, however, six weeks before, in the crowded fortnight when the Commons were hammering the charges into shape in debates instructive less for the factual information contained in them than for the glimpses which they offer both of the mentality of members and of the methods employed to bring an unpopular Minister to book. Whether by accident or design, the particular grounds on which the Treasurer was first arraigned were supplied by a subject which the House had much at heart, and on which he himself had in the past been heard with respect.

Business conditions, though no longer in 1624 the nightmare of 1621, still caused alarm. The House had, for that reason, recently taken steps to ensure that the reports of the Standing Commission on Trade appointed in 1622, as well as the views on the subject expressed in the last Parliament, should be made available to its Committee for Trade.[1] In introducing on 2 April a Report from that Committee, its chairman, Sir Edwin Sandys, seized the opportunity to launch a frontal attack on the minister by whom, more than by any other, the financial measures of the Government were held to be inspired. He disclaimed the intention either to reopen the old question of the legality of impositions or to reduce the revenue of the Crown. Lower duties, with a larger volume of trade, would, in his view, advantage King and subject alike; but, whatever the verdict on that point, the sacrifice of commercial to fiscal interests could not be allowed to continue. It was true, no doubt, that a variety of different causes had contributed to the depression still afflicting the country. Unquestionably, however, he insisted, the screw turned on trade by the exorbitant demands of the Exchequer must be given a high place among them. The so-called praetermitted customs had been one case in point. The decision of the Treasurer to rub salt into that still painful wound, by harassing London business with a duty which doubled the already stiff tax on imported wines, and provincial enterprise with a charge on groceries[2] from which the outports—so it was alleged—had hitherto been exempt, was another, and more glaring one. Nor was the mere magnitude of the imposition

---

[1] *C.J.* vol. I, p. 728, 4 March 1624. In addition to the *Commons Journals*, two other sources, an anonymous diary of the Parliament of 1624 in the *Gurney MSS.* (cited below as '*Anon. Diary*') and the notebook of Edward Nicholas (cited below as 'Nicholas') *S.P.D. Jas. I*, CLXVI, throw light on the proceedings against Middlesex in the House of Commons. My thanks are due to Mr Robert C. Johnson, of the University of Minnesota, who kindly allowed me to consult his extracts from them.

[2] See below, p. 251, n. 1.

on wines its most objectionable feature. Justified by the Government as an emergency contribution to the necessities of Palatinate defence, it had subsequently, by a manœuvre suspiciously like a breach of faith, been slipped into the permanent tariff contained in the Treasurer's new Book of Rates, which, though temporarily withdrawn from circulation, could, whenever he thought fit, be given effect. In view of the £60,000 odd by which, as Sandys alleged, the duties levied at the ports had in recent years been increased, and of the precedents now set for further additions to them, what was the future of a commercial nation to be? 'This conceived to be the reason of the decay of trade. Not a burden on the merchant alone but upon the whole realm.... If the burdens continue they will tend to the utter destruction of the kingdom.'[1]

The object of Sandys' opening rounds was to make it inevitable that the Treasurer's conduct should be brought under review. He focused attention, therefore, on its economic aspects, to the exclusion of the delicate issue of the Crown's right to impose, and of the allegations of corruption in connection with the surtax on wines, which were subsequently to overshadow the resentment aroused by the imposition itself. The lengthy denunciation three days later by the member for Launceston, Sir Miles Fleetwood, the Receiver of the Court of Wards, of the supposedly oppressive and fraudulent innovations forced on a reluctant department by its tyrannical Master, opened a second, and not less threatening, front.[2] The House of Commons possessed in its well-developed committee system a powerful engine of investigation. The dual indictment of the Treasurer brought the formidable machine into action. Under the leadership of Coke and Sandys, the chairmen respectively of the Committees for Grievances and for Trade, evidence was collected; witnesses examined; further misdemeanours brought to light; and a Committee appointed to

---

[1] *C.J.* vol. I, pp. 752–3, 2 April 1624.

[2] *Anon. Diary*, 5 April 1624. Fleetwood prefaced his remarks on the Court of Wards by more general complaints, e.g. the alleged sale of offices by the Treasurer, his harsh dealings with creditors, and the fact that he 'procured a grant that nothing should pass in England and Ireland without his certificate and special allowance'. The last statement was presumably a reference to Cranfield's attempt to economise by controlling grants at the source. Fleetwood's charges specifically relating to the Court of Wards were four: (1) the new orders issued by Middlesex as Master, (2) the transfer of some duties from the Clerk of the Court to the secretary, (3) Middlesex's reduction from three years to one of the period after which the Master received compositions for concealed wardships, (4) the use of a stamp, which he entrusted to his secretary. On these points see below, pp. 255–7.

determine the responsibility both for the advice given to the Crown to approve the obnoxious wine duty, and for the intimidation used to silence the victims' complaints. The result of these and subsequent inquiries was not merely to strengthen with corroborative detail the accusations with which the attack had begun. It was to add to the economic counts allegations of bribery, peculation and extortion[1] —'the enriching of himself and his servants to the detriment of the King'—and thus to pillory the offender, not only as the author of fiscal burdens mischievous to trade, but as odiously avaricious and corrupt. It was not till 12 April that the charges were systematically marshalled under six heads, and that a Select Committee was entrusted with the task of reducing them to a form suitable for presentation to the Lords.[2] To judge, however, by the reception given to the proposal in earlier debates, the resort to impeachment was a foregone conclusion within a week of Sandys' initial speech.[3]

That course, it was evident, was not without its risks. James had not concealed his disapproval of proceedings which he regarded as designed to victimise a loyal officer for services to himself. In the long dispute on impositions each side had developed its own *mystique*. The subject could not be avoided, but the House would defeat its own aims if, by appearing to trench on the prerogative, it provoked the intervention of the King, and thus, in the words of one of the culprit's fellow-ministers, were to 'open a gap for him to lay hold of the horns of the altar'.[4] A resolution formally repudiating the intention to challenge, on this occasion, the King's legal right to impose was accordingly passed; while the provocative reference to the alleged breach of the royal word involved in its recent use was, for the same reason, dropped. The former disclaimer ran the gauntlet of weighty criticism including, it seems, though on different grounds, that of Selden and of Sandys himself. It was accepted by the majority as a precaution necessary to safeguard the performance of their immediate task. Finally, in order to avoid the appearance of reflecting on the Council, the communication sent to the Lords was to emphasise that the Treasurer was 'the first propounder' of the imposition on wines.[5]

For the rest, the moving spirits in the attack on the Treasurer

---

[1] *Ibid.* 5 April (Fleetwood). [2] See below, p. 243, n. 3.
[3] *C.J.* 8 April (Spencer and Coke); *Anon. Diary*, 9 April (same speakers and Phelips).
[4] *C.J.* 12 April (Chancellor of the Duchy).
[5] For the points mentioned above see *C.J.* 8 and 12 April; *Anon. Diary*, 9 and 14 April; and Nicholas, 14 April.

held a strong hand. Backed in their course by Buckingham, who used his influence to forward the investigations of the Select Committee,[1] they could dismiss as negligible the danger of a blow from without, in the shape of a premature dissolution, of which an apprehensive colleague warned them.[2] The asset supplied by their immunity from serious opposition in the House was equally secure. The two most intimate of the Treasurer's parliamentary friends, Ingram and Brooke, did for him what little they could.[3] Weston, the Chancellor of the Exchequer, his usual channel of communication with the House, while disclaiming all knowledge of the new Book of Rates, appears to have shown a reasonable objectivity in the interpretation which he offered of his chief's actions and views.[4] Some independent-minded members, while prepared to proceed with charges for which a *prima facie* case had been established, were nauseated by the circulation *ad invidiam* of damaging imputations, probably unprovable and certainly unproved. The indignation with which, in particular, Seymour and Hayman denounced as monstrous the attempt to saddle Middlesex with the responsibility, not only for the imposition on wines—for which, as the former remarked, the Council, having accepted his advice, should bear an equal share of blame—but also for the last dissolution and subsequent benevolence, was an example of parliamentary *moral* at its best.[5] The sense of the House, however, was all the other way.

[1] *Anon. Diary*, 8 April, information from Solicitor-General that Buckingham signified that the King allowed the books of the farmers of the customs to be seen, but wished them to be viewed by a Select Committee, because many things were not fit to be published.

[2] Phelips: 'Presently acquaint the Lords...and not to stay for more matters, lest they stay till the Parliament has ended suddenly before the rest can be prepared' (*ibid.* 9 April).

[3] Ingram states that the Treasurer told him that the new Book of Rates was not yet published. Stayed because of composition for grocery wares. Had issued no warrant for levying it since printing of Book of Rates (*C. J.* 8 April). Brooke asks on behalf of Treasurer for more time to prepare his case. Says that Treasurer should not be heard here, but before Lords (*ibid.* and Nicholas, 9 April).

[4] See, for example, *C. J.* 2 April, when he explained that the imposition on wines was intended to last no longer than the present Parliament.

[5] Sir Frances Seymour stated that to say, like the Secretary, that the Council accepted with 'implicit faith' the Treasurer's advice as to the imposition on wines was to 'lay an imputation upon them'; that to make the latter responsible for the last dissolution was dishonourable to the House as 'censure upon surmise', which the King's speech had contradicted; and that 'for the benevolence the Treasurer did no more than the rest of the Council, and we can charge him with no more'. Sir Peter Hayman said that the Treasurer had not pressed the benevolence, 'nor was so forward as other Lords in that business' (*Anon. Diary* and Nicholas, 14 April).

Respected figures, among whom Phelips[1] was the weightiest, were at one with Coke and Sandys in insisting that the impeachment should go forward. With the exception of Weston, Cranfield's colleagues in the Government, Calvert, the Secretary of State—who cast on the Treasurer the whole odium of the wine duty by emphasising the Council's 'implicit faith' in his economic wisdom —Heath, the Solicitor-General, and May, the Chancellor of the Duchy, threw him to the wolves.[2] Not only Fleetwood, who was venomous, but other officials, such as Rudyard, Wardour and Pye, were unfriendly to him. The group of his critics on the Select Committee appointed to investigate his misdeeds was more than a handful.[3] The merchants who contributed to the debates appear to have been few, but hostile. The Recorder of London, who, though not one of them, presumably reflected City opinion, did not mince his words in urging that the Treasurer's case should be sent to the Lords. Another City member, Bateman, a prominent Merchant Adventurer, who had served on the Committee appointed in 1621 on the depression of trade, confirmed the allegations of Sandys that the autocrat had heightened resentment at his exactions by giving complainants the rough side of his tongue.[4] The two Devonshire paladins, Delbridge and Neale, with whom Cranfield had crossed swords in the Parliament of 1621, appear on this occasion to have held their peace;[5] but Guy of Bristol, who had negotiated with him on behalf of his city for the withdrawal of the duty known as the composition for groceries, and who probably voiced sentiments shared by other western out-ports, took the chance to have his say.[6]

[1] *C.J.* 8 and 12 April; *Anon. Diary*, 5, 9, 12, 14 April; Nicholas, 5 and 11 April. Glanvill and Selden seem rarely to have spoken, but it is clear from what little they said that they supported the impeachment. More frequent speakers in the same sense were Hoby, Cavendish and Spencer, the last more violent in his language than most.

[2] For Calvert, see Nicholas, 9 April (where he refers to the 'implicit faith' of the Council in the Treasurer) and 14 April (where he defends the phrase); for Heath, *C.J.* 7 April, *Anon. Diary*, 8 April; for May, Nicholas, 9 April, and *C.J.* 12 April.

[3] For Fleetwood and Rudyard see *Anon. Diary*, 5, 7, and 12 April and Nicholas, 5, 7, 9, and 10 April. Wardour and Pye sat on the Select Committee appointed 8 April. and later gave evidence unfavourable to the Treasurer before the Lords. The Select Committee consisted of twenty-seven members, plus the Solicitor-General and the Recorder.

[4] *Anon. Diary*, 12 April.

[5] They were, however, members of the Select Committee appointed on 8 April.

[6] *Ibid.* 12 April. Particulars given by Guy of the levying of the composition in Bristol and of the action taken by him on behalf of the city are contained in *L.J.* vol. III, pp. 365–6 (10 May). Pitt, M.P. for Poole, produced in the Commons evidence against the Treasurer in the shape of a warrant to levy composition there (*C.J.* 8 April).

It is difficult, in fact, to find, among the thirty to forty members whose views on the Treasurer are known, more than four or five who had a good word to say for him.

The consensus of opinion is impressive. Middlesex, it must be confessed, was not an easy client to defend. We cannot say whether Coke's[1] contemptuous reference to the written memorandum submitted by him should be read with the grain of salt which some of that professional pugilist's performances might suggest; but it is difficult not to feel that, if that and other animadversions were heard by an audience predisposed against their object, the latter was himself largely to blame. It would appear, indeed, that at this stage of the proceedings the Treasurer not only allowed his case to go almost by default, but conducted himself in a manner which fortified his critics and embarrassed his friends. The supercilious self-confidence of his public reactions to the attack gave an impression of arrogance, which harmed him.[2] His failure, after requesting to be heard in person by the House, to appear on the day appointed was resented as disrespectful.[3] The suggestion made by him through Weston that the Commons should transmit their charges to the Lords, without themselves expressing an opinion on the case, touched an assembly jealously defensive of its precedents on the raw.[4]

Such indications, as they seemed, of a cavalier contempt for the Lower House lent colour to the suspicion that Middlesex's sins were 'not accidental, but a trade'. Combined with the baseless rumours already afloat as to his part in the last dissolution, their effect was to cause improprieties or illegalities which, as isolated lapses, might have been condoned, to be seen in a more sinister light, as symptoms of a political mentality so radically vicious as to make its possessor's continuance in public life a danger to the State. The outburst of a member—'never heard any man speak of any virtue in the Lord

---

[1] *C.J.* 15 April.   [2] McClure, *Letters of John Chamberlain*, vol. II, p. 553.

[3] Chancellor of Exchequer presents Treasurer's... desire that he may have a day to answer. Ordered: he is to have copies of both the charges and attend tomorrow afternoon (*Anon. Diary*, 9 April). Statement by Brooke that Treasurer desires 'a little favour in circumstance of time...offers no delay, but necessity urges him to it'. Objection by Cavendish. Resolved that he be heard this afternoon (*C.J.* 10 April). Chancellor of Exchequer apologises for not sooner informing House that 'the Treasurer saith he could not in so short a time instruct his Counsel and make his answer'; states that he desires to be heard on Monday next. Protests by members that his failure to appear is an affront to House (Nicholas, 10 April).

[4] Statement by Chancellor of Exchequer that Treasurer desires that 'this House will suspend the delivering of any opinion of his Lordship, but will transmit it to the Lords as it now stands' (*ibid.* 10 April).

Treasurer...thinketh he hath no affection to Parliament, nor ever will'[1]—was ingenuously phrased; but the conviction that matters of graver import than particular derelictions of duty were at stake was widely held. It prompted both the thunder of Coke and Phelips' prediction that the time was at hand when such 'wicked instruments' would be destroyed by the wrath of a reunited King and people.[2]

Thus the case opened by Sandys' strictures on the disastrous effects of fiscal burdens on trade had, before it was half-way through the Commons, become involved, as James foresaw that it must, in the fundamental issue of the balance of political power. It is not surprising that, in such an atmosphere, Eliot's lofty rhetoric—'Remove this strange and prodigious comet, which so fatally hangs over us'— should have found in the Treasurer's tainted reputation an easy target. The House voted the same day the charges to be laid before the Lords, and appointed a Committee to formulate them in precise terms.[3]

3. THE CASE BEFORE THE LORDS

At the moment when Coke and Sandys were expounding to the Upper House the Commons' 'crying complaints', the object of these animadversions was for other reasons under a cloud.[4] Both as a Commissioner for the Navy and as Treasurer, Middlesex had long had a hand in the tangled affairs of the small Office of Ordnance. By a coincidence too apt to be fortuitous, the Committee appointed by the Lords to report on the state of the country's munitions had recently received information associating his name with a characteristic specimen of the scandals from which that much-bedevilled department seems rarely to have been free.[5] Questioned by the

---

[1] *Ibid.* 14 April (Sir John Savile).

[2] *Anon. Diary*, 14 April (Coke), and 12 April (Phelips).

[3] *Ibid.* and *C.J.* 12 April. The charges then listed were: (1) a bribe of £500 from the farmers of the Petty Customs, (2) a bribe of £500 from the farmers of the Great Customs, (3) malpractices in the Court of Wards, (4) the imposition on wines, (5) the matter of the sugars, (6) the composition for grocery. On 15 April Coke delivered to the House the report from the committee appointed to give the charges a logical shape. The conference with the Lords took place the same day.

[4] Except where otherwise stated, the following account is based on *L.J.* vol. III, 13 April to 13 May 1624.

[5] Middlesex referred to Sir Robert Pye, whose brother, Sir Walter, was attorney of the Court of Wards, as having been the moving spirit in the part of the charge which related to the lands of Dallison, a former Master of the Office of Ordnance (*ibid.* 13 April). Sir Robert Pye, a Rembrancer of the Exchequer, had attacked the Treasurer in the Commons (see above p. 243). For Cranfield's complaint of a plot see Hist. MSS. Comm., *Buccleugh MSS.* vol. III, pp. 228-43 and especially 235-7.

Committee, he complained indignantly to the House of a 'plot and conspiracy against him' of a kind which, if allowed to pass unchallenged, must mean that no public man was safe. The allegations concerned, however, were included in the Report submitted to the Lords on 12 April by the Committee's chairman, the Archbishop of Canterbury, with the result that it was instructed to put the charges against the Treasurer into due legal form; and it was with these revelations in mind that the Peers heard on 16 April the Lord Keeper's account of the conference between the Houses held the preceding day. Confronted by a fresh sheaf of accusations, they took the obvious course. They strengthened the Munitions Committee by the addition of five new members and a legal expert. They then entrusted to that reconstructed body the preparation of a case incorporating, together with the alleged Ordnance Office misdemeanours, the graver and more comprehensive indictment formulated by the Commons.

The alacrity with which that initial step was taken did not last. The Committee, it is true, did its work with creditable speed. In just over a week[1] it had conferred with the experts whom it had been ordered to consult; had decided what points to dismiss and what to include; and had reduced a mass of allegations of varying degrees of plausibility to a list of specific charges which, though later found to require amplification, was, as far as it went, logical, lucid and coherent. That first phase over, a second began; and here both the character of the business and the atmosphere in which it was handled imposed powerful brakes. Before the trial could open, certain unavoidable prerequisites must be got out of the way. It was necessary that the defendant should receive a formal statement of the charges against him; that he should transmit a written reply; that the prosecution should communicate such supplementary charges as it might think fit; that depositions should be taken on behalf of both parties and that each should supply a list of the witnesses whom it desired to be called, together with interrogatories to be administered to them. To judge by the date[2] first fixed for the Treasurer's appearance at the bar, the design of those in charge had been to drive the proceedings through at a pace whose impetus would carry all before

---

[1] Its Report was presented to the Lords on 24 April 1624.

[2] On 24 April it was ordered by the Lords that the Treasurer should appear on Thursday next, i.e. 29 April. Later, the date for his appearance was changed to Friday, 7 May.

it. If such was their strategy, it failed. Within a week their time-table had broken down. It did not suit even the prosecution, which presumably was no friend to delay, but which produced two new charges on 29 April, the day originally assigned for the trial, and added a third on 1 May.[1] Still less was it acceptable to the defence.

It was of the nature of the crisis that, both before and during the impeachment, a battle of personalities and interests should rage behind the scenes. Each front reacted on the other; and Middlesex, at last alive to his danger, was in arms on both. James, lonely, disillusioned and ill, but detesting both on personal and public grounds a conspiracy, as he thought it, against a trusted servant, nerved himself by fits and starts to ineffectual efforts to rally his few friends among the Peers.[2] Charles, with a disloyalty ominous in conservative eyes for the future of the monarchy, played his reckless part of Opposition Whip against his father.[3] Buckingham bullied the one and egged the other on. The Treasurer, until debarred by order of the Prince, who feared his hold on James, from access to the Court, both besieged his master with prayers to intervene,[4] and simultaneously—since everything depended on winning time for the King to take his courage in his hands—fought a series of delaying actions with his adversaries in the Lords.

In some he was defeated; in others he was on strong ground and got his way. His requests for permission to be heard by counsel and to be supplied with copies of hostile depositions were rejected with contempt; nor was favour shown to his suggestion that the examination of witnesses might be deferred till the House had received his reply to the charges against him. On the other hand, his pertinacity in pressing petition after petition for three days on end[5] had some successes to show. It secured him leave to employ counsel in an advisory capacity; an extension of the period allowed for the

---

[1] The first two related to the Treasurer's conduct at the Wardrobe and failure to pay drawbacks to merchants re-exporting sugar; the third to the additional imposition of 10s. per cwt. on hops imposed by him in October 1622.

[2] James 'courted many to take side with the Treasurer, and prevailed little' (Hacket, *Scrinia Reserata*, pp. 189–90).

[3] 'The Prince...compassed suffrages to condemn him' (*ibid.*). '[Parliament] does every day grate so much upon the King's prerogative as I do much doubt hardly it shall be recovered....It is very strange to see the Prince...applauding...their doings' (Hist. MSS. Comm., *Sup. Rep. on MSS. of Earls of Mar and Kellie*, Kellie to Mar, 15 May 1624).

[4] McClure, *op. cit.* vol. II, pp. 555–6, 30 April 1624.

[5] *L.J.* 27, 28, 29 April.

preparation of his answer and interrogatories; and the postponement by more than a week of his appearance at the bar. Unfortunately, as far as his hopes of a royal rescue were concerned, his prodigies of procrastination—'never hare near her end made so many doubles'[1] —produced no more impressive result than the involved and spiritless appeal for clemency addressed to the Lords on 5 May by James. There were observers who thought that the King's advocacy had done his Minister more harm than good.[2]

The influence on political thought and practice of the renaissance of historical studies is a familiar theme. The resurrection of an antiquated weapon, which produced some forty impeachments between 1621 and 1688, is an example of their power. Between its employment for the chastisement of Mompesson, Mitchell and Bacon and its last preceding use under Henry VI a century and three quarters had elapsed.[3] Precedents, therefore, were dim. Irregularities surprising in a judicial process suggest that, when Middlesex faced his judges, the technique of the formidable, but rusty, blunderbuss required to be learned or invented in the course of discharging it.[4] For the formal aspects of the proceedings a few words must suffice. The hearings, to which all else was prologue, began on 7 May, and lasted six days. The Treasurer's old enemy, the Lord Keeper, presided. The counsel for the prosecution were two notabilities appointed by the Lords, Sir Randall Crewe, a former Speaker of the Commons and now Chief Justice of the King's Bench, and Sir Thomas

---

[1] McClure, *op. cit.* vol. II, p. 552, 10 April.

[2] For the King's speech on 5 May see the report in *L.J.* 7 May, and for comments on its alleged ambiguity, McClure, *op. cit.* vol. II, pp. 559–60, 13 May. As a matter of fact, in spite of Chamberlain's statement that the speech might be 'diversely construed', it made clear enough the King's opinion that Middlesex was a valuable public servant in danger of suffering for his virtues.

[3] 'It seems true to say that there is no case of impeachment between that of the Duke of Suffolk in 1449 and that of Sir Giles Mompesson in 1621' (F. W. Maitland, *The Constitutional History of England* (1909), p. 246).

[4] See the words of Frances Hargrave, in the Introductory Preface (1796) to Sir Matthew Hale's *The Jurisdiction of the Lords House of Parliament*: 'The criminal accusations of the Commons, and the proceedings upon them of the Lords, had not reached the sort of formality of accusation, defence and trial which belongs to impeachments in more modern times.' He instances four innovations in the impeachment of Middlesex, of which the most important were two, that the charges were presented by the King's counsel, not by managers appointed by the Commons, and that 'the benefit of counsel was harshly, and, as it seems, against precedent, denied to him'. Middlesex's contemporary, John Selden, in his posthumous *Of the Judicature in Parliament*, written, apparently, before August 1627, had also referred (pp. 101–3) to examples of the 'variation from the ancient course' which occurred in the Treasurer's impeachment.

Coventry, like him long a member of the Commons House, from which he had retired on being promoted in 1621 from Solicitor- to Attorney-General. The defendant's legal advisers, Nicholas Hyde and William Hakewell, were also well-known figures, who combined professional eminence with long parliamentary careers. The second had, on occasion, as in the impositions controversy of 1610, and again in 1621, been among the leaders to whom the House deferred.

Of the charges against Middlesex all, save one, contained several counts; but the subjects[1] to which they related were six, of which two were handled by the Attorney-General, and the remainder by Crewe. Unlike Bacon, the Treasurer was required to attend at the bar of the House and to answer for himself. The procedure included, in general, an opening speech for the prosecution; the reading by the clerk of supporting depositions; the defendant's answer; the reading of depositions in his favour; and the examination of such witnesses as were called, followed, on occasion, by a recapitulation on the part of the prosecution and a further rejoinder by the defence. The time occupied by different parts of the case varied with the subject concerned; but five days sufficed to see all six of them through. There followed on 12 May, a concluding statement by Middlesex in which, in addition to underlining points made in his preceding replies, he dwelt on the gravity of the financial embarrassments with which he had wrestled and on the services rendered by him to the Crown; a retort by the Lord Keeper—inevitably, Williams being what he was, an unmannerly retort—and the recording of six successive votes on the charges one by one. With the pronouncement next day of their judgment by the Lords, and its communication to the Commons, the trial concluded.

When, before approaching more controversial topics, the reader turns from these procedural aspects of a famous case to consider its content and substance, certain preliminary commonplaces are likely at once to strike him. It is evident, in the first place, that in the month which had elapsed since impeachment was first proposed,

---

[1] In the order, not of their importance, but of their presentment to the Lords, the subjects in question were the Wardrobe; the bribes alleged to have been received from the Petty and Great Farms; the abuses in connection with the sugar farm; the composition for groceries; the Ordnance Office; and the Court of Wards. The charges under the second and fifth of these heads were opened by the Attorney-General, those under the remainder by Sir Randall Crewe. In the following pages the more trivial charges are touched on first, and the more important later.

the gravamen of the indictment had somewhat changed. Not only had two new charges,[1] one of them formidable, been added to those listed by the Lower House, but an important item among the latter had been set in a more sinister light than that in which it had at first been seen. The attack on the Treasurer had opened with denunciations of the disastrous effects of his additions to the tariff; and when, on 15 April, Coke and Sandys expounded his offences to the Lords, the latter had made the commercial ruin portended by 'impositions upon impositions' the burden of his theme. During the trial itself, apart from reminders to Middlesex that the responsibility for the obnoxious wine duty sanctioned by the Council rested, not on it, but on him and him alone, these economic grievances play a minor part. The efforts of the prosecution are concentrated on establishing, not the injury to enterprise or injustice to merchants resulting from the Treasurer's operations, but the incidental bribery alleged to have accompanied them. The business charlatan, affecting a spurious infallibility on matters of trade, temporarily recedes from view. The hardened rogue remains.

A second, and not less significant, feature of the impeachment is the breadth of the front on which the prosecution's batteries played. The actual or potential victims of Middlesex's alleged misdemeanours included, in addition to the royal benefactor reported to have been robbed by him, the senior staffs of three or more departments; commercial and financial interests in London, in particular the customs-farmers, as well as purveyors to the Crown; metropolitan and provincial exporters and importers; landowners whom their affairs brought into undesired contact with the Court of Wards; courtiers thirsting to secure pensions or trembling to lose them; and a heterogeneous host of minor officials and business men. The majority of the deponents for the prosecution belonged to one or other of the first two groups, but some evidence was drawn from quarters less distinguished. A third and equally obvious consideration deserves perhaps a word. It will be observed that the offences for which Middlesex was called to answer differed from each other, not only in degree, but in kind. Some consisted of crimes punishable, if proved, by law; others of sharp practice which, in different

---

[1] Those relating to the Wardrobe and to the alleged refusal to pay the drawback due on re-exported sugar were added on 29 April. The third new charge, referring to an additional duty of 10s. per cwt. on imported hops imposed in October 1623, was added on 1 May, but does not appear to have been included in the charges heard at the trial.

circumstances, might properly have formed the ground of a civil action; others, again, of administrative innovations on which more than one opinion might reasonably be held. In view of the role of impeachment as an all-purposes weapon for the punishment of great offenders, the mixed bag of sins deposited at the Treasurer's door need cause no surprise. It is conducive to clarity, however, to distinguish between the varying footings on which different charges stood.

Space does not permit a detailed account of the manner in which the prosecution unfolded its case. Posterity can profitably observe the sparks from the controversial clash, but to assess the merits of argument and counter-argument is beyond its power. On two of the issues raised little, happily, need be said. In spite of the militant emotions of the western out-ports led by Bristol, the so-called composition for grocery[1] proved on inspection to be a storm in a tea-cup. Partly as a result of a communication from the King, the famous sugar scandal,[2] at first sight more gross, was, rightly or wrongly, dismissed as equally a mare's nest. The impression made by these two heads of the indictment on an audience not too friendly to the defendant is shown by his acquittal on both.

Whatever—to turn to weightier matters—the faults of Middlesex, his reputation as an administrator stood high. The first of the graver charges against him may occasion, in view of it, some surprise.

[1] The composition for grocery was levied in lieu of purveyance on a list of imported groceries. London and the majority of ports had agreed to pay it. Certain others in the west and south-west alleged that they had not. Middlesex showed that precedent supported the collection of the due from all but one of the complainants; that in the case of Bristol, though acting in good faith, he had been misinformed; and that, on learning of the special settlement made by his predecessor, Salisbury, with that city, he had at once cancelled the obnoxious warrant.

[2] The allegation was that Middlesex, at a time of financial stringency, had used public money to buy out the lessee of the farm of the sugar duties, Herriott, the late Queen's jeweller; that he had then secured the lease for himself at a rent ($£2000$) so preposterously low that, by sub-letting (for $£6000$), he cleared $£4000$ a year; and that he had refused the customary drawback on re-exported sugar. He replied to the first point that, while Herriott and the Crown had been mutually indebted, a balance was due to the former, which he could have repaid himself by witholding part of his rent, and that Middlesex had merely transferred its repayment to the tobacco farm, thus spreading it over a term of years. The second assertion was disposed of by a message from the King affirming that he had given his approval to the terms of the lease. Middlesex answered the third by stating that he would be happy to pay the drawback to any re-exporter of sugar who applied for it, which none as yet had. It should be added that the message from James, though a bar to further action, cannot be regarded as morally exonerating Cranfield. If the terms of the lease were of dubious propriety, it was he who was responsible for commending them to the King.

During his three years at the Wardrobe, the Treasurer, Sergeant Crew told the House, not only had pocketed £8000 a year, plus a *douceur* of £6000 on retirement, but had brought the office, which the King had summoned him to reform, 'into confusion, far from its old state' under, presumably, its preceding virtuous Master. The reference to Hay—of all people—as a model of economy and efficiency must have tempted the noble augurs to exchange some surreptitious winks; but the evidence supporting the criticisms on his successor was not of a kind to be lightly dismissed. The tale of woe rehearsed by a dozen witnesses, from the principal officer in charge and an auditor of the Exchequer to the small fry of clerks and artisans, paints a picture of an office afflicted by every vice which a Supply Department should shun. Deliveries habitually behind time; inferior qualities supplied; prices to producers arbitrarily cut; creditors languishing unpaid—such was the story. Even the elementary precaution of registering orders, purchases and issues had, it was complained, been thrown to the wind.

To one familiar with the imperious minister's ways, the probability that, even had he been as punctilious as he was alleged to be the reverse, his career in a sedate department would have earned his colleagues' applause must seem remote. Impatient, relying, when he could, on his personal staff in preference to slow-moving officials, and not afraid, as one outraged dignitary groaned, to turn 'the whole frame and course of the office' upside-down, it is not surprising that Middlesex should have been as popular at the Wardrobe as a pike among trout. To complaints on points of detail he naturally replied that, as far as materials, buying, business methods, and the rest of it were concerned, he had forgotten more than his critics ever knew. The most damaging charge, however, was that of financial laxity; and here, characteristically, his defence was a counter-attack. It was to point to the conditions on which alone he had consented to accept a thankless post, and to his positive achievements while he held it. In return for an undertaking to keep annual expenditure down to a maximum of £20,000—an improvement of roughly one-third on his predecessor's offer and of more on his practice—he had been authorised to retain the results of such further economies as he could contrive to introduce. The singular bargain had admittedly paid the Crown. Provided that he kept within the limit fixed, why, the Minister asked, should he be expected to account in detail for monies which, by the terms of his patent, were his own?

The retort was technically sound, morally questionable, and politically in the last degree inept. The truth was that, at the time of Middlesex's appointment, neither he nor the King had realised that Hay's mismanagement had been on a scale so portentous as to enable a competent successor to effect savings of the dimensions actually achieved. The Treasurer, as he virtually admitted to Buckingham,[1] was himself surprised by the magnitude of the windfalls which had come his way. Prudence, as well as conscience, should have caused him to suggest a review of the conditions which produced them. The King, when, some months after the trial, he at last grasped the facts, was indignant. His officer, James complained, had conducted the Wardrobe as though it were a property granted him in a fee-farm.[2]

'At a time when', in the words of the Attorney-General, 'all Christendom, except ourselves, was in combustion',[3] the condition of the Crown's Munitions Department was a matter of some moment. The reader who turns to the charge brought against Middlesex under the head of the Ordnance Office observes, with some surprise, that the aspect of the subject with which the prosecution opens its case is not the question of the adequacy of that organ to its task, but an apparently irrelevant topic, which an accident of personal history had caused to be associated with it. A former Master, Sir Roger Dallison, had run heavily into debt both to the Crown and to his officials. As a result, part of his lands had to be sold, and the remainder granted in lease to the department,[4] the salaries of whose staff were perpetually in arrears. At this point Middlesex, who had an eye for speculations in real property, had intervened. He compounded with the Office for its lease; pacified some other claimants to an interest in Dallison's lands, partly with cash, partly with promises of lucrative concessions; and employed more forceful

---

[1] 'The Lord Treasurer then told his Grace that his gains in that office had been £8,000 per annum, nay more than he could tell' (L.J. 7 May, Lord Keeper's speech).

[2] S.P.D. Jas. I, CLXX, no. 36 (21 July 1624).

[3] L.J. 11 May 1624.

[4] For the affair of Dallison's lands, see L.J. 12 April (petition of Sir Thomas Dallison); 24 April (charge as stated by Lord's Committee in report of that date); 1 May (Treasurer's reply); 10 May (Attorney-General's speech and defendant's answer); S.P.D. Jas. I, CLXXV, no. 37, November (?) 1624 (statement of the original debts of Sir Roger Dallison, for which Sir Thomas Monson was bound, etc.). My excuse for the mis-leading brevity with which the subject is here treated must be partly the intricacy of the transactions concerned, partly the fact that Middlesex's share in the matter, though it shocked the King (ibid. CLXX, no. 36), did not form a major part of the case against the Treasurer.

methods to silence those less easily appeased. The consequence was a cry of protest from the victims of these manœuvres, with the heir of the unfortunate Sir Roger at their head, that 'using the power of his place and the countenance of the King's service', the voracious leviathan had grown fat at their expense.

Into the ramifications of this too briefly summarised mystery of iniquity it is needless to enter. It offered, if confirmed, a glaring example of the contrast between the defendant's inhuman concentration on 'his own private profit' and his equally shameless neglect of 'that which concerned the public'. It was inevitable that the prosecution should use assertions of the former failing in order to throw the latter into high relief, and should work the unedifying antithesis for all it was worth. Granted, however, the sharp practice alleged, the indifference of Middlesex to the finer shades of economic ethics was, after all, a secondary issue. The important question was not whether, as earlier episodes in his career suggest may well have been the case, his treatment of the Dallisons of the world had been business-like to excess. It was the degree to which, in his dealings with the department concerned, his responsibilities as a minister had been competently discharged. The counts against him on that point can be simply stated.

The Office of Ordnance had a dismal history of waste and inefficiency behind it. Middlesex, it was alleged, had added another discreditable chapter. Instead of observing either the standard of expenditure fixed in 1617 by the Council or the amended figure prescribed two years later by the Commissioners of the Navy, of whom he himself had been one, he had, during his two and a half years at the Exchequer, systematically under-spent; had left unpaid the accounts of Evelyn, the Crown's powder manufacturer, with the result that supplies destined for the Government had been diverted elsewhere; and had allowed the reserves of explosives essential to national safety to run down. As a consequence, the department was impotent either to munition the critical Irish front, or, at a moment when Europe was plunged in war, to meet emergencies elsewhere. The reply to these complaints was a series of blank denials. So far from being due to him, the disorders of the Office had been, the Treasurer insisted, at their height at a period when his public career had barely begun. The Council's Orders had been issued four years before his first contact with the department had been made. The so-called 'settlement' of 1619, consisting as it did of mere proposals unconfirmed either by Council or King, had not, in fact, been a settlement at all. Finally, he invoked figures to clinch his argument. Those cited by him proved that more had been spent on powder during his Treasurership than during the whole of the preceding seven years; that arrears of debt had at the same time been reduced; and that stocks were actually higher at the end of March 1624, than they had been when, at Michaelmas 1621, he entered his present office. Thus the deadlock was complete. The conflicting evidence of witnesses did nothing to resolve it.

Another, and more formidable, charge of a ministerial breach of trust found its target in the regime established by Middlesex at the Court of Wards.[1] Stated in prosaic terms of specific abuses, the blots on this chapter of his career lost, it is true, the taint of unscrupulous malignity imputed to them in the thunderous generalities of Coke. Unquestionably, however, the financial triumphs of the Master's reforming zeal, on which his enemies were silent, had been won at the price of animosities within the office and suspicions outside it, which were grist to their mill. The counts in the indictment of his work at the Court of Wards were inspired by both.

The capital grievance, with which the prosecution opened this part of its case, consisted of the revolution held to have been effected in the traditional procedure of the Court by the new Instructions imposed on it in 1622 by its innovating chief. It was only, it was alleged, by a dishonest trick that the King's consent to them had been obtained. Promising to lay his proposals before a Committee of the Council, the Master had gone behind its back, forced his draft through a docile meeting of intimidated officials, and used his victory to establish a dictatorship equally injurious to subjects and to King. Under the despotism erected by him, parties who had business with the Court no longer, as in the past, had it handled gratis by the clerk. Before their petitions[2] could be entered by the latter, they must now go to the Master, and from him to his secretary, who, in addition to charging an exorbitant fee, might, on one pretext or another, hold up applications and leave their authors in the dark as to whether their requests had been duly recorded or not. The present Master, in the second place, unlike his predecessor, claimed a share in the management of the business of Liveries, with the

---

[1] See on this charge, in addition to *L.J.* 11 May, *S.P.D. Jas. I*, CLXV, no. 1, 'Information of Sir Miles Fleetwood, against the Lord Treasurer touching the Court of Wards'.

[2] The 'petition' was the first stage in the application for a wardship.

result that costs to the client, which formerly consisted of a single payment to the Surveyor, had been doubled by the addition of a fee to himself. Not less significant, the permission given by the new Instructions to treat as 'concealed' a wardship unnotified within one year of a ward's death, instead of, as previously, within three, put a premium on jobbery. It was an invitation to the secretary to procrastinate for twelve months, and then to pocket the reward for discovering a 'concealment' perpetrated, in effect, by himself. The arrogance of the Treasurer in manufacturing a stamp with his signature, and his irresponsibility in entrusting it to his myrmidon, the secretary, were the last straw. 'What mischief and oppression may be both to King and subject when both the signing and settling and whole trust of the Court of Wards shall be committed to the hands of the secretary, who...hath thereby the power to alter and antedate as he pleaseth!'

The arraignment revealed the hand of the Zimri of the department, Fleetwood, the Receiver. The defendant's rejoinder was not couched in an apologetic vein. Appointed to the Court of Wards with orders to compel a torpid nag to pull its full financial weight, Middlesex had quickly realised that the first necessity was a tight hand on reins which easy-going predecessors had allowed to slip. What more natural than that the resulting centralisation of control should infuriate officials accustomed to 'share the Master's power and authority among themselves'? One sinister suggestion he could afford to ignore. A message from the King declared, with a categorical precision unusual in James, that so far from having been smuggled through without his knowledge, the new Instructions had been debated at length in his presence by the officers of the Court and enforced with his approval.

The merits of the unpopular innovations were, of course, a different question; and here, where the Treasurer fought his own battle, he did not pull his punches. He conceded that, as a result of an increase in the so-called fees for continuance—the occasion of his never-forgiven *gaffe*, 'it is the King's grace to the people, let them pay for it'—suitors to the Court might be a trifle out of pocket; but, with that small exception, his reforms, he insisted, were as much in the interest of subjects as of King. The provisions that petitions should be lodged, in the first instance, with the Master, not his clerk, and that wardships unrevealed within a year could be classed as 'concealed', not only contributed to a much-needed increase in the revenue of the Court, but saved the time of all resorting to it. Surmises were not evidence; and the allegations of extortionate fees demanded, bribes accepted, and 'concealments' manufactured by his secretary and himself were, at most, he contended, no more than complaints of hypothetical possibilities, unsupported by facts. The crowning scandal of the stamp he treated with a gravity more galling than contempt. The pernicious instrument had been employed by the venerable Burghley, and was at the moment in use in offices so respectable as those concerned with subpoenas and outlawries. If it was right to permit a subordinate to attach a seal, why should permission to him to add a signature be wrong? The clients of the Court complained that the despatch of their business was purposely delayed. Was it reasonable to keep them kicking their heels ten days on end merely because the Master had been too busy at the Exchequer, or the Council or the Commission on Spanish Affairs to sign with his own hand a document which in any case, if stamped with his signature by his secretary, would be passed for approval to other members of the office staff?

Had these issues been all, Middlesex would have emerged from the battle scarred, but not too badly battered to fight again. The charge which, though financially a bagatelle, did most to bring him down was more subtly conceived. As told by the Attorney-General, the story of bribes squeezed from customs-farmers was a drama with a double plot. No notice, it appears, had been given by the Government of its choice of 19 January 1622 as the appointed day for the enforcement of the fateful imposition on French wines. Harried by the revenue officers with demands for payment before the new stocks which, in ignorance of the duty, they had just laid in, could be landed from the wine fleet in the Thames, the importers naturally raised a storm. It was temporarily allayed by a guarantee of higher prices wrung by the Council from their customers, the vintners. A more formidable group of victims was not so easily appeased.

The concessionaires of the wine farm had signed their lease[1] on the assumption, which a clause in their patent confirmed, that during its nine and a half years' currency no new burdens should be laid on the trade. Now, with the increased cost of wines, they saw a cheerless vista of stagnant markets and profits tumbling down. Ten months of fruitless expostulations with the Treasurer were followed in

---

[1] The lease, which had been signed on 30 September 1619, was to run for nine and a half years from Michaelmas 1621.

December 1622 by an appeal to the King; that step again, by negotiations between the farmers and Middlesex, supported by Weston, the Chancellor of the Exchequer, which secured to the farmers a rebate of £1000 a year on their rent of £29,900 odd; and these, in their turn, by another five months of exasperating procrastination, during which the warrant from the Treasurer required to implement the new arrangement was unaccountably witheld. In the meantime, the much more important farm of the Great Customs was also in the doldrums. Alarmed by forecasts of a deepening of the depression, and suspicious of the personalities by whom the syndicate was controlled, five of the prospective partners had declined to take up their shares. A reasonable precaution required that the participants in the farm should give security for the payment of the rent due to the Crown, and that, before the grant became operative, the Treasurer's approval of the guarantee proffered should be notified to the proper quarter.[1] The four patentees made no difficulty about themselves taking over the shares and liabilities renounced; but, once more, the Treasurer's reluctance to complete his part of the formalities produced paralysis. How break the ice? The directorates of the Petty and Great Farms interlocked. At a conference held towards the middle of 1623, and attended by the leading figures in both, the decision already taken by the Petty farmers to stimulate the unwontedly lethargic minister with a gift of £500 was capped by a resolution to the same effect on the part of their colleagues. Abraham Jacob, a member of both groups and an old factotum of the Treasurer, was instructed to 'gratify' him with a lump sum of £1000. What more glaring example could be conceived of honest speculators blackmailed into bribery by a grasping officer of State?

Middlesex did not deny the facts alleged, but put a different construction on them. He conceded the delay in the issue of the warrant in favour of the Petty farmers, but ascribed it partly to the consideration then being given to the desirability—an alternative known in other connections to appeal to him—of substituting for the farming of the wine duties direct administration by officials, partly to the fact that the first warrant prepared had been incorrectly drawn. Admitting with equal frankness the receipt of the £1000, he stated that, in accepting it, he supposed it to be paid him as the price of four £250 shares in the Great Farm recently resold by him to the patentees, and that, till informed by Jacob that half the sum

[1] I.e. to the King's Remembrancer.

had been contributed by the Petty farmers, the idea that the latter were involved had never crossed his mind. These assertions, if confirmed, disposed of both the bribery counts at once. Their refutation, therefore, was vital to the prosecution's case.

Led by Wolstenholme, Garway and Dawes, the magnates of the Great Farm presented on that issue a united front. They agreed that Middlesex had at one time coquetted with the project of acquiring an interest in the farm, but were emphatic that he had quickly changed his mind, with the result that, when they went to allotment, the question of assigning to him shares had never even arisen. The principal evidence rebutting their assertion was circumstantial. It was that if, as alleged by these potentates, Middlesex did not invest in the farm, circles closely in touch both with him and with them had acted, in some cases with the encouragement of the farmers themselves, on the assumption that he did. Ingram stated that the Treasurer had to his knowledge reserved a block of six shares to be distributed as a *solatium* among members of the rival syndicate, formed by Ingram at the minister's request before the old gang got the contract, to bid up the rent in the interest of the Crown. A less suspect witness testified that a share, which he believed to have been procured him by Middlesex, was still in his possession. Two others declared that, on applying for shares to Wolstenholme and Garway, they had been advised by them to have recourse to Middlesex, with the remark that he held shares of which he might be willing to dispose. Finally, the Chancellor of the Exchequer, who himself for a time had money in the farm, recounted in convincing detail a conversation of the preceding June between himself and the Treasurer. The latter, he asserted, when driving home to Chelsea, had given him a lift, and, in chatting on this and that, had boasted with glee of the £1000 just cleared by him through the sale of his holding of four shares in the Great Farm. Weston had seen Middlesex at close quarters for over two years, and was neither an innocent nor a Quixote. It is difficult to believe that nine months later, when the pack was closing in for the kill, he gratuitously concocted a fiction to prop his chief's falling fortunes at the peril of his own.

Against these inferences and recollections there were hard facts to be set. The entry of the fatal gratuities in the farmers' books, combined with the absence from the accounts of the Great Farm of any reference to Middlesex's alleged investment, was one. The story told by the intermediary through whose hands the money passed, added others. Abraham Jacob—'my Lord's necessary creature and petty chapman', as Coke contemptuously called him—stood too near the Treasurer to escape the odium of the latter's supposed misdeeds.[1] His assumed reluctance to reveal their full enormity had earned him, a month before, black looks from the Commons' Committee on Grievances, but, under the educative influence of an interview with the Solicitor-General[2]—whose arguments we do not know, but can guess—he had so far 'recollected himself' as to promise to 'tell all the whole naked truth'. Included by the Treasurer, as a confidant on whose reliability he could count, among the witnesses to be called for the defence, he ended by giving evidence designed, it seemed, to aid the prosecution. He may fairly be numbered among those of whom an observer wrote that 'many of his accusers were his bosom friends'.[3] The fallen minister's bitter outburst in the Tower—'I have many enemies and great ones... I have few friends and those dare not appear for me.... The examinations and inquisitions clear me, for I am not troubled in those kinds or any other, save those which Jacob hath forsworn me into'[4]—shows that the turncoat's dagger had struck home.

Actually, Jacob's testimony pointed more than one way. He agreed with his fellow-farmers that the initial wish of Middlesex to obtain shares in the Great Farm had quickly died down, but added that later, in the summer of 1623, when, with the return of the East India fleet in August, business prospects were looking up, it had again come to life. The patentees, however, dreaded the associates[5] whom the Treasurer might, they feared, bring with him. Their part in the gratuity was depicted by Jacob as intended less, as they had declared, to accelerate the long overdue acceptance of their security than to buy off a possibly embarrassing partner. His account of the crucial interview at which he informed Middlesex of the sources of the sum subscribed is at once instructive and ambiguous. The outburst of angry astonishment—'You have done me wrong. This will trench into mine honour. I received of you £1000 as my part of

---

[1] Jacob had, for example, been employed by Middlesex to levy the composition for groceries in London and the out-ports (*L.J.* 10 May).

[2] *C.J.* 8 April.

[3] McClure, *Letters of John Chamberlain*, vol. II, pp. 55–6 (Chamberlain to Carleton, 10 April).

[4] *Cranfield MSS.* no. 2456 (28 May).

[5] The individual whom they were determined to keep at a distance was Middlesex's old friend, Arthur Ingram (Statement of Abraham Dawes, *L.J.* 7 May).

the Great Farm, and it had no reference to the Petty farmers'—
with which the Treasurer was reported by him to have greeted his
statement that the Petty farmers had contributed half the £1000
was susceptible of two interpretations.[1] It could be regarded either
as yet another smoke-screen on the part of a hardened hypocrite or
as the genuine dismay of an honest man, horrified to discover the
false position in which, without his knowledge, he had been placed.
In his written answer of 1 May, even more effectively than in his
subsequent reply to the Attorney-General, Middlesex had hammered
home the second view with indignant force. Jacob, if he did not
state, insinuated the first. The impression made by the unhappy
wretch is of one a prey to fright, but tormented to the last by agonies
of doubt of whom it is his interest to be frightened most.

It is possible, therefore, though not certain, that the reader, while
grateful to the trembler for the vivid details supplied by him, should
take his testimony with some grains of salt. Whether that be so or
not, one fact, at least, is beyond dispute. It is that the precautions
taken by the Treasurer to ensure that his conduct should be seen
in the most favourable light made it doubly inevitable that the
worst construction should be put upon it. Alarmed early in 1624 by
the approach of a Parliament of whose members many, as he rightly
foresaw, would be under Buckingham's thumb, Middlesex set himself to obliterate all traces of transactions which his enemies might
use against him. On the one hand, he extracted from Jacob a letter
written in January of that year, but antedated to June 1623, in which
the £1000 handed him by Jacob was stated to be the price of four
£250 shares in the Great Farm. On the other, he gave orders that
the compromising £500 contributed by the Petty farmers should be

---

[1] It obviously makes a difference to the view taken of these transactions whether it
be thought that Middlesex knew, at the time when he accepted the £1000, the two sources
from which that sum was derived, or that he did not learn till later that half of it came
from the Petty Farm. Jacob's narrative is compatible with either interpretation. Middlesex, in his written answer of 1 May was, of course, emphatic that the true interpretation
was the second, not the first. He stated that Jacob offered him £1000 for the four shares
in the Great Farm, an offer which he accepted; that Jacob and his partners, instead of
paying for these shares out of their private accounts, improperly entered the payment
for them in the books of the two farms, £500 being debited to each as a gratuity to the
Treasurer, 'who little knew of this their unjust proceeding'; that, on discovering what
he professed to regard as a dishonest trick, he reproached Jacob, who promised that all
should be put right; and, finally, that the patentees then 'restored back the money which
they had taken' to the Petty and Great Farms. According to Middlesex, therefore, he
did not know that £500 of the £1000 came from the Petty Farm till after he had accepted
the £1000 as payment for four shares in the Great Farm.

transferred to the accounts of the Great Farm, and that copies of the uncorrected accounts already in circulation should be called in and destroyed. He insisted, in short, to put it bluntly, that the books of both farms should be cooked—or, as he would have said, corrected —in such a way as to show, not what according to his enemies had occurred, but what Middlesex thought should have occurred, and what for a time, till enlightened by Jacob, he may have believed actually to have occurred. It is astonishing that a man of his experience should, if innocent, have resorted to such manœuvres, and hardly less astonishing if he was guilty. Neither step, of course, could be concealed. Both were gifts to the prosecution.[1]

The votes recorded by the peers under these half-dozen heads showed more discrimination than the previous proceedings might have led an observer to expect. On three charges and part of a fourth they pronounced the defendant guilty.[2] Partly, perhaps, in deference to royal representations, they acquitted him on the remainder. If, however, the verdict allowed him on some points the benefit of the doubt, the judgment on his conduct as a whole was unqualified by similar refinements. Declaring that the allegations of 'bribery, extortion, oppression, wrong and deceipt' had been proved to the hilt, and dismissing as, not merely negligible, but noxious, his alleged services to the Crown, it depicted the delinquent as a monster of corruption and greed, unredeemed by the pedestrian virtues of industry, business ability and devotion to duty, which the King had attempted, in his address to the House, to throw into the scales. The sentence which followed, though in detail more severe than that passed on Bacon, was in essentials the same. Of the fine of £50,000 part would certainly be remitted; nor was the criminal's detention in the Tower likely to be long. The important point, both for him

---

[1] The above account omits one minor item of the bribes alleged to have been extorted from the customs-farmers. Middlesex, on receiving from the Petty farmers their customary New Year's gift, a tun of wine, is stated to have turned up his nose at the triviality of the present, with the result that they offered him in addition £100 in cash, which he accepted. In his reply he admitted by implication the truth of the story, but denied that he had mentioned any specific sum.

[2] The charges on which Middlesex was convicted were (1) his mismanagement of the Wardrobe; (2) bribes received from customs-farmers; (3) misconduct in connection with the Office of Ordnance by (a) oppression and extortion in the case of Dallison and other parties, (b) failure to keep the Office adequately supplied; (4) two counts in the charges of misconduct in the Court of Wards, viz. (a) double fees for 'continuances' resulting from the addition of a fee for the Master to that paid to the Surveyor, (b) the entrusting of a stamp to his secretary.

and for the prosecution, was not the particular penalties imposed. It consisted in the ruin of Middlesex's reputation and the termination of his public career.

4. THE AFTERMATH

'Seldom', writes Gardiner of another episode of the early 1620's, 'has the unfitness of the Lords to act as a judicial body been more clearly brought out'.[1] A retrial of the Treasurer by posterity would clearly be absurd; but it is not irrelevant to inquire whether the peers showed to greater advantage as judges of a minister impeached by the Commons than in a case, like that of Yelverton, referred to them by the King. Discretion had caused Middlesex, while he had something still to hope, to distinguish between the chicanery, as it seemed to him, of the Attorney-General and 'the just and honourable dealing' of the Lords; but once the issue was decided, his conviction that his trial had been a caricature of justice was no longer concealed. On the one hand, the procedure, he protested—in particular his summons to the bar, the employment against him of the Law Officers of the Crown, and the denial of counsel to speak for him—offered the unedifying spectacle of a judicial tribunal throwing precedent to the winds. On the other, he was indignant at a conduct of the case at once indulgent to his opponents and harsh, to the point of inhumanity, to himself.

Both reactions were natural in the hour of his humiliation; neither can be dismissed as the cry of a fallen greatness alone. Weighty legal opinion, from Selden's contemporary work to the rules for the management of impeachments summarised half a century later by Sir Matthew Hale, and from Hale to Hargrave's application of his doctrines to the Treasurer's case,[2] can be cited in support of Middlesex's complaint that traditional usage had been jettisoned in order the more easily to bring him down. On the second point, a matter, not of law, but of convention, courtesy and fair play, comment is hardly needed. The utterances of the Lord Keeper; the insulting scepticism with which the defendant's request for a day's respite on account of illness was received; the alleged tampering with witnesses; the

---

[1] Gardiner, *History of England, 1603–1642*, vol. IV, pp. 116–17.

[2] See the works of Selden, Hale and Hargrave, mentioned above (p. 248, n. 4). The Lords virtually admitted the justice of one of Middlesex's complaints by making an order after the trial that counsel should be allowed to delinquents in cases of impeachment (Selden, *op. cit.* p. 103, and Hargrave, *op. cit.* pp. xxxiv–v).

canvassing for votes and occasional oral interventions of the Prince, tell their own story. Nor, it may be added, was the action of the Lords in appending to their judgment a series of denunciations of the defendant's services to the Crown—a matter on which they had heard no evidence and possessed no special qualification to pronounce—calculated to strengthen confidence in their scrupulously judicial temper. Middlesex, on his side, was not of those who turn the other cheek; nor, in his retorts to the 'unchristianlike dealing' of advocates who 'make white black and black white', did he mince his words. 'Baited all day by two mastiffs', he too, on occasion, showed his teeth.

These aspects of the impeachment occasion at first sight some surprise, as a symptom of passions disproportionate to the issues at stake. An occasion is reported on which, in preaching in St Paul's before his master on the text, *Again the devil taketh him up into an exceeding high mountain...*, one of the royal chaplains concluded an eloquent exposition of the proceedings of the demons who administer the finance department of Hell, by pointing to Middlesex, and remarking, much to James' entertainment, 'that man that makes himself rich and his master poor, he is a fit treasurer to the devil'.[1] One may sympathise with the preacher's tribute to the venerable doctrine of the presumptive wickedness of the rich, but regard it, nevertheless, as of some importance to determine the methods by which, in particular cases, the wealth which damns them is obtained. Not the least peculiar features of the indictment of Middlesex are, on the one hand, the almost ludicrous minuteness of the sums for which, on the charges of which most was made, the ambitious worldling was alleged, not only to have sold his soul, but to have ruined his career, and, on the other—since, though not in the first flight, he was by this time a man of means—the failure to reveal the sources from which the fortune which made him 'odious to the people' was derived. The statements of the prosecution do not enable the plunder imputed to him to be expressed in exact terms of cash received; but, even on the assumption of the veracity of the charges held by the Lords to have been proved, it is difficult to rank his predatory exploits as approaching in brilliance the triumphs of a master-brigand like Suffolk, who, after being sentenced in the Star Chamber for extortion, now sat, a respected figure, among the judges who

[1] The story is told by Arthur Wilson, 'Life and reign of James I', in *A Complete History of England* (1719), p. 729.

condemned him.[1] In reality, it may be suggested, the results of an attempt to test the Lords' sweeping judgment by a cold-blooded appeal to facts are less illuminating than a foreign observer's impressionist picture of the conflicting animosities and fears from which the sentence emerged. 'The objects of the inquiry differ with different people. Some act for the punishment of guilt; some to abase a Spanish partisan; some from desire of change; some to profit by the confiscation of his goods to use them for public purposes; and all are moved by his unusual unpopularity as a man of low birth raised by the King's favour to the dignities of Treasurer and an Earldom, [who] behaved very haughtily in the latter, and proved very stingy in making payments in the former. The Prince and Buckingham are his chief enemies.'[2] Given such an atmosphere, discussions of the impeachment in terms either of the legal merits of the procedure employed, or of the delinquent's pecuniary gains, are beside the point. The issues which counted most were on a different plane.

In his final defence before the Peers, Middlesex remarked that, having devoted his public life to reform, it was not surprising that he should be threatened by a reformer's fate. The views of the handful of contemporaries, whose opinions we know, were equally *terre-à-terre*. They treated the famous trial as a tactical stroke in a political campaign; dismissed with a shrug of the shoulders as, coming from such a quarter, mere ritual patter, the prosecution's disquisitions on the sin of greed; and focused their attention on an unpopular Minister's struggle for survival against an alliance between ambitions bent on sweeping an obstruction from their path and interests whose economic nerves the dictatorial, parsimonious parvenu had set on edge. It was partly that cynical attitude to the impeachment as the last round in a pugilistic contest which prompted the sympathy expressed for the defeated champion. It was natural that Goodman[3] should vindicate the memory of a life-long friend; but the incurably quixotic—and at times, it must be added,

---

[1] A contemporary report of Suffolk's trial (A. B. Grosart, *Lismore Papers*, second series, vol. II, pp. 160–80) puts the losses caused the Crown by his depredations at approximately £30,000, exclusive of his frauds in connection with the Crown's jewels. As he had been pardoned for the latter by the King, no figure for the jewels was stated in Court; but gossip put it at £240,000. For another estimate of his peculations see *D.N.B.*

[2] *Cal. S.P. Ven. 1623–5*, no. 351, 26 April 1624.

[3] Goodman, *The Court of James I*, vol. I, pp. 227–9.

feather-headed—Bishop was not alone in holding that the virtues of Middlesex had done more to wreck him than his sins. 'Very much prosecute and, some say, persecute...the grounds of the censure are not such as deserved so great and severe a sentence'[1] was the comment of a Scottish peer who, while thinking royal favours to the Treasurer overdone, was shocked by the persistence of the Prince in pursuing a vendetta odious to the King. The offences ascribed to him, wrote a correspondent to the former diplomat, Sir Dudley Carleton, when the hearing before the Lords was about to begin, 'are not very heinous or inexcusable in these days, but he must be sacrificed unless the King interferes; there has been no man in England these two hundred years whose ruin has been so thirsted after by all sorts of people'.[2] The biographer of Williams had much in praise of his unpleasant patron to say; but he does not seem to have regarded the Lord Keeper's part in the impeachment as a feather in his cap. 'He [Middlesex] was charged with corruption and sordid bribery', but 'many sages contended that the charges came not to full discovery...I spake with few, when it [sc. the trial] was recent, who were contented with it, except the members of the House, who would not dislike their own work.'[3] 'Perdidit Fides; he was lost at Court', wrote a younger contemporary, 'for his fidelity to King James in sparing his treasure, and not answering the expensiveness of a great favourite.'[4] In Chamberlain's view, Middlesex had suffered less for his offences than for his temerity in denying them. Dismissing the former as peccadilloes which an indulgent eye would have overlooked, the critic remarked that few previous holders of the Treasurership would have emerged from so searching a scrutiny unscathed. But, himself obsequious to servility, he was shocked beyond measure by the audacity with which Middlesex outfaced prosecution, peers, and his two august opponents, and not only prophesied, but hoped, that a pride so Satanic would have a fall. When all was over, he was still ill at ease. Had the fall been profound enough? The proprieties had been vindicated, but was it certain that they were safe? Shorn of power and wealth, why had not the defeated, but still haughty, Lucifer been stripped of his titles as well?

[1] Hist. MSS. Comm., *Sup. Rep. on MSS. of the Earls of Kellie and Mar*, pp. 200–2 (letters of Kellie to Mar, 13, 22 May 1624).

[2] *S.P.D. Jas. I*, CLXXII, nos. 56 and 60, 14, 15 April 1624.

[3] J. Hacket, *Scrinia Reserata*, pp. 189–90.

[4] Thomas Fuller, *The Church History of Britain* (1845), vol. III, pp. 288–9, *Perdidit Fides* is said to have been Middlesex's motto, conspicuously displayed at Copt Hall.

'Having failed to crush him low enough when they might, he may live to be a pestilent instrument, and crush some of them.'[1]

Rumour lent for a time some colour to these alarms. The chronic malady depicted in the Venetian Embassy's variations on the theme 'desperately short of cash' could neither last for ever nor cure itself. Would not darkening financial horizons compel the recall to some unspectacular, but influential, post, of the pilot whose 'alacrity and industry' had weathered previous storms?[2] Such surmises—the tittle-tattle of gossip-mongers—missed the moral of the Treasurer's fate. In reality, the motives of high policy, which impelled his enemies to liquidate an opponent with the ear of the King, made it even more essential, as their plans unfolded, to perpetuate his eclipse. The prospect which had appalled the finance minister was a diplomatic revolution issuing in war. During the critical six weeks of his ordeal at Westminster events on other fronts[3] had made the nightmare of yesterday the reality of today. Buckingham's new line abroad had as its domestic corollary a short way with opposition at home. The elimination of Middlesex, stripped not only of the Treasurership, but of his Mastership of the Wards, of his seat on the Council, and even of so humble an office as that of Commissioner of the Subsidy, must be seen in that context.[4] In spite of its decorous legal drapery, it was a particular case of the same repressive policy as that which silenced dissent on the Council; and, while holding the most formidable of its critics, Bristol—whom Buckingham wished, but did not dare, to send to the Tower—under virtual home arrest, entrusted the national finances to the amiable nonentity, Ley; rewarded with a peerage the sycophantic Conway; and welcomed, if it did not prompt, the retirement of his Catholic fellow-secretary, Calvert, to make room for the anti-Spanish stalwart, Morton. In such circumstances, the ex-Treasurer might be called

---

[1] McClure, op. cit. vol. II, pp. 559–60 (Chamberlain to Carleton, 13 May 1624).

[2] Cal. S.P. Ven. 1623–5, 14, 21 June, 12 July 1624.

[3] E.g. the final rupture with Spain (6 April); the conditional promise of troops to Mansfeld (18 April); the appointment of a Council of War (19 April); Carlisle's mission to Paris to negotiate a marriage treaty with a view to joint action against Spain (17 May).

[4] Pending the appointment of Chief Justice Ley as Treasurer on 20 December 1624, the Treasurership was in commission, Weston, the Chancellor of the Exchequer, doing most of the work (Gardiner, op. cit. vol. v, p. 310). Naunton succeeded Middlesex as Master of the Wards in October 1624 (McClure, op. cit. vol. II, p. 582). Middlesex remained nominally a member of the Council till 9 April 1625, when, together with Bristol and Suffolk, and certain other members, he was discharged (ibid. p. 609). He had been excluded from the Commission of the Subsidy in June 1624 (ibid. p. 564).

on for confidential advice; but both short-term considerations and long, both the tactical exigencies of the moment and the sentence of the Peers, made nonsense of prognostications that the actor hissed in May 1624 off the public stage would quickly reappear among the leading figures on it. Actually, sixteen years were to elapse before, on the eve of another and more formidable crisis, he was allowed once more to take his seat in the Lords.[1]

The letters of Middlesex show that the plunge, at the height of his powers, from eminence to ignominy hit him hard. At the moment, however, he had more to do than lick his wounds. Released from the Tower early in June, within three days of the prorogation of Parliament on 29 May, he found himself confronted, not, of course, by poverty, but by financial liabilities of an indeterminate amount, which time and adroitness would be required to meet. Convention made the fine of £50,000 rather a demonstration of disapproval than a statement of cash to be paid. But would the King follow precedent in remitting a substantial sum? In the fortnight following the trial, a Bill introduced in the Lords had been rushed through both Houses, which made the fallen minister's real property liable, not only for the fine, but also for whatever other debts, whether to the Crown or private persons, might hereafter come to light, as well as—a comprehensive rubric—for restitution to all parties wronged.[2] James accompanied his *pro forma* assent to a measure which he obviously disliked with admonitions intended to blunt its edge. He uttered words of sympathy with his former protégé, whom he exonerated from the charge of accepting bribes; questioned the justice of the sentence passed on him; declared that

---

[1] That is, assuming that the date of his readmission as given by the *D.N.B.* (4 May 1640) is correct; on the other hand, the name of Middlesex appears later in that year, in a list of absentees, as still 'under the censure of this noble House' (*L.J.* vol. IV, 16 November 1640).

[2] *L.J.* vol. III, 14, 15 May, and *C.J.* vol. I, 19, 28 May 1624. The Act did not, so far as the Crown was concerned, remain a dead letter. It was designed to compel Middlesex to pay its creditors, under the pain of the survey and sale of part of his lands. See Hist. MSS. Comm., *Fourth Report*, App., p. 288 (Ley and Weston to Middlesex, 1 January 1625); *S.P.D. Jas. I*, CLXXXII, no. 34 (Middlesex to Ley and Weston, 23 January stating that he is pressed to impossibilities by the creditors of the Household and the Wardrobe); CLXXXIII, no. 37 (same to Sec. Conway, 10 February, Lord Steward pressing for an extent of lands); CLXXIV, no. 27 (same to same, 21 February 1625, Lord Steward persecutes him extremely, so pressed by creditors that he would rather be in his grave); Hist. MSS. Comm., *MSS. of the Earl Cowper*, vol. I, p. 182, 29 January (the King resolved to have the £20,000 paid; the Lord Steward to send particular creditors to the Earl; if the Earl refuses an accord with them, H.M.'s pleasure is that the extent should proceed without further delay).

he would not in future permit the conduct of his officers to be questioned in Parliament; and stated that, in the present case, he himself would proportion the punishment to the crime.[1] But here again, what exactly, in pecuniary terms, did these consolatory qualifications imply? Finally, an order by the House of Lords added a few straws to the load. It required the payment by the ex-Treasurer, in instalments of £1000 odd a year, of over £13,000 to a dozen officers of the Ordnance, together with damages of an unspecified amount to three of the more influential victims in the same department alleged to have been defrauded by him.[2]

It will be seen that the sums in which Middlesex might be mulcted, if not crushing to one with his resources, were more than a mere trifle. The total, though uncertain, would unquestionably much exceed the pecuniary penalties levied on Bacon and Suffolk; while he must meet it at a moment when the loss of profitable posts had, by his own account, reduced his income by approximately one-half. Of the possible claims on him, that which at once most perturbed him and seemed least incapable of readjustment was the fine. From his creditors he could expect no mercy; but he had hoped that the Crown's demand might be waived, and Weston's news of the King's first decision on the subject was a shock.[3] The result was a round of appeals, rebuffs, concessions, compromises, further rebuffs and renewed appeals, in which quotations fluctuating between zero and a figure well above that fixed by the Lords were watched by the small world of interested observers with the animation readily aroused in it by the exhilarating spectacle of lengthening and shortening odds. Lady Middlesex, who was not a miracle of discretion, fought the battle for total remission, not wisely, but too well. Not content with letting loose her detrimental brother, Arthur Brett—by this time in high quarters a red rag to a bull—she engaged in tearful pilgrimages from Chelsea to Theobalds, and from Theobalds to Royston, till at last James, whose taste in bores, though catholic, was his own, politely, but firmly—'Madam, you shall not need to

[1] S.P.D. Jas. I, CLXV, nos. 60 and 61 (29 May 1624) and CLXVII, no. 10 (2 June); McClure, op. cit. vol. II, pp. 561–2.

[2] L.J. 20, 25, 28 May 1624. The officers were to be paid £1062 down, plus £500 half-yearly from Lady day 1623, till £12,000 should have been paid over and above the initial £1062, plus interest at 10% on payments in arrears. The three parties mentioned by name were Sir Roger Dallison, Sir Thomas Monson and Sir Philip Cary.

[3] Harl. MSS. 1581, f. 208, Weston to Buckingham, n.d. but latter part of May 1624, where Middlesex is described as extremely dismayed by the news of the King's pleasure respecting the fine, which was contrary to his expectation.

trouble yourself further'—showed the suppliant the door.[1] The preliminaries over, the ground was clear for business. The Government's financial prospects had gone, since the Treasurer's incarceration, from bad to worse. Whether for such pecuniary reasons, or from fear of his favourite's reproaches,[2] or because, as he alleged, a further study of the trial had convinced him that his initial leniency had been overdone, the King's attitude had stiffened.[3] Middlesex, on his side, though he still had some turning movements up his sleeve, had come by the summer to the conclusion that a frontal attack on the principle of a fine was hopeless, and, the better to bargain as to figures, called his uncompromising wife to heel. July 1624, therefore, saw a more realistic phase of the discussions begin.

It opened with a notification from the Crown that the fine had been fixed at £30,000, and an order that full particulars of the petitioner's financial position should be supplied. The result was a return by Middlesex putting his income at £8000 to £10,000, of which by this time more than half came from real property, and his net debts, largely to Van Lore and the officers of the Ordnance, at £34,000 odd. He added a note to the effect that he was encumbered with marriageable daughters entitled to a portion of £8000 apiece, and—since his long suit was not humour—concluded with a prayer that, if the King must add a fine to his other penalties, he would at least, greatly reduce it, and not, after seventeen years of service, turn an old employee, his wife and three prospective heiresses adrift to beg.[4] The figure of £30,000 had been sufficiently firm for its allocation between the Navy, Wardrobe and Stables to be provisionally determined; but James' resolutions were rarely built upon a rock. During the next three months the fine began to crumble, and by

[1] Hist. MSS. Comm., *Fourth Report*, App., p. 28 (Nicholas Herman to Middlesex, July 1624).

[2] For the anxiety of the King to conceal from Buckingham and the Prince the receipt, via Holderness, of a letter from Middlesex, see *ibid*. 10 January 1625.

[3] *Cal. S.P.D. 1623–5*, CLXX, no. 26, Conway to Weston, 21 July 1624. Weston is to inform Middlesex that, after three readings of the charges and answers at the trial, the King is shocked by those relating to the Court of Wards and the Office of Ordnance. He has, therefore, fixed the fine at £30,000. Weston is to ascertain the value of Middlesex's estate.

[4] *Ibid.* CLXX, no. 82, Weston to Conway, 31 July 1624. Thinks that Middlesex's account of his landed property is correct, but that some parts of the personal property are omitted. *Ibid*. no. 82, I, petition of Middlesex to King. Protests that he is unable, owing to debts, and loss of offices, to pay £30,000. Begs for total remission or, at least, further substantial reduction. *Ibid*. no. 82, II, statement by Middlesex of his property and debts.

November was down by another third. There, for a time, it stuck. Middlesex denounced £20,000 as the largest penalty ever exacted; protested that it would involve him in the sale of £30,000 worth of land; and, in the hope of further reductions, begged that payment might be made by him in annual instalments to the Exchequer, which the King might later reduce, and not by assigning the Crown's claim on him to its creditors, who would naturally demand the uttermost farthing. James, however, for once stood firm. Early in the following year he told the Council that £20,000 was the lowest figure which he would accept; and six weeks later the Lord Steward, who had Household debts to meet, was pressing, in default of immediate payment, for a survey, with a view to the sale of Middlesex's property. In the language of the malicious Venetians, the ex-Treasurer was to be sold up.[1]

At this point other influences intervened. The road to the royal heart lay through the Grand Vizier, whose part in his opponent's ruin was an open secret. While the culprit still languished in the Tower, Weston, presumably with his approval, had appealed to the favourite to speed his release; and later, in September, Middlesex himself suggested an interview for mutual explanations in a dignified letter which, apparently, elicited no reply.[2] Among the friends who stood by him in adversity were two, who, for personal reasons, had the Duke's ear. One, Lord Cromwell, a soldier who had seen service in Ireland, and who relied on the Viceroy, as he had virtually become, to push his career, was sufficiently intimate with his patron to convey to him hints of the public attitude towards his one-man regime in language of a bluntness not always, it seems, too well received, but which, to judge by Cromwell's appointment on the staff of the ill-fated Spanish expedition, did him no harm.[3] The other, Dr John More, was a Catholic physician, to whom we find the

---

[1] On the above see McClure, *op. cit.* vol. II, p. 580; *S.P.D. Jas I*, CXXIV, no. 41 (Weston to Conway); Hist. MSS. Comm., *MSS. of the Earl Cowper*, vol. I, p. 182 (Sir J. Coke to Buckingham); *Cal. S.P. Ven. 1623–5*, no. 787, 31 Jan. 1625.

[2] *Harl. MSS.* 1581, f. 206 (Weston to Buckingham, 29 May 1624); *S.P.D. Jas. I*, CLXXII, no. 8 (Middlesex to Buckingham, 5 September 1624).

[3] For the intervention of Cromwell, see three letters from him to Middlesex of June 1624 (Hist. MSS. Comm., *Fourth Report*, App., p. 288) and of 17, 26 Aug. (R. Davies, *op. cit.* pp. 100–2). The writer reports that Buckingham has received Middlesex's letter. He hopes to arrange a meeting between them; begs Middlesex to tell him what he can offer Buckingham that may be worth the latter's acceptance, e.g. Chelsea House, and urges Middlesex to disclose the plots of enemies who have intrigued to bring Buckingham, as well as Middlesex, down.

Duchess referring a relation for a report on her health,[1] and who, whether as the family doctor, or on grounds of religion, had the entrée at the Buckinghams' house. Acting independently, first Cromwell and later More set themselves to ascertain the conditions on which the Duke could be induced to secure for his now prostrate foe a settlement less onerous than that announced by James. Buckingham, they both seemed aware, was not the man to serve the Lord, or any one else, for nought; but, if appeals to sentiment were futile, might not a lure which tickled vanity and appetite at once cause the sullen fish to rise? On the fall of his friend, the Chancellor, the Duke, who was not fastidious, had pressed him to sell York House, the mere thought of parting with which, as its unhappy owner wrote, was a misery to him.[2] Might not a similar morsel tempt the rapacious favourite now?

Conscious that he held the whip hand, the subject of these speculations was in no haste to state his terms. It gradually became apparent, however, that the augurs had divined aright. The prize which allured Buckingham and his wife, for whose marriage with the favourite their victim believed her to have had largely himself to thank,[3] was the mansion at Chelsea originally erected in 1520 by Sir Thomas More, reconstructed by Sir Robert Cecil in the 1590's, and purchased in 1619 by Cranfield from Spenser's friend, at once man of letters and adventurer, Sir Arthur Gorges. If Buckingham's intervention was to be purchased, the conveyance of Chelsea Great House to the Duke, either directly or via the King, must be part of the price. Into the haggling between these harpies and More; Nicholas Herman, Middlesex's secretary; and Lady Middlesex, it is needless to enter.[4] The settlement which finally emerged in May from the recon-

---

[1] *S.P.D. Chas. I*, IV, no. 140, 28 July 1625. For further references to Dr John More see *ibid.* CXXII, no. 48, and CCLV, no. 135.

[2] On Bacon's refusal to sell him York House, Buckingham appears to have endeavoured to induce him to sell it to Middlesex, and Bacon agreed to that course (Spedding, *The Letters and the Life of Francis Bacon*, vol. VII, pp. 342–3, 346–7.

[3] In a draft letter to the Duchess, possibly not sent, of 1631 (R. Davies, *The Greatest House at Chelsey*, p. 130) Middlesex reminded her of the events preceding her marriage when, in March 1620, 'you by your act reduced yourself into as distressed an estate as you have brought me and mine.... My bowels then did yearn on your behalf...in so much as if it had not been for my advice, fortified with reasons, on the one side, and the now Lord Savage, his discretion and stoutness, on the other, I may truly affirm you had never been the Duke's wife.'

[4] For the discussions, see letter to Middlesex from More of 3 November 1624, and 27, 28 April 1625, and from Herman, 4, 6, 7, 10 January 1625 (Hist. MSS. Comm., *Fourth Report*, App., p. 288; R. Davies, *op. cit.* pp. 104, 107–8).

ciling formula proposed by More killed three birds with one stone. Its essence was the reduction to £5000 of the fine to be exacted in cash, accompanied by the transfer to the King both of Middlesex's patent for the farm of the sugar duties, which still had sixteen years to run, and of Chelsea House, which was quickly presented to the favourite.[1] Thus the hard-pressed debtor escaped the necessity for large-scale sales of land. The Crown secured an asset of greater value than the £20,000 fine. Not least important, since the heart of the King was in his hand, the coveted property was acquired gratis by the Duke.

Middlesex had driven in his day too many hard bargains to be entitled to sympathetic tears; but his outburst—'Naboth's vineyard was justly gotten in respect of Chelsea'[2]—may be pardoned. It is a question whether he ever forgave Buckingham, whom he charitably believed, or affected to believe, to have gone to his grave tormented by the thought of wrongs done to a friend;[3] but he renewed polite, if distant, relations with him. We cannot say whether he deserved Goodman's praise for his generosity in declining, at a moment when the Duke seemed to be threatened by a fate resembling his own, to fortify the opposition with the inside Treasury information which he was peculiarly qualified to supply,[4] but his refusal to seize the opportunity of avenging his personal injuries[5] was in agreeable contrast with the vindictive malice shown by influential colleagues to himself. His reserve was the more creditable because the favourite's

[1] McClure, *op. cit.* vol. II, p. 619, 21 May 1625. The suggestion that he should compound for his fine by resigning the sugar farm, said to be worth £4000 a year, had been made by Middlesex, but unfavourably received, in August 1624 (*S.P.D. Jas. I*, CLXXI, no. 25, 7 August 1624), and Cromwell in the same month had mentioned as a possibility the gift of his house to Buckingham. More's plan combined the two proposals.

[2] R. Davies, *op. cit.* pp. 110–12 (abstracts of letters from Middlesex to Harman, 29 April and 1 May 1625).

[3] In his draft letter of 1631, Middlesex reminded the Duchess of her statement that the Duke had told her that 'he pulled me down, but withal confessed he never had a good day since'. He also cited Lord Savage to the effect that Buckingham 'was resolved to make me reparation, and was so troubled until he had done so that it struck a dagger to his heart that he did but name me'.

[4] See letter of October 1631, from Goodman to Middlesex, printed by G. I. Soden in *Godfrey Goodman, Bishop of Gloucester, 1583–1656* (1953), pp. 189–91. The writer reminded Middlesex that 'when the good Duke was troubled in Parliament, and that especially concerning the King's treasure, when as no man could have informed so much as yourself, yet was your Lordship then not only silent, but did furthermore search for some notes, which did abundantly serve to acquit and justify the good Duke'.

[5] Letters printed in R. Davies, *loc. cit.* in which Middlesex expresses his reluctance to testify as to the Duke's attitude in the matter of his fine.

mounting megalomania filled, on public grounds, the former Treasurer with dismay. Himself a member of the House in the year which had seen the youthful Villiers' début at Court, he was convinced, as in May 1626 he wrote to an ecclesiastical acquaintance,[1] that Buckingham's only hope was to endeavour to recapture the confidence of Parliament, and that threats to break it would end in its breaking him. The letter preceded by three months the ceremonial banquet at Chelsea House at which the King and Queen honoured by their presence its new proprietors. By that time the writing was already on the wall.

A curious episode revealed somewhat later how nearly full circle the wheel had by that time come. At a meeting, in May 1626, of the Commons Committee appointed to investigate the revenues extracted by the Duke from the Crown, Sir Robert Pye, whose hatred of his brother's former chief was still unappeased, proposed that, since Middlesex had made hay at high speed to the tune of £112,000, he too should be examined. Eliot, who was in the chair, had crossed swords with the ex-Minister in the days when the latter was a power; but Pye's inveterate malignity to a fallen foe was too much for him. He remarked, in effect, with agreeable astringency, that he neither knew nor cared whether the speaker's statement was true, but that one fact, at least, was beyond dispute. It was that 'Middlesex had merited well of the King, and had done him that service that few had ever done'.[2]

---

[1] Hist. MSS. Comm., *Fourth Report*, p. 288, Middlesex to Francis White, then Dean of Carlisle, and later Bishop of Carlisle, Norwich and Ely.

[2] *Ibid.* p. 289 (3 May 1626). It may be added that time seems to have induced a similar change of attitude in some of the City magnates whose evidence at the trial had helped to bring Middlesex down. The unanimous opinion at a dinner attended by Sir Abraham Dawes and Sir John Wolstenholme, reported ten years later by Burlamachi to Nicholas Herman, the ex-Treasurer's Secretary, was that 'no man ever suffered for so little as the Earl of Middlesex' (*ibid.* p. 293, 8 Aug. 1637).

CHAPTER IX

CONCLUSION

Eliot's tribute was an epitaph on the public labours of one whose private life had still another nineteen years to run. There are careers which leave on the observer an impression of consistency and completeness, as of the unconscious logic of a continuously unfolding plan. Cranfield's brilliant, but broken, course, a collection of striking torsos, not a finished work, has no such unity to show. His reputation in the City, and the prestige attaching to 'the great wit and understanding in all the mysteries of trade',[1] for which, a generation later, Clarendon had an admiring word to spare, survived his political eclipse; while the qualities which caused the resourceful minister's advice to be invoked, if too rarely followed, by James continued, in the graver crises of the ensuing reign, to make him a counsellor confidentially consulted by his former master's son.[2] The fact remains that the comment passed on the morrow of the catastrophe which stayed at fifty the Treasurer's forceful hand—'a man forgotten clean'[3]—was not, during the culprit's life, reversed by time. As the tree fell, so it lay; and few biographical watersheds are more abrupt than that which divides the toils and contentions of Cranfield's stormy youth and middle age from the dignified and opulent obscurity of his closing decade at Copt Hall. A final verdict must obviously take account of both. There is something to be said, however, for pausing for a moment at the cross roads of his fortunes to ponder the lessons of the race already run. How, in that limited perspective, does the record look?

Cranfield was, of course, a more complex personality than a study restricted, like the present work, to his business and public activities suggests. His City experience, it may readily be conceded, left its mark on him for life, and must be given in all accounts of his career a conspicuous place. Nothing, however, can be more superficial

[1] Clarendon, *The History of the Rebellion*, ed. W. D. Macray, vol. I, p. 26.
[2] Goodman, *op. cit.* vol. I. p. 327, and below, p. 293.
[3] A. B. Grosart, *Lismore Papers*, 2nd ser., vol. III, pp. 114-15 (Sir John Leeke to Earl of Cork, 15 August 1624).

than the *naïveté* which, having classified an individual by his occupational or social group, insists on discovering in him at every turn the traits, and nothing but the traits, conventionally supposed to be characteristic of an artificially constructed type. Granted the significance of Cranfield's twenty years in commerce, it remains to consider what manner of commercial man he was. To that question a mere recital of his economic interests provides no adequate reply.

Not the least attractive feature of the London of Elizabeth and her two successors was the zeal for the advancement of education and culture shown by figures, eminent and obscure, in business life. Cranfield did not imitate his fellow Adventurer, Gresham, in founding a college, or, like Billingsley, Stow, Speed, and other less familiar names, such as Grafton and Nicolls, himself contribute to learning or scientific thought; but the continued hold on him in middle life of the scholastic influences of his youth, the friends of his leisure hours, and, as his means increased, the environment and manner of existence that he used them to create, add a touch of mingled realism and humanity to a portrait based on his professional pursuits alone. Like his choice of books to buy; his occasional visits to the theatre as an antidote to days and nights at the Exchequer; and, not least, the library—'the treasure of a Lord Treasurer'—later housed at Copt Hall, by the gift of whose war-worn remains the third Earl was to win the heart of that lovable book-worm, Fuller, they suggest that the man of docquets and trade returns was not immune to the civilised tradition of which the achievements of merchants with literary or scientific leanings and historically-minded craftsmen were the fruit.[1] *The Gruicampus* of a comic Latin poem is a welcome

---

[1] For books see Hist. MSS. Comm., *Cranfield Papers, 1551–1612*, pp. 179, 213, 232, 236,256. Those mentioned between 1608 and 1612 include works by Cicero, Tacitus and St Augustine, together with the productions of such moderns as de Comines, Bacon, the anonymous authors of treatises on the History of the Netherlands and the Treaty with Spain, and two volumes of Andrewes' sermons. For visits to the theatre see *ibid.* p. 213, and Goodman, *op. cit.* vol. II, p. 215 (letter from Cranfield to Buckingham, 4 December 1621, where the recently appointed Treasurer writes of the crushing load of work at the Exchequer). For the library at Copt Hall, see T. Fuller, *The Church History of Britain*, ed. J. S. Brewer (1845), vol. III, pp. 3–6, containing the dedication of the fifth book of the *Church History* to Lionel, third Earl of Middlesex. The dedication describes the first Earl, whose second son the third Earl was, as one who 'by his mere natural parts and experience acquired that perfection of invention, expression and judgement to which those who make learning their sole study do never arrive'. Copt Hall was searched for arms by the parliamentary troops 12 July 1644 (Hist. MSS. Comm., *Fourth Report*, App., p. 296).

figure among the choice and lively spirits invited to 'the philosophical feast' of a circle which includes, in addition to well-known officials and members of Parliament, Donne, Inigo Jones, Richard Martyn, a celebrity whose eloquence and wit had made him the orator chosen by the City to voice the capital's enthusiasm at the first appearance in it of the King, and the jester and butt of the group, Thomas Coryat of the *Crudities*. What Coryat's banker thought of his eccentric client we do not know; but the fervour of the comedian's tribute to 'my sincere and entire friend, Mr Lionel Cranfield, the original and principal animator' of the publication of his book, speaks for itself.[1]

The truth is that, judged by his ambitions and style of life, the failings of the 'base fellow'[2] floated by wealth to undeserved distinction proved, to the annoyance of some among his critics, to be in some respects the antithesis of those which convention had taught them to expect. The merchant of contemporary literature varied both with his creator's predilections and with the tastes at different times in fashion among the heterogeneous publics for whom dramatic authors wrote; but a favourite target of satire was the sanctimonious niggard whose occupational disease of meanness wrung a groan from him at every penny spent. The meticulous record of the *minutiae* of Cranfield's personal outlay kept, under his supervision, by a trusted employee is a tribute to the vigilance of the master's eye, and later his war on royal bounty to ornamental parasites was to arouse indignant cries at Court; but his personal affinities were with the class to whom expenditure, rather than income, was the mark of social status and whose foible was display. Once success was on the way, his outlay was as lavish as his nose for gain was keen, and the parsimony which, as a minister, he preached did not long remain conspicuous among the virtues practised in his private life. The new house in Wood Street which he launched at the age of twenty-eight, was hardly, to judge by the bills received, a monument to thrift. Pishobury, whose home farm was his hobby, was meant, like his other ventures, to pay its way; but his reiterated injunctions as to the lay-out of its gardens combine an eye to utilitarian considerations

---

[1] The officials included John West, secondary to the King's Remembrancer in the Exchequer, and one Master Connock, Auditor of the Prince; the M.P.'s (i.e. members of the Parliament dissolved February 1611), Sir Robert Phelips, Sir Henry Neville, Sir Henry Goodere and Mr Hoskins. See Hist. MSS. Comm., *Cranfield Papers*, p. 271; *S.P.D. Jas. I*, LVII, no. 2 (September 1611); I. A. Schapiro, 'The Mermaid Club', in *Mod. Lang. Rev.* vol. LXIV, no. 1, January 1950.

[2] *Cal. S.P.D. Jas. I, 1611–18*, p. 406 (Sherbourne to Carleton, 18 November 1618).

with more than a touch of the solicitude of Bacon's famous essay to make the most of aesthetic charms. He intended to make Chelsea Great House the palace of a merchant prince, with which no other private residence in London could compete; and, once in possession, gave his appetite for magnificence free rein, arranging for the gateway to be designed by Inigo Jones, and spending apparently more on the reconstruction of the mansion and its surroundings than it had cost him to buy. His reward was the applause with which Sir Henry Wotton, in presenting to him the recently published *Elements of Architecture*, saluted a fellow-enthusiast whose 'noble love' of the enchanting art almost equalled his own.[1]

It was inevitable that a dominating personality, marked by traits so distinctive and pronounced, should leave, as it ploughed its way through the muddy waters of the Court, a turmoil in its wake. In the days of Cranfield's power, he was loved, it seems, by some, envied and disliked by more, and an offensively intimidating figure, perhaps, to most. No man could desire a warmer tribute of affection than the description of him given by his friend and fellow-labourer in the stony wilderness of Irish reform, Sir Dudley Norton: 'very gentle and good in all his courses, being far from offering injury and as far from enduring any, not willing to engage himself in suits, but very earnest in them if they be once begun'.[2] There were quarters, on the other hand, where the Treasurer's haughty independence was resented as 'a sullen and proud humour',[3] doubly unbecoming in 'a fellow'—so the usual slander ran—'of so mean a condition that none but a poor-spirited nobility would have endured his perching upon that high tree of honour'.[4] Subordinates were apt to tremble at 'his over-swaying greatness',[5] and petitioners to grumble that he was 'surly and of hard access'.[6] The apology for these failings—'that he sat in great places, not to be popular and get affection, but to be just and to husband the revenues of the Crown with prudence'[7]—came

---

[1] L. Pearsall Smith, *The Life and Letters of Sir Henry Wotton* (1907), vol. II, p. 285 (Wotton to the Earl of Middlesex, April (?) 1624).

[2] A. B. Grosart, *op. cit.*, 2nd ser., vol. III, no. CCLXXVI (Sir Dudley Norton to the Earl of Cork, 18 November 1621).

[3] A. Wilson, *A Complete History of England*, p. 787.

[4] Goodman, *op. cit.* vol. I, p. 297. The sneer is that of the incorrigible Sir Anthony Weldon.

[5] Hist. MSS. Comm., *MSS. of the Earl Cowper*, vol. I, p. 176 (Sir Guildford Slingsby to Sir John Coke, 29 November 1624).

[6] Hacket, *Scrinia Reserata*, p. 189.

[7] *Ibid.*

from the biographer of one between whom and Middlesex little love was lost. It was, nevertheless, the answer to critics which, had he troubled to notice them, the alleged curmudgeon would himself have made, and if insufficient, it was true.

His most admirable quality, the foundation of all other political virtues, was courage of a kind never too common, and conspicuously rare at the sycophantic court of James, combined with a public spirit and sense of duty to the State, more native to an earlier generation than to his own; but there were occasions when these gifts would have served their owner better if ridden on the curb. Denounced by the Bishop of Cloyne for robbing the Church, by Strafford for defrauding the State, and by Lady Raleigh, whom her husband's death made an easy prey, for devouring widows' houses, Richard Boyle, later Earl of Cork, was a type of colonial capitalist with whom Middlesex may be pardoned for falling out;[1] and the rupture with Buckingham, which ruined him, was also to his credit. But his quarrels with Bacon, with Digby, and possibly even with the double-faced Williams, are less easily condoned. Whether he was so exclusively a child of this world as his reputation would suggest we cannot say. He appreciated the importance of the Church as a political institution; refused, when Treasurer, to countenance a scheme for plundering it yet further for the advantage of the Crown;[2] took, if Goodman may be trusted, the initiative in launching the plan for the repair of St Paul's; and, in a programme of administrative reform prepared by him for James, gave a larger space to the ecclesiastical than to the secular aspects of his theme;[3] but he was not of those who wear their convictions on their sleeve. It is with something of a shock that, in turning over his papers, the reader discovers, scrawled by him on the back of a dull business letter, the well-known lines ascribed to Raleigh on the night before his execution:

Even such is Tyme wch tackes in trust...[4]

[1] For the views of the persons mentioned on the Earl of Cork, see A. B. Grosart, *op. cit.*, 2nd ser., vol. IV, pp. 164–5, 183–7 (Bishop of Cloyne), vols. III, pp. 206–15, 246–59, IV, pp. 174–80 (Strafford) II, pp. 157–60, III, p. 105–6 (Lady Raleigh).

[2] Goodman, *op. cit.* vol. I, pp. 327–9; T. Fuller, *The Church History of Britain* (1845), vol. III, pp. 288–9.

[3] *Cranfield MSS.* no. 4847 (1617).

[4] *Ibid.* no. 6118. The business letter in question is dated 27 October 1618 and is from one Richard Blackall at Exeter. It is accompanied by an account (*ibid.* no. 9007) showing receipts of £313 odd from the import of Spanish wines, in which Cranfield was interested, landed at Exeter, 25 March to Michaelmas 1618. The lines as given in *Cranfield MSS.* no. 6118, differ slightly from other

The quotation comes as near, perhaps, to a confession of faith as the unbending minister's reserve allowed.

On Cranfield's political conceptions it is needless to dwell at length. A product neither of the study of the wisdom of classical antiquity denounced as foolishness by Hobbes, nor of converse in an Inn of Court with counsel learned in the law, nor of wrestlings with Apollyon in the waste places of the soul, Cranfield, 'his own University' as an admirer called him,[1] is primarily not a theorist, but a man of affairs who intends to make his way, and who, once in public life, wins the confidence of his superiors by using his business experience and reputation to rectify abuses threatening, if neglected, the stability of the regime. The compliment paid him by a foe— 'it is a brave thing to see a gentleman by his own wisdom and virtue raise himself to the height of honour and office that he so admirably hath done'[2]—may well have been insincere, but, even so, it hit the nail on the head. His concern with questions of principle is restricted to those directly relevant to the immediate tasks in hand. Like Bacon on a loftier plane, he is keenly interested in the art of government, but feels little need for a philosophy of the State.

Given such a disposition, it is not surprising that energy in action and conservatism in thought should, in the Treasurer's case, have travelled hand in hand, and that the note of his political outlook

---

versions, e.g. Oldys and Birch, *The Works of Sir Walter Raleigh*, vol. VIII, p. 729, and Gardiner, *History of England, 1603–1642*, vol. III, p. 152. They are as follows:

> Even such is Tyme wch tackes in trust
> Our Yowth, our Joyes, and all we have
> And payes us but with Adge and dust,
> W^{ch} [?] in the darck and silent Grave
> When we have wandred all our wayes,
> Shuttes up the story of our dayes,
> And from wch Earth and Grave and dust
> The Lord shall rayse me up I trust.

Raleigh was executed on 29 October 1618. For the tradition that these lines were written by him during the preceding night see D. Bush, *English Literature in the earlier Seventeenth Century, 1600–1660* (1945), pp. 96–7. Did Cranfield, on hearing them, commit them to the first scrap of paper that came to hand on his desk?

[1] T. Fuller, *The History of the Worthies of England* (1840 ed.), vol. II, p. 66.

[2] *Cranfield MSS.* no. 6866, 28 November 1621, the Earl of Cork to Sir Dudley Norton. Cork was at this time seeking the assistance of Norton, whom he knew to be a warm friend of Cranfield, in persuading the latter to abandon his claim to some Irish properties coveted by Cork. It is, perhaps, characteristic that in August 1641 Cork was still complaining to the Long Parliament that Cranfield had done him out of £1000 odd twenty years before (Hist. MSS. Comm., *Fourth Report*, part I, App. 98, 25 August 1641. Petition of Richard, Earl of Cork).

should have been, not the originality which challenges accepted doctrines, but a determination, by applying their full rigour, to compel these cautious formulae to serve the State's turn and his own. For us, who know the event, it is tempting to assume that questions concerning the relations between Parliament and Crown were already, by the later years of James, the overshadowing issue which subsequently, when the problem of sovereignty could no longer be evaded, they were destined to become. In reality, it may be suggested, up to and beyond the close of Middlesex's public career political opinion lagged behind political facts, with the result that the majority of thoughtful men would have replied to inquiries on their attitude to the increasingly contentious partners that they owed an equal loyalty to both. Where topics of that kind are concerned, Cranfield resembles Poins in being 'a blessed fellow to think as all the world thinks'. His veneration for 'our great and glorious master' —*majestas salutis imperii tutela*[1]—as the bulwark of national unity and social solidarity is quite in the lofty Tudor vein. He sees in the monarch the representative of 'the general good of the whole kingdom'[2] against sectional interests, individual and class cupidities, and disruptive ambitions of region, family or creed.

It is in obedience to such convictions that he grapples with the administrative problems daily brought before him—that he rejects, for example, as 'of dangerous consequence' the favourite's demand for the grant to a needy peer of 'many thousands of acres belonging to a multitude of poor and clamorous people' who hold them from the King;[3] and presses for the reconstruction of the government of Ireland on the ground that 'it is now high time [that] that kingdom should no longer be made to serve particular turns, to the detriment of his Majesty and the danger of both kingdoms'[4]; and at an early stage of his official career, by way of marshalling his conclusions for a mass attack, prepares for the eyes of James a paper on the tasks of a reforming monarchy. Drafted with a severe and uncompromising trenchancy foreign to his usual style, the memorandum defines, with the curt precision of a military manual, the duties to be enforced on different categories and grades of servants of the Crown, from ecclesiastical dignitaries, privy councillors and

---

[1] *Cranfield MSS.* no. 2330 (1616).   [2] *Ibid.* no. 582 (March 1618).
[3] *Ibid.* no. 39 (24 January 1624).
[4] *Carte MSS.* Bod. Lib. f. 135 (Middlesex to Buckingham, 18 November 1622). I am indebted for this reference to Mr V. H. Treadwell.

judges, at one end of the scale, to privy chamber employees at the other. The scandal of clerical poverty to be ended by employing unused or misused impropriations to provide livings for lecturers willing to conform; all bishops and deans to reside in their sees; the temptation to misapply endowments for the benefit of relatives to be exorcised by making celibacy the rule for the archbishops, the six senior bishops and all heads of colleges and halls—such are among the tonics prescribed to revivify the Church. The rules— to turn to secular matters—of Privy Council procedure—secrecy, majority decisions, no attempt by the defeated minority to obstruct their application—are to be strictly observed. Judges must regularly report to the king on the quality of the *personnel* of subordinate courts. The Presidents of the Councils of Wales and the North, Lord Lieutenants of counties, Wardens of the Cinque Ports and other office-holders must reside within their charges. Conscious, finally, of the key position occupied by the Justices of the Peace, the author is alarmed by symptoms that their attitude to the Crown is no longer the unquestioning deference of his youth. It is essential, he insists, that the gentry should be made to feel 'their immediate dependence on the King', and that opportunities for 'the censuring of his Majesty's actions and his government by daily meetings' should be drastically curtailed. The first point is to be secured by a heightened rigour on the part of the Council in sifting and resifting the names of possible Justices to be submitted to the King. In order to safeguard the second, a reality must be made of the venerable, but obsolescent, procedure of a royal proclamation at the end of each term, ordering noblemen, gentlemen and justices to abandon the delights of the capital for the duties of their country homes.[1]

It might have been expected that Cranfield's conviction of the virtues of a centralised discipline imposed by a vigilant Executive would have impressed on his attitude to individual rights, to public opinion and to Parliament an unregenerately authoritarian stamp. In reality, while insistent that the Crown must use with energy all powers that the law confers, he is equally alive to the importance of the legal restrictions which circumscribe their scope. The regime of his devotion is not an autocracy ruling by arbitrary

---

[1] *Cranfield MSS.* no. 4847, 'Considerations humbly offered to his Majesty'. Both in style and in substance this paper is noticeably different from such other of Cranfield's writings as I have read. It is ascribed by Professor Newton, on internal evidence, to the autumn of 1617.

decrees, but, in the language of the day, a 'mixed' or 'limited' monarchy; and the portrait of a would-be dictator arrested in mid-career by a liberty-loving parliament is a caricature. Occasions, it is true, can be cited when interference of a kind not easy to defend may fairly be charged to his account;[1] but it would be difficult to find in his record either a programme of governmental control so comprehensive as that prepared in 1559 for Burghley or an instance of a stroke of policy resembling, in its combination of chicanery and *force majeure*, the last minute embargo on the Merchant Adventurers' cloth fleet by which an earlier adviser of the Crown, Thomas Gresham, had extorted from the Company a reluctantly conceded loan.[2] The truth was, of course, that the two generations which had elapsed since that much vaunted exploit had seen a silent, but significant, advance in the power of London business, and that statesmanship had, as a rule, no choice but to follow suit. It is not surprising, therefore, that both the views expressed by Cranfield and his conduct of affairs should, in general, reveal a strong repugnance to action to divert or override the ordinary course of law. As minister he throws his weight against the disturbance of established business expectations by patents or other concessions from the Crown; dismisses with a growl—'this project doth smell too much of a monopoly'—a proposal submitted to him as Treasurer and later, in the 1630's, partly carried out, to make England the entrepôt for trade between Spain and her Netherlands dominions;[3] and, still haunted by memories of the noxious Cockayne, damns, as a variant of the disastrous dyeing and finishing racket, a grandiose scheme for capturing from the foreigner another branch of commerce coveted by English rivals.[4]

Mercantilism, if that term is still to be employed, varied in content and method from period to period and State to State; but one

[1] E.g. the seizure of goods and alleged intimidation of persons in connection with the collection in 1622 of the additional imposition on imported wines, and the part played by him in the negotiations preceding the confiscation of the Virginia Company's charter.

[2] See Tawney and Power, *Tudor Economic Documents*, vol. I, pp. 325–30, and G. Unwin, *Studies in Economic History* (1927), pp. 154 and 165–6.

[3] *Cranfield MSS.* no. 8434 (1622). The proposal was in effect to vest the trade between Spain and the Spanish Netherlands in a single company. The marginal comments criticising the plan appear to be by Cranfield. After the Cottington Treaty of 1630 the shipment of bullion from Spain to the Spanish Netherlands was for a time conducted by agreement via England.

[4] *Ibid.* no. 4581 (1617, Cranfield to Lord Treasurer Suffolk, on a fishing project, described by the writer as 'much of the nature of that of the dyeing and dressing').

distinction between its different species deserves more attention than it commonly receives. It is between the authoritarian versions of the policy, primarily designed to meet the fiscal needs of rulers, of which—to refer only to England—some imposing, but short-lived, specimens were nursed into unpopular existence under Charles I, and its business varieties, prompted by a concern for the interests of the commercial classes, which, though they had, of course, a longer life behind them, came at the Restoration conspicuously to their own. That 'the City is the King's chamber' was the motto of the first. That, if merchants were left to look after trade and measures for promoting it, the Exchequer would look after itself was the argument of the second. Cranfield's programme took its stamp from both; but holding, as he did, that political stability had as its condition a prosperous economy and a contented City, it was normally the latter which was uppermost in his thoughts. His so-called mercantilism, therefore, was a modest and unpretentious plant, than which nothing could be more remote from the later all-embracing *étatisme* of Colbert and his continental imitators. Its characteristic traits were not privileged monopolies and manufacturing establishments owned or licensed by the State, but such unexciting expedients as tariffs planned to attract foreign raw materials, while keeping foreign manufactures out, and monetary controls to ensure that the payment for such imports is made, not in specie, but in English manufactured goods. With this mild and unaggressive protectionism Cranfield's style in most, though not quite all, financial matters, is much of a piece. He takes credit for achieving in his first two years of office an increase in the royal revenue; but the triumph which, in his own words, 'crowns the service', and which he makes his special boast, is his success in securing the additional income 'without clamour, and by advancing the public good'.[1] Indignant at the 'lavish grants and gifts' extorted 'by fraud and deception'[2] from the King, he would have wished to see the concessions voided and the swindlers brought to book; but, here again, he will not hear of either course except as the result of proceedings in the Courts. The idea of employing methods other than due process of law to compel the surrender of ill-gotten gains is foreign to his thought.

[1] *Cranfield MSS.* no. 4463 (5 August 1615); see also nos. 4069 (June 1613), where he claims to have advanced the revenue, 'without any strain of power, but by justice intermingled with much mercy', and 4321 (October 1614).

[2] *Ibid.* no. 2330 (1616).

Cranfield's utterances on public opinion and Parliament strike, save on rare occasions, an equally sober and legalistic note. The former—though he does not use the phrase—is for practical reasons rarely absent from his mind. His concern for it is occasioned by his conviction that the achievement of financial stability is a psychological, even more than an economic, problem, and that, unless the public is reasonably well-disposed towards the Government, the solution of fiscal enigmas is beyond the wit of man. As long, he argues, as James insists on spending on his pension list three to four times the sum which had satisfied the Queen, appeals to the tax-payer to part with his hard-earned cash will inevitably fall on stony ground. They provoke the unanswerable retort that, in such conditions, grants to the ruler benefit, not him, but the leeches who suck him dry, and that even if the public has a duty to keep the King afloat, it is under no obligation to do the same for whatever mob of greedy undesirables the father of his people may choose to take in tow. Cranfield, whose written comments do not mince their words, and who, according to Goodman,[1] was equally blunt in his personal expostulations with James, shares that view. His struggle against royal prodigality is partly, in fact, an effort to deprive the public of the argument which does most to keep its pockets closed.

It is natural—to turn to the third point—that the events of Middlesex's closing year of office and the language used at his impeachment should create the impression of a Minister predisposed against the rising power of the House of Commons, and for that reason regarded by it as an enemy to be destroyed. How much weight should be attached to accusations of an anti-parliamentary bias made in an attack on him planned by strategists outside the House, whose leader was destined two years later to be more odious to the Commons than the fallen Treasurer himself, is fair matter for debate. The important question, after all, is the political outlook of Cranfield and the tenour of his policy, not in the closing months of his career, but throughout his public life. On that point the facts are not open to dispute. It is true that, at moments during the debates of 1621, he was short, to the point of discourtesy, with what he regarded as querulous or ill-informed complaints, and that on one occasion, he was guilty of the folly of threatening the House with royal displeasure. The majority of his references to Parliament are, however, in a different key. They treat it with respect; describe a

[1] Goodman, *The Court of James I*, vol. I, p. 201.

recourse to it at moments of financial stress as 'the most honourable, just and certain way' that the King can pursue;[1] and insist that, when particular reforms, for example the proposed reconstruction of the impositions, are the order of the day, it is with Parliament, not with the Council, that the final word must rest. On the few occasions during Cranfield's eleven years of public life when the expediency of convening a Parliament is the subject of debate in circles round the King, his influence, such as it was, appears to have been thrown in favour of that course. In 1615–16, when the reform of the tariff is for a moment in the air, it is on a meeting of Parliament that his hopes are set. Four years later he is among the Privy Councillors who welcome, in the autumn of 1620, the rumours heralding the Parliament which assembles on the last day of January 1621. When accused at his impeachment of having intrigued to procure its premature dissolution, he has no difficulty in proving, with the aid of a letter from the King, that his advice had been the opposite of that alleged.

As far, therefore, as matters of constitutional principle were involved, Middlesex trod, with the majority of his fellow-countrymen, not, indeed, a clearly-defined, but a familiar and, for all its uncertainties, a tried and trusted track. A favourite formula of the day depicted the characteristic virtue of English institutions as their maintenance of a 'balance' between the royal prerogative and popular rights. Accepting that fashionable, if ambiguous, view, but holding that, in recent years, the scales had been tilted to the prejudice of the ruler, he regards it as the first duty of a loyal servant of the Crown to endeavour to promote the financial reforms required to ensure that the equipoise shall be restored. The kernel of the problem, he holds, is neither the poverty of the nation, whose real income, he insists, has greatly increased during the present reign,[2] nor the inadequate endowments of the King. It consists in a maladministration, long continued and condoned, which causes the royal receipts to be ruinously less than, with energetic and intelligent management, they should have been, and the royal expenses ruinously more. He admits, in mitigation of the charge of official incompetence and dishonesty, that for some of the alleged shortcomings the King has only himself to blame. Too often he fails to back his ministers, stultifies the labours of zealous officers by withdrawing his support from reforms

[1] *Cranfield MSS.* no. 6770, October [1621].   [2] See above, pp. 18 and 193.

which he had approved and which they are toiling to apply, and leaves them with the impression that the appeasement of influential nonentities is a surer road to fortune than the honest service of the State.[1] The fact remains that, granted bad examples in high places, 'the unfaithfulness of officers', denounced, together with royal prodigality, as 'the bane of his [the King's] estate',[2] is one of Cranfield's recurrent themes, and that his exasperation at the laxity and confusion of departmental procedures is almost equally unrestrained. It is possible that he painted the shadows too black, and that his censures, if valid for some offices, in the case of others overshot the mark. It is fair to add, however, that, where matters of this kind were concerned, his strictures were rarely bows drawn at a venture. In most cases they were the sequel to detailed investigations in which not only he, but other persons of experience and weight, had taken part.

The Treasurer was not alone in thinking that, since the accession of James, not only had the cost of the public services risen beyond all reason, but their morale and efficiency had declined. His constructive labours are primarily devoted, therefore, to ensuring that the Crown receives the maximum revenue to which it is legally entitled; that none of the funds collected are improperly diverted to private ends; and that the machinery of receipt and disbursement is reasonably economical and efficient. When all is going well, the performance of these functions might not seem an exacting task; but it was precisely the preceding quinquennium of mounting deficits and debt which in 1617 had caused the Surveyor-General's aid in restoring the Crown's finances to be invoked. He is required, in short, not merely to supervise a smoothly working system, but to effect the changes needed in order to produce one. The resulting revisions upwards of the terms on which customs-farms are let; the more stringent code of regulations with which collectors of the land revenue are required to comply; the overhaul of the personnel and organisation of some six or more government departments, including the Court of Wards; and, in general, reductions in inflated defalcations and allowances, not to mention the unhappily abortive struggle for the rational control of grants—such measures formed together a heavy programme which it is surprising that Cranfield, the leading spirit in most of it, should

---

[1] Hist. MSS. Comm., *Fourth Report*, App., p. 284 (Calvert to Cranfield, 'many things shall be mended if the King will support his ministers'), and *Cranfield MSS.* no. 7887 (October 1621).　　　　[2] *Ibid.* no. 6770.

have been able to pilot to such qualified success as it attained. Administrative achievements are apt to lack the lustre which arrests the eye; nor is it easy, in observing them, to distinguish between the commonplace improvements of the industrious hack and the creative strokes which reveal the master's hand. Some of the qualities displayed by Cranfield—promptitude to decide and act, candour in stating brutal truths to favourite and king, the pertinacity which, on grounds of public advantage, held without deviating an unpopular course—were predominantly of the first type. Though admirable in themselves, they amounted, it may reasonably be said, to little more than the exhibition of 'the ordinary powers possessed to an extraordinary degree' of the disillusioned politician's recipe for success. On the other hand, in the higher ranges of administration, which were his special field, policy and its execution cannot easily be kept apart, and other features of his schemes have a touch of originality which lifts them out of the common rut. Examples include the pains taken by him to show, by comparison with the past, the scale and causes of present fiscal disorders, so that the price of continued inertia may be plain for all to see; his insistence on quantitative data as the condition of effective action; the mixed sub-commissions of officials and business men invented by him as a device for turning bureaucratic flanks, and his reiterated demand that, in the crucial matter of grants to private persons, not the King, but the Treasurer and his department shall have the decisive voice. It may be added that, in spite of the storm which the fourth point aroused, the acceptance in principle of a procedure analogous to that for which it contended was not, at least on paper, long delayed.[1]

Middlesex did not, of course, plan and act unaided. In some of his reforms he owed much to the help of Exchequer officials, in particular Sir Francis Gofton and Sir Richard Sutton, the Auditors of the Prests; to Weston, the Chancellor, who had not yet run to seed; and to his secretary, Richard Willis, a Puritan with literary tastes[2] who served in the same capacity Fulk Greville, Lord Brooke, for a time Chancellor of the Exchequer, and later, after Middlesex's

---

[1] An order (date not certain, but probably 1641) provided that in future all grants emanating from the Crown should be signed by a Secretary of State or other responsible minister; see *Cal. S.P.D. Chas. I, 1641–3*, pp. viii–ix and 491, and E. F. Churchill, 'The Crown and its Servants', in *Law Qu. Rev.* XLIV, 1926.

[2] See, for example, his *Mount Tabor* (1639) which contains, among other things, a charming account of the author's childhood and his schooldays at Christ's School in Gloucester.

fall, Lord Keeper Coventry; and, not least, to the co-operation of City acquaintances, such as Sir William Russell, Sir John Wolstenholme and Sir Thomas Smythe. Of his relations with his fellow members of the Council the same cannot be said. 'Les gens de qualité', remarks Mascarille, 'savent tout sans avoir jamais rien appris.'[1] Cranfield's groan—'great men not fit for work of labour'[2]— epitomises, unhappily without the wit, an equally distressing truth. He did not bear noble, or other, fools gladly, and, as Goodman lamented, was wont to speak his thoughts when they had better been left unsaid. A scene of the kind which the Bishop may have had in mind is described in an account, sent to Falkland in Ireland by his London agent, of the angry outburst with which the Treasurer greeted the Lord Deputy's appeal for funds. The Council has just risen, and Middlesex, standing by the Council Chamber fire, is pressed by his colleagues to do for Falkland what he can. 'Let his lordship pay his debts, but not with the King's money', is the heartless Minister's reply, followed by a statement that, if the Lord Deputy thinks the Treasurer's office preferable to his own, he can have it and welcome.[3] Such behaviour was not calculated to win affection, but the causes which made the speaker a rock of offence lay deeper than a rasping manner. In all his work, whether departmental economies, or the effort to bring the navy up to date or the more efficient management of the Court of Wards, or the amalgamation into larger units of customs-farms previously distinct, or the attempts to subject royal munificence to bring grants to suitors under Treasury control, the dominant note throughout was the need for systematised procedures in accordance with a preconcerted plan. Easy-going officials, speculators alert to squeeze them, patrons with would-be concessionaires to push, actual and prospective grantees, had little to hope from such an attitude, and much to fear; nor could it be expected that an ambitious pro-consul in Dublin, proud of his authority and alive to the opportunities offered by it of making useful friends, would welcome the interference of a distant potentate in Whitehall.[4] The Treasurer's centralising propensities, it may be suggested, were not the least of his administrative virtues. They were certainly among the greatest of his unforgiven political and social sins.

[1] Molière, *Les Précieuses Ridicules*, sc. x.   [2] *Cranfield MSS*. no. 4872 (May 1618).
[3] *Add. MSS*. no. 11033, f. 16 (21 December 1622). I am indebted for this reference to Mr V. H. Treadwell.
[4] *Cal. S.P. Ireland, 1615–28*, pp. 569–70, 10 March 1625, Lord Deputy to Privy Council.

The financial services of Middlesex, though not easily expressed in figures,[1] are no longer in dispute. On the more general question of the place to be assigned him in the history of his day agreement has hardly yet been reached. Gardiner, while commending his industry, his head for business, and the unremitting zeal with which he served the Crown, thought that, at times, he sailed so near the wind as to offer openings for a charge of malversation which his enemies could hardly fail to seize, and, apart from that alleged failing, that 'the higher question of statesmanship' was quite beyond his grasp.[2] The tendency of more recent studies, it is, perhaps, true to say, has been to make less of the Minister's occasional lapses, and more of the constructive labours by which he kept a not too stable edifice erect. Professor D. H. Willson, for example, praises Cranfield's enlightened economic policy and gifts of lucid and incisive speech, while deploring the too frequent frustration of these virtues by their possessor's quarrelsome temperament and discourteous ways.[3] Professor Newton's verdict both on his personality and on the part which he played in public life puts him on a higher plane. Citing Clarendon on the shock given by his impeachment to the authority of the King in his choice of ministers, he salutes Cranfield as 'the last Tudor servant of the State', with whose overthrow not only an individual career, but a system of government, neared its close. His comparison of James's Treasurer with famous financiers of a more recent date summoned, like him, on the eve of a revolution to adapt an ancient system to novel needs, indicates, at least, the angle from which Middlesex's record of achievements and defeats may best be approached. It not only underlines the importance of the fallen minister's role, but suggests the further question whether, had he been maintained in office and his policy supported by the King, he might not conceivably have found a method at once effective and acceptable of arresting the financial *débâcle* before it was too late.[4] Other authorities have seen Cranfield's battle for solvency in a less inspiring light, as the effort of an

---

[1] See App. 4.

[2] Gardiner, *op. cit.* vol. III, pp. 199–200; vol. V, p. 230.

[3] D. H. Willson, *The Privy Councillors in the House of Commons, 1604–1629,* pp. 85–7.

[4] An MS. paper by A. P. Newton on 'Cranfield as Treasurer' (unnumbered, but in *Cranfield MSS,* bundle 1100–1199) suggests an analogy with Turgot. The comparison with Necker, which was made in conversation with the present writer by Professor Newton, though less complimentary to Cranfield, was, perhaps, more felicitous.

industrious clerk rather than of a leader animated by large, constructive aims. Why, it is asked, did the reformer concentrate his energies on the small change of economies which, even if realised, would yield an unimpressive sum, instead of grappling boldly with the capital problem of substantially augmenting the ordinary revenue of the Crown? Compared with the policies of Salisbury, have not Cranfield's expedients a negative, thin and unconvincing air?

Such questions cannot here be discussed at length, but a comment may be permitted on the last. A familiar view of the revolution of the 1640's sees it as primarily the product of discontents provoked since the dissolution of March 1629. The significance of the famous eleven years was obviously profound; it may be suggested, nevertheless, that tendencies already visible before the death of James make a too exclusive emphasis on the follies and misfortunes of his son difficult to accept. Among these tendencies not the least important, evidenced not only by the attitude of successive parliaments, but by similar criticisms mentioned in the despatches of ambassadors,[1] in an occasional pamphlet, and here and there in Cranfield's papers, was the decline in the prestige of the monarchy. To say that the Jacobean regime brought the Crown into general contempt would be an exaggeration; but it can hardly be denied that the later years of James saw its dignity compromised and its reputation cheapened. Pym's famous description in the Parliament of 1621 of 'the State of Monarchy' as 'the perfectest State of Government'[2] must have suggested to some among his hearers how singularly remote from the orator's ideal the reality known to them had become.

The policies of the day, financial and other, must be seen in the light, partly of that fatal loss of moral authority by the ruler, partly of the varying conditions of different periods of his reign. In its first sanguine phase, when economic seas were calm, and tension between Parliament and Crown not yet the deadlock that later it became, a minister might without presumption anticipate a term of office sufficient to allow him to see his measures yield some fruits. It was natural, in such conditions, for Salisbury to make an increase of revenue his chief financial aim, though unfortunate that, in the matter of expenditure, he should have given James his head. By the

[1] For remarks by ambassadors, see, for example, D. H. Willson, *King James VI*, p. 428.
[2] *Proceedings and Debates in the House of Commons in 1621*, vol. II, p. 238.

time when Cranfield took his task in hand, the situation had profoundly changed. A serious depression during a substantial part of his period as minister; more than half his years of office accompanied by a European war; intransigence in the Commons more pronounced when Parliament reassembled in January 1621, than when, six years before, its predecessor was sent about its business—such were among the ingredients of the atmosphere which he breathed. In those circumstances some additions to the Crown's ordinary income could, no doubt, be made by exacting more favourable terms from customs-farmers, and by heightened vigilance in the administration of the land revenue and the Court of Wards; but even a convinced reformer might be pardoned for holding that to press for larger measures of a kind already rejected could serve no useful end. The most striking of Salisbury's financial schemes—his proposal for the substitution for the so-called feudal incidents of a parliamentary grant—had come to grief in 1610. In view of the subsequent movement of opinion and events, would not the inevitable result of an attempt twelve years later to resuscitate it, or some version of it, have been the sacrifice to an impracticable Utopianism of all hopes of constructive work?

In the matter of major improvements of the revenue, therefore, the regime had shot its bolt before Cranfield enlisted in its service. A policy of drastic retrenchment was for that reason all the more essential. In that sphere considerable things were done; and, had James been an Elizabeth, it is possible that a tight hand on domestic expenditure, combined with a prudent foreign policy, might have delayed, if it could not arrest, a further slide downhill. It was, perhaps, on some such hopes that Cranfield built; if so, he deceived himself in two respects. By nature a planner and executant, not a politician, he was the victim, in the first place, of an illusion which may be called, perhaps, the administrator's fallacy—the belief, that is to say, that efficient management, combined with public spirit and a logically unanswerable case, can hold its own against interests and ambitions wielding personal and political power. Enjoying almost to the end the confidence of James, Middlesex both exaggerated, in the second place, the value of the King's support and underestimated the capacity for mischief of the royal entourage. His proposals for abolishing superfluous offices, for further departmental economies, for pruning grants and pensions, and for transferring patronage from King to Treasurer were obviously sound sense; but, not less obviously, they were odious to influential individuals and groups who had the royal ear. It is not surprising, therefore, that they should have fallen on stony ground, and that the few of them which were partially adopted should not have long survived their detested author's fall.

Thus the second road towards solvency was blocked, as well as the first, and the financial irresponsibility which was the characteristic vice of the dual fiscal system, pursued its evil course unchecked. Commons and King alike were parties to the mischiefs which its continuance entailed, for both, with a handful of exceptions, were equally sterile of remedies to cure its vices and of alternatives to take its place. The former might criticise and complain, but there was nothing, it is probable, which members of the Commons House desired less than additional taxation to ease the tasks of an Executive whose policies they distrusted and whose misuse of its existing resources they were impotent to check. The latter could fairly argue that the ordinary income of the Crown was absurdly out of date; but, apart from the recklessness which frittered much of it away, few prophecies could be more certain of fulfilment and less agreeable when fulfilled than that, if Parliament provided more to pay the piper, it would assert with redoubled emphasis its claim to call the tune. In the meantime, whatever the long-term solution of these enigmas, funds must be found to keep the Government afloat. In view of that necessity, the frustration of the Treasurer's commonplace, but necessary, economy proposals was a disaster. Its result was an accelerated rush into the morass of 'shifts and bargains',[1] a resort to which, during his period of power, he had striven, not wholly without success, to hold at bay, and which was to reach its zenith in the ensuing reign.[2]

Chance has preserved a paper in which, long after, when the Long Parliament was less than four years off, Middlesex, in obedience apparently to a command from Charles, stated his views both on the consequences to which, at long last, that policy had led and on the principles to be observed in order to meet existing needs.

---

[1] *Cranfield MSS.* no. 2330 (1616).
[2] See Clarendon, *The History of the Rebellion*, vol. I, p. 32, writing of the years immediately following James' death. His words, 'new projects were every day set on foot for money, which served only to offend and incense the people, and brought little supply to the King's occasions', hit the nail, as Cranfield saw it, on the head.

The situation, as he saw it, was unquestionably grave—the ordinary revenue barely sufficient to cover current outlay; nothing in hand to clear off anticipations, or pay pressing debts, or replace depleted stores; the Narrow Seas in danger; France, Spain and the Netherlands on the watch; military and naval preparations, in the shape of men, fortifications and equipment, urgent; and, again, nothing in the extraordinary account to foot the bill. Yet never had greater ingenuity been exercised in diverting along new and devious channels fresh funds to the Exchequer. What had gone wrong? What must be done to put it right?

The retired veteran's answer to those questions differed little from the reply which the Minister would have given in his prime. For the pecuniary trickles laboriously wrung from questionable sources he had nothing but contempt. The root of the trouble was simple. It was the prolonged mismanagement which allowed monies due to the Crown to remain unpaid and which wasted monies received. The attempt in such circumstances to keep the Treasury in funds was as hopeful as the effort to fill a cistern riddled with unstopped leaks. 'Projects and extraordinary courses?' Moonshine. Their total yield was less than the sums thrown away through maladministration since the death of James.[1] Ship money? A mirage, and a treacherous one at that. So far from being enabled by it to cover the costs of retaining the command of the Narrow Seas, the King had found it necessary for that purpose to supplement from his personal resources the proceeds of the novel and unpopular tax.[2]

Expedients of this kind, Middlesex argued, were not only futile, but noxious as well. They combined the minimum advantage to the Crown with the maximum exasperation of the public. The essential thing was not to devise stratagems for screwing further funds from a reluctant nation, but to treat it as a partner and to win its confidence, in which case the funds required would not fail to be supplied. 'Every footman can raise money for the King by the King's power, with the alienating of his subjects' hearts; but that is so far from service

---

[1] *Cranfield MSS.* no. 8218 (*c.* 1637). 'The King hath lost more by the miscarriage and abuse of his own revenue, which his father left, than he hath gained by all the projects and extraordinary courses.'

[2] Middlesex's comments on ship money suggest that he under-estimated both the proceeds yielded by it and the contribution made by it to English naval strength, the purpose to which it was confined. See M. D. Gordon, 'The Collection of Ship Money in the Reign of Charles I', in *Trans. R.H.S.* 3rd series, IV, pp. 141–62, and Dietz, *English Public Finance, 1558–1641*, pp. 274–81.

as it is treason of the worst kind, even Judas' treason, who betrayed his master with a kiss, as these men [the projectors] do under pretence of service.' The course of wisdom was the opposite. It was first—a characteristic touch—to ascertain the precise facts as to the amount of the deficit to be extinguished, and next to provide promptly for the reduction in the ordinary expenditure and, if necessary, for the increase in the ordinary revenue required to meet it. Above all, whatever the fiscal technique employed, it was to convince the public that, so far from threatening liberty and property by playing fast and loose with Magna Carta and the Petition of Right, the King and his advisers acted exclusively '*pro salute rei publicae*, wherein is contained the safety of his Majesty, his Crown and posterity, and of them and their children, their lands and goods, and —which is above all—the true religion professed.' If Charles will strike a bold and generous note—if he will make it evident that the supplies demanded are raised and spent with a single eye to the public good—he will receive from his subjects a return more precious than increased financial contributions. He will 'have their hearts and their love, wherein consists the real glory and safety and content of the kingdom'.

APPENDIX

1. Note on Opinion in London, 1619

One of Cranfield's duties was to keep the Government informed on the attitude of public opinion. The following extract from MS. no. 6774 (November 1619), shows his view of the state of mind of the City at the date concerned.

...the King's speeches and promises are not valued as it is fitting for want of performance. The Privy Council orders not respected because altered upon private information and extraordinary direction from Court.

Witness:

The great business of sending ships into the Narrow Seas. All the fault imputed to my Lord, who is said to be the cause of all.

Whereby:

The City is undone;
The trade of the kingdom lost;
The merchants are ruined, and, to use their own terms, 'bought and sold';
The shipping, being the strength of the kingdom, wrecked;
Our neighbours', the Hollanders', shipping thereby improved.

By which of necessity must follow:

Danger to our kingdom;
Great loss to his Majesty's revenue by impairing his customs;
General discontent in the subjects, and, in particular, disaffection in the City to his Majesty, which God forbid.

The new impositions upon cloth by the States.

The remedy:

To impose upon all commodities that come out of Holland in the like proportion to bring them to a parity.

Never so unfit a time to discontent the Merchants, in regard:

Of the general decay of trade;
The impositions not yet digested;
The praetermitted custom lately imposed;
Prejudice in farming of the Great Customs now to be let in farm;
The merchants' bankruptcy.

All, this, and whatever else will fall out to the prejudice of trade, is and will be affirmed to be occasioned by the abandoning the merchants, and all is laid upon my Lord of Buckingham. Whether this be a good preparation to the meeting of the parliament, and friendly advice to thrust my Lord upon such a sort as to bring the envy of the whole kingdom upon him, I leave to his judgment.

Proposition made to sell the Adventurers and consequently the trade of the East Indies to the Hollanders.

This damnable proposition approved.

2. Note on Financial Conditions as Seen by Cranfield, October 1621

(a) *Revenue*. Cranfield, on taking up his duties at the Exchequer in October 1621, found awaiting him a return prepared for his predecessor, Viscount Mandeville, with the heading, 'My Lord President of the Council, his book about his Majesty's Revenue. Received October 1621'. The document in question, *Cranfield MSS*. no. 6894, gives the gross ordinary revenue from Michaelmas 1620 to Michaelmas 1621 as £485,804. This does not include the income from the praetermitted customs, for which a heading is included, but the amount is left blank. Two other documents (nos. 7225 and 7223, 22, 29 October 1621) show that their yield in 1620–1 was slightly over £12,000. On the other hand, a deduction of about £16,000 must be made for defalcations to sundry farmers. With these adjustments the gross ordinary revenue amounts to about £482,000, which may be compared with the figure of £495,658 given in Hist. MSS. Comm., *Fourth Report*, Pt. I, App., p. 281. Much of this money never found its way into the Exchequer, being assigned directly to meet specified expenditure. The whole revenue of the Court of Wards, for instance, is assigned to three spending departments (the Cofferer, the Wardrobe and the Chamber) and to the payment of annuities and pensions to various individuals and other allowances, 'the money never coming into the Exchequer'. The actual revenue 'paid in clear and ready money into the receipt of the Exchequer' is put at £208,408. This does not include the receipts from tobacco and praetermitted customs, which are left blank. The revenue from tobacco is given as £15,600 in the account of the gross revenue and there are no defalcations or assignments, so that presumably the whole amount is received in the Exchequer. Adding this figure, together with £12,000 odd for the praetermitted customs, the total so received would be about £236,000. A further item, the so-called 'monthly payments', increased the receipts from the great customs, the new impositions, and the imposition of 3d. upon strangers' goods. The value of the 'monthly payments' in 1621 is unstated. In 1612, when the total rent had been £136,626 odd, it had been £2500 per month or £30,000 per year (R. Ashton, *Government Borrowing*, p. 243).

(b) *Expenditure*. The total gross ordinary revenue, therefore for the year 1620–1 was in the region of £482,000, and the total paid in cash into the Exchequer perhaps something over half that figure. Our information on the expenditure side of the ordinary account in the year before Cranfield's entry on the Treasurership is even more meagre. Nothing on the subject is contained in *Cranfield MSS*. no. 6894. The account of the ordinary expenditure, including 'excesses upon the ordinary', which put it in Michaelmas 1620–1 at £385,136 (*ibid.* no. 7908, September 1622) clearly understates the total; possibly it relates exclusively to disbursements by the Exchequer. The figures of £459,187 for the issues, and of £495,658 for the receipts of 1620–1 (Hist. MSS. Comm. *Fourth Report, loc. cit.*) are more plausible. The claim implied in the assertion later made by Mandeville that in September 1621, at the end of his nine months as Treasurer, 'I left the state of the revenue much better than I found it' (quoted Dietz, *English Public Finance,* p. 184) need not be taken too seriously. It is true, however, that, as James had told Parliament in January 1621 (see above pp. 173) the administrative reforms launched in 1617 were beginning to bear fruit. There is nothing surprising, therefore, in the existence in 1620–1 of the small credit balance shown above.

(*c*) *Anticipations. Cranfield MSS.* no. 6894 puts the anticipations in October 1621 at £123,000, the equivalent of about a quarter of the gross ordinary revenue. The principal revenues charged were the great farm of the customs (£58,000), other customs-farms and the new impositions (£33,700 odd), and the first instalment of the subsidy due in November 1621 (£29,000). For similar, though slightly different figures, see *ibid.* no. 6485 (29 September 1622).

(*d*) *Debt.* 'His Majesty', declared Cranfield in October 1621, 'can neither borrow in City nor country, considering the great debts he owes in both' (*ibid.* no. 6770). The statement was not literally correct; but it puts in a nutshell one of the new Treasurer's alarms. The debt, which had stood early in the preceding year at just over £700,000, had grown, on his estimate, at the time when he started work as Treasurer, to over £900,000, and was destined to rise before his fall in 1624 to approximately £1,000,000. (For references see Dietz, *English Public Finance,* pp. 191–2, 271). The structure, as distinct from the amount, of the debt is illustrated by an analysis in *Cranfield MSS.* no. 6294 (21 July 1619). The then total of £829,000 had consisted of two main parts, first, moneys borrowed to the amount of £375,000 odd together with just under £15,000 interest, and second, undischarged liabilities in the shape of payments due for goods and services. The debts under the first head were (1) Loans by privy seals, £112,000, (2) loan by City, £96,000, (3) advances by four individual capitalists to the amount of £10,000, (4) anticipations, £117,344. They reappear in 1621 though, owing to the growth of anticipations, in slightly different proportions. The liabilities under the second head were payments due from government departments to contractors, tradesmen, etc., and also to employees for salaries and wages in arrears. It was a feather in Cranfield's cap that, at the end of his first two months as Treasurer, he could boast that the Crown was on this occasion free from the reproach of sponging on its officials and workmen to keep itself afloat (Goodman, *op. cit.* vol. II, pp. 210–18, Cranfield to Buckingham, 4 December 1621).

APPENDIX

3. COMPARISON OF CERTAIN HEADS OF REVENUE AND EXPENDITURE IN THE LAST YEARS OF ELIZABETH AND 1620–1

Cranfield MSS. *no. 6894 concludes with 'A brief report of the revenue of the crown as it was delivered to the Lord High Treasurer of England by the several officers of the Land revenue, anno 44 Eliz.'. The object was presumably to facilitate a comparison between the amount and resources of the revenue in 1601–2 and 1620–1. Other documents in the* Cranfield MSS. *e.g. no. 6987 (October 1621), no. 541 (2 May 1622), and earlier, no. 4458 (? 1615), are concerned with the same point, but no. 7887 (? 1621) treats it, perhaps, with most effect.*

The paper in question runs as follows:

'REMEMBRANCES TOUCHING THE KING'S ESTATE.

To maintain the King's ordinary charge with his own without falling upon the people, two things must be principally looked into;

    1. The upholding and husbanding of his revenues,

    2. The well-ordering of his Majesty's expense.

The Revenue must needs be much decayed when in the certain rents of lands of the Crown, which in the last year of Queen Elizabeth were 128,257 l. and are now (with 23,310 l. assigned to the Prince) but 95,403 l. In all there is a diminution of 32,854 l.

Casual revenue, in these 5 heads: of Recusants, Fines upon Leases, Temporalties of Bishoprics, Forfeitures upon penal Statutes, and Fines of the Star Chamber, these which was then 17,834 l. is now but 7,700 l, to the abatement of 10,134 l.

Total 42,988 l. per annum.

And the Expenses have been exceedingly increased in the ordinary; as by comparison of these few heads will appear:

	By a Medium of the last 5 years of Queen Elizabeth	By the Balance 1621
	£	£
Privy Purse	1,304	5,000
Great Wardrobe	6,891	20,016
Master of the Robes (New: brought in in 2° of the King)	—	4,000
Treasurer of the Chamber	10,000	26,000
Cofferer of the Household	29,452	54,081
Band of Pensioners	4,161	6,000
Foreign Ambassadors and Agents	4,253	12,000
Office of the Works	7,729	10,000
Fees, Pensions and Annuities	28,386	96,434

So as the pensions alone come now to as much as were then the charge of Pensions, Privy Purse, the Wardrobe, Chamber, Cofferer, Pensioners,

299

Ambassadors and Works, and in these 9 heads the excess has grown to per annum 141,254 l.

Besides extraordinary The Prince's ordinary 53,177 l.	By this may appear how hard it is in this decay of the revenue and increase of the ordinary charge to keep up the one, to balance the other: and how heavy the last addition of charge must needs be that is laid upon the revenue, which is surcharged already.'

Proposals for remedies follow:

'REMEDIES:

To bring these disproportions into better harmony, His Majesty may be graciously pleased constantly to resolve upon these heads:

1. That no suit be hereafter admitted upon the King's lands, either by lease in reversion, grants in fee farm or otherwise, it being expressly prohibited in the Book of Bounty.

2. The like for all suits upon fines of the Star Chamber, or other parts of the casual revenue, and all Grants of Bounty to cease for a time.

3. That the pensions already granted may die with the parties, and not be revived afterwards to others and so made perpetual.

4. That such as the King hath given parks unto for any term or estate may discharge all reparations themselves, according to Mr Hugh May's example in Moate Park in Windsor forest.

5. That his Majesty will be pleased to limit the restitution of Bishops' temporalties to the day of their admittance, whereas now they carry all from the death of their predecessor.

6. Forbear the defraying of foreign ambassadors here, which in the King's first 5 years stood in 17865 l. more than in the last 5 years of the Queen.

If his Majesty, will observe these things both for England and Ireland, there will be the more hope that his officers may do good, whose care and providence will otherwise be altogether fruitless. And then may they consider of each head of the revenue, to improve it, and of the charge, to diminish it, as may stand with his Majesty's honour and service.

ADVANCING THE REVENUE AND RECEIPTS:

In the revenue of recusants which (when the time is fit) will be brought to 20,000 l. per annum, with more contentment to them, and more security of them.

In raising moneys by fines of leases.

In better looking to the fines of Star Chamber and other forfeitures.

In collecting the temporalties of Bishoprics, *sede vacante*.

In wood sales and settling the neglected revenue of the woods.

In the Hanaper, by not admitting the usual word, *Abseque*, etc., *Eo quod*, etc.

DIMINISHING THE ORDINARY CHARGE

In all the great offices, as is already done in the Navy and Wardrobe, and hath been and is in hand for the Household.

Examination of unprofitable and unuseful officers in collecting the Revenue and elsewhere, for ceasing their fees.

Settling the charge of castles and forts in order.'

The document concludes by returning to the lesson suggested by Elizabeth's closing years, but this time in connection with the Extraordinary, not the Ordinary, account.

'THE EXTRAORDINARIES:

In the 5 last years of Queen Elizabeth her yearly charge for her Navy, Ireland and the Low Countries came to, by the medium, 380,618 l. which stands the King now but in 50,000 l. per annum or thereabouts.

But to sustain those 5 years charge of those 3 heads, which came to about 2 millions, she was fain, besides all other helps, to sell so much land as in her last 4 years brought into the Exchequer 362,694 l.

So as extraordinary disbursements will require extraordinary supplies. By:

Subsidies and fifteenths of Parliament.

Settling the revenue of Ireland to bear its own charges.

A fine of one or two years fee, to be paid for all offices granted by letters patent.

Query? for the revenue of Scotland.

Refining of lead and lead-ore before it is exported.

Imposition upon lead and herrings to be exported.'

4. NOTE ON EFFECT OF SOME OF CRANFIELD'S FINANCIAL REFORMS

Statistical evidence as to the effect of Middlesex's financial reforms is too fragmentary and ambiguous for confident conclusions to be based on it. All that is attempted here is to summarise such few data as exist.

In his opening speech to Parliament on 30 January 1621, James gave figures purporting to show the reductions of departmental expenditure under certain heads between that date and the start of the economy measures set on foot in the latter part of 1617. The figures in question (Notestein, Relf and Simpson, *Commons Debates in 1621*, vol. II, pp. 8–9; IV, p. 4; V, p. 428) differ slightly in the different diaries reporting them. The conclusion reached by the editors is that, by the date of James' speech, expenditure on the Household had been reduced by £18,000; on the Navy by £25,000; and on the office of ordnance by £20,000. No figures of expenditure on the Wardrobe were given by James; but, three years later, in May 1624, Cranfield in his concluding speech at the trial stated that, when Master of the Wardrobe, he had made from its receipts a contribution—meaning, probably, an annual contribution—of £6000 to the king's extraordinary expenditure. Figures given by Dietz (*English*

Public Finance, p. 405), from the Exchequer papers, show that during three years of Cranfield's Mastership, viz. Michaelmas 1618 to Michaelmas 1621, his annual outlay on the Wardrobe averaged £13,300 odd, as compared with an annual assignment of £20,000, and an annual outlay on the part of his predecessor of £28,000 odd. Middlesex's contract with the Crown allowed him to retain all savings below the assignment of £20,000. As these averaged for the three years in question approximately £6750 per year, an annual contribution of £6000 from the Wardrobe to the Crown was, during Cranfield's Mastership, quite within its means.

In his final speech before the Lords (*L.J.* 12 May 1624, Middlesex stated that he had 'advanced the profits of the Crown at least £80,000'. The above-mentioned savings on four departments of £60,000 to £70,000 were a long step in that direction. Increases in revenue, in the form not of reduced costs of collection, but of larger sums raised, either by making existing taxation more productive, or by new taxation, also played their part. Examples of the first are the stiffer terms exacted from farmers (e.g. the Great Farm, and silk and other farms grouped with it in 1621, and also the tobacco farm), and the increase during Middlesex's Mastership in the current receipts from the Court of Wards (see above, pp. 183, n. 4, and 207, nn. 1 and 2). An example of the second are the praetermitted customs (first imposed in 1619: yield in 1620–1 £12,000 odd). Finally there are some unclassifiable items, of which the most substantial was probably the £60,000 which, on Middlesex's own account (last speech at trial), his financial *expertise* enabled him to save the Crown on the exchange operations required to provide funds for the maintenance of troops for the defence of the Palatinate.

BIBLIOGRAPHY

I. MANUSCRIPT SOURCES (INCLUDING CALENDARS AND INDEXES OF MSS.)

1. *Publications of the Historical Manuscripts Commission*

Buccleuch MSS.: The MSS. of the Duke of Buccleuch and Queensbury (Hist. MSS. Comm. Series 44 and 45, 1897–9).

The MSS. of Earl Cowper at Melbourne Hall (Hist. MSS. Comm. Series 23; twelfth Report, Apps. I, II and III, 1888–9).

Cranfield Papers, see *Sackville MSS.*

The MSS. of the Earl of Egmont (Hist. MSS. Comm. Series 63, 3 vols, 1905–1909).

Fourth Report, Part 1. Appendix (Hist. MSS. Comm. Series 3, 1784).

The MSS. of the Earl of Mar and Kelly at Alloa House, Clackmannanshire (Hist. MSS. Comm. Series 60, 2 vols, 1904–30).

Middleton MSS.: The MSS. of Lord Middleton, formerly at Wollaton Hall, Notts (Hist. MSS. Comm. Series 69, 1911).

Sackville MSS.: The MSS. of Lord Sackville at Knole. Part I: *Cranfield Papers, 1534–1612* (Hist. MSS. Comm. Series 80, 1940).

The Salisbury (Cecil) MSS. at Hatfield. Parts III and IV (Hist. MSS. Comm. Series 9, 1889–92).

Third Report, Appendix (Hist. MSS. Comm. Series 2, 1872).

Various Collections, vol. VIII (Hist. MSS. Comm. Series 55, 1913).

2. *State Papers, etc.*

Acts of the Privy Council of England, new series.
Calendar of State Papers relating to Ireland. James I.
Calendar of State Papers (Venice).
Calendar of State Papers, Domestic, Elizabeth.
Calendar of State Papers, Domestic, James I.
Calendar of State Papers, Domestic, Charles I.
State Papers, Domestic. Elizabeth.
State Papers, Domestic. James I.
State Papers, Domestic. Charles I.
The Commons Journals.
The Lords Journals.
The Parliamentary Diary of Edward Nicholas, 1624 (State Papers Domestic. James I, vol. CLXVI).

3. *Other Manuscripts*

British Museum
Additional MSS.
Cottonian MSS.
Egerton MSS. (especially MS. 2541, ff. 39–44: Anon. 'A true discovery of the decay of trade and decrease of money, with the remedy

303

thereof'), n.d. Cat. states temp. James I: reference to praetermitted customs shows that document is subsequent to 4 November 1618.

Harleian MSS. (especially MS. 2204, no. 2, ff. 89–109; Anon. 'A discourse on trade', 1622; and MS. 2204, no. 3: William Sanderson, 'An excellent treatise of a state mercant or merchandising state'), n.d.

Lansdowne MSS. (especially MS. 798, no. 3, ff. 78–104: Keymer, 'Book of Observations...touching trade and traffic beyond the seas and in England, etc.' *c.* 1620 or 1623; and MS. 811, no. 3, ff. 17–43, 'considerations of Entercourse, 1630', probably by William Sanderson, which is another version of *Harl.* 2204, no. 3, *supra*).

Stowe MSS, MS. 32.

Public Record Office

Court of Wards. Receiver General's Accounts.

Exchequer. King's Remembrancer. Port Books.

Exchequer. Lord Treasurer's Remembrancer. Enrolled Accounts.

Sackville MSS., Cranfield MSS., unpublished.

The National Library of Wales

The Wynn Papers.

Keswick Hall, Norwich

Anonymous political diary in the *Gurney MSS.*

II. PRINTED PRIMARY SOURCES AND CONTEMPORARY WORKS

Allen, W. Cardinal. *The Letters and Memorials of William, Cardinal Allen*, ed. by Fathers of the Congregation of the London Oratory, with intr. by T. F. Knox (London, 1882).

Aulicus coquinariae in *The Secret History of the Court of James I*, ed. Sir W. Scott, 2 vols. (Edinburgh, 1811).

Bacon, Francis, Viscount St Albans. *The Works of Francis Bacon.* Collected and edited by J. Spedding, R. L. Ellis and D. D. Heath, 14 vols. (London, 1857–74). Note: vols. 8–14 have the additional title: *The Letters and Life of Francis Bacon.*

Barozzi, N. and Berchet, G. (eds.). *Relazioni degli stati europei lette al senato dagli ambasciatori veneti nel secolo decimosettimo.* Ser. 4. Inghilterra (1863).

Basilikon Doron, see James I.

Beale, R. *A Treatise of the Office of a Counseller* (1592) in *Complaint and Reform in England 1436–1714*, ed. W. H. Dunham and S. Pargellis.

Behemoth. The history of the civil wars of England from the year 1640 to 1660 (by Thomas Hobbes), in *Select tracts relating to the Civil Wars in England*, ed. F. Maseres (London, 1815).

Bernard, St, Abbot of Clairvaux. *De Consideratione*, in his *Opera omnia*, ed. J. P. Migne, 4 vols. (Paris, 1864).

Béthune, M. de, Duc de Sully. *Economies royales* (Paris, 1888).

Birch, T. (compiler). *The Court and Times of James the First*, 2 vols. (London, 1848).

Buck, Sir G. *The Third University of England* (1615).

Cabala, Mysteries of State (1654).

Chamberlain, J. *The Letters of John Chamberlain*, ed. N. E. McClure (American Philosophical Society. Memoirs, vol. 12, 2 vols. Philadelphia, 1939).

Clarendon, 1st Earl of. *The History of the Rebellion*, ed. W. D. Macray (1888).

—— *A Commission with Instructions and Directions...to the Master and Council of the Court of Wards...for compounding for Wards, Idiots and Lunaticks* (Brit. Mus. E, 80, 3).

Cotton, Sir R. B. *Cottoni Posthuma*, ed. J. Howell (London, 1651).

Dekker, T. *Dramatic Works*, 4 vols. (London, 1873).

D'Ewes, Sir S. *Autobiography and Correspondence*, ed. J. O. Halliwell. (1845).

Digges, Sir D. *The Defence of Trade* (London, 1615).

Discourse on Trade in *Early English Tracts on Commerce*, ed. J. R. MacCulloch (Cambridge, 1954).

Dunham, W. H. and Pargellis, S. (eds.). *Complaint and Reform in England, 1436–1714* (New York, 1938).

Du Plessis, A. J., duc de Richelieu. *Testament politique*, ed. L. André (Paris, 1947).

Fortescue Papers, see Gardiner.

Gardiner, S. R. (ed.). *The Fortescue Papers* (Camden Society, new series, vol. 1, 1871).

—— *Parliamentary Debates in 1610* (Camden Society, old series, vol. 81, 1862).

Godfrey, W. H. (ed.). *The Book of John Rowe* (Sussex Record Society, vol. 34, Cambridge, 1928).

Goodman, G., Bishop of Gloucester. *The Court of King James the First*, ed. J. S. Brewer, 2 vols. (London, 1839).

Greene, R. *A Quip for an Upstart Courtier* (1592) in *Harleian Miscellany*, vol. II.

Grosart, A. B. (ed.). *The Lismore Papers*, 10 vols. (London, 1886–8).

Hacket, J. *Scrinia Reserata* (1693).

Hale, Sir M. *The Jurisdiction of the Lords House*, ed. I. Hargreave (London, 1796).

Hall, H. and Nicholas, F. J. (eds.). *Select Tracts and Table Books Relating to English Weights and Measures (1100–1742)* in *Camden Miscellany*, vol. 15 (Camden Society, 3rd series, vol. 41).

Hanserecesse, see Ropp, G. von der (ed.).

Harleian Miscellany, 8 vols. (London, 1744–6).

Heylin, P. *Cyprianus Anglicanus* (London, 1671?).

Howell, J. *Epistolae Ho-Elianae: Familiar Letters, Domestic and Forren* (London, 1678).

Hutchinson, L. (ed.). *Memoirs of the Life of Colonel Hutchinson* (Everyman's Library, 1908).

James I, King of England. *Basilikon Doron*, Bk. II in his *Opera Regia* (1619).

—— *Trew Law of Free Monarchies* (1598).

Jonson, Ben. *The Alchemist* (1610).
—— *The Devil is an Ass* (1616).
—— *The Staple of News* (1625).
Leake's Treatise on the Cloth Industry (1577) in *Tudor Economic Documents*, ed. R. H. Tawney and E. E. Power, vol. III.
Legg, *A Relation of a short Survey of 20 counties observed in a seven weeks journey, 1634* (1904), ed. Wickham.
MacCulloch, J. R. (ed.). *Early English Tracts on Commerce* (Cambridge, 1954).
Malynes, G. de. *Consuetudo: vel, Lex Mercatoria* (London, 1656).
—— *The Maintenance of Free Trade* (1622).
May, J. *A Declaration of the Estate of Clothing now used within this Realm of England* (London, 1613).
Milles, T. *The Custumers Apology* (1599?).
—— *The Replie or Second Apologie* (1604).
Misselden, E. *The Circle of Commerce* (1623).
—— *Free Trade or the Means to Make Trade Flourish* (1622).
Molière, J. B. *Les Précieuses Ridicules*.
Moryson, F. *An Itinerary* (*1617*), 4 vols. (Glasgow, 1907–8).
Mun, T. *England's Treasure by Forraign Trade* (1664).
—— *A Discours of Trade* (1621) in *Early English Tracts on Commerce*, ed. J. R. MacCulloch (Cambridge, 1952).
Naunton, Sir R. *Fragmenta Regalia* (1642) in *A Collection of Scarce and Valuable Tracts*, Baron Somers and others, vol. 5.
Notestein, W. and others (eds.). *Commons Debates, 1621* (Yale Historical Publications. MSS. and edited texts, 14, 1935).
Oglander, Sir J. *A Royalist's Notebook*, ed. F. Bamford (London, 1936).
Oldys and Birch, *see* Raleigh, Sir W.
Overbury, Sir T. *The Observations of Sir Thomas Overbury in his Travels* in *The Harleian Miscellany*, vol. VIII.
Pepys, S. *Diary*.
Petty, Sir W. *The Economic Writings*, ed. C. H. Hull, 2 vols. (Cambridge, 1899).
—— *The Petty Papers: Some Unpublished Writings of Sir William Petty*, ed. Marquis of Lansdowne, 2 vols. (London, 1927).
Pickard, P. *Memoirs of the Life of Mr Nicholas Ferrer* (Cambridge, 1790).
Proceedings and Debates in the House of Commons in 1620 and 1621, Collected by a Member of that House [Sir Ed. Nicholas], 2 vols. (Oxford, 1766).
Raleigh, Sir W. *The Works of Sir Walter Raleigh now First Collected, to which are Prefixed the Lives of the Author by Oldys and Birch*, 8 vols. (Oxford, 1829).
Richelieu, *see* Du Plessis.
Roberts, L. *The Merchants Mappe of Commerce* (London, 1638).
—— *The Treasure of Traffike* (1641).
Robinson, H. *Certain Proposals in Order to the People's Freedome and Accommodation in Some Particulars* (London, 1652).
—— *England's Safety, in Trades Encrease* (London, 1641).

Roe, Sir T. 'Speech in Parliament', in *Harleian Miscellany*, vol. IV.
Ropp, G. von der (ed.). *Hanserecesse von 1431–1476*, 7 vols. (Leipzig, 1876–92).
Saville, G., 1st Marquis of Halifax. *The Complete Works*, ed. W. Raleigh (Oxford, 1912).
Selden, J. *Of the Judicature in Parliaments* (London, 1690?).
Shakespeare, W. *The Sonnets*, ed. H. E. Rollins, 2 vols. (1944). (The New Variorum edition of Shakespeare.)
Smith, L. Pearsall. *The Life and Letters of Sir Henry Wooton*, 2 vols. (Oxford, 1907).
Smith, Sir T. *De Republica Anglorum*, ed. L. Alston (Cambridge, 1906).
Somers, J., Baron Somers. *A Collection of Scarce and Valuable Tracts*, 2nd ed. by W. Scott, 13 vols. (London, 1809–15).
Spedding, J., *see* Bacon, Francis.
Stow, J. *The Annales, or Generall Chronicle of England*, 3 parts (London, 1615).
—— *A Survey of London*, ed. C. L. Kingsford, 3 vols. (Oxford, 1908–27).
Stubbes, P. *The Anatomie of Abuses* (London, 1583).
Sully, duc de, *see* Béthune.
Tawney, R. H. and Power, E. E. (eds.). *Tudor Economic Documents* (University of London Historical Series, no. 4, 3 vols. 1924).
Tom Tell-Truth, a Free Discourse Touching the Manners of the Times (1622) in *Harleian Miscellany*, vol. III.
Watts, Sir J. *A Discourse upon Trade* (1625). (Quoted in Hist. MSS. Comm. 3rd Report, Appendix, p. 66.)
Wheeler, J. *A Treatise of Commerce* (1601), ed. G. B. Hotchkiss (Facsimile Text Society, New York, 1931).
Willis, R. *Mount Tabor* (1639).
Willson, D. H. *King James VI and I* (London, 1956).
Wilson, A. *The Life and Reign of King James I* in *A Complete History of England* (3 vols., London, 1706), vol. II.
Wilson, T. *A Discourse upon Usury...[1572]*, ed. R. H. Tawney (London 1925).
—— *The State of England, Anno Dom. 1600*, ed. F. J. Fisher (Camden Society, 3rd ser. vol. 52, *Camden Miscellany*, 16, 1936).

III. SECONDARY WORKS

1. *Published works (other than articles in periodicals)*

Albion, R. G. *Forests and Sea Power: the Timber Problem of the Royal Navy, 1652–1862* (Cambridge, Mass. 1926).
Allen, J. W. *English Political Thought, 1603–1660*, vol. 1: 1603–1644 (London, 1938).
Ashley, M. P. *Financial and Commercial Policy Under the Cromwellian Protectorate* (Oxford Historical Series, 5, London, 1934).
Baddeley, W. St C. *A Cotteswold Manor: Being the History of Painswick* (London, 1907).

20-2

BIBLIOGRAPHY

Bang, N. E. *Tabeller over skibsfart og varetransport gennem Øresund, 1497–1660: Tables de la navigation et du transport des marchandises passant par le Sund, 1497–1660*, 2 vols. (Copenhagen, 1906–22).

Barbour, V. *Capitalism in Amsterdam in the Seventeenth Century* (Johns Hopkins University Studies in Historical and Political Science. Series 65, no. 1. Baltimore, 1950).

Barker, Sir E. and others (eds.). *The European Inheritance*, 3 vols. (Oxford, 1954).

Beaven, A. B. *The Aldermen of the City of London*, 2 vols. (London, 1908–13).

Bezançon, M., *see* Martin, G. L. and Bezançon, M.

Black, J. B. *The Reign of Elizabeth, 1558–1603* (Oxford, 1936).

Braudel, F. *La Méditerranée et le monde méditerranéen à l'époque de Philippe II* (Paris, 1949).

Burgon, J. W. *The Life and Times of Sir Thomas Gresham...Including Notices of Many of his Contemporaries*, 2 vols. (London, 1839).

Bush, J. N. D. *English Literature in the Earlier Seventeenth Century, 1600–1660* (Oxford History of English Literature, vol. 5, Oxford, 1945).

Cambridge Economic History of Europe, see Postan, M. M. and Rich, E. E. (eds.).

Carlisle, N. *A Concise Description of the Endowed Grammar Schools in England and Wales*, 2 vols. (London, 1818).

Christensen, A. E. *Dutch Trade to the Baltic about 1600: Studies in the Sound Toll Register and Dutch Shipping Records* (Copenhagen, 1941).

Clapham, Sir J. H. *A Concise Economic History of Britain from the Earliest Times to 1750* (Cambridge, 1949).

Clark, Sir G. N. *Guide to English Commercial Statistics 1696–1782;... with a Catalogue of Materials by Barbara M. Franks* (Royal Historical Society. Guides and Handbooks, no. 1, London, 1938).

Cokayne, G. E. *Some Account of the Lord Mayors and Sheriffs of the City of London During the First Quarter of the Seventeenth Century, 1601–1625* (London, 1897).

Craven, W. F. *Dissolution of the Virginia Company: the Failure of a Colonial Experiment* (New York, 1932).

Davies, G. *The Early Stuarts, 1603–1660* (Oxford, 1937).

Davies, R. *The Greatest House at Chelsey* (London, 1914).

Dictionary of National Biography. Article on Lionel Cranfield, Earl of Middlesex, by C. H. Firth.

Dietz, F. C. *English Public Finance, 1558–1641* (New York, 1932).

—— *The Receipts and Issues of the Exchequer During the Reigns of James I and Charles I* (Smith College Studies in History, vol. 13, no. 4, N'ton, Mass., 1928).

Ehrenberg, R. *Hamburg und England im Zeitalter der Königin Elizabeth* (Jena, 1896).

—— *Das Zeitalter der Fugger: Geldkapital und Creditverkehr im 16. Jahrhundert.*

Elton, G. R. *The Tudor Revolution in Government* (Cambridge, 1953).

Foster, Sir W. *England's Quest of Eastern Trade* (London, 1933).

Friis, A. *Alderman Cockayne's Project and the Cloth Trade* (Copenhagen, 1927).

Fuller, T. *The Church-History of Britain*, ed. J. S. Brewer, 6 vols. (Oxford, 1845).

—— *The History of the Worthies of England*, new ed. by P. Austin Nuttall, 3 vols. (London, 1840).

Gardiner, S. R. 'Britain under James I', in *The Cambridge Modern History*, vol. III, pp. 549–78.

—— *History of England from the Accession of James I to the Outbreak of the Civil War, 1603–1642*, 10 vols. (London, 1883–4).

Gibbon, E. *The History of the Decline and Fall of the Roman Empire*, ed. J. B. Bury, 7 vols. (London, 1897–1901).

Girard, A. *Le commerce français à Séville et Cadix au temps des Habsbourg* (Paris, 1932).

Giuseppi, M. S. *A Guide to the Manuscripts Preserved in the Public Record Office*, 2 vols. (London, 1923–4).

Gras, N. S. B. *The Evolution of the English Corn Market from the Twelfth to the Eighteenth Century* (Harvard Economic Studies, vol. 13, Cambridge, Mass., 1915).

Hamilton, E. J. *American Treasure and the Price Revolution in Spain, 1501–1650* (Harvard Economic Studies, vol. 43, Cambridge, Mass., 1934).

Harper, L. A. *The English Navigation Laws: a Seventeenth Century Experiment in Social Engineering* (New York, 1939).

Hauser, H. 'Le sel dans l'histoire', in *Les Origines historiques des problèmes économiques actuels* (Paris, 1930).

Heaton, H. *Economic History of Europe* (rev. ed. New York, 1946).

—— *The Yorkshire Woollen and Worsted Industries* (Oxford, 1920).

Heckscher, E. F. *Mercantilism*, 2 vols. (London, 1934).

Johnson, A. H. *The History of the Worshipful Company of the Drapers of London*, 5 vols. (Oxford, 1914–22).

Jordan, W. K. *Men of Substance: A Study of the Thought of two English Revolutionaries, Henry Parker and Henry Robinson* (Chicago, 1942).

Judges, A. V. 'Money, Finance and Banking from the Renaissance to the Eighteenth Century', in *European Civilisation*, ed. E. Eyre (7 vols, London, 1935–9), vol. V.

Keynes, J. M. *A Treatise on Money*, 2 vols. (London, 1930).

Khan, Sir S. A. *The East India Trade in the XVIIIth Century in its Political and Economic Aspects* (London, 1923).

Knights, L. C. *Drama and Society in the Age of Jonson* (London, 1937).

Krannhals, D. *Danzig und der Weichselhandel in seine Blütezeit vom 16. zum 17. Jahrhundert* (Leipzig, 1942).

Krishna, B. *Commercial Relations Between India and England, 1601 to 1757* (London, 1924).

Kulischer, J. *Allgemeine Wirtschaftsgeschichte des Mittelalters und der Neuzeit.* Band II. *Die Neuzeit* (Munich, 1928).

Lejeune, J. *La formation du capitalisme moderne dans la principauté de Liége au XVIe siècle* (Paris, 1939).

Lintum, C. Te. *De Merchant Adventurers in de Nederlanden* ('s Gravenhage, 1905).

Lipson, E. *The Economic History of England*, vol. 2, *The Age of Mercantilism* (London, 1931).

Lodge, E. *Portraits of Illustrious Personages of Great Britain*, vol. IV (1849).

Lopez, R. S. 'The Trade of Medieval Europe: the South', in *The Cambridge Economic History of Europe*, vol. II, ed. M. M. Postan and E. E. Rich.

Maitland, F. W. *The Constitutional History of England* (Cambridge, 1926).

Martin, G. L. and Bezançon, M. *L'histoire du crédit en France sous le règne de Louis XIV*, vol. I, *Le crédit public* (Paris, 1913).

Mendenhall, T. C. *The Shrewsbury Drapers and the Welsh Wool Trade in the XVI and XVII centuries* (London, 1953).

Nef, J. U. *Industry and Government in France and England, 1540–1640* (American Philosophical Society, Memoirs, vol. 15, Philadelphia, 1940).

—— *The Rise of the British Coal Industry*, 2 vols. (London, 1932).

Notestein, W. *The Winning of the Initiative by the House of Commons* (British Academy. Raleigh Lectures on History for 1924. 1926).

Oppenheim, M. *A History of the Administration of the Royal Navy and of Merchant Shipping in Relation to the Navy from 1509 to 1660* (London, 1896).

Postan, M. M. and Rich, E. E. (eds.). *The Cambridge Economic History of Europe*, vol. II (Cambridge, 1952), especially chapter 4 by M. M. Postan and chapter 5 by R. S. Lopez.

Posthumus, N. W. *De geschiedenis van de Leidsche lakenindustrie*, 3 vols. ('s Gravenhage, 1908–39).

Price, W. Hyde. *The English Patents of Monopoly* (Harvard Economic Studies, vol. 1. Boston, Mass., 1906).

Reade, H. G. R. *Sidelights on the Thirty Years War*, 3 vols. (London, 1924).

Richards, R. D. *The Early History of Banking in England* (London, 1929).

Rogers, J. E. Thorold. *A History of Agriculture and Prices in England*, 7 vols. (Oxford, 1866–1902).

Rutkowski, J. *Histoire économique de la Pologne avant les partages* (Paris, 1927).

Schanz, G. *Englische Handelspolitik gegen Ende des Mittelalters*, 2 vols. (Leipzig, 1881).

Scott, W. R. *The Constitution and Finance of English, Scottish and Irish Joint-Stock Companies to 1720*, 3 vols. (Cambridge, 1910–12).

Simiand, F. *Recherche anciennes et nouvelles sur le mouvement général des prix due XVIe au XIXe siècle* (Paris, 1932).

Soden, G. I. *Godfrey Goodman, Bishop of Gloucester, 1583–1656* (London, 1953).

Te Lintum, C., *see* Lintum, C. Te.

Thrupp, S. L. *The Merchant Class of Medieval London, 1300–1500* (Chicago, 1948).

Toynbee, A. J. *A Study of History*, 10 vols. (London, 1935–54).

Unwin, G. 'The Merchant Adventurers Company in the reign of Elizabeth', in *Studies in Economic History, the Collected Papers of George Unwin*, ed. R. H. Tawney (London, 1927).

—— 'London Tradesmen and their Creditors', in *Finance and Trade under Edward III*, ed. G. Unwin (Manchester, 1918).

Vincent, W. A. L. *The State and School Education, 1640–1660 in England and Wales* (London, 1950).

Wiebe, G. *Zur Geschichte der Preisrevolution des XVI und XVII Jahrhunderts* (Leipzig, 1895).

Willson, D. H. *The Privy Councillors in the House of Commons, 1604–1629* (Minneapolis, 1940).

Woodworth, A. *Purveyance for the Royal Household in the Reign of Queen Elizabeth* (American Philosophical Society Transactions, new series, vol. 35, part 1, Philadelphia, 1945).

2. Unpublished Works

Ashton, R. *Government Borrowing Under the First Two Stuarts, 1603–42* (University of London, Ph.D. Thesis, 1953).

Hall, B. *The Trade of Newcastle-on-Tyne and the North-east Coast, 1600–1640* (University of London, Ph.D. Thesis, 1933).

Harper, W. P. *Public Borrowing, 1640–1660* (University of London, M.Sc. (Econ.) Thesis, 1927).

Pilgrim, J. E. *The Cloth Industry in Essex and Suffolk, 1558–1640* (University of London, M.A. Thesis, 1939).

IV. ARTICLES IN PERIODICALS

1. *In the* Economic History Review

Andrews, J. H. 'Two Problems in the Interpretation of the Port Books', 2nd ser. vol. IX, no. 1, August 1956.

Ashton, R. 'Deficit Finance in the Reign of James I', 2nd ser. vol. X, no. 1, August 1957.

—— 'Revenue Farming Under the Early Stuarts', 2nd ser. vol. VIII, no. 3, April 1956.

Aylmer, G. E. 'The Last Years of Purveyance, 1610–1660', 2nd ser. vol. X, no. 1, August 1957.

Belof, M. 'Review of *The Rebuilding of London After the Great Fire* by T. F. Reddaway', vol. XIV, 1944–5.

Beresford, M. W. 'The Common Informer, the Penal Statutes and Economic Regulation', 2nd ser. vol. X, no. 2, December 1957.

Bowden, P. J. 'Wool Supply and the Woollen Industry', 2nd ser. vol. IX, no. 1, August 1956.

Carus-Wilson, E. M. 'Review of *The Wiltshire Woollen Industry in the Sixteenth and Seventeenth Centuries*', by G. D. Ramsay, vol. XVI, no. 1, 1946.

Clark, G. N. 'Early Capitalism and Invention', vol. VI, no. 2, April 1936.

Fisher, F. J. 'Commercial Trends and Policy in Sixteenth Century England', vol. X, no. 2, November 1940.

—— 'The Development of the London Food Market, 1540–1640', vol. V, no. 2, April 1935.

—— 'London's Export Trade in the Early Seventeenth Century', 2nd ser. vol. III, no. 2, 1950.

Gould, J. D. 'The Royal Mint in the Early Seventeenth Century', 2nd ser. vol. V, no. 2, 1952.

—— 'The Trade Depression of the Early 1620's', 2nd ser. vol. VII, no. 1, August 1954.

Hamilton, E. J. 'The Decline of Spain (Revisions in Economic History, 8)', vol. VIII, no. 2, May 1938.

Heckscher, E. F. 'Mercantilism (Revisions in Economic History, 5)', vol. VII, no. 1, November 1936.

Hill, C. 'Soviet Interpretations of the English Interregnum', vol. VIII, no. 2, May 1938.

Hinton, R. W. K. 'The Dutch Entrepot Trade at Boston, Lincs.', 2nd ser. vol. IX, no. 3, April 1957.

—— 'The Mercantile System in the Time of Thomas Mun', 2nd ser. vol. VII, no. 3, April 1955.

Hurstfield, J. 'The Profits of Fiscal Feudalism', 2nd ser. vol. VIII, no. 1, August 1955.

Kerridge, E. 'The Movement of Rent, 1540–1640', 2nd ser. vol. VI, no. 1, August 1953.

Moir, E. 'Benedict Webb, Clothier', 2nd ser. vol. X, no. 2, December 1957.

Nef, J. U. 'Prices and Industrial Capitalism in France and England, 1540–1640', vol. VII, no. 2, May 1937.

—— 'The Progress of Technology and the Growth of Large Scale Industry in Britain, 1540–1640', vol. V, no. 1, October 1934.

—— 'War and Economic Progress, 1540–1640', vol. XII, nos. 1 and 2, 1942.

Ramsay, G. D. 'Industrial *Laisser Faire* and the Policy of Cromwell', vol. XVI, no. 2, 1946.

Rich, E. E. 'The Population of Elizabethan England', 2nd ser. vol. II, no. 3, 1950.

Schenk, W. 'A Seventeenth-century Radical', vol. XIV, 1944–5.

Stone, L. 'The Elizabethan Aristocracy—a Restatement', 2nd ser. vol. IV, no. 3, 1952.

—— 'Elizabethan Overseas Trade', 2nd ser. vol. II, no. 1, 1949.

—— 'State Control in Sixteenth-Century England', vol. XVII, no. 2, 1947.

Supple, B. E. 'Currency and Commerce in the Early Seventeenth Century', 2nd ser. vol. X, no. 2, December 1957.

Viner, J. 'Review of *Mercantilism* by E. F. Heckscher', vol. VI, no. 1, October 1935.

Wagner, D. O. 'Coke and the Rise of Economic Liberalism', vol. VI, no. 1, October 1935.

Walker, P. C. Gordon. 'Capitalism and the Reformation', vol. VIII, no. 1, November 1937.

Willan, T. S. 'The River Navigation and Trade of the Severn Valley, 1600–1750', vol. VIII, no. 1, November 1937.

Wilson, C. '"Mercantilism": Some Vicissitudes of an Idea', 2nd ser. vol. X, no. 2, December 1957.

Wilson, C. 'Review of *Dutch Trade to the Baltic About 1600* by A. E. Christensen', vol. XVI, no. 1, 1946.

Wren, M. C. 'The Chamber of London in 1633', 2nd ser. vol. I, no. 1, 1948.

2. *In Other Periodicals*

Ansiaux, M. 'Histoire économique de la prospérité et de la décadence de l'Espagne au XVIe et au XVIIe siècles' (2 parts), *Revue d'Economie Politique*, vol. VII, 1893.

Churchill, E. F. 'The Crown and its Servants' (3 parts), *Law Quarterly Review*, vol. XLII, 1926.

Fisher, F. J. 'The Development of London as a Centre of Conspicuous Consumption in the Sixteenth and Seventeenth Centuries', *Transactions of the Royal Historical Society*, 4th series, vol. XXX, 1948.

George, M. D. 'Notes on the Origin of the Declared Account', *English Historical Review*, vol. XXXI, no. 121, January 1916.

Hamilton, E. J. 'American Treasure and the Rise of Capitalism', *Economica*, vol. XXVII, 1929.

Hurstfield, J. 'Lord Burghley as Master of the Court of Wards, 1561–98', *Transactions of the Royal Historical Society*, 4th ser. vol. XXXI, 1949.

Knoop, D. and Jones, J. P. 'Masons' Wages in Medieval England', *Economic History*, vol. II, no. 8, January 1953.

Marston, G. G. 'English Ships in the Reign of James I', *Transactions of the Royal Historical Society*, new ser. vol. XIX, 1905.

Newton, A. P. 'The Establishment of the Great Farm of the English Customs', *Transactions of the Royal Historical Society*, 4th ser. vol. I, 1918.

Schapiro, I. A. 'The Mermaid Club', *Modern Language Review*, vol. LXIV, no. 1, January 1950.

Van Dillen, J. G. 'Amsterdam als wereldmarkt der edele metalen in de 17de en 18de eeuw' (2 parts), *De Economist*, August and September 1923.

Viner, J. 'English Theories of Foreign Trade Before Adam Smith', (2 parts), *Journal of Political Economy*, vol. XXXVIII, no. 3, June 1930 and no. 4, August 1930.

INDEX OF SUBJECTS

INDEX OF PERSONS

INDEX OF PLACES